FLESHING THE SPIRIT

Fleshing the Spirit

Spirituality and Activism in Chicana, Latina, and Indigenous Women's Lives

Edited by
ELISA FACIO AND IRENE LARA

THE UNIVERSITY OF
ARIZONA PRESS

TUCSON

The University of Arizona Press
© 2014 The Arizona Board of Regents
All rights reserved

www.uapress.arizona.edu

Library of Congress Cataloging-in-Publication Data

Fleshing the spirit : spirituality and activism in Chicana, Latina, and indigenous women's
lives / edited by Elisa Facio and Irene Lara.
    pages cm.
  Includes bibliographical references and index.
  ISBN 978-0-8165-3097-7 (pbk. : alk. paper)
  1. Hispanic American women—Religious life.   2. Indian women—Religious life.
3. Spiritual life.   4. Spirituality.   5. Social justice.   I. Facio, Elisa.   II. Lara, Irene.
  BL625.7.F556 2014
  204.082—dc23

                                                          2013039492

Publication of this book is made possible in part by funding from San Diego State University's Department of Women's Studies' Wertz Carstens Faculty Professional Development
Grant, the University of Colorado–Boulder, and by the proceeds of a permanent endowment created with the assistance of a Challenge Grant from the National Endowment for
the Humanities, a federal agency.

♻

Manufactured in the United States of America on acid-free, archival-quality paper contain-
ing a minimum of 30% post-consumer waste and processed chlorine free.

To my valiant sister Cynthia Facio Ortiz, lifelong friend Diane Gutierrez, beloved tia Maria Isidorita "Dora" Esquibel, who crossed over on May 7, 2013, and to all those who have guided and continue to guide me on this spiritual journey.

To my daughters, Belén and Xóchitl Lara-Trejo, and every single other one of my precious teachers and students, past, present, and future.

Contents

A Mindful Invitation / *Una invitación consiente*   xi
    INÉS TALAMANTEZ

Foreword: A Meditation   xiii
    INÉS HERNÁNDEZ-AVILA

Acknowledgments   xxi

Introduction: Fleshing the Spirit, Spiriting the Flesh   3
    IRENE LARA AND ELISA FACIO

PART 1. THE EAST: NEW BEGINNINGS   19

The East   21
    CINTHYA MARTINEZ

Writing with Crooked Lines   23
    LAURA E. PÉREZ

Toward a Spiritual Pedagogy along the Borderlands   34
    MARIA FIGUEROA

Spiritual Roots of Chicana Feminist Borderland Pedagogies:
A Spiritual Journey with Tonantzin/Guadalupe   43
    C. ALEJANDRA ELENES

Spirit Journey: "Home" as a Site for Healing
and Transformation   59
    ELISA FACIO

Part 2. The West: Feminine Energies   73

Queeranderismo   76
BERENICE DIMAS

Methodologies of the Spirit: Reclaiming Our Lady
of Guadalupe and Discovering Tonantzin Within
and Beyond the *Nepantla* of Academia   81
BRENDA SENDEJO

Saints in the Cuban Heat   102
OLIVA M. ESPÍN

Sensing the Serpent in the Mother, *Dando a Luz la
Madre Serpiente*: Chicana Spirituality, Sexuality,
and Mamihood   113
IRENE LARA

Part 3. The North: The Direction of the Elders   135

Sacrificios   137
FELICIA MONTES

Chicana in the Zendo: Love and Power on the Spiritual Path   138
ALICIA ENCISO LITSCHI

"Pero tu no crees en dios": Negotiating Spirituality,
Family, and Community   150
MICHELLE TÉLLEZ

Healing Introspections: Reaching Inside
and Reconstructing Myself   157
ROSA MARÍA HERNÁNDEZ JUÁREZ

Nepantla Spirituality: My Path to the Source(s)
of Healing   167
LARA MEDINA

Part 4. The South: The Direction of Youth   187

The Woman Within   189
SARAHI NUÑEZ-MEJIA

Contents · ix

Creosote and Lavender   191
ANGELITA BORBÓN

Coming Full Circle   195
BEATRIZ VILLEGAS/ILHUICATLAHUILI-BEA

Living La Vida Santa: My Chicana Spirituality
and Activist Scholarship   202
NORMA E. CANTÚ

Anatomy of Learning: *Yauhtli, Peyotzin, Tobacco,*
and *Maguey*   218
PATRISIA GONZALES

References   241
Contributors   257
Artist's Statement   263
Index   265

A *Mindful Invitation*

Una invitación consiente

Inés Talamantez

It is the sun with its *bitole*, rays, that brings us new life
It is the moon's radiance that watches over us during the night
It is the female rain that gently washes away our fears
It is the breeze that caresses our skin making us strong as we walk on the
    land
On this sun day I offer my thoughts for all of our journeys to succeed.
This is hard labor
The ancestors knew we were coming
They left work for us
Now we carry their wisdom forward.
Know who you are, *sabe quien eres*
Know your land, *conoce tu tierra*
Learn your language, *aprende tu idioma*
Follow the beliefs of your people, your spiritual culture
Do not let spells affect you.
Like every other achievement of human thought
We have emerged culturally and religiously
We are still exploring the possibilities for future growth
Seeking and testing, we take time to measure our generations and know
    that through working together we continue to build decent conditions
    for our people
This is our obligation
Never give up.

Foreword

A Meditation

Inés Hernández-Avila

I am deeply honored to have been asked to write the foreword for this book. As I write, I pay my respects first to the Patwin people, who are the original peoples of this land where I live. May they always be blessed. I give thanks for this day of life, for all the lessons I have learned, and all the blessings I have received. I give thanks to Spirit for working with me on this foreword, for my *guias personales* who inspire my thinkingheart, for the signs I have received as I write, for the songs that have come to me, for the singing of the birds when I go outside to smoke a sacred cigarette, for the singing copal I have burned with sage, cedar, angelica, for the image of Gloria next to me on my left and the votive candle in the purple glass holder. Grácias.

Fleshing the Spirit: Spirituality and Activism in Chicana, Latina, and Indigenous Women's Lives is a labor of love, yes, a birthing labor, with analysis, *autohistoria, testimonio,* poetry, art. As Norma Cantú says, "Every step along life's journey is indeed a step along a spiritual path" (202). The *caminos* are distinct for each contributor; some caminos intersect more directly than others. The path is winding *como una serpiente,* sometimes smooth, tender, sometimes arduous, immensely painful, almost unbearable, full of anguish, *llanto, gritos de coraje.* With this birthing, though, there is joy, rapture, *cariño,* relief, healing, *y amor, mucho amor.* Patrisia Gonzales writes, "Indigenous natural law(s) stress generosity, mutuality, and interdependence" (221). The editors of *Fleshing the Spirit* have brought together a collective of voices that represent these attributes.

As I read the manuscript, discovering the many references to the Earth, the female sacred, the goddesses, the saints, the folk saints, the sweat lodge, known in the north as "Grandmother" and called by women's names in Mexico, I saw in front of me a familiar image. When I was Director of the Chicana/Latina Research Center at the University of California-Davis, I chose for the website an ancient Mesoamerican image from Teotihuacan, a mural fragment (http://clrc.ucdavis.edu/). I wrote,

> The image is of the Great Mother birthing Coyote. The Great Mother is the Female Principle of the universe, present in all of life. . . . [T]he act of birthing has to do not only with the physical act of giving birth, but also with personal creativity and the creative spirit of the universe. Coyote is the Trickster par excellence, and as such she/he is fitting to represent the radical, transforming, subversive, cutting edge work that is being done by Chicana, Latina, and indigenous women scholars. The divine hands of the Female Principle are also shown, and for us, they represent everything we do, writing, living, loving, being.

Fleshing the Spirit reflects an intimate understanding of this principle.

Even though there is no direct mention of Coyote or Trickster energy, I find threads of playfulness, directness, boldness, risk, outrageousness, danger. The Trickster, if anything, trusts herself/himself and goes for it, *punto*. The writers in this collection do the same. It is part of being *nepantleras*. In a way, nepantleras are in step with the cosmos, because they recognize that the space/place of *nepantla* is definitely not static, but utterly dynamic, slippery, sometimes rocky, sometimes flowing. Negotiating this space requires alertness, often choosing at a moment's notice what to do, having a clear sense of self (with all our flaws and virtues), shrugging our shoulders when mistakes are made (sometimes remembering what did not work, sometimes forgetting and repeating the mistakes), laughing at ourselves and at life, longing, wanting what is prohibited, what seems absolutely unachievable, sometimes saving ourselves and others miraculously, with grace and compassion, sometimes surprising everyone with our generosity, wit, and wisdom, picking ourselves up, putting ourselves back together when we are knocked down or destroyed, moving on, always moving on. This is Trickster energy, Coyote energy (I can say this, because I am Nimipu/Nez Perce, so I am a daughter of Coyote). This is nepantlera energy.

As many of the writers have indicated, Chicana/Latina/Indigenous women's spirituality, the fleshing of the spirit and the spiriting of the flesh, are linked intrinsically to social, environmental and global justice, to the well-being of us as women, to our communities and all of life, to all of our relations. What is the creative impulse that drives this need, this search? *Amoridolor*, a term coined by some of us in the 1970s in Texas, a contemporization of the Nahuatl "*difrasismos.*"

Amoridolor. We love deeply so we feel pain from the suffering of our generations (as Berenice Dimas notes in her poem) and, I would add, the suffering of the Earth. And we feel pain because we love. They are inseparable.

Amoridolor. This is what moves us to create, to write, to be, with *"sabor a rebeldía"* (Dimas, 76). Dimas's poem reminds me of the Zapatista saying that I cherish: *"Somos la Dignidad Rebelde"* ("We are the Rebellious Dignity"). Sí. Perhaps most importantly, we love language and we have learned to *name* in many languages at many intertwined levels—academically and otherwise–we have found our voices and we have exercised them, as truthfully as possible, knowing what we know, trusting what we know, willing to reflect on what we know, always, as we grow. The contributors to this volume know that naming, as Elisa Facio notes, is spiritual as well as political. It is a naming through and for the generations. But the naming itself belongs to each and every one of us as individuals, also.

This is indeed an important collection of writings, *la palabraespiritú de cada quien, la palabraespiritú que se mueve, busca, complica, clarifica, transforma.* Each writer offers her self to the whole. Each contributor expresses her autonomy through the creative act of writing, Spirit writing, as Laura Pérez says, and in the union of the individual autonomous manifestations of self a collective of *personas completas* emerges. As Alicia Enciso Litschi states, "There is no spiritual ideal. With that discovery comes a momentary taste of freedom" (147). Autonomy, creativity, spirituality, are the tools of self-realization. These are the tools that bring us as close as possible to Moyocoyani, or Ometeotl Moyocoyatzin, the Female/Male Creator who invents Herself/Himself, in the ancient Nahuatl philosophical tradition. Moyocoyani, *El[/Ella] Que Se Inventa a Si Mismo.*[1] These are also the tools that give us the *camino* by which to achieve "spirited desire and erotic spirit" (Lara and Facio, 75). Erotic spirituality or the spiritual erotic is the very energy of the Creative Spirit, known by many names, the one who is "the sacred source and great mystery of life and death" (Medina, 167).

This is why nepantla is so useful to us today, and we are using it in the ways Gloria Anzaldúa so brilliantly intended—she is such a *guía* and *Maestra* to so many of us. I believe it is safe to say that all of the writers express nepantla in their work, some explicitly, some implicitly. In Native American studies we are firmly committed to validating Indigenous knowledge systems, as many of the contributors to this book are. This concept of nepantla that Gloria took to heart, and delved into, immersing herself in its potentialities, is one of her most profound strokes in a truly inspired life. For at least five hundred years or more (and even before, as humanity, whether we called it nepantla or not), we have been in the midst of transition, change, shape shifting—not to mention horror, terror, and atrocity—up to the present. Nepantla is this place of chaos, disjuncture, disorder, but it is also the space of possibility, creativity, heightened imagination, consciousness, and spirituality. It is the place where we do create "more equitable, personal, social and dare I say it, yes, *cosmic* change" (Lara, 130). It is the space where we can say, with Brenda Sendejo, "[M]y soul took a long, deep breath" (94).

In *danza Conchera*, we learn that Life is Dance and Dance is Life. Sometimes we might not know the steps perfectly, but we should at least move harmoniously, without crashing. Fluidity, nepantla can be about fluidity, not collisions. And home, sometimes home can be its own nepantla, so we bridge, we negotiate (Téllez), by honoring, with compassion.

East. West. North. South. By its divisions into the four directions, each direction as described by the editors, the book creates a cross. A balanced cross. Each of us is at the center of this cross—each of us, from the moment we take bodies and begin to be fleshed spirits on this Earth in this life, emanates from this center towards the four directions, but also towards the EarthMother and the Sky-World. Four directions. Seven points. Four times seven. Twenty-eight, the lunar cycle/circle. Woman's Time. According to some elders of the danza Conchera (adding to the descriptors offered by the editors), the East represents the body, the West, the Spirit, the North, the mind (or consciousness), the South, the will, and the center represents the heart.[2] Lara Medina writes "[M]y heart has intelligence" (168), and that it is important to trust the body and the heart as well as the mind (and spirit). I was happy to see, in Rosa María Hernández Juárez's essay, a reference to will, in her discussion of where Faith comes from. "My mom later said she knew I would be fine because of my will-power. I believe that Will is Spirit and the reverence that my mothers and fathers instilled in me, Faith" (161). Body, Spirit, Mind, Will, Heart, Earth, Sky. Wholeness. Integrity. Returning to ourselves. Forgiving ourselves. Standing up for ourselves. Loving ourselves.

"[I]t is the female rain that gently washes away our fears" (Talamantez, xi). "I will sing a thousand songs / And write a hundred poems / All in one night" (Martinez, 21). "Spiritual awareness works like a muscle" (Pérez, 27). "As I lit the blue candle a gentle collective silence blanketed the classroom" (Figueroa, 38). Tonantzin "represents female power" (Elenes, 53). "To heal involves a radical transformation of the body" (Facio, 62). "I was a curandera before birth / Healing layers of pain / From generations within" (Dimas, 76). "I was adamantly and in some ways defiantly redefining myself and my place in the world" (Sendejo, 81). "Joan of Arc 'saved me'" (Espín, 110). "May we be gifted with the healing knowledge of la Serpiente" (Lara, 131). "Flesh offerings / Come daily in Xicana ceremonies" (Montes, 137). "This realization of self-betrayal is a ferocious fire of initiation" (Enciso Litschi, 154). "Pero tu no crees en Diós" (Téllez). "I felt I had found my Curandero" (Hernández Juárez, 165). "[M]y body can talk to me . . . art is healing . . . the earth is alive . . . plants and animals have spirit" (Medina, 168). "I am free to smile" (Nuñez-Mejia, 190). "My first memory is the sound of a woman sobbing wailing muffled *llantos al cielo*" (Borbón, 191). "When we dance, we are making the prayer with our feet, song and spirit" (Villegas, 200).

"TRUST" (Cantú, 206). "Plants are part of our oldest 'body memory' and reveal a profound story about the human condition" (Gonzales, 223). These are only some of the compelling words of the contributors.

In the late seventies I wrote the following poem that begins with a verse from a song titled "Solo le pido a Diós" by León Gieco (of the Latin American New Song Movement). As I reread the poem, I see my wish in my last stanza has been fulfilled by reading this book:

Oftentimes My Voice

"Solo le pido a Dios
que la guerra no me sea indiferente
es un monstruo grande y pisa fuerte
toda la pobre inocencia de la gente"

Oftentimes my voice
wants more
than what it must say
oftentimes I feel
the need to sing of other times
to come
to move with eyes
across the strip-mined territories
of the present
with steps that miss the traps
diffuse the bombs and
carry us across
the way
where peace is
not perversion
where language is not a tool
of death
where harmony is not a fantasy
where the days won't fly by
in mere sensation
and titillation
is not all that matter is

my voice tires
yet my voice must reach

must seek
other voices who know
of what I speak.

"Solo le pido a Dios
que la guerra no me sea indiferente
es un monstruo grande y pisa fuerte
toda la pobre inocencia de la gente."

While I was working on this foreword, I was listening to Pandora.com, to a *vallenato* "station." Suddenly, out of the blue, while I was writing, Gieco's song came on. I did a double-take and checked the music, still vallenato, but what came through right at the time I was writing was this song that has been dear to me for decades. Perhaps I called it to me. I had thought of it as I was reading Laura Pérez's essay. I knew from this sign I was doing what I was supposed to be doing. There were signs in the writings of the contributors as well.

Timing is everything. As my Grampa Tom would have said, it is important to be with the rhythm—he meant the rhythm of the cosmos. This foreword marks my reentry into my writing life. I am done being department chair, and on July 1, 2013 I began a sabbatical. I can think of no more beautiful transition from the grueling demands of administration to the freedom and *disciplina* that will be most fulfilling for me than to have read this manuscript, lived with it, been with it, and written these words. I give thanks to SpiritHeart for this gift. I know that the writings, the *obra(s)* in this book will be bountiful gifts to its readers.

Regarding timing, we are now in the *Sexto Sol*, according to the Nahuatl tradition, or the new *Baktun*, as the Maya would say. The Sexto Sol is called *Nahui Coatl, Cuatro Serpiente*, Four Serpent, this is what I know from the *Conchero* dance tradition. This sun, I was told, will be one of high spirituality and spiritual understanding. My friend and mentor, artist George Longfish (Seneca/Tuscarora), has said that the planet is vibrating at almost pure love, and that everything is moving at an accelerated speed—we should match our energy to the energy of the change. This collection represents a working out of and working through issues of the mind-body-spirit-heart-will splits that have occurred (over the centuries) through the "Conquest" and resulting colonization. As we work to decolonize and reinvigorate ancient knowledges that resonate with the Earth and our contemporary lives, we take careful, thoughtful steps. *Fleshing the Spirit* does just this.

I must close by affirming my immense love and respect for Inés Talamantez, Mescalero Apache/Chicana, *mujer completa, mujer de palabra sagrada*, wise woman, older sister, elder—Maestra. For what she has created, for what she has birthed, for what she has accomplished as a spiritual warrior for the people(s), gracias. Gracias a Irene Lara and Elisa Facio for having her do the Blessing for this book. Inés's life has been dedicated to Spirit. Her main work has focused on the Mescalero Apache young woman's puberty ceremony(ies). Her passion and *compromiso* are to understand, teach, and write about the rite of passage from girlhood to womanhood. She speaks to us as women in her blessing. In her "Mindful Invitation" she writes, "The ancestors knew we were coming / They left work for us / Now we carry their wisdom forward" (xi). So we come full circle, again and again. As Felicia Montes says, "Becoming holy sacrifices / Within our own temples of worship" (137). We must honor those sacrifices and be at peace with them, for we are here now, in present time, on this Earth that needs us so. *Serpiente iluminada con la flecha de la conciencia, con la Luz. Serpiente que es de la tierra, que ama a la tierra, que se mueve sensualmente sobre la tierra, que hace caso a la tierra. Cada una de nosotras.*

Notes

1. One of my ongoing research projects focuses on Ometeotl Moyocoyatzin (Hernández-Avila 2006).
2. The heart is central to many Indigenous traditions (Hernández-Avila [1997] 2000; Shanley 1999).

Acknowledgments

As with any long-term labor of love, many people have helped this anthology come to fruition. Thank you to all of the contributors and additional supporters who have believed in the project throughout the years. Thank you also to our audiences at MALCS (*Mujeres Activas en Letras y Cambio Social*), NACCS (National Association for Chicana and Chicano Studies), and NWSA (National Women's Studies Association), our anonymous reviewers, and editor Kristen Buckles and support staff at the University of Arizona Press for your invaluable feedback and encouragement.

Muchisimas gracias a las maestras Inés Talamantez and Inés Hernández-Avila for opening the *camino* to this work with all of their own fierce trailblazing in Chicana, Latina, Indigenous, and Native American studies, in addition to contributing their beautiful "A Mindful Invitation / *Una invitación consiente*" and "Foreword: A Meditation" to the anthology. I, Irene, still vividly remember being a first-year graduate student squeezing into a standing-room only panel session at the 1997 NACCS featuring "las Ineses" presenting on spirituality, and being forever transformed by the eloquence and integrity of their presence and words. These *madrinas* to many are among the first academics and poets who spoke from their thinking hearts to my whole body-mindspirit, in essence lighting my lifelong devotion to creating spirit-infused scholarship and pedagogy.

I also thank my colleagues and students at San Diego State University (SDSU), with whom I have shared my journey. In particular, I cherish my healing *pláticas* with Sophia Arredondo, Jessica Heredia, Eneri Rodriguez Arauz, Maria de la Luz Ibarra, Victoria Gonzalez-Rivera, Alejandra Gonzales, Carolina Prado, Carmen Rodriguez, Sophia Lujan Rivera, Alicia Chavez Arteaga, and all other "CuranderaScholarActivists." In addition, I thank SDSU's College of Arts and Letters and Department of Women's Studies, the Ford Foundation's Postdoctoral Grant, and the Career Enhancement Fellowship for Junior Faculty (funded by The Andrew W. Mellon Foundation and administered by the Woodrow Wilson National Fellowship Foundation) for the funding they have awarded me over the years enabling me to research, write, and coedit this anthology, as well as travel to conferences to present on related work.

My family and friends *de alma y corazón* have also been essential in nurturing me as a person, scholar, writer, teacher, and mother. Thank you, *hermanas*: Laura Jiménez, Luz Herrera, Yolanda Venegas, Bianet Castellanos, Rosa María Hernández Juárez, Christina Grijalva, Macarena Hernández, and Maria Figueroa. Thank you, *madrinas*: Ana Castillo, Gloria Anzaldúa, AnaLouise Keating, Laura Pérez, Patrisia Gonzales, Luz Alvarez Martínez, Angelita Borbón, and Griselda Sesma. A special thank you to my family, whose unconditional love sustains me every day: my love Raúl Trejo, my daughters Belén and Xóchitl Lara-Trejo, my parents Rigoberto and Dolores Lara, my second parents Raúl and Edda Trejo, my Grandma Linda, my Tia Maria, my brother Rigo, my extended sisters Edda Maria, Xenia, and Michelle, and their families, my nieces, nephews, *tias, tios, primas, primos, todos*.

In particular, I, Elisa, wish to acknowledge University of Colorado-Boulder faculty members Emma Perez, Arturo Aldama, and Reiland Rabaka for their consistent encouragement throughout the development of this anthology. A number of community spiritual teachers and guides, including Belinda Garcia, Christina Segala, Roberta Maldonado and Maria Cuevas provided unconditional love and support, which sustained my health and productivity. Also, Rocky Rodriguez, Robert Cross, and David Young played instrumental roles as my guides, teachers, and relatives during this spiritual process. And I am honored by and indebted to my communal Indigenous family for providing me the opportunity to pray with them regularly throughout the seasons in *temazkalli*. I extend my heartfelt thanks to Erica Padilla, Cynthia Diaz, Brianna Mestas, Miranda Encina, LeRoy Saiz, Vanessa Gordilla, Blake Angelo, Robert Carney, Andres Aragon, Anthony Luta Ginn, Peter Oswalt, Ara Cruz, and Zach Serrano. My *comadres* Adaljiza Sosa Riddell, Patrisia Gonzales, Elsa Holguin, Paula Espinoza, Deborah Mendez Wilson, and Adrianna Abarca created and provided critical healing spaces that enabled me to negotiate a challenging healing journey. Also, my compadres Bill Flores, Augustine Hernandez, Concepcion Herrera, and Stephen Medina played a vital role throughout my spirit journey. Finally, I want to thank the College of Arts and Sciences' allocation of the Dean's Fund from 2009–2011, which allowed me to attend conferences to present this work, and also assisted with general research expenses.

Unfortunately, two of our initial contributors passed over into the spirit world during the evolution of this anthology: Karen Holliday and Elena

Avila. Their passing deeply pains us, but their scholarly and creative work is a reminder of the medicine we all have within ourselves. Thus, their presence is always with us.

Elisa Facio
Irene Lara

FLESHING THE SPIRIT

Introduction

Fleshing the Spirit, Spiriting the Flesh

Irene Lara and Elisa Facio

This anthology foregrounds scholarly, activist, and creative reflections on spirit, spirituality, and "spiritual activism" (Anzaldúa 2002a) from the perspectives of Chicana, Latina, and Indigenous women.[1] We, the coeditors Elisa Facio and Irene Lara, have been studying Chicana, Latina, and Indigenous women's spiritualities and, just as significantly, living our own spiritualities since the 1990s. Through our distinct yet interweaving paths as spiritually identified Chicana scholar-activists from working-class backgrounds, we are committed to decolonizing the academy that largely devalues or misunderstands spirituality, both as a serious academic topic *and* as an integral aspect of being alive.[2]

We have encountered many others who are also committed to a life of inquiry, teaching, writing, cultural activism, or social justice that values a spiritual perspective and praxis grounded in the decolonial histories, politics, and dynamic cultures of our Indigenous and mestiza/o ancestors and in solidarity with Indigenous people and people of color, across constructed "races" and "nations." Built on the supposition that spirituality often plays a decolonizing role in creating meaning, inspiring action, and supporting healing and justice in our communities, this anthology contributes to an emerging body of knowledge focused on voicing and understanding spirituality through an intersectional, interdisciplinary, and nonsectarian lens.

Although they are widely perceived to be a religious or spiritual group, until recently there have been few works that address the gendered, sexualized, classed, and racialized spiritualities of Chicanas, Latinas, and Indigenous women, particularly through their own voices. As discussed in theology and

3

religious studies, being spiritual certainly can go hand in hand with being religious (González 2009, Dreyer and Burrows 2005a). However, being "religious" connotes participating in a religious institutional structure and following specific religious tenets and canonical practices, even if in popular or hybrid cultural forms (Rodríguez 1994; Irwin 2000; Aquino, Machado, and Rodríguez 2002; Matovina and Riebe-Estrada 2002; León 2003; Espinosa and García 2008). Acknowledging the historical and ongoing role that some religious beliefs have played in empire building and (neo)colonial struggles for dominance over land and resources—as well as in justifying ideological and material control over the bodymindspirits of people, especially girls and women, the impoverished, and the sexually, nationally, ethnically, and racially "othered"—we join others in focusing on the ways "spirituality promotes liberation" (Comas-Díaz 2008, 13) and socially equitable well-being for all.

With the specter of the living legacy of patriarchal and (neo)colonial control over the spirits and bodies of women of color as a backdrop, Ana Castillo asserts that recuperating, refashioning, and combining spiritual and healing knowledge(s) and practices in the process of proclaiming one's spirituality is a liberatory, empowering act: "We will determine for ourselves what makes us feel whole, what brings us tranquility, strength, courage to face the countless— not for one moment imagined—obstacles in the path on our journey toward being fulfilled human beings" (1994, 147). Indeed, for most of the contributors in this volume, forging a personal and communal spirituality is distinct from engaging in an official religion. In this sense, spirituality is a conscious, self-reflective way of life and a way of relating to others, to ourselves, and to "s/Spirit" (L. Pérez 1998 and this volume) in a manner that honors all of life as an interconnected web.[3]

Lara Medina defines spirituality similarly, as "the multiple ways in which persons maintain and nurture balanced relationships with themselves, others, the world, and their creator or creation" (2006, 257). As C. Alejandra Elenes asserts in her essay in this volume, "Spirituality, then, means more than one's relation with a God or a Creator because it is tied with struggles for social justice and gender equality. Spirituality is a way of understanding someone's (or a community's) position in the world by trying to make sense of unfair economic conditions and gender inequality, and to do something about it." As such, one's spirituality includes what we think and do in regards to knowing ourselves to be "related to all that lives," as Inés Hernández-Avila elaborates in her work (2002, 532).

Indeed, for many women who identify as Chicanas, Latinas, and/or Indigenous, the claiming of their spirituality goes hand in hand with a deep sense of respect for and accountability to their communities, including a specific land base or specific traditions, as seen in Hernández 1988; Talamantez 1995;

Hernández-Avila [1997] 2000; Moraga 2000; Broyles-Gonzáles and Khus 2011; and Gonzales 2012. As discussed by various authors in this anthology, part of practicing and making sense of one's spirituality entails navigating the potential tension between personal and familial or community well-being and critically understanding the power relations at play in defining spirituality, community, and well-being. Among women of color, such tensions have included resisting the racism, sexism, classism, and homophobia within, and directed toward, their communities, as well as dealing with challenges regarding appropriation and authenticity, including the right to, and related responsibilities associated with, (re)claiming one's dynamic ancestral traditions and making ethical connections with other cultural spiritual traditions.

Accustomed to assembling interdisciplinary readings for our classes, conducting our own research with community healers, and seeking like-minded *almas afines*, "kindred spirits" (Anzaldúa [1981] 1983b) with whom to deeply dialogue about these issues, we recognized the need to bring together such reflections intentionally within one text. In creating a supportive space to engage spirituality unabashedly from personal, activist, critical, and creative perspectives, this anthology documents our living theories, knowledge/ *conocimientos*, and practices. In fact, when we solicited submissions, we did not directly define spirituality; instead, through a series of prompts, we invited contributors to engage spirituality for themselves from their diverse cultural, historical, and social locations as Chicana, Latina, and Indigenous women.[4]

Not only does this anthology gather well-known scholars, activists, healers, and other women who integrate all of these identities, it introduces new and emerging writers. All are contributing to the flourishing of knowledge about Indigenous, US Latina/o, and women's spiritualities in general, and Chicana, Latina, and Indigenous women's spiritualities in particular.[5] In this time of great need for social and ecological consciousness and transformation, may our voices and actions harmonize with those of others in solidarity.

The anthology project was conceived during Elisa's severe battle with cancer. What follows is a brief synopsis of the creative process that evolved:

During my cancer journey, family and friends of various spiritual expressions crossed my path sharing their beliefs and values about resisting, healing, and surviving. Such medicinal gifts were pivotal in my physical, spiritual, and emotional survival. Subsequently, given the significant impact of these spiritual expressions in my life, I became interested in learning more about the place of spirit and spirituality in the lives of Chicanas, Latinas and Indigenous women. In August 2004, I attended the MALCS (Mujeres Activas en Letras y Cambio Social) Summer Institute in Seattle,

Washington, where I actively sought guidance and direction in learning more about Chicana, Latina, and Indigenous women's spirituality.[6] My inquiry began by presenting a paper titled "Living and Writing Spirituality," which was well received, but only a few truly understood my intentions. For example, in spite of the title of the presentation, conference organizers were inclined to place this paper on a general panel titled "Religion." Therefore, those in attendance were not quite sure how to react. My work was a theoretical engagement of spirituality and how we live spirituality, not about religion per se.

These initial reactions are very telling about the ambivalent and complex place of spirit and spirituality in the academy. Indeed, as critically discussed by trailblazing scholars of Chicana, Latina, and/or Indigenous spiritualities such as Inés Talamantez, Inés Hernández-Avila, Oliva Espín, Gloria Anzaldúa, Ana Castillo, Jeanette Rodríguez, Lara Medina, Laura Pérez, and Patrisia Gonzales (many of whom are contributors to this anthology), the silences, distortions, and questions surrounding Chicana, Latina, and Indigenous women's spiritualities are deeply rooted in the legacies of colonial racism, (hetero)sexism, and classism and modernity's emphasis on the mind, reason, and science set in dualistic opposition to spirit, intuition, passion, and the sacred. In spite of such ambivalence, however, a growing number of publications, conference panels, and college courses are addressing the importance of spirituality, as distinct from and/or in relationship to religion, as an epistemology, and its role in cultivating "whole" human beings who see themselves as "related to all that lives" (Hernández-Avila 2002) and advancing social and ecological justice on local and global scales.

Many writers have elucidated the connection between the embodiments of a spiritual worldview and actively engaging the world, coined as "spiritual activism" by Gloria Anzaldúa (2002a) and discussed in detail by AnaLouise Keating (2005; 2008).[7] In her essay in this volume, Norma Cantú also discusses the ways her "activism springs directly from [her] spiritual practice": "I am drawn to work on projects and to exercise certain tasks as a sense of mission" (215). Defining "activist spirituality" as "living a holistic life focused on issues of social justice," she claims that "we touch the spirit when we change the world with our actions, and it is spirit that 'inspires' right action, especially our social justice actions" (216). They join others who have recently explored the motivating and generating role of spirituality in social justice movements (Fernandes 2003; Huerta 2008; Doetsch-Kidder 2012; Maparyan 2012; Garcia Lopez 2012).

On the wings of Chicana, Latina, Indigenous and other activists, artists, scholars, and healers of color from the social justice movements before and after the 1960s and 1970s, and the women and men in our familial and community genealogies who have been our primary teachers of spirituality, inspiring our "right action[s]" (Cantú, 216), we are part of a tide of women transforming the academy and society in general. More specifically, we insist on the intellectual and political significance of analyzing spirituality and activism within transcultural and historical contexts.

What follows is the continuation of Elisa's narrative of her personal path to coediting this anthology:

At the Seattle MALCS conference, I was excited to attend the few panels that marginally addressed the importance of healing or, more specifically, the idea of human revolution in order to transform society guided by Anzalduan concepts of spirit, spirituality, and spiritual activism. But I felt disappointed that I could not locate a critical site of discourse. Finally, one late afternoon during a conference break, I met with Inés Hernández-Avila, noted Indigenous Chicana scholar, to discuss my health journey and my interest in deepening an understanding about spirit and spirituality as feminist and culturally constructed concepts. Inés recommended speaking with Irene, who had recently completed her dissertation on Chicana/ Latina spirituality, sexuality, and healing. At our first meeting in Seattle, we immediately connected through our similar, spiritually grounded scholarly, teaching, and activist commitments.

Irene recalls her entrance into the project:

I distinctly remember feeling honored that Elisa followed her intuition and although she had just met me, asked me, a junior scholar, to collaborate with her as a coeditor of what has been nurtured into this anthology on spirituality. Trusting our path to each other, it was then that we decided we would work on a collection addressing Chicana, Latina, and Indigenous women's spirituality. It is particularly fitting that we initiated our work as coeditors at MALCS, an organization supporting Chicana, Latina, and Indigenous women scholars, activists, and artivists whose vision includes creating a space for such collaborations to take place. The timing was also auspicious for me because my first daughter Belén had recently been born and I had decided that attending MALCS would be my official reentry into my academic life after focusing on transitioning into new parenthood for a few months. Committing to work on this project seemed to me the perfect way to mindfully integrate my scholarly research and my desire to approach life grounded in a holistic spiritual perspective, and has created a space to continuously reflect on that very process.

By the next MALCS in 2005, we had our call for papers ready and began circulating flyers at a spirituality panel on which we both presented. While spiritual/religious topics had certainly been presented in previous MALCS Summer Institutes, every year we began to notice that more and more panels centering on spirituality were being organized and that spirituality, spiritual activism, and/or healing began to be listed as possible themes in the call for proposals distributed by the organizers of the annual institutes. Indeed, through the enlivened discussions that our solo and collective academic presentations and teaching experiences have elicited throughout the years, we have found widespread interest in this undertheorized topic that holistically attends to the whole student/reader/audience member by addressing the bodymindspirit from a Chicana, Latina, and Indigenous women's epistemology, which takes into account a rich decolonial history and politics.

Curiously, while there have been several interdisciplinary anthologies spotlighting specific themes within Chicana, Latina, and/or Indigenous women's studies, such as sexuality, popular culture, education, health, and mothering (such as Alarcón, Castillo, and Moraga 1993; Trujillo 1991; Cantú and Nájera-Ramírez 2002; Gaspar de Alba 2003; Delgado Bernal et al. 2006; Chabram-Dernersesian and de la Torre 2008; Silva 2011), and at least one textbook (Broyles-Gonzáles 2001), that have included some spirituality-themed work, this is the first anthology to entirely focus on Chicana, Latina, and Indigenous women's spiritualities.

Moreover, while many spirituality-related scholarly articles, creative works, and *testimonios* have inspired our contributors, there are only a handful of single-authored books that center on the spiritualities of Chicana, Latina, and/or Indigenous women. The interdisciplinary work of scholars, such as Oliva Espín's *Latina Healers: Lives of Power and Tradition* (1996), focusing on Santeras and Espiritistas, and Lara Medina's *Las Hermanas: Chicana/Latina Religious-Political Activism in the U.S. Catholic Church* (2004), for example, has contributed knowledge about the diverse ways women practice spirituality within, outside of, and/or while bridging religious, familial, and political institutions. Moreover, Latina theologians have also been trailblazers in exploring spirituality from social justice perspectives. In addition to the early work of Ada Isasi-Díaz and Yolanda Tarango (1988) and Jeanette Rodríguez (1994) on Our Lady of Guadalupe as a source of empowerment for Latinas, one can turn to the theological work anthologized in *A Reader in Latina Feminist Theology: Religion and Justice* (Aquino, Machado, and Rodríguez 2002) and *Feminist Intercultural Theology: Latina Explorations for a Just World* (Aquino and Rosado-Nunes 2007) for further examples of the many ways women theorize and practice spirituality. Indeed, Chicana, Latina, Indigenous and other women scholars of color writing at the crossroads of "feminist," womanist, or mujerista spiritualities and liberation theology have been at the forefront of making claims for social justice, as have the women they write about (in works such as Isasi-Díaz 1993; Isasi-Díaz 1996; Medina 2004; Aquino and Rosado-Nunes 2007; Pui-lan 2010).[8]

Women considered spiritual practitioners, healers, and/or ceremonial leaders by their communities have also blended scholarly writing with testimonio to write their own book-length works. For example, in *Altar of My Soul: The Living Traditions of Santería* (2000), Afro-Boricua Santería practitioner and cultural activist Marta Moreno Vega vividly describes the process of becoming a Santera, and the late curandera and poet Elena Avila documents the centuries-old legacy of Aztec *curanderismo* in *Woman Who Glows in the Dark: A Curandera Reveals Traditional Aztec Secrets of Physical and Spiritual Health* (1999). More recently, Patrisia Gonzales, trained as a birth attendant and herbalist in the traditions of Indigenous medicinal knowledges, utilized "a *promotora-investigadora* (community health worker-researcher)" model to innovatively research and write *Red Medicine: Traditional Indigenous Rites of Birthing and Healing* (2012, 9), from which we have excerpted a chapter.

In addition, recently published books by B. Marie Christian (2005), Laura E. Pérez (2007), Elizabeth de la Portilla (2009), Theresa Delgadillo (2011), and Clara Román-Odio (2013) center spirituality and/or healing from interdisciplinary cultural studies, literary, or anthropological perspectives. For example, in *Chicana Art: The Politics of Spiritual and Aesthetic Altarities* (2007), Pérez theorizes the relationship between spirituality and power in the work of more than forty Chicana artists between the 1970s and 1990s. In *Spiritual Mestizaje: Religion, Gender, Race, and Nation in Contemporary Chicana Narrative* (2011), Delgadillo conducts a close analysis of several fictional and testimonial texts and two films that also broaden our understanding of spirituality. Long at the center of innumerable feminist spirituality studies, the "Goddess of the Americas" (Castillo 1996) Guadalupe-Tonantzin is at the heart of Róman-Odio's text, *Sacred Iconographies in Chicana Cultural Productions* (2013).

Together, Pérez, Delgadillo, and Román-Odio document a long list of creative writers, performers, filmmakers, and multimedia visual artists who have infused Chicana, Latina, and Indigenous women's spirituality studies with their evocative cultural expression.[9] While these recently published texts largely focus on Chicana experiences, many scholarly articles, poems, and visual, performance, and fictional artworks specifically address spirituality from Puerto Rican, Cuban, and other Caribbean, Latin American, or US Latina women's perspectives in the United States.[10]

The field of Chicana, Latina, and Indigenous women's studies, which insists on critically documenting and analyzing the gendered, racialized, and classed experiences and expressive cultures of women, largely from decolonial feminist perspectives, has been developing for several decades. So why has it taken this long to directly explore Chicana, Latina, and Indigenous women's spiritualities in a full-length manuscript? The time lag suggests that focusing on this theme from personal, activist, creative, and critical perspectives can be just as provocative and thus as risky as spotlighting sex and sexuality, or even more so.[11] In fact, lesbian and queer artists and scholars have been at the vanguard of exploring spirituality, particularly in relation to the socializing role of religion in constructing and constricting sexual identity and behaviors within heteronormative confines.

As Carla Trujillo notes, "Chicana lesbians . . . take on the sacred contexts of religion and family. . . . For our own survival, Chicana lesbians must continually embark on the creation or modification of our spirituality and *familia*, usually implying alteration of the traditional, since these institutions, by their very nature, profess to be antithetical to the Chicana lesbian existence" (1991, x). As theorized by several writers, oppressive attempts to control sexuality go hand in hand with control over spirituality, and thus the resistance, healing, and transformation of such oppression must engage both sexuality and spirituality as constitutive of each other (Moraga 1983, Castillo 1994, Lara 2005, Lara 2008c). However, only a few contributors to the anthology directly address sexuality as part of their engagement with spirituality, suggesting that such discussions are still difficult to have.

In any case, as women writers of color have insisted, it is crucial that we write about all aspects of our lives and honor how our reflected-upon experiences are valid forms of scholarship and knowledge (Moraga and Anzaldúa 1983; Morales 1998; Latina Feminist Group 2001). Given the legacy of oppression against people of color, and queer people of color in particular, to proclaim that *our* flesh deeply matters and, moreover, is a source of profound knowledge, is a radical and healing act. A "theory in the flesh," as discussed by Cherríe Moraga in *This Bridge Called My Back*, is "one where the physical realities of our lives—our skin color, the land or concrete we grew up on, our sexual longings—all fuse to create a politic born out of necessity" (1983, 23). Investigating the spiritual realities of our lives is just as significant. Our spirit also matters. And, contrary to some dominant views that assume that being spiritual is a passive, apolitical state, we are affirming that as deployed within a "spiritual activist" worldview, it is active, it moves us into further action, and sustains the multiple ways we participate in social justice.

Aligned with a growing number of artists and scholars creating work that explores reality from holistic, spiritual perspectives, the contributions in this collection equally value and attend to material and spiritual conditions. In fact, we see those conditions as interconnected. As a result, we offer new theories of flesh and spirit, or, more accurately, of fleshed spirit and spirited flesh, for part of what these works do is heal the colonial-modern, patriarchal separation between flesh and spirit. Like our radical "foremothers," we are interested in "pursuing a society that uses flesh and blood [and spirit] experiences to concretize a vision" of healing and justice (Moraga and Anzaldúa 1983, 23).

Anzaldúa's writings courageously naming and exploring spirituality since the late 1970s have been vital in seeding this ground (Anzaldúa 2000; Keating 2009). Risking censure and misunderstanding from fellow women of color, white "allies," and others who argue she is romanticizing or appropriating spirituality or who have possibly internalized dominant views against spiritual worldviews as naïve, "New Age-y," and apolitical, Anzaldúa has repeatedly insisted on addressing spirit and spirituality as essential aspects of reality (Keating 2000; Keating 2005; Pérez 2007). Moreover, by insisting that we engage both our bodies and spirits, we shun so-called New Age dehistoricized approaches focused on transcending our flesh. Concretizing our spiritual lives through words and image, and in turn, spiritualizing our material lives, allows us to paint a fuller picture of our realities. This work resists dominant western thought that would have us split our bodies, our flesh and bones and cells, from our spirits—the invisible, yet felt aspect of our beings that is part of our life force—as if they were separate or opposite. As a decolonizing feminist project, it works to transform all racist, classist, sexist, heterosexist, patriarchal religious thought that denigrates the flesh—associated with the feminine, the queer, and all "others"—as inferior.

Saying "to flesh" and "to spirit" acknowledges that spirituality is something we do; it is part of creating culture and the production of meaning. Not only do we share insights and provide concrete details about our "spirit" or spiritual lives, we also recognize that knowledge about our "flesh," bodies, lives, and work expands and develops when we deliberately approach it as a spiritual endeavor. As such, to flesh the spirit and spirit the flesh heals. The writing and artwork in our volume is our humble contribution to such decolonizing healing work. Like the women described in Lara Medina's study, these contributors "utiliz[e] their intuition, gut, and intellect" to "discern the multiplicity of ways they can decolonize their spirits in order to heal and be healed" (1998, 191).

The initial call for work stated the anthology's attempt to document the legacy of Chicanas, Latinas, and Indigenous women who bridge spirituality with progressive worldviews. Acknowledging that many of us draw on spiritual resources as we work toward personal and social well-being, we invited contributors to examine spirituality from any traditions—such as Catholicism, other Christian faiths, Native and African-based religions, and Buddhism—that guide our spiritualities. Some refer to this journey as being on the red road; others call it Xicana, mestiza, hybrid or *nepantla* spirituality.[12] Others do not call it spirituality at all, yet live their lives within the context of a spiritual worldview that values the interrelationship among all life. True to the interdisciplinary nature of Chicana, Latina, and Indigenous studies, we invited women to submit critical essays, short stories, poems, personal narratives/testimonios, photographs, and artwork that address our many understandings of spirit and spiritualities, as well as investigate the personal and collective practices of how spirit and spirituality shape our everyday lives.

It is important for us to acknowledge that various dialogues, heart-to-heart *pláticas*, throughout the years and conference presentations at the National Association for Chicana and Chicano Studies, the MALCS Summer Institute, and the National Women's Studies Association were also instrumental in the development of the contributors' essays and our project overall.[13] After many discussions regarding the need for our anthology to be created in a spiritually mindful manner and not simply be a place that collected work on the subject matter, we invited Chicana, Latina, and Indigenous contributors to participate in conferences where they could share and have their works assessed in a woman-of-color-centered environment. All of our panels, roundtables, and discussion groups or talking circles have been extremely well attended. We feel our collective efforts have been productive in that women, and some men, exposed to our works are finding a community with which to engage in critical discourse on spirit and spirituality through the lens of Chicana, Latina, and Indigenous theory and practice. We have observed a deep intellectual and emotional need for such work while we simultaneously advance this subfield, particularly within Chicana and Chicano studies, Latina and Latino studies, Native American studies, ethnic studies, and women's studies.

The anthology begins with the premise that in the context of the universalization and homogenization of culture, as well as that of the economy, turning to the particular or local is a defense of place, culture, history, and individual experience. This anthology creates a space for women who identify as Chicana, Latina, or Indigenous to discuss their responses to social, political, cultural, and spiritual conditions that threaten the survival of their communities. As such, overall, the contributors' work focuses on several themes: negotiating personal, political, and/or cultural understandings of the concept of spirituality; healing one's identity and body; elucidating personal and social transformation; and subsequent practices rooted in various traditions. Moreover, throughout the anthology, contributors address spirituality as a valid way of knowing and creating knowledge, reflect on the decolonization of the bodymindspirit, and examine the role of spirituality and spiritual activism in moving toward a spiritually democratic society.

In general, the essays, poetry, and short stories document each writer's spiritual journey by discussing particular life events and how these events lead to their awareness of spirituality, negotiation and engagement with their understandings of spirit and spirituality, and subsequent ideologies and practices. These processes guided them to develop spiritual knowledge, deploy tools toward decolonizing the spirit, and ultimately to undertake a lifelong journey of spiritual-political transformation as human beings. Finally, the essays are grounded in critical feminist thought with an emphasis on Anzalduan theory and methodology. Most notable is the implementation of *autohistoria-teoría* (Anzaldúa 2000) and testimonio (Latina Feminist Group 2001) as methodological approaches. The tenor of the narratives moves from and between elucidating spirituality in relation to identity, the family, the academy, spiritual or religious communities, and the Earth; to analyzing cultural dimensions of spirituality, particularly the preeminent Virgin de Guadalupe-Tonantzin and other sacred feminine figures; to the deployment of spiritual identity in various sites, beginning with the body as a place of interrogation, negotiation, and healing.

"We Are All Radically Interconnected": Honoring and Calling to the Four Directions

Throughout our discussions, we realized that many of the contributors practice or are reflecting on some form of spirituality associated with the Four Directions.[14] As taught within many Indigenous worldviews, the Four Directions—East, West, North, and South—represent particular life energies and elements.[15] For example, the East represents "New Beginnings" and the energy of sun or fire. The West represents the "Place of Women" and is associated with water. The North represents the "Place of Elders" and the energy of wind. And the South is the "Place of Youth" and associated with earth. To honor and learn from this ancestral Indigenous knowledge while shedding light on the significance of our spiritual testimonios within this worldview, *con respeto*, we organized our anthology into the Four Directions by grouping contributions that generally share energies that pertain to one of the directions.

In prefaces to each of the four sections, we introduce the grouped texts and elaborate on their connection. Some texts, however, may reflect one or more directions. Situating the poems and essays into the Four Directions represents our collective commitment to personal and societal transformation. Building on Anzaldúa, the contributors' works clearly indicate they are "ready for change" (2002a, 576). This process involves creating a community of spiritual activists consistently engaging and negotiating the nepantla state, as discussed by Inés Hernández-Avila in the foreword and by several contributors. Thus, the anthology's organization into the Four Directions is an act of spiritual activism; namely, a communal prayer and ritual to incite radical social change (Anzaldúa 2002a; Avila 1999).

Our realization of the anthology's potential energies is best exemplified in the following conference gathering. The first roundtable of anthology contributors we organized as coeditors was held at the NACCS conference in San José, California in spring 2007. We desired to share our work in progress publicly and to create a space to exchange ideas and support one another. For many, participating in the roundtable served as an opportunity to meet others who were also thinking and writing about spirituality, and thus to find affirmation and inspiration to continue with their own work. For others who already knew each other, it was a reunion that served to deepen our relationships and commitment to develop our like-spirited work. Rearranging chairs, we transformed the conference room into a *círculo* and sprinkled ourselves throughout it, sitting among the audience. Flowing from one to another, we each began to discuss our unique yet connected essays.

We soon realized that the direction of the West and the energy of the water were undeniably with us. For soon after Irene finished introducing her essay, her "water broke." The symbolic amniotic fluid in this funny case poured out of a bottle of mineral water that frothed over into her lap, down her legs, and onto Tonantzin—Nahuatl for Our Mother, the Earth—when she opened the cap. Without skipping a beat, the two *comadre* birth attendants, Angelita Borbón and Patrisia Gonzales, proclaimed, "you know, once your water breaks, there is no turning back until the baby is born." Everyone bore witness to this communal prebirth as we all had a good healing belly laugh. Tlazolteotl—the sacred energy in Nahua thought that guides and protects midwives, birthing women, and newborns and who is "the Great Weaver and Parturient of Life," as described by Gonzales (2012, 30)—among other *comadres,* was right there with us, also merrily laughing and creating warmth in the midst of wetness.

Interpreting Irene's water bursting as the inevitability of the birth of this collection is also a sign of the spiritual power of our creativity. With these works we offer another perspective on this familiar metaphor in feminist artist and women's studies communities of birthing creativity and ourselves. So there we were and here we are several years later, joyous women in the midst of collectively *dando a luz* this anthology for our audience to critically engage and enjoy. May it elicit needed conversations on s/Spirit, spirituality, and spiritual activism, inspire further scholarship and creative expression, and contribute to the ongoing decolonial feminist project of radically healing and transforming lives and the Earth. In sum, like Anzaldúa's intentional ritual and prayer to the Four Directions, this anthology is organized in such a way as to engender "increased awareness of s/Spirit, our interrelatedness, and work for healing and transformation" (2002a, 574).

Notes

1. Although we are both Chicanas and most of our scholarship focuses on Chicana studies, our research is also comparative and our politics is inclusive. Thus, we intentionally sought to include the perspectives of Latinas and Indigenous women to deepen and broaden the discussion, and also because—although our lived experiences are as different as they are similar—we share many cultural and historical commonalities. Moreover, as "Chicanas," we acknowledge the multiple strands of our Indigenous or mixed-race ancestries, recognizing the historical and political contexts of (neo)colonialism that have led to many Chicanas becoming detribalized Indigenous women. This means that although many Chicanas know we have Indigenous genealogies and experience the transcultural *sobrevivencias* of Indigenous practices, including healing knowledges in our families, some may not have a direct generational link to a specific tribal identity or land base, while others do. Hence, for some Chicanas, to state they are Indigenous is considered redundant, while for others to identify as Xicana or Chicana Indígena is to explicitly claim their indigeneity in the face of racist (neo)colonial powers who benefit from cultural erasure, amnesia or denial.

However, we also recognize that ongoing dialogues between and among women who identify as Indigenous and/or Native and/or Chicana about what constitutes "indigeneity" are sometimes fraught with dissension and misunderstanding. Issues discussed include: the complexity of cultural identity, worldviews, and overlapping racist colonial histories and resistance to such histories and their political legacies; a decolonial approach to mestizaje; the problematics of Indigenist ideologies, which can work against Indigenous peoples' needs; the need to understand the diversity and differences of privilege and power between and among Indigenous peoples, Chicanas, and Latinas, throughout the Americas and globally, and act on that awareness; concern regarding appropriation in juxtaposition to ethical connections and/or acknowledgment of ongoing cross-cultural formation; an understanding of Indigenous peoples in present time (not only as existing in the past); and the politics of sovereignty, including land rights, reproductive rights, language rights, and other human rights. We also acknowledge how colonial processes have contributed to genocidal constructions of colonial categories of indigeniety. Unfortunately, a vast majority of Indigenous and mestiza/o peoples have assimilated these ideas about indigeniety due to the brutal and inhumane denial of the transference of traditional knowledges and a spiritually democratic educational system.

For related and additional perspectives on these matters, see, for example: Hernández-Avila 1992; Broyles-Gonzáles 2001; Talamantez, Guerrero, and Waters 2003; Denzin, Lincoln, and Tuhiwai Smith 2008; Latorre 2008; McNeill and Cervantes 2008; Luna 2011; Castellanos, Gutiérrez Nájera, and Aldama 2012; Gonzales 2012.

2. There is a growing discussion of the need to engage spirituality (as distinct from religion) critically as part of the decolonizing education of the "whole" student, as well as teacher. See, for example, Lara 2002; hooks 2003; Delgado Bernal et al. 2006; Rendón 2009; Gonzales et al. (forthcoming); Elenes and Figueroa, this volume.

3. Following Laura E. Pérez (1998; this volume), we write "s/Spirit" with a lowercase "s" and uppercase "S" to reference a simultaneous understanding of the reality of "spirit" as part of the self and life in general and "Spirit" as suggestive of an immanent "God" or

"Creator" or "Life" itself. In addition, by including "(s)," Pérez cross-culturally acknowledges the potential plurality of "the s/Spirit(s)" (1998, 37, 38, 45).

4. Contributors were asked to consider the following prompts as starting points: Define your spiritual roots and the sources that (re)define your spirituality. Does your practice integrate different traditions, and if so, how? Describe (a) formative moment(s) in your relationship to spirituality. How does your spirituality manifest itself in your intellectual work, family life, sexuality, and/or creativity? How has your spirituality assisted you with personal and/or political experiences of healing? How do you decolonize spirituality, personally, politically and/or socially? Describe the relationship between your spiritual practice and feminism.

5. Several recent anthologies address spirituality more broadly. On women's spiritualities see, for example, Rayburn and Comas-Díaz 2008; Agyeong et al. 2011. On US Latina/o and/or Chicano/Mexican American spiritualities see, for example, Garcia-Camarillo, Rodriguez, and Gonzales 2002; Menes 2004; De La Torre and Espinosa 2006; Espinosa and García 2008. For anthologies on Indigenous spiritualities in the United States and globally, see, for example, Irwin 2000; Pui-lan 2010; and Marcos 2010. All of these texts are largely focused on poetry and fiction, personal narrative, or scholarship, and do not merge all genres as this anthology does.

6. As described in their mission statement, *Mujeres Activas en Letras y Cambio Social* (MALCS, Women Active in Letters and Social Change), founded in 1982, "is an organization of Chicanas/Latinas and Native American women working in academia and in community settings with a common goal: to work toward the support, education and dissemination of Chicana/Latina and Native American women's issues. Chicanas/Latinas and Native American women from a variety of institutions gather at this yearly Summer Institute to network, share information, offer support and re-energize." See http://www.malcs.org/.

7. As Keating elaborates, "spiritual activism is a visionary, experientially-based epistemology and ethics, a way of life and a call to action. At the epistemological level, spiritual activism posits a metaphysics of interconnectedness and employs nonbinary modes of thinking. At the ethical level, spiritual activism requires concrete actions designed to intervene in and transform existing social conditions. Spiritual activism is spirituality for social change, spirituality that recognizes the many differences among us yet insists on our commonalities and uses these commonalities as catalysts for transformation" (2005, 242). For more engagement with spiritual activism, see Fernandes 2003; Lara 2005; Maparyan 2012; Sendejo 2013.

8. We place "feminist" in quotes to acknowledge that it has long been a contested term among women of color and Indigenous women. Indeed, because of the historical marginalization of women of color within mainstream women's movements and the desire to (a) use a more culturally resonant term and/or (b) clearly signal that one's framework is intersectional and expands beyond a monist emphasis on sex and/or gender by also accounting for other social categories of difference and inequality (e.g. class, sexuality, race, ethnicity, citizenship status, religion, ability), many prefer and/or simultaneously use the self-referents feminista, womanist, mujerista, and/or Xicanista (Delgado Bernal et al. 2006; Isasi-Díaz 1996; Comas-Díaz 2008; Castillo 1994; Luna 2011). We use "feminist" to describe the practice of working to understand the lives of people in general, and girls and women in particular, through an intersectional lens that tries to account for the complex ways one's multiple social categories and identities can influence lives with the aim of advancing social justice for everyone.

9. Some of the artists and writers engaged by Pérez 2007, Delgadillo 2011, and Román-Odio 2013 are: Kathleen Alcalá, Gloria Anzaldúa, Santa Barraza, Ana Castillo, Yreina Cervántez, Denise Chavez, Sandra Cisneros, Ester Hernández, Alma López, Yolanda Lopez, Amalia Mesa-Baines, Pat Mora, Lourdes Portillo, and Liliana Wilson. For a complete list see the texts cited above. For additional literature and/or art-based analyses of spirituality and/or religion, see Christian 2005; Alvarez 2007; Blake 2008; Garcia Lopez 2012; Romero 2012. Notably, in 2010, a Triton Museum of Art exhibition, "Xicana: Spiritual Reflections/Reflexíones Espiritúales" featured the artwork of six California Bay Area artists: Pilar Agüero-Esparza, Betta A. Davis, Celia Herrera Rodriguez, Consuelo Jiménez-Underwood, Viviana Paredes and Patricia Rodriguez. See http://www.tritonmuseum.org/exhibitions_Chicana.php (accessed July 1, 2013).

10. See for example the fiction of Judith Ortiz Cofer, Nicholasa Mohr, Loida Maritza Pérez, Julia Alvarez, and Cristina Garcia, the essays of Aurora Levins Morales (1998), and the art of Ana Mendieta.

11. Akin to the experiences of the editors of *Compañeras: Latina Lesbians* (Ramos 1987), *The Sexuality of Latinas* (Alarcón, Castillo, and Moraga 1993), and *Chicana Lesbians: The Girls Our Mothers Warned Us About* (Trujillo 1991), who responded to the need for a cohesive publication centered on the diverse sexualities of Chicanas and/or Latinas, we noticed a resounding gap in the literature on Chicana and/or Latina spiritualities. Getting Chicana/Latina writers and artists to submit work focused on sex and sexuality was indeed challenging in the 1980s and early 1990s, as described by some of the coeditors of these trailblazing editions, but it has undoubtedly helped to open critical and creative doors, as we continue to see this field develop in new and exciting directions (e.g., Gaspar de Alba 2003, Esquibel 2006, Blake 2008, Asencio 2010).

We share a similar hope and envision many more texts engaging the diversity of Chicana, Latina, and Indigenous women's spiritualities, including more work that integrates sexuality and spirituality, Afro-Latina, Muslim, Jewish, non-Catholic Christian, Buddhist, atheist or humanist spiritualities, and Indigenous spiritualities across the hemisphere and globe, among other themes not thoroughly addressed in this text. Promisingly, as we prepare this manuscript, a call for submissions for an anthology on Queer Xicana/o and Chicana/o spiritualities edited by José M. Aguilar-Hernández circulates.

12. See, for example, L. Pérez (1998; 2007) and Delgadillo (1998) on "hybrid spirituality," Medina (2006; this volume) on "nepantla spirituality," Anzaldúa (1987), Rodríguez (2004), and Delgadillo (2011) on "mestiza spirituality," and Castillo (1994), Luna (2011), Moraga (2011), and Medina (this volume) on "Xicana" spirituality.

13. At MALCS in 2006, we facilitated a "talking circle;" at both NACCS in 2007 and MALCS in 2011, we held two roundtables. Most recently, we held panels at NWSA (2012) and MALCS (2013).

14. Gloria Anzaldúa (2002a) and AnaLouise Keating (2005) explore the concept of the radical interconnectedness between and among all beings as an essential component of spiritual activism or a politics of spirit.

15. We are thankful for the teachers who have shared their knowledge of the Four Directions with us. Drawing largely from the Mexica tradition, they include: Griselda Sesma, Inés Hernández-Avila, Luz Alvarez Martínez, Elena Avila, Gloria Anzaldúa, Ana Castillo, Patrisia Gonzales, Rocky Rodriguez, Maria "Dora" Esquibel, Roberta Maldonado, Inés Talamantez, Belinda Garcia, and Christina Segala. Many have also noted that there are seven directions, including above, below, and center.

PART ONE

The East

New Beginnings

We begin with the East, the place of the sun, associated with new beginnings and vision. Critical engagement with dominant modern-colonial and ancient, dynamic, spiritual ideas, as well as the related desire for spaces that legitimate spirituality as a way of knowing and being within academia and our daily lives, is a common theme interweaving these initial texts. Cinthya Martinez's poem "The East" sets the tone for the anthology as she poignantly describes her relationship to energies associated with the East. This poem in particular situates the overall spiritual journey or red road reflected in the following essays. The intentionality of seeking guidance to heal and move toward happiness and transformation is characteristic of Eastern energies. Martinez's poem thus provides the contributors a space from which to engage new beginnings.

Undergirding Laura E. Pérez's "Writing with Crooked Lines" is a call for a traditionally materialist, masculinist, hierarchical, profit-driven, and fragmenting academia and dominant society in general to forge a new beginning that embraces ancient, cross-cultural spiritual knowledges, focused on the generative role of harmony, love, and justice. Indeed, as an astute global observer and social justice theorist, she prophetically suggests that the dominant world order is already crumbling. Pérez weaves together wisdom from many of the world's spiritual traditions that have informed her spirituality, including the Mayan philosophy of In Lak'ech, the Tibetan Buddhist "spiritual warrior" ideal, and the nonviolent, social-liberatory applications of Hinduism and Christianity—as lived out, for example, by Gandhi in India and some US civil rights activists. Challenging post-Enlightenment thought's delusions that we "are unrelated, gulfs apart from nature, from other people, even from parts of our own selves, as if our interdependence on all these levels were fantasy," Pérez focuses on the need to learn how to decipher and embody the "spirit writing" that *knows* working to synchronize "humanity to the rest of the natural world is sane, healthy, necessary," and is at the heart of a decolonial politics of spirit.

Contesting the modern notion that colleges should be disenchanted institutions, Maria Figueroa offers an essay titled "Toward a Spiritual Pedagogy along the Borderlands." Interweaving *testimonio* and theory grounded in Gloria Anzaldúa's (1987) geopolitical and creative concept of the "borderlands," this essay addresses the issues that arise in the author's path to integrate her spiritual practices as a *danzante azteca* into her pedagogy as a professor. Borrowing from what Anzaldúa calls *autohistoria*, where history is presented as a serpentine cycle rather than linearly, the essay examines how this conceptual and practical borderlands framework helps the author to seek new methods of facilitating knowledge with her students. How can "teachinglearning" be a spiritual endeavor that consciously examines the historical, social, and political implications of the borderlands? What are the pedagogical possibilities, risks, and limits of integrating one's whole identity and spirituality into the classroom?

Addressing the interrelationship between Chicana feminist pedagogies and epistemologies with respect to the author's own spiritual journey, C. Alejandra Elenes discusses how her spirituality has evolved throughout her adulthood. Indeed, in "Spiritual Roots of Chicana Feminist Borderland Pedagogies: A Spiritual Journey with Tonantzin/Guadalupe," Elenes shows us how she has come to understand—through her scholarship and interrogation of, and relationship with, Tonantzin/Guadalupe—that her own activism has meaning because it is related to a feminist spiritual understanding of the world. For Elenes, as for other contributors, practicing one's spirituality must include asking questions concerning the reasons for social injustice and what one can do to transform such inequities, here on earth.

Grounded in Anzaldúa's concept of "*autohistoria-teoria*," Elisa Facio's essay, "Spirit Journey: 'Home' as a Site for Healing and Transformation," illustrates her negotiation with Chicana feminism and spirituality during a bout with cancer. The metaphor of "home" is used to engage how particular places—sites—became spiritually significant in healing and transformation processes. The sites of home include places such as her birthplace, to meeting Mexican Indigenous family members, to attending *inipi* and *temazkalli* ceremonies, to negotiating her body as a spiritual medium. Her body now serves as a site of home where she has incorporated a fluidity of revolutionary and spiritual love into her life essence. Drawing from Anzaldúa's ideas of "spiritual activism," Facio thus argues that a relationship between Chicana feminism and spirituality is essential for the healing and transformation of Chicana, Latina, and Indigenous communities.

The East

Cinthya Martinez

The East
The place of new beginnings
Here I contemplate the mystery of life
I don't know when my death will arrive
And tap me on the shoulder
I accept my mortality and vitality
All at the same time
I don't know what lies ahead of me
But I openly embrace it
I determine nothing
I'm no longer a prisoner of the rigidity
That existed within me
For so long.
I consciously release the uncontrollable
And here I meet with Quetzalcoatl
As he covers me in his blanket of a million stars
I will sing a thousand songs
And write a hundred poems
All in one night
I am grateful for my essence
This is the place of air, of my breath
I inhale my resignation
Because I am my greatest friend
I am the love of my life

I am whom I have been waiting for
No one can complete me
Because I can complete myself.
The East
The place where I welcome the many rising suns that greet me
The place of new beginnings

Writing with Crooked Lines

Laura E. Pérez

Dedicated to my father, David "Miguel" Pérez Ordaz
(February 4, 1931–April 20, 2010)

My friend Father Eddie Fernandez, a Jesuit doctor of theology, once said to me in response to my worries about the possible errors and confusion that writing about hybrid spiritualities could cause, "God writes with crooked lines." This is so, Father Eddie explained, because *"Dios es bueno."* God is good. What turns up most often if you Google is the phrase, "God writes straight with crooked lines." But it occurs to me that it isn't just that God fixes our mistakes. God writes crookedly. The natural world and human nature as a part of it are neither really straight nor straightforward. The natural world is in constant motion—fluid, porous, changeable, inexhaustibly enigmatic.[1] And our handiwork, the social worlds and all the cultural objects humans create within these, including our individual and collective ways of being through the cultural, are likewise continually improvised, never fully decipherable, contours.

Spirit Writing

Split as we are into various shades of unhappiness by the tension between undomesticated being and desire and how we have been socialized to be and want, we are taught to embody, to produce reality as binary.[2] We live on the crumbling faith act, the historically specific aftereffect of colonization of the Americas and the rationalization of racialized, gendered, and sexed hierarchical orders in post-Enlightenment thought—that we are unrelated, gulfs apart from nature, from other people, even from parts of our own selves, as if our interdependence on all these levels were fantasy, delusion, superstition, or the demonic.[3] And so, swept away are the ancient cross-cultural imperatives to know ourselves, to be true to ourselves, and to care for others as our own selves.[4] Discovering ourselves, nonjudgmentally, is dismissed as useless navel gazing rather than the indispensable road to respectful coexistence with others.[5]

Perhaps, therefore, the crooked lines of our living are a spirit writing, traces that life forces some of us call spirit(s) and/or Spirit(s) leave, testifying to that which is disincarnate in us, not quite killed yet not fully born in us, yet the marrow of our being.[6] Traced in us and by us is a different alphabet, markings between and beyond the social text of dominant, dominating orders: a spirit writing. Winding, returning, spiraling and seemingly dead-ended jagged paths characterize the pilgrimage toward understanding that the (re)harmonization of the mind-body-spirit and the synchronizing of humanity to the rest of the natural world is sane, healthy, necessary, a craft work that is not solely personal, but perhaps the most pressing ideological and political work, the heart of the "decolonial."[7]

Working to undo or shift to a different form of consciousness beyond the racializing, patriarchal, homophobic, and classist ordering of social reality and being in the westernized world is, by necessity, a journey through the dark forest of human power gone awry. The hypnotic suasion of ideological discourses of supposed superiority that have rationalized power and exploitation of one kind of human over another, and of humans over other beings in nature, dehumanizes us; that is, we are desensitized and alienated from what is natural within and to us. Social disempowerment occurs in tandem with disempowerment at the level of individuality, within our psyches, and more generally within our entire being's multiple sources of intelligence and our capacity to "know" through our contact with human and nonhuman life forms. Gloria Anzaldúa (1987; 2002a) called this extrarational knowing "*la facultad*," and "*conocimiento*"—"the faculty" and "cognizance"—but numerous writers alongside her speak of intuitive awareness and the multiple, simultaneous, complex forms of knowing that our different senses produce beyond the more obvious capacity to consciously reason through the intellect (for example Gardner 2006).

Interpellating Love and Integrity

Art, spirituality, and traditional popular wisdom rooted in timeless truths remind us that love is the source of all life, and its lack the source of error, psychological, somatic, and social suffering, and illness. The intention and practice of loving care seems to be a fundamental, harmonizing expression of the natural, perduring, and enigmatic reality of which we form part, signified cross-culturally as energy, the vital life force, *aché, qi/chi, shakti, kora,* s/Spirit(s), and by the names of numerous deities and natural entities in ancient and surviving "mythologies" and theophilosophies.[8]

Elders from different cultural traditions, including scientists, have long cautioned that to the degree that we collude in disrespect, exploitation, and oppression of others, humanity destroys itself and our planetary habitat.[9] Such collusion depends upon our own fragmentation, which is another way of thinking about our "interpellation" (Althusser [1971] 2001) as subject(ed)s within modern western(ized) culture that consents in various degrees to the interests of dominating economic, political, and social classes rather than to our personal, humanity's, and the planet's greater good.[10] We are inculcated with the historically recent credo that there are no essences, let alone a "quintessence" connecting all life forms, and that the only "real" forms of power are guaranteed by the threat or enactment of violence and the amassing of economic, social, and cultural powers. A "successful" life is therefore the succumbing of our will, the "consent" to perform socially prescribed roles and in other ways coproduce the "world" that domination over others has imagined and continually re-utters like a mantra through the dominating circulation of its imaginary as the blueprint of social and psychic reality. In this psychic landscape, out of which political ideologies of the Left and the Right alike are fabricated, we are alive, as if alive.[11] We are the simulacrum, walking billboards of unreal reals; the vitality, creativity, resiliency of genuinely meaningful existence dwindling, as if these natural impulses were mere fancies and delusions.[12]

I gather that the task of thinkers, artists, storytellers, spiritual students and elders, *curanderas/os,* and all manner of healers, by whatever names and functions these are defined in different cultures, involves perceiving through, sensing beyond, understanding in spite of culturally and historically specific veils, and acting within and upon the social body to ensure harmonious relations based on enduring realities and truths derived from the careful observation of human and nonhuman nature, notwithstanding the ultimately enigmatic nature of Nature.[13] From this perspective, the cross-cultural injunction of wisdom traditions to know one's self results in both psychological healing and ideological and political empowerment, for the practice of integrating a psyche that has been splintered as a consequence of the psychological and social violence of racializing, classist, patriarchal, and heteronormative socializing processes, for example, returns power to us as individuals and thereby as active, meaningfully engaged members of the human ecosystem as well as the planetary ecosystem.[14]

For Audre Lorde, the erotic, arising from our authentic and deepest nature and expressed as love of self and other and the joy and knowledge these bring, is both regenerative and liberatory: "For as we begin to recognize our deepest feelings, we begin to give up, of necessity, being satisfied with suffering and self-negation, and with the numbness which so often seems like their only alternative in our society. Our acts against oppression become integral with self, motivated and empowered from within. . . . In touch with the erotic, I become less willing to accept powerlessness, or those other supplied states of being which are not native to me, such as resignation, despair, self-effacement, depression, self-denial" (1984, 58).[15]

Decolonizing Heart and Hearth

My own journey towards decolonized and decolonizing consciousness germinated in a childhood and youth during the 1960s and 1970s of much spiritual, intellectual, and social diversity, cross-pollination, and openness to change. I was raised in a Catholic, Spanish-speaking Mexican home in Chicago in which my mother respected the pantheons of different religions and spiritualities as she became aware of them. In her childhood mestiza home in Mexico, she learned Indigenous worldviews and healing practices, which she conveyed within our home. Part of this philosophy is an openness to truth and knowledge in different traditions; in her case, particularly regarding healing and spiritual assistance. In time, her pantheon included the Buddha and a Hindu guru; she invoked the latter successfully for healing purposes. My mother's principal practice, however, has been prayer, the powerful and intelligent use of intention as directed, positive energy to help herself and others. This openness in my mother to universal truths in culturally different spiritual traditions was modeled by my father with respect to thought more generally. From him I learned to think critically about social and political realities in different parts of the world. I learned that learning is a continual process, one that involves discussion, reflection, and revision of one's opinions, aimed most importantly towards the transformation of individual practices. I learned that intelligence is reflected in the prudence of how well we live in relation to our families, our relatives, our communities, and in the personal tranquility with which we live our daily lives.

I have also been nourished by feminist and queer thought (especially women of color's) and the theophilosophies of diverse Native American (especially Nahua and Maya), African-diasporic (especially Santería and African American women's spirituality), Hindu (especially through Gandhi), and Buddhist (especially Tibetan and Zen Buddhist) systems of thought, and by European esoteric holistic writings of the "perennial philosophy" (particularly relating to the teachings of Pythagoras) and those of early Christian desert church fathers and mothers and other Christian mystics, including modern ones such as Thomas Merton. I have greatly benefitted from reading the poetry of the Sufi mystic Rumi and of poets of every culture and tradition. I have been particularly attentive to the role and function of creativity in spiritual-intellectual personal and social transformation.

From childhood, I have been increasingly surrounded by cultural difference, and not only mine, vis-à-vis Euro-American culture. The lived experience of on-the-ground, co-inhabited cultural diversity has functioned as a fluid, omnipresent, alternative and global social imaginary always-in-the-making. This is different from cultural appropriation; this is multicultural coformation, cross-cultural synchronization, sympathetic attraction to the humane against the dehumanization of beliefs and practices from dominant cultures. It has been the affinity for truth and meaning.[16]

In my experience, I observe that spiritual awareness works like a muscle, growing clearer and stronger with attentive use. I work to realign my overworked brain and my underworked muscles with the heart, as vehicles of spiritualized consciousness. I also observe that the body regenerates through the circulation and exchange of spiritual or vital life-force energy within itself and between itself and other life forms; otherwise it is increasingly depleted on every level.

I find myself in an ongoing process that is decolonizing within me, detecting and releasing binary habits of thought and inflexibility, rebuilding psychological-spiritual boundaries, recuperating my energy from self-deprecating, other-centered ideologies still occupying and colonizing me, and increasingly trusting my intuition and creative impulses. I have felt internal tectonic plates shifting, as old thoughts are released and others remembered, as in Irene Perez's image of the once-dismembered Coyolxauhqui healed, with the piecing back together of my own severed psychic members. This has happened every time I have gone back to important places where I have lived, with the express intention of psychically calling myself back through gratefully recollecting how I grew and received gifts there, rather than focusing on losses sustained in these places. I have gone back for the "good," leaving behind the "bad," as a Diné elder once advised a small group of us, to count my blessings, as my father urged in the face of sadness, depression, and the feeling of being overburdened. Instead of my old habit of racing forward to the future, without grieving for what is left behind, and without fully gathering all of my pieces to take with me on my journeying, I have found that it is good to reclaim my scattered being and with it, my life energy as my inner hearth.

"Interbeing," "Spiritual Warriorship," and "In Lak'ech"

"Making Face, Making Soul,"[17] Gloria Anzaldúa's (1990) version of the Nahua concept of personhood and integrity, (*in ixtli in yollotl*; face, heart = person), speaks to aligning one's spirit-directed heart to the countenance by which the world is faced and engaged.[18] The antidote to the *susto* (spirit fright/psychic loss) of culturally induced mind-body-spirit fragmentation is in the pilgrimage to the Self within self, to Nature within one's own unique nature. It is in the reclamation of one's social shadow, in Jungian terms, of one's cultural, gender, sexual desire for expression of s/Self, and any other aspects of being that have been shamed, repressed, misunderstood, or punished. It is reassembling the essential tool kit natural and unique to us, the gifts necessary to realizing our fullest potential.

Integrity is tied to interdependence in the writing of the Zen Buddhist monk Thich Nhat Hanh, who expresses this relationality as "interbeing":

> It is difficult to find English or French words which convey the same mean-
> ing as Tiep Hien. There is a term from the Avatamsaka Sutra, "interbeing,"
> that conveys the spirit, so we have translated Tiep Hien as interbeing. In the
> sutra it is a compound term which means "mutual" and "to be." Interbeing
> is a new word in English, and I hope it will be accepted. We have talked
> about the many in the one, and the one containing the many. In one sheet
> of paper, we see everything else, the cloud, the forest, the logger. I am,
> therefore you are. You are, therefore I am. That is the meaning of the word
> "interbeing." We "interare." ([1987] 2005, 88)

Similarly, Chogyam Trungpa writes that "inner authentic presence comes from exchanging yourself with others, from being able to regard other people as yourself" ([1984] 2009, 160). Tibetan Buddhism emphasizes compassion (Latin: *com-* "together" + *pati* "to suffer"), care for the psychological, physical, and social well-being of others, and understanding that we are all interrelated and therefore interdependent. For me, the Sacred Hearts of Jesus and Mary convey this teaching as well. From hearts pierced with compassion and crowned with the thorns of suffering, roses bloom, and the flames of spiritual awareness and power blaze.

Chogyam Trungpa's "spiritual warrior," Mahatma Gandhi's morally powerful, politically victorious anticolonial activism, the lunch counter sit-ins, Freedom Rides, and other disciplined acts of noncooperation with southern racism by James M. Lawson, Jr.'s carefully trained Student Nonviolent Coordinating Committee (SNCC) are all characterized by a paradoxical, highly active, and effective "meekness," a nonviolent ethics and politics that is none-theless steadfastly committed to socially transformative action.[19] The nonvio-lent activism of the spiritually disciplined occupies another, a different, a "third," an "*x*" space beyond good-evil and other dichotomized perceptions of reality that call for reactive solutions that are ultimately within the logic of dominant paradigms. Nonviolent spiritual activism performs a shift of con-sciousness, enacting differently imagined social realities and ecological rela-tionships and actualizing into being a different worldview and logic, one based on harmonious, respectful relationships of diversity-within-unity.[20]

Based on the spiritually discerned understanding of the nature of the interrelationship of all planetary life forms, nonviolent being performs not as repetition of the status quo, nor only as disidentification with dominant, oppressive orders, but as identification, as reharmonization with respect to a different, wilder, undomesticated, natural, lush, rich, plural, multiple, trans-formative, continually hybridizing and interconnected reality.[21] This gentle-ness, this acceptance of a natural drifting towards each other, called sympathy, attraction, affinity, and love, is founded on the knowledge that we are made of the same stuff, resonant in the beautiful and powerful Mayan concept of *In Lak'ech, tú eres mi otro yo*: you are my other me.[22] Writing in the shadow of the atomic bomb, Maya linguist and scholar of Amerindian languages Domingo Martínez Parédez dedicated his scholarly efforts to the circulation of this concept, in the hope that humanity could learn to peacefully coexist. He observed:

> esa manera de concebir al Ser Absoluto y su manifestación matemática, como el Ser de todos y no ser de nadie, evitó esas odiosas divisiones raciales y trajó como consecuencia admirable el que el pensador maya llegase a la genial conclusión de que EL TU es mi OTRO YO, con la expresión IN LAK'ECH, ERES MI OTRO YO. (1960, 19; see also 129, 141, and 153) [that manner of conceiving Absolute Being and its mathematical manifes-tation, as the Being of all and of none, avoided those odious racial divisions and had the admirable consequence that the Maya thinker arrived at the genial conclusion that the you is the other me, in the expression *In Lak'ech*, you are my other me.]

We are Power

Elder, philosopher, and activist Grace Lee Boggs, ninety-eight years old this year, witness to and participant in more than half a century of social change movements, speaks of the necessity of seizing our own power *now* and alongside growing numbers of people across the nation and globe, meaningfully recreating devastated communities *ourselves*, reinventing work, education, and culture *ourselves*. Rebuilding community and the self as a communal being in ways that make sense for our varying local conditions, she urges us to be the change we wish to see. She writes:

> At this point in the continuing evolution of our country and of the human race, we urgently need to stop thinking of ourselves as victims and to recognize that we must each become a part of the solution because we are each a part of the problem. . . . Each of us needs to undergo a tremendous philosophical and spiritual transformation. Each of us needs to be awakened to a personal and compassionate recognition of the inseparable interconnection between our minds, hearts, and bodies; between our physical and psychical well-being; and between our selves and all the other selves in our country and in the world. Each of us needs to stop being a passive observer of the suffering that we know is going on in the world and start identifying with the sufferers. Each of us needs to take a leap that is both practical and philosophical, beyond determinism to self-determinism. . . . Despite the powers and principles that are bent on objectifying and commodifying us and all our human relationships, the interlocking crises of our time require that we exercise the power within us to make principled choices in our ongoing daily and political lives—choices that will eventually although not inevitably (since there are no guarantees) make a difference. (2011, 29; 33–34)

Serpentine Writing

Writing with the crooked lines of our lives against the grain of dominating cultures is a serpentine journey of embodied, increasingly aware, spiritualized being. It is a multiply sourced feeling-sensing-thinking-being of constant growth and fluidity that seeks to make harmonious connections across time and space, across cultures and geographies, across the span of the living and the discarnate, in search of deeper truths—the kinds of truths that will allow us to recapture the power and energy necessary to transform self, humanity, and society for the greater good.[23] Shedding the old skins of profoundly wounded and wounding excessively profit-driven and materialist culture, s/Spirit which is l/Life escapes moribund ideologies, with the heart as a compass, shifting in transformation, enacting the yes that lies within our powers.

Notes

1. As Masanobu Fukuoka states, "Nature is in constant transition, changing from moment to moment. People cannot grasp nature's true appearance. The face of nature is unknowable. Trying to capture the unknowable in theories and formalized doctrines is like trying to catch the wind in a butterfly net" (2009, 145).

2. As Robert A. Johnson says, "We are all born whole but somehow the culture demands that we live out only part of our nature and refuse other parts of our inheritance. We divide the self into an ego and a shadow because our culture insists that we behave in a particular manner. . . . But the refused and unacceptable characteristics do not go away; they only collect in the dark corners of our personality" (1971, 4). For the importance of integrating the wild or natural under patriarchy, particularly for women and the feminized, see Estés 1996.

3. For elaboration, see Gregory Cajete's *Native Science*: "All of nature, not only humans, has rights. This is the essential 'cosmological clash' between the foundations of Native culture and those of modern society. . . . The cosmology that has shaped the evolution of the West with its focus on dominion over nature, the hierarchy of life, and a transcendent male God, has also shaped modern people's perception of the 'real world.' . . . an essentially dysfunctional cosmology, a cosmology that can no longer sustain us at any level" (2000, 53).

4. See Chogyam Trungpa, who writes, "If we try to solve society's problems without overcoming the confusion and aggression in our own state of mind, then our efforts will only contribute to the basic problems, instead of solving them. . . . The warrior's journey is based on discovering what is intrinsically good about human existence and how to share that basic nature of goodness with others. There is a natural order and harmony to this world, which we can discover" ([1984] 2009, 126).

5. See *Is There No Other Way? The Search for a Nonviolent Future* (2001) by Michael N. Nagler, Gandhi scholar and cofounder of the program in Peace and Conflict Studies at the University of California, Berkeley.

6. By "s/Spirit(s)" I mean to indicate that different cultures and historical eras define "spirit," "spirituality" and related concepts differently and that therefore these are not universally synonymous or translatable concepts. Thus, for example, in some cultures one might speak of spirits rather than spirit, or of both a creator Spirit and manifestations of this as "spirits," and so on. All of this is quite apart from what indeed might be universal across cultures and times, and apart from specific discussions of how s/Spirit(s) is or are understood in different cultural traditions.

7. See Estela Román: "El ser humano, ya separado y dividido de sí mismo, se ha vuelto incapaz de entender los mensajes de la Tierra y ahora es más factible de ser manipulable, de ahí que las visiones que se le presenten como mensajes se vuelvan solo una historia creada. La oscuridad, se vuelve, cada vez más la condición cotidiana del ser humano" (2012, 40).

[The human being, already separated and divided from self, has been incapable of understanding the messages of the Earth and is now more vulnerable to being manipulated, and because of this the visions which present themselves as messages are taken only to be created fiction. Darkness becomes, increasingly, the everyday condition of the human being.] (All translations are mine.) Also, "from a Taoist alchemical perspective, the body/mind split is a pathological state because there is blockage when the qi cannot transform freely from yin form to yang formlessness, from yang formlessness to yin form.

An excess accumulates on one side, bringing deficiency and exhaustion on the other. . . . Traditional Chinese medicine regards these splits and blockages as the cause of all disease and pain" (Dechar 2006, 18).

8. See the work of Dr. Masaru Emoto (2005) for the harmonizing, beneficial effects of loving thoughts and the destructive effects of negative thoughts on the molecular structure formation of water crystals. Pearce (2002) offers further insight with respect to the science of the body's fields of energy and interaction with those outside of itself, and the centrality of the heart..

9. These warnings date in the Americas to the warnings of Native American elders during the European invasions of the continent. For a more recent message from the Kogi Indigenous people of Columbia, see Alana Ereira's 1992 documentary, *The Heart of the World*. Most recently, authorized Mayan elders have been traveling throughout the world to dispel the 2012 doomsday scenarios of unauthorized writers and filmmakers, and to instead emphasize humanity's power and responsibility to transform the dangerous ecological and social disharmonies of the planet. In the San Francisco Bay Area, that message was conveyed by Don Miguel Angel Chiquín in April 2011.

10. "Interpellation" (Althusser [1971] 2001) refers to the shaping of the subjectivity of individuals through the circulation of dominant cultural ideology to reflect the interests of the economically, politically, or socially powerful.

11. The Greek etymological root of the word *psyche* is soul, as psychologists like Carl Jung and Jungians like James Hillman, Robert A. Johnson, and Clarissa Pinkola Estés have emphasized. By "psychic," I refer to the psychologically conscious and unconscious, to the intuitive and "paranormal" potentialities of the body, but also more broadly to the mind as a multidimensional, organ-wide system of awareness, as discussed in work such as Pearce's (2002).

12. As Jean Baudrillard states, "Abstraction today. . . . [s]imulation is. . . . the generation by models of a real without origin or reality: a hyperreal. The territory no longer precedes the map, nor survives it. Henceforth, it is the map that precedes the territory—precession of simulacra—it is the map that engenders the territory. . . . It is the real, and not the map, whose vestiges subsist here and there, in the deserts which are no longer those of the Empire, but our own. The desert of the real itself" (1998, 166–84).

13. That patriarchal, heteronormative, and racist scientists have constructed narratives that serve their own ideological interests as to what is "natural" does not mean we cannot know something of what in fact is natural. The ancient unbroken sciences of India, China, the Maya and Nahua and other Native American peoples, for example, are the basis of their philosophical and spiritual beliefs.

14. For more in this regard, see Nagler 2001; Trungpa ([1984] 2009); Thich Nhat Hanh ([1987] 2005, 2010); Mani 2009.

15. As Audre Lorde states: "The very word erotic comes from the Greek word *eros*, the personification of love in all its aspects—born of Chaos, and personifying creative power and harmony. When I speak of the erotic, then, I speak of it as an assertion of the lifeforce of women; of that creative energy empowered, the knowledge and use of which we are now reclaiming in our language, our history, our dancing, our loving, our work, our lives" (1984, 55).

16. Mindful of dominant culture's ethos of rationalized appropriation of the land, beliefs, and even bodies of the colonized and enslaved in the Americas, I have asked Mexica and Maya spiritual elders if I, and if we Chicana/os and Latina/os, have a right to "know," participate, and reclaim Indigenous ways of being, and I have been told both

that we do, and that Maya spirituality is for humanity, not just the Maya. Furthermore, my experience with all people of wisdom is that our intention in humbly and sincerely seeking guidance for the greater good, rather than for personal aggrandizement or enrichment, is the heart of any deeply meaningful and nourishing act of cultural exchange and of imparting/receiving knowledge. Knowledge is not to be tricked out of people, obtained falsely, or otherwise ill gotten.

17. This section title makes reference to *Making Face, Making Soul: Haciendo Caras, Critical and Creative Perspectives by Women of Color*, the anthology edited by Anzaldúa in 1990, and more to the point, her reclamation of the Nahua concept of personal, social, and cosmic integrity; the alignment of the inner or unseen soul self with the outer and social self or "face." The concept of nonviolent, spiritually and mentally disciplined conduct akin to the discipline of a warrior comes from Chogyam Trungpa ([1984] 2009).

18. See Anzaldúa's introduction to *Making Face, Making Soul* (1990). Drawing on the codices, Miguel León-Portilla (1992) wrote about this concept in many of his works on Aztec philosophy and literature.

19. Hogan (2007) provides an account of the crucial, spearheading role of Lawson and this civil rights organization.

20. Nagler (2001) and Thich Nhat Hanh ([1987] 2005, 2010) elaborate on this concept of "diversity in unity."

21. Performance as repetition and therefore coproduction of socially prescribed roles and disidentification in cross-dressing and other queer practices as only partial and subversive identification with these are theorized in Butler (1993) and Muñoz (1999).

22. The concept of In Lak'ech was circulated in Chicana/o literature and culture by playwright Luis Valdez (1990) in his 1971 essay "Pensamiento Serpentino." Valdez took many concepts, including that of the title of his theological-philosophical poem and the *ars poetica* of his theater, from Domingo Martínez Parédez's *Un Continente y una Cultural* (1960), which he cites. Martínez Parédez traces the linguistic and theological-philosophical unity of Mesoamerican and southern Indigenous cultures, characterized by "*pensamiento serpentino*," serpentine thought. In *Hunab Kú, Síntesis del Pensamiento Filosófico Maya* (1964), Martínez Parédez writes of the cosmic rather than tribal or nationalist concept of *Hunab Kú*, an absolute being who represented cosmic dynamism and unity in plurality (40). Mayan elder Don Miguel Angel Chiquín confirmed the meaning of the concept of In Lak'ech to me and of Maya theophilosophy as "cosmic," that is, as belonging to all of humanity, in April 2011. He further confirmed that Maya thought has been safeguarded through the centuries orally by generations of Maya elders.

23. Consider Fukuoka:

Culture is usually thought of as something created, maintained, and developed by humanity's efforts alone. But culture always originates in the partnership of man and nature. When the union of human society and nature is realized, culture takes shape of itself. Culture has always been closely connected with daily life, and so has been passed on to future generations, and has been preserved up to present times. . . . Something born from human pride and the quest for pleasure cannot be considered true culture. True culture is born within nature, and is simple, humble, and pure. Lacking true culture, humanity will perish. . . . When people rejected natural food and took up refined food instead, society set out on a path toward its own destruction. This is because such food is not the product of true culture. Food is life, and life must not step away from nature (2009, 138).

Toward a Spiritual Pedagogy along the Borderlands

Maria Figueroa

Testimonio #1: Pidiendo Permiso

Como Xipe Totec
me visto en piel ajena
protective regalia of designer glasses
pencil skirts, collar blouses and
binding shoes

my only desire
is for the rising sun of the east
witness the new ritual
a sundance for shedding and offering my skin
in a renewal and rebirth

like vibrant sun rays
mis plumas de quetzal
cultivan semillas de luz y consciencia
offering regenerative breath into
mindbodyspirit

                        Ometeotl

I begin with the death of a cultural warrior as an acknowledgement of those who have come before me and as a reminder of what is to come. Gloria

Anzaldúa, the cultural warrior and spiritual philosopher, who sought to borrow from the traditional epistemological structures of learning and moved towards including a diverse genre as a new mode of expression and inquiry, died in the spring of 2004. However, her pedagogical legacy will live on in *Borderlands/La Frontera*. In her introduction to the second edition of *Borderlands* (1999), Sonia Saldívar-Hull asserts it "opens up a radical way of restructuring the way we study history. Using a new genre she calls *autohistoria*, Anzaldúa presents history as a serpentine cycle rather than a linear narrative" (2). It has been through careful examination of Anzaldúa's work and my own process as a teacher that her conceptual framework helps me to seek new methods of facilitating knowledge for my students. The borderlands are historical experiences with deep social and political implications. They are also metaphoric possibilities for knowledge not yet uncovered.

Therefore, I am searching for ways in which I can make my teachinglearning a spiritual endeavor by essentially applying a nonlinear, nontraditional pedagogy. My guide becomes Anzaldúa's metaphor of the serpentine cycle, which implies a dynamic and retrospective process. This is the spirit of the borderlands. By approaching the discussion and enacting a borderlands experience, I am situating my pedagogy in an untraversed process where traditional pedagogy becomes linear and spiritual pedagogy becomes serpentine.

History of the Borderlands

Perhaps a careful examination of the greater vision of borders and borderlands is appropriate. Academia's cultural codes perpetuate borders, enabling privilege for a few and disenfranchising many. As exposed in borderlands literature, the borderlands are literal and metaphoric spaces where one can venture into complex diversity. The borderlands are where the personal becomes the political. Where the personal is rooted in the historical. Where the spiritual is political and historical. In the Americas, the borderlands have been "in process" for over five hundred years. Five-hundred-plus years of colonization have left a people, Native Americans (Chicanas and Chicanos included), searching for roots in the land once rightfully theirs. The historic violation and dishonoring of the Treaty of Guadalupe Hidalgo (1848) and subsequent legislation rendered Mexicans living in the United States second-class citizens, Native Americans on reservations, Blacks still slaves, and Asians excluded.

What the cultural warrior Anzaldúa so keenly saw was a way to bridge the many historical memories and traumas of people, and more specifically of women of color. At the root of her thinking and writing is an attempt to reclaim the human element that embodies a spirit and whose legacy remembers.

Historical acts of colonization, slavery, and exclusion are rooted in masqueraded attempts to acknowledge spirit and divination, as in the case of Manifest Destiny. In practice, however, these acts served to perpetuate a lack of consciousness void of spiritual accountability. Anzaldúa's journey from the physical into the spirit world reminds us that with life comes death; it is the balance of all things. With colonization and marginalization comes rebellion, liberation, and social transformation; hence, the journey to seek balance.

The Face of Spiritual Borderlands Pedagogy

My journey continues as I seek the balance between the traditional demands of academia—read, lecture, and listen—and the more spiritual approaches to academic knowledge—read, think, feel, discuss, and think again. In her groundbreaking text, *Sentipensante (Sensing/Thinking) Pedagogy* (2009), Laura I. Rendón reiterates Parker J. Palmer's (1998) references to the split between the inner and outer landscape of teaching and learning. She observes, "In education the *outer* is what we do with our minds, and is usually associated with intellectualism, rationality, and objectivity. The *inner* privileges subjectivity, intuition, emotion, and personal experience" (7). The spiritual approach seeks to make the learning and teaching experience more holistic where one aspect of learning depends on the other.

By analyzing the borderlands from a sociological perspective, and enacting the spirit of the borderlands within my holistic approach to teaching, thinking, and learning, my students and I are honoring the *inner* essence in higher education. We are emotional beings engaged in the spiritual. C. Alejandra Elenes's notion of "border/transformative pedagogies"—as also referenced in the following essay in this collection—complements Rendón by claiming that "Border/transformative pedagogies involve cultural politics that incorporate as social practices the construction of knowledge(s) capable of analyzing conflicts over meaning" and by further identifying "these pedagogical practices as border or borderlands because they blur many distinctions artificially created in cultural productions and classroom practices" (2006, 247).

Elenes's and Rendón's work reminds us that traditional pedagogical models all too often overemphasize logical thought guided by the ever-present knowledge of the professor and discourage emotional or personally driven questions from coming to fruition as legitimate subject matter. As a result, traditional pedagogy omits the spiritual entity (a connection of body, mind, and spirit) of the individual and collective, by ignoring the emotional connection inherent in the subject matter. Traditional pedagogy fragments the parts of the whole in order to seek objectivity and reason, thereby invalidating any kinesthetic or emotively driven reactions to learning. Recognizing teachinglearning as a spiritual entity calls for acknowledging that teachinglearning is a sacred act as well. bell hooks makes this connection best when she convincingly argues, "That learning process comes easiest to those of us who teach who also believe that there is an aspect of our vocation that is sacred; who believe that our work is not merely to share information but to share in the intellectual and spiritual growth of our students" (1994, 13). Hence, teachinglearning as a spiritual sacred act is ceremony put into motion. The serpentine cycle has commenced.

Anzaldúa's death prompted me to share the tragic news with all of my students, especially with my literature students. After all, they had read "Mestiza Consciousness/La conciencia de la mestiza" from her *Borderlands* text. The text is a difficult one for any student of literature, let alone for first year undergraduates who are mostly unfamiliar with literary conventions. After careful, lengthy, genuine, and critical discussion, my students arrived at the conclusion that Anzaldúa's vision for social transformation was simple yet complex when implemented. Social transformation happens when we seek new paradigms based on equality and inclusivity.

With Anzaldúa's death fresh on my mind and my students' analyses of her work, I performed my usual routine. I prepared my notes for class, gathered my books, reviewed and graded papers, sipped some coffee, and paused as I contemplated packing the blue candle, shell, framed picture of Our Lady of Guadalupe Tonantzin, and *Borderlands*—the book. All of these items sit on my office altar to remind me of our humanity and spirit when swamped with overwhelming numbers of student essays. Because I am careful about not offending and respecting students and colleagues of all walks of life, my office altar is humble and not intrusive. It rests on an overflowing metal bookcase adjacent to my desk, draped in crimson southwestern pattern material. It holds the heartfelt stories of those students who sit in my office, with tears in their eyes and joy in their tone. My altar also acknowledges fear in their look, curiosity in their inquiry, and abuse on their bodies. It creates a sanctuary in a nontraditional space for my students and me, as well as serves to encourage me to contemplate my role as an educator.

Once I finished packing, the walk to my class was one of evaluation and fear of not knowing how my students would react to my decision to build an altar in honor of this writer. Would they walk out of class, report me to the dean for possibly imposing religious dogma, or would they maybe just listen and be engaged in a familiar act of altar building in honor of the dead? I am reminded of Anzaldúa's potent words, "La mestiza constantly has to shift out of habitual formations; from convergent thinking, analytical reasoning that tends to use rationality to move towards a single goal (a western mode), to divergent thinking, characterized by movement away from set patterns and goals and toward a more whole perspective, one that includes rather than excludes" (1999, 101). This citation implies that *la mestiza* is always in process, seeking those paradigms of inclusivity.

By allowing my fears to dictate my actions, I would have violated my personal journey towards inclusive spiritual pedagogy. How could I not seek another way of facilitating knowledge with my students? Why would honoring the academic, cultural, and feminist legacy of this author be seen as so different from honoring Shakespeare, Whitman, Woolf and others? My fears spoke to my own internalized "rationality to move towards a single goal." The western model would have me walk into a classroom full of students awaiting knowledge from the "know-it-all-teacher," as if they were mere open vessels free of emotional perspective and prepared to rationalize the day's lecture.

There have been moments when I have had the urge to internalize linear and spiritless models for the sake of keeping teachinglearning "safe" and streamlined. As a means of remedying these urges, I call on Anzaldúa's suggestion for "divergent thinking" by honoring her academic and spiritual work and further echo Ayala, Herrera, Jiménez, and Lara's groundbreaking dialogical approach to transgressing the constructed borders between the community and the academy, particularly Lara's recollection of feeling fear when challenging pedagogical strategies. In her response to the question "What have been our most memorable teaching experiences?" Lara remarks, "We felt fear, yet we knew how important it was for us as instructors to break down the hierarchy of knowledge by being ourselves, being vulnerable in front of the students. . . . We showed them a different way to be teachers and learners, a way that values the whole self, feelings included" (2006, 270).

Contextualizing both the students' and teacher's wholeness in the process of teachinglearning serves as a vehicle by which I can bridge the analytical "convergent thinking" with the practical and spiritual.

My fears and reservations subsided when I explained to the students the reasons for this spiritual pedagogical act of altar making. Instantly they responded with their bodies and minds. They became engaged. As I lit the blue candle a gentle collective silence blanketed the classroom and my students' bodies shifted from morning fatigue to lively curiosity. The light in their eyes, mixed with sympathy, cued permission to continue with an explanation of the shell as a symbolic presence of the feminine and of the waters the spirit of Anzaldúa would travel across into the spirit world. It was also imperative to explain Anzaldúa's cultural and literary connection to Tonantzin as the Mexica or Aztec deity of earth and fertility. At this moment, I realized that the time to engage in a spiritual experience had arrived and the opportunity to connect all the parts of the whole presented itself. We responded to Anzaldúa's work through the analytical and intellectual lens, while also allowing for the emotional and mindbodyspirit connection to happen. It was a spiritual moment in the classroom. This class continued for three more hours that day, and another paradigm of inclusivity had been traversed.

Testimonio #2: La Ofrenda

The spring semester seems to be a time when my teaching experiences are more in harmony *con la naturaleza*. Time does not feel as oppressive. Teaching is enlightening. The presence of more light throughout the day enables for more light and lightness in the teachinglearning. Spring brings a rebirth of ideas and cleansing energy.

In the spring of 2005 I taught "La Chicana," an elective course originally conceptualized by the early feminist efforts of Chicanas who saw a need to bring the voices and experiences of Chicanas in Aztlán into academia. Their courageous efforts gave fruit to an academic dialogue never experienced before. Wanting to pay homage to these women who essentially paved the path for me as an academic, I was committed to organizing this course in such a way as to connect historical context with current social, political, and cultural issues relating to and affecting Chicanas. In addition, when organizing the course content, it was imperative for me to contextualize Chicana subjectivity within an Indigenous framework, in order to construct and deconstruct our Indigenous identity and practices.

In an attempt to reconcile the demands of addressing the *outer* landscape of academia, I turned to the course outline, which surprisingly called for a potential *inner*-landscape-like topic. This topic was Chicana Indígena Spirituality. I immediately seized the mental opportunity to consider broaching discussions on traditional Aztec Danza (or *danza azteca*) and *curanderismo*. As in the previous testimony, I was still uncertain as to how my students would react to reading about curanderismo and danza azteca. Having been raised with my maternal *abuelita*'s Indigenous Mexican healing practices and being a traditional *danzante* for over sixteen years, my vision was to unveil my personal relationship with Chicana Indígena Spirituality so that my students in turn could potentially identify with their own.

This class in particular had a demographic of fourteen Chicanas/Latinas who were between the ages of eighteen and twenty-five years old, two elderly Mexicanos, and two white males in their early twenties. Embracing the demographic represented in my classroom, I trusted that perhaps my students had heard of and/or experienced treatment by a curandera/o and had seen danza azteca, and maybe even had an inclination to accept their own Indigenousness despite the fact that they may have been socialized to reject their Indian roots. My fears fed into the dominant paradigms inherent in academia where spirituality is confused with religion. Multiple doubts inflated into overwhelming fears. I feared my students would equate curanderismo with *brujeria*; I feared they would only see danza azteca as entertainment and not as a ceremonial practice; I feared they would confuse my Chicana Indigenous identity with an attempt to "fit in" with the exotic and more interesting "other" because to be Indigenous is somehow more interesting than to be simply Mexican.

These fears of disturbing and debunking the acceptable codes also fueled an even deeper reservation to expose myself (the professor) as a traditional danzante azteca. To expose myself as such meant I had to explain the reasons for devoting my life to danza as well as explaining the fundamental spiritual aspect of the tradition. It meant I also had to model the process of shedding all reservations and trust that checking in and engaging in *palabra* (the word)—sharing from the heart and being spiritually present—modeled the type of spiritually informed pedagogy we were attempting to manifest.

To disclose my own spirituality as it connected to danza azteca humanized my own experiences and also indicated that I too have had to travel a spiritual journey in order to trust my devotion in the practice. How do you explain "coming to consciousness" when in the middle of *Aguila Blanca,* a traditional dance, *copal* smoke moves in the same direction as your bodily prayers? How do you explain humility and empowerment among hundreds of danzantes in full regalia, while *huehuetels* and *caracoles* invoke permission to offer these ancient dances from the four directions, Mother Earth and Father Sky? How does one describe feeling the presence of the divine once your bare feet caress *la madre tierra* during an *ofrenda*? How does one explain that each step is a word, a syllable composing spiritual language?

None of the above fears or reservations became a pressing issue. Instead, I embraced the thought that my students might see this unit as a fresh approach to learning and would even welcome the thought of exploring familiar subject matter.

Coming back to the memory . . .

Soy danzante por amor
A mis ritos y a mi dios

Es mi danza, esperanza
Es bonanza, es pudor[1]

Within the danza tradition, peer danzantes become *comadres* or *compadres*. We refer to each other as *comadrita* or *compadrito*, identities in the Spanish diminutive that emphasize these are terms of endearment and point to familial connection. Therefore, I invited two of my closest comadritas, Eva Sandoval and Erendira "Endy" Bernal, as guest speakers on the danza azteca tradition. While I mostly assumed the role of facilitator between the guests and students, I also spoke on my experiences and knowledge of the tradition. As is customary, I lit the *popxcomitl*, an incense burner, by lighting a piece of coal and placing copal on top of the burning coal. Once the copal began to burn and fill the classroom with white smoke and its cleansing aroma, the energy in the classroom completely shifted. A sense of security, timelessness, and lightness blanketed the classroom. Immediately, one of the women in the class commented on the smell of the burning copal. She associated its smell with Catholic mass and the burning of frankincense during Easter services and other significant religious holidays. This was the first sign that all would be fine.

We proceeded with the evening's agenda. Eva and Endy continued to share and explain the reasons for lighting the popxcomitl. They clarified that when lighting the popxcomitl, we are initiating a ceremonial endeavor where all those present are part of the experience equally represented within the circle. My students attentively listened. The white smoke, *izta cuauhtli*, flowed around the room, blessing each student it touched, reminding them of their Indian connection. As a means of connecting the theory with the practical, my comadritas and I agreed to offer a dance in honor of the Mexica female deity and Madre Tierra, Tonantzin, who is traditionally venerated as the Catholic Virgin of Guadalupe. Endy and I dressed our ankles with our *chachayotes*, bared our feet and faced each other as Eva drummed. We initiated the ofrenda with an opening *cruz*, asking the four directions for permission to offer this dance, and proceeded with the danza.

Being in the confines of the classroom, with desks surrounding you, green chalkboards and the possibility of other instructors invading your space because the drumming and rattles are creating too much noise, presented some challenges. It challenged me as the instructor/professor to measure how far I was willing to push the professional envelope per se and risk criticism from faculty and administration. Silvia Toscano Villanueva suggests in "Teaching as a Healing Craft: Decolonizing the Classroom and Creating Spaces of Hopeful Resistance through Chicano-Indigenous Pedagogical Praxis" (2013) that "to reclaim the classroom as a healing space centered in Chicano-Indigenous frameworks is a decolonial act" (33). The decolonial act of baring my feet to the earth and to my students literally and metaphorically speaks the spiritual language inherently created in what Villanueva calls "ceremonial epistemology" (37), revealing to them (my)self in mindbodyspirit.

Offering this danza in honor of Mother Earth and in honor of my students brought the spiritual into the classroom and enabled the creation of a spiritual space. Without imposing a religious dogma or predominant spiritual philosophy, the rhythm of the drum, the sound of our rattling chachayotes, and the movement of our bodies taught a different lesson and created the possibility for a new spiritual academic discourse. In its serpentine shape, the copal collectively guided our untraversed process.

Notes

1. The *alabanza* is a sacred, traditional song usually sung during an all-night prayer vigil known as the *sagrada velación*. The velación acts as the precursor to the next day's danza ofrenda where all participating danzantes offer their danzas as prayer. The alabanzas are therefore offered during the velación as prayer songs to welcome and honor the ancestors and bring focus to the ceremony. The widely sung alabanza, cited "Soy Danzante," speaks to the love, respect, modesty, and spiritual/cultural prosperity one gains as a danzante, as well as to the strength, empowerment, and devotion one has to the tradition of danza. See Moncada 2009.

Spiritual Roots of Chicana Feminist Borderland Pedagogies

A Spiritual Journey with Tonantzin/ Guadalupe

C. Alejandra Elenes

Living on borders and in margins, keeping intact one's shifting and mul-
tiple identity and integrity is like trying to swim in a new element, an
"alien" element.
—GLORIA ANZALDÚA, *BORDERLANDS/LA FRONTERA: THE NEW MESTIZA*

Spiritual activism begins with the personal yet moves outward, acknowl-
edging our radical interconnectedness. This is spirituality for social change,
spirituality that recognizes the many differences among us yet insists
on our commonalities and uses these commonalities as catalysts for
transformation.
—ANALOUISE KEATING, "CHARTING PATHWAYS,
MAKING THRESHOLDS . . . A WARNING, AN INTRODUCTION"

Spirituality, for me, is the way I understand my position in the world in relation to larger existential questions about the meaning of life and death.
Through spirituality one is connected with the world, with one's ancestors and
descendants, and one's contemporary relations. My spirituality has evolved
throughout my adulthood and childhood experiences, after years of seeking
"something" that I am now able to name as a quest for spirituality. It is through
my relationship with and interrogation of Tonantzin/Guadalupe that I have
come to understand that my activism, my work toward social justice, my academic career, and my family life have meaning because they are related to
feminist spirituality. My relationship with Tonantzin/Guadalupe has changed

43

over the years. I was raised Catholic, and as I grew up, I eventually rejected the strict sexual and patriarchal rules of the Catholic Church. My first understanding of the Virgin of Guadalupe was based on the Church's patriarchal definitions. In recent years, as a result of my research on Guadalupe, I have come to understand her as a feminist figure.

In this chapter, I address how my spiritual journey inspires my scholarship, which in turn is also inspired by my spiritual understanding of the world. I examine the relationship between Chicana feminist pedagogies and epistemologies vis-à-vis my spiritual journey. I also show how my life history informs my epistemological outlook and the reasons for having chosen to develop and apply borderland theories to my scholarship on Chicana feminist pedagogies and epistemologies. I will focus first on Chicana feminists' interpretations of Tonantzin/Guadalupe. Then, I narrate my spiritual journey. Finally, I will connect how La Virgen de Guadalupe and my spirituality inform my analysis of Chicana feminist pedagogical praxis.

Tonantzin/Guadalupe and Chicana Feminist Spiritualities

For many women of Mexican descent, La Virgen de Guadalupe is an important expression of their spirituality. This understanding of spirituality goes beyond organized religion and the traditional dogma of the Catholic Church. Chicana feminist theologian Lara Medina (2004) proposes that "spirituality emphasizes the multiple ways people relate to the world around them, to their source of life of their Creator, and to themselves" (124). Spirituality, then, means more than one's relation with a God or a Creator, because it is tied with struggles for social justice and gender equality. Spirituality is a way of understanding someone's (or a community's) position in the world by trying to make sense of unfair economic conditions and gender inequality, and to do something about it. This is precisely why Gloria Anzaldúa (2000) believed that for oppressed people, spirituality is a weapon of protection. It is a guiding source for understanding one's position in the world and giving meaning to one's life in relation to one's community.

As Medina describes it, "For women struggling not only to survive but also to prosper spiritually, culturally, and economically, the manner in which they engage in this struggle becomes key to understanding their spirituality" (2004, 124–25). Indeed, while some women find themselves struggling to survive, many of them invoke their spirituality to engage in social change. In this sense, spirituality is linked to a person's core; as Jeanette Rodríguez points out, "Spirituality contains our deepest beliefs and thoughts" (2002, 114). Spirituality can also be understood in terms of how a person relates to the totality of life (De Luna 2002).

One of the ways in which many Chicanas reclaim their Indigenous roots and spirituality is through their worship of the Virgen de Guadalupe.[1] This is part of a "spiritual *mestizaje*" that combines Catholic imagery and Indigenous practices (Delgadillo 2011). The spirituality associated with La Virgen de Guadalupe understands that Guadalupe and various Nahua female deities such as Tonantzin, Tlazolteotl, and Coatlicue are interrelated. Tonantzin is "our mother," while Tlazolteotl is linked to the cycle of life, "birth, growth, undoing, renewal and returning" (Gonzales 2012, xiv). She is the guardian of midwives, women who are pregnant, and infants (Gonzales 2012). In Catholic colonial discourse, she is depicted as the goddess of dirt and filth (Robelo 1951).[2]

Tlazolteotl is also depicted in westernized viewpoints as the goddess of fertility and sex, and as such, she is considered the Venus of Nahua mythology (Robelo 1951) and linked to Eve (Lara 2008a). In the colonial Catholic imaginary, her ability to make people lustful but also to remove impurities and forgive after public or private confession (Fernández 1992) associates her with sin, especially in terms of sexuality (Lara 2008a). Linking Tlazeolteotl with dirt constructs a sinful view of sexuality, particularly female sexuality. However, she has a regenerative principle associated with balance, action, and repose (Gonzales 2012). A more complex and feminist analysis of Tlazolteotl does not equate sexuality with sin, but rather associates her regenerative principles with transformation (Lara 2008a).

Coatlicue was/is the mother of Huitzilopochtli and Coyolxauhqui, described by some Chicana feminists as *La Hija Rebelde* (the rebel daughter) (Cisneros 1996). For Chicana feminist writer Sandra Cisneros, the interrelationship of these figures helps her understand the multifaceted aspects of Guadalupe. Cisneros, who in her youth was angry at the unattainable expectations for women represented in the traditional Virgin, also believes that La Virgen was "damn dangerous, an ideal so lofty and unrealistic it was laughable. Did boys have to aspire to be Jesus? I never saw evidence of it" (1996, 48). By rediscovering the antecedents of Guadalupe in pre-Columbian deities, she was able to associate Guadalupe with sexuality and women's freedom. Cisneros further writes: "Perhaps it's the Tlazolteotl-Lupe in me whose *malcriada* spirit inspires me to leap into the swimming pool naked or dance on a table with a skirt on my head. Maybe it's my Coatlicue-Lupe attitude that makes it possible for my mother to tell me, *No wonder men can't stand you*. Who knows? What I do know is this; I am obsessed with becoming a woman comfortable in her skin" (50).

Chicana feminist playwright Cherríe Moraga's spirituality is part of her drive to write and to search for the whole woman who is "A free citizen of Aztlán and the world" (1996, 70) and as one who prefers to pray to *La Hija Rebelde*, rather than to Coatlicue, whom she views as a male-identified mother.

Tonantzin and Guadalupe are generally seen as the same figure. Ana Castillo proposes that most Mexicans and Mexic-Amerindians recognize La Virgen de Guadalupe as Tonantzin, who as "Our Mother" is present in every mountain summit (1996, xvi). Tepeyac is the summit where she appeared to Juan Diego and where she insisted that her Temple be built. Castillo also believes that La Virgen de Guadalupe, through her connection to Coatlicue, is a symbol of life and death; that she represents a dual force. Gloria Anzaldúa contends that the Catholic Church "desexed" Guadalupe and split her positive and negative duality (1987, 49).

Chicana spiritual practices, which, as Laura E. Pérez reminds us, are similar to Amerindian and African practices, recognize that there is a spiritual interconnectedness among all beings. This spiritual belief is antithetical to ideologies that claim there are essential and hierarchal differences that justify the subjugation, exploitation, and abuse of racially different people (L. Pérez 1998). When Chicana feminist theorists, cultural workers, and everyday women rearticulate La Virgen as a feminist figure, they claim their rights not to be discriminated against and exploited because of their gender and sexuality. Moreover, when Chicanas invoke these spiritual practices in their cultural productions, they are linking them to a politics of memory aimed to maintain one's consciousness about Indigenous practices that recall and reintegrate the spiritual in everyday life. Therefore, Pérez joins many others in claiming them as decolonizing practices.

Yolanda Broyles-González (2002) argues that Indigenous communities adopted Catholic figures, including the Virgin of Guadalupe, as a form of concealment in order to maintain their spiritual traditions. Similarly, Rodríguez's *Our Lady of Guadelupe* (1994) documents how women who are devoted Catholics prefer to pray to *La Virgen* as they believe that Guadalupe understands them better and in ways that God the Father and Jesus Christ are not able to understand because she is a woman and a mother. Indeed, Castillo proposes that the feminist writers who contributed essays to her anthology *Goddess of the Americas* (1996) emphasize recapturing La Virgen's omnipotence to offer "spiritual orphans" a spirituality of love, transformation, and hope (xxi).

The mother figure represented in La Virgen de Guadalupe is part of a decolonial spirituality. For Castillo the conquered Indigenous peoples may have turned to the mother to bring comfort, assurance, and hope after the

Spanish conquest. The male gods "became silent," and La Virgen represents the archetype of the mother figure "that appears and speaks with such melodic tenderness that it was compared to the singing of birds, flor y canto—that is, beauty and truth. It sounded like music never heard before" (1996, xvii). La Virgen de Guadalupe was adopted by Indigenous peoples and mestizas/os as a spiritual figure through which they could reclaim their humanity. Moreover, Castillo understands La Virgen de Guadalupe as "mythistory" that shares similar characteristics with Chicana feminist spirituality (xviii).

Jeanette Rodríguez also sees that La Virgen de Guadalupe represents the power of memory, which stands for justice and solidarity with the oppressed. She quotes Clodomiro Siller-Acuña, who uses the image of the *yollo* (heart), which is what moves individuals to action and to have agency in the world, which must be done with heart and for the benefit of the people. For Rodríguez, if the devotion to La Virgen de Guadalupe is not accompanied with solidarity with the poor, then the devotion is not "authentically Guadalupana" (1996, 30). Chicana feminist spirituality is multifaceted and its sources of inspiration are varied. Yet these are spiritual practices that are connected with the quest for social and gender justice and for women to express their agency as complete beings.

For some Chicana scholars, theologians, and cultural workers, spirituality is related to culture, history, and economic and material conditions, as well as epistemology. Spirituality is formed, in part, by "family, teachers, friends, community, class, culture, gender, social location and historical moment" (Rodríguez 2002, 117). In a 1998 essay, Medina proposes that among some Chicanas, spiritual practices emerge from the integration of creative inner resources and diverse cultural practices that feed the soul and psyche. Many Chicanas link their spiritual beliefs with service to others, especially their communities. Indeed, spirituality entails a "liminal space of crossing, and conocimiento" linked to theories of consciousness (Delgadillo 2011, 23). My spirituality follows a similar path: my family, the communities in which I grew up and lived, as well as social consciousness, inspire my spiritual journey.

My Spiritual Journey: A Borderland Narrative

My life has persistently entailed the crossing of borders in both a material and metaphorical sense: physical, linguistic, cultural, and religious borders. As the product of a Mexican father and an American white mother, and raised in the 1960s and 1970s in México, I have constantly negotiated and traversed different worlds. Border crossing informs who I am and is one of my sources of strength. These border crossings have led to my understanding and embracing of Chicana feminist spirituality, in which Tonantzin/Guadalupe occupies a central space. To understand how I came to my spiritual awakening, I need to delve into my own story and that of my parents.

The story of my family is one of crossing borders, with one of the initial border crossings going in "reverse"—from the United States to México. My mom moved to México City in 1953, where she married my dad. My parents met in the early 1950s when they were traveling by transatlantic ship to Europe. My father did not speak English and my mother did not speak Spanish, yet they found a way to communicate. After they arrived in Europe, they went their separate ways. While in Paris, my father happened to see my mom and a friend she was traveling with having dinner in a restaurant; he spotted them through a window and kept walking, but then changed his mind and decided to return to the restaurant to say hello to the "two girls" from the United States. I believe my parents and my mom's friend traveled together in Europe and when the trip was over each went home. My dad returned to Mexico City and my mom to Milwaukee. Two years later, my mom traveled by car with some friends to Mexico City to visit my dad. She did not return to Milwaukee until twenty-seven years later! She married my dad and had four children: three girls and a boy. I am the third and middle child, as my brother is the eldest and I am in the middle of the girls.

My parents settled in Mexico City and started to raise a culturally (and religiously) mixed family. In an era when the Catholic Church did not accept mixed marriages, my parents had to make a decision about the religion in which we would be raised. Because we lived in Mexico, a country that to this day is predominantly Catholic, my parents opted to baptize us in the Catholic Church. The decision was purely a pragmatic and social one, as they felt our integration into the society would be easier if we were Catholic. My mother was raised Lutheran and now attends a Methodist Church, and my father was Catholic. And while neither was particularly religious, they were not willing to change religions. I was baptized when I was about five or six years old and not as a baby, as is the tradition in the Catholic Church, because my parents waited to make the decision about our religious upbringing. Obviously, then, I remember my baptism. I grew up going to Mass in Spanish and I only know the prayers in Spanish. To this day, Mass is much more (or maybe only) meaningful in Spanish.

When I was about six or seven years old, we moved from Mexico City to Monterrey. Monterrey of the 1960s and 1970s was still provincial in spite of being México's third largest city, and a bastion of conservatism and capitalism, earning the designation of the industrial capital of the country. As a middle-class family, my parents were able to afford private education, and because of a lack of public school options my siblings and I attended Catholic schools. We were enrolled in the schools that were closest to our house and that meant that we, the girls, ended up in a *Guadalupana* school, a Catholic school run by the *Hijas de María Inmaculada* (see http://www.Guadalupanas .com). Here is where I first learned about the miracle of La Virgen de Guadalupe. But instead of bringing me closer to La Virgen, the repressive environment of the school, due to strict gender roles and religious dogma, helped me reject her. Similar to others, such as Brenda Sendejo who also discusses her journey to La Virgen in this volume, once I developed a feminist consciousness later on in my life I understood that I initially rejected her due to the patriarchal meanings with which she was associated. The nuns taught us that the Virgen was a model of femininity, piety, and passivity to which we should aspire if we wanted to become "good" wives and mothers.

It is a tradition in Mexico to make pilgrimages to the sanctuary of La Virgen, particularly La Basilica in Mexico City. But most cities and towns in México have a church that is dedicated to La Virgen de Guadalupe, where people can conduct the ceremonies on and in the days before December 12 if they cannot travel to Mexico City. The ceremonies are a mixture of Indigenous traditions with Catholicism, and oftentimes children are asked to bring flowers to La Virgen. The flowers are symbolic because part of her miracle was that she made flowers grow in December in a harsh environment. For the nuns, taking the elementary-school girls to offer flowers, especially roses, to La Virgen every December 12 was an important ceremony. For me as a kid, it was a nuisance. I hated the school's yearly trips to offer flowers to the Virgin because it was always too cold (and we had to wear thin white uniforms) and because they required us to travel in crowded school buses. As I was growing up, I was not able to grasp why growing roses was such a miracle.

One of the highlights of those yearly pilgrimages was that I could take beautiful roses from my mom's garden. They bloomed beautifully in December, and while we were in northern México, roses also bloom in the winter in Mexico City. Eventually I started to question the miracle. Now, I wish I had understood the spiritual meaning of offering flowers to La Virgen, and in hindsight I realize that the nuns did not teach us or help us see how beautiful and spiritual the ceremony could be. The Nahua ceremonies of *flor y canto* were transferred to the veneration of Guadalupe. Thus, not knowing better, by middle school, I had had enough with the Church and La Virgen de Guadalupe, as the ideals of feminine perfection were impossible to attain; so I begged my parents to let me go to a secular high school.

Going to a Catholic school in the 1960s and 1970s in an extremely conservative environment with a Protestant mother was not easy. The nuns were very hostile to Protestants, so I had to learn early on how to negotiate these two different worlds. For the nuns in the Catholic school, it seems that Martin Luther had just called for the reformation of the Church: *Protestants were not to be trusted.* They were, it seemed, akin to devil worshipers. At times, I hid my mom's religion from the nuns and some zealous classmates. I was never embarrassed, much less ashamed, but sometimes I just did not want to deal with the absurd questions and dirty looks. For example, one day the nuns decided to ask each of us to tell the date of our baptism. I was not in the mood to be lectured by the nun that I should have been baptized as a baby so I could have gone to heaven in case I died. After all, the whole issue did not make sense, given that I survived early childhood and was baptized. So I made up a date two or three months after my birthday. Perhaps living those glaring contradictions between messages of love and compassion and disparaging an important aspect of the person I loved most in my life was the beginning of my questioning of the Catholic Church and organized religion. As a child, of course, I could not articulate my thoughts and feelings in such a way. I just knew there was something wrong, and started my quest for "something," not knowing it would be years before I found what I yearned for.

By my teenage years, I was really fed up with the Church and with the unattainable prescriptions of Guadalupe. The 1970s Mexican Catholic Church campaign to fundraise the building of the new Basilica in Tepeyac included a slogan that said *"Todos los mexicanos somos guadalupanos."* The first time I heard this slogan, I reacted viscerally. Today in my academic jargon, I would say that I reacted to the essentialism of the statement. But as a sixteen- or seventeen-year-old, obviously I had not heard of the concept. In hindsight, I probably reacted to a message that dictated and prescribed what my identity should be, and who I should pray to. After all, I already rejected Guadalupe, and resented being told that to be Mexican I had to be a Guadalupana. I had many Mexican friends who also left the Church and did not blink when they heard that slogan.

Throughout my childhood, whenever I needed to explain my background I would tell people that my mom was Americana and that I was half "gringa."[3] I recognized that I was not a full Mexican, but at the same time I never felt white (and I still do not after more than twenty years living in the United States). I am Mexican, and have always been. But for me being Mexican included a mixture of Mexicaness with Americaness, both identities delicately layered and interwoven. I think that is why I reacted to a slogan that so blatantly promoted an "essentialist" definition of Mexican cultural identity.

At the time, I rejected the connection between Mexican identity and *Guadalupanismo* because I rejected the Church. The slogan and the campaign were a good excuse for me to move away from the strict prescriptions of the

Church. From that moment on, I would live a secular life. And while I am something of an agnostic, I cannot declare myself an atheist or a totally secular person. But for many years, especially during graduate school, I avoided going to church as much as possible.

Yet I kept yearning for a sense of purpose and spirituality, which I looked for in different places. It was not until two dear friends, Steve Casanova and Inés Hernández, introduced me to Indigenous spiritualities, also during graduate school, that I had a better understanding of their relationship with Mexican and Chicana/o culture. I found a connection with Indigenous spiritualities because of their association with the earth and all living things. This is when I also started to have a better understanding of myself. And to my surprise I was pulled back to the Catholic Church and to Tonantzin/Guadalupe. No matter how far I go from Tontantzin/Guadalupe she is always there and does not let me stray too far. I do not fight her any more; I embrace her and realize that she is a very important figure in my life.

My early feminist awakening occurred when I was in my early twenties and working for the private sector in Monterrey. However, my feminism is also grounded in my upbringing and the lessons that my mom taught me. My mom raised her three girls to be independent. Education was very important in my house, and good grades a must. There was no question that all of us would go to college, and nobody would get married until they finished college. And going to college was a goal in and of itself; we, the girls, were not going to college to find husbands, as was customary for middle-class young women. We would go to college so we could find good-paying jobs and not depend on a man. I was also fortunate enough to grow up in a house full of books, and one of the books on my mom's shelf was Simone de Beauvoir's *The Second Sex* (which I did not read until I got involved in women's studies).

In 1982 the economic outlook in Mexico was bleak as a result of the devaluation of the peso after President López Portillo nationalized the banks. Moreover, my parents had recently divorced and my mom decided to move back to Milwaukee. My grandmother was aging and sick and my mom decided that she also wanted a college degree. In 1983, when my mom came back to Monterrey for my brother's wedding, seeing that I was unhappy, she suggested that I move to Milwaukee. Years earlier, during a trip to visit Grandma in Wisconsin, we had gone to Madison because I wanted to see the campus I had heard of so many times. At the time, 1976, the campus still had its aura of activism and "crazy hippies." I fell in love, and deeply desired to attend college there. So in 1983, I left my boyfriend, sold my car, packed the few things I had, and embarked on a new adventure. I moved to the United States with a college degree but few skills. My English was very poor, as

I had never studied the language, and unfortunately I had to make a living out of writing. I needed more training, so graduate school at the University of Wisconsin–Madison was my salvation.

It was in Madison, Wisconsin, of all places, where I was introduced to the Indigenous ancestry of my Mexican identity. It was also in Madison where I began to identify as a Chicana. Having grown up navigating two different worlds, I felt that I finally met people who understood my world when I met Chicanos for the first time. Like me, Chicanos and Chicanas navigated at least two worlds, two languages, two different cultures. They belong to these two worlds and to none. Like Chicanos, I have never been completely Mexican or American, yet I was/am both. I also understood very soon in my stay in the United States that racism continued to exist in spite of the civil rights struggles. I am a US citizen by birth, and my mom registered us at the US embassy in Mexico City after we were born. As a US citizen, she passed her citizenship to us even though we were born outside the country. When each one of us turned 18, we had to choose if we wanted to be US or Mexican citizens and we all opted to be "Americans."

Yet when I was about to board my plane in McAllen, Texas to Milwaukee and was saying good-bye to my dad and sister, I had a rude awakening on US racial and ethnic politics. As I was saying in Spanish "I hope to find a job soon," INS agents seemed to come from every corner like in a movie (in all honesty I think there was only one or two) and immediately demanded that I show proof of citizenship or legal residency. They accepted my documents, and I boarded my plane. But I knew that my accent and Mexican mannerisms marked me as not "American." And this became very evident my first year in the United States.

In 1985, the Chicano Studies Program at Madison put together a conference on Chicana and Native American women. One of the featured speakers was Inés Hernández, who helped me understand my Indigenous roots. Through many conversations we had in the 1980s, Inés helped me understand that as a Mexican woman, not only should I learn about my Indigenous ways, but that Indigenous spiritualities belong to me. Without Inés and my subsequent studies of Mexica and Mayan cultures, I would not have been able to see La Virgen de Guadalupe as Tonantzin.

For several years I have been studying La Virgen de Guadalupe/Tonantzin, Malintzin/Malinche, and La Llorona (see Elenes 2011). I first approached this work in order to understand how Chicanas reclaimed these traditionally patriarchal figures as feminist ones. I was interested in demonstrating that La Virgen de Guadalupe was a myth created in order to Christianize Indians in Mexico. However, reading and learning about Guadalupe's association with Nahua deities, in conjunction with analyses of contemporary cultural productions depicting the image of the Virgen, helped me view her differently. I realized that whether the Virgen appeared or not, whether there was a miracle or not, was not important. What mattered is that she exemplifies a very powerful spirituality that is very different from what the nuns had taught us. Through my research on La Virgen de Guadalupe I found out that her appearance symbolized the subjectivity of Indigenous peoples in México. She is a protector against illness and natural disasters. But more importantly, she gives hope to the poor and disenfranchised that it is possible to struggle for social justice. That is, the hope and humanity that Tonantzin/ Guadalupe brings is not only that the poor will go to heaven and thus should accept their lot in life, but that they are entitled to social justice in the here and now.

Soon, after I started to understand and embrace Indigenous spiritualities, I found myself praying to La Virgen and surrounding myself with images of her from Chicana feminist interpretations to traditional *veladoras*. For me, La Virgen de Guadalupe represents female power, not the passive image that the nuns and Catholic Church taught me.

This feminist meaning of Tonantzin/Guadalupe centers my spiritual beliefs on the circularity of life. Philosophically, my beliefs are similar to Indigenous spiritualities in that I see the connection between mind, body, and spirit with the earth and universe. The mind, body, and spirit should be in balance, without privileging one over the other. If the body is alienated from the spirit, for example because of paying too much attention to material things, we run the risk of losing sight of what is important in life. On the other hand, we cannot ignore the body in the service of the spirit because that would lead us to ignore the social condition of many people, and even our own health. To me, Tonantzin/Guadalupe represents this balance; as a spiritual figure she symbolizes the humanity and subjectivity of Indigenous people and the need to work toward social justice that would satisfy the material needs of people. As a female figure, the needs of women take center stage.

I have learned to embrace my mixed spirituality and returned to the Church. I normally go to Mass on Sundays with my husband and son. Mass is important for my husband, as I believe it gives him peace and also a spiritual outlet. And I strongly believe that children should be taught and exposed to spirituality and religion. For cultural and spiritual reasons, my husband and I are raising our son in the Catholic Church. Recently, my son made his first Communion and confirmation. Going through the process gave him a spiritual outlet and as a result he took it very seriously. Tellingly, the church we go to is called Our Lady of Guadalupe and maintains a connection with Indigenous culture (Yaqui). My participation in the Church is one more contradiction in my life, of living between different borders.[4]

Chicana Feminist Pedagogies as a Spiritual Praxis

My educational philosophy and my approach to scholarship are guided by spirituality. That is, in the same way that spirituality is essential in my life, it is also influential in my academic activities. Therefore, I believe that educational practices committed to social justice cannot rely exclusively on objectivist educational theory and practice. Unfortunately, dominant discourses on education follow a western model that separates the mind from the body and the spirit. The quest for objectivity and the reliance on rationality do not permit the theorization of the nonmaterial elements of education.

bell hooks, in her book *Teaching Community: A Pedagogy of Hope* (2003), links spirituality with transformative education. In doing so, she critiques traditional or conventional educational practices because the quest for an objective education promotes and values teaching practices that disconnect the body and mind, which alienates many students. As a young undergraduate at Stanford University, hooks learned that in elite schools what mattered was the work of the mind. Taking care of the soul or the spirit had to take place in private. As a working-class student, hooks's vision of education was shaped by an understanding of the intellectual as someone who sought a union of the mind, body, and spirit. It is through this union, as Gloria Anzaldúa also made clear and Maria Figueroa discusses in this volume, that transformative education can take place. Chicana feminist pedagogies are similar to hooks's vision of transformative education. Such transformative education must be linked with social and gender justice, which in turn are based on feminist spirituality.

Recognizing that spirituality has a central place in the way people construct their subjectivity is a necessary step in the formation of Chicana feminist pedagogies. Recent works on Chicana feminist pedagogies (such as Delgado Bernal 2006; Godinez 2006; Ayala et al. 2006; Rendón 2005; Lara 2005; Trinidad Galván 2001, 2006) have recognized the importance of spirituality in Chicana feminist education. Unlike traditional western epistemologies that separate mind and spirit, the practice of many Chicana feminist scholars does not separate the mind from the spirit and the body.

Transformative education is a form of educational praxis that honors wholeness and spirituality in "the practice of freedom" (hooks 2003, 181). hooks proposes that many students of color are disconnected from their education when it is too dominated by western values because these values can undermine the significance of spirituality. Chicana feminist educators have found that for some Chicana students the source of their educational success was their ability to link their education with spirituality. That is, they were able to find the wholeness that hooks says is necessary for a transformative educational practice.

As Dolores Delgado Bernal points out in a 2006 article, some of the Chicana college students in her study linked their spirituality with community service and their education. Similarly, Francisca Godinez "found a thread of spirituality" that linked young Mexican high school students in their "identities and worldviews" (2006, 30). Godinez discovered that the young women in her study learned through their families' cultural knowledge how to make sense of their realities as first generation immigrants in the United States in ways that "create meanings and strategies with threads of cultural virtues, spirituality, life energy, vitality and desire, and relational behaviors in *trenzas de identidades multiples*, 'braids of multiple identities'" (32). By combining an awareness of their structural position within US society with cultural knowledge and spirituality, the young women were able to see that their education not only benefited their personal future, but also that of their communities.

Chicana spiritual practices connect mind and body, integrating creativity and sexuality. Chicana feminist scholar Irene Lara embraces what she calls *bruja* or *brujandera* spirituality, which incorporates spiritual epistemologies. She writes, "Though we aim to transform our selves and our worlds, the reality is that we are part of a society still largely organized around racist and sexist binary ways of knowing. As we carve transformative spaces in a profession built on a rigid foundation of reason that invalidates and binarizes itself with spiritual intuitive knowledges, we are still judged by that value system" (2005, 28). Chicana higher education scholar Laura Rendón puts into question the basis of western thought and educational scholarship that separates intellect from spirituality. She proposes "to create a new dream of education" in which "the foundation of this dream is a more harmonic, holistic vision of education that honors the whole of who we are as intellectual, compassionate, authentic human beings who value love, peace, democracy, community, diversity and hope for humanity" (2005, 81).

This is a dream that is intellectually and spiritually based. Such spirituality honors our humanity in its wholeness connecting mind, body, and spirit. Rendón's exhortation to bring a spiritual dimension into educational research and practice is based, in part, on Indigenous epistemologies. Her research into spirituality includes ancient Mexica and Mayan knowledges. Similarly, as Inés Hernández reminds us, spirituality is connected with Indigenous knowledge about how to be humble, honest, and hard working. Spirituality is also about showing consideration toward individuals and societies, and respecting each other's sovereignty (Hernández 1988).

According to bell hooks, a way to bring spirituality to education is through experience. Based on the work of Steven Glazer, who writes that "spiritual identity arises in and of itself from identification with experience rather than submission to a particular set of beliefs" (2003, 182, quoting Glazer 1999), hooks credits women's studies, cultural studies, and black studies in developing pedagogies that are holistic and connected with spirituality. As a women's studies faculty member, I bring my understanding of the world and spirituality into my teaching and scholarship. Bringing spirituality to teaching does not entail explaining to students the basis of one's spirituality. Rather, spirituality emerges out of praxis. In this sense, praxis refers to the process by which one puts into action the theory(ies) that frame one's work.

As Gloria Anzaldúa (2000; 2002a) argued, spiritual activism is necessary for the development of feminist and critical pedagogies, even though these are not always specifically articulated. Spirituality is an important aspect of intellectual development. From an epistemological and pedagogical perspective, spirituality is an avenue to take people's subjectivity into account as a whole and as a source of transformation. In the same way that some Indigenous peoples of Mesoamerica adopted the Virgin of Guadalupe as a spiritual figure to help them reclaim their humanity, educators should also reclaim their spirituality in order to make their education whole. In my scholarship on Chicana feminist pedagogies, I proposed the development of border/transformative pedagogies because they "offer a cultural critique of material conditions of subaltern communities that invoke politics of change to transform society in order to become truly democratic" (Elenes 2006, 247). And spiritual activism is meaningful for border/transformative pedagogies because it is a source of transformation that links "feminist praxis, spirituality, and education" (Elenes 2011, 65). The commitment to social justice and the agency in Chicana feminist praxis are examples of how spirituality can be incorporated into educational scholarship.

Classroom or cultural practices that recognize the significance of personal experience are much more capable of accepting spirituality and activism within their praxis. For example, classroom practices where abstract theory, praxis, and agency are linked open the possibilities for students to see the ways in which they are capable of acting in the world. This acting in the world can be done in the service of others or for the greater good. Connecting analytical thinking, which addresses social problems and issues as complex, with a sense of purpose in the world that goes beyond the mere accumulation of material goods can also enable students to think of their spirituality. They can start to make connections between who they are, how they interpret the world, and how they can act in the world in ways that are fulfilling—that is, spiritual. This is my spirituality—a connection between the mind, the body, and the spirit.

Fleshing the Spirit, organized by the four directions (East, West, North, and South), places this essay on pedagogy in the East. This is such a fitting place for pedagogy, as teaching and learning is about the cycle of beginnings and endings. As we learn new things the process of transformation takes place, which leads to new beginnings. I close my essay evoking the East's transformative power of fire and its renewal energy.

Epilogue

Spirituality helps me to make sense of life during difficult times. On a Friday morning in January 2009, I received an e-mail from Mario Compeán letting me know that Steve Casanova had passed and journeyed to the spirit world. Words to express the loss and grief over Steve's passing are hard to come by and I still cannot find them. Sometimes, I cannot believe he does not walk the earth with family and friends. But when such grief strikes, I remember that his spirit lives with his family (especially his two sons Stevie and Amado) and in the legacy of his work with his students and colleagues at St. Cloud State. I knew Steve for about twenty-five years; we started graduate school the same year at the University of Wisconsin–Madison. Steve not only helped me edit innumerable papers and gave necessary support to continue in graduate school when I found the task difficult; more importantly, he helped me get in touch with my spirituality and Indigenous roots.

During Steve's funeral on a beautiful winter day in San Antonio, Texas, when we prayed to the Christian God and to our Indigenous ancestors, I felt a stronger spiritual connection to the earth and the sky. I also connected with friends I had not seen in a long time, particularly Tess Arenas, Mario Compeán, and Delia Enriquez. Spending time together was bittersweet; it was so nice to reconnect and know that friendships endure over time; it was hard to do so because we had "lost" our dear friend Steve.

My spiritual journey owes a lot to Steve, and I am very grateful for the friendship we shared over so many years. To end this chapter, I want to extend a *mil gracias* to Steve for helping me get in touch with the spiritual side that I was neglecting when I arrived in Madison for graduate school. Without his help, I would not have been able to write this chapter (which I told him about once), and certainly my research on Tonantzin/Guadalupe would have been very different.

Notes

I wish to extend a special note of *agradecimiento* to many individuals who gave me spiritual support and who provided invaluable feedback for this chapter. Special thanks to Gloria Cuádraz, Shari Collins, Anna Guevarra and Michelle Téllez for their feedback to the early drafts of this essay. I am so grateful to Elisa Facio and Irene Lara for putting together this wonderful anthology and for their invaluable comments to my chapter, and to the anonymous reviewers for their insighful comments and suggestions. Andrea "Tess" Arenas and Mario Compeán and his sister Felipa gave me so much needed emotional and spiritual support, as well as shelter during Steve Casanova's funeral. This chapter, and my spiritual journey, could not have happened without my family. I cannot thank them enough, especially my mother LaVerne Steven and my father Mario Elenes (who journeyed to the spirit world in 2003). Finally, many thanks to Manuel de Jesús Hernández-G. and H-Tubtún (Tuni) Hernández-Elenes for being part of this incredible spiritual journey.

1. In this chapter I am claiming that a significant number of Chicanas who reclaim La Virgen de Guadalupe do so by also reclaiming their Indigenous roots. However, I do want to point out that not all Chicanas who reclaim this spirituality also reclaim their Indigenous roots.

2. Cecilio Robelo attributes this description to Fray Bernardino de Sahagún.

3. Oftentimes in México people use the term Americano or Americana to refer to people from the United States, as I did as a child to refer to my mom's nationality, even though most people recognize that the term refers to the whole continent. A more appropriate term is *estadounidense*, but for children this is a mouthful.

4. At this point maintaining a relationship with the Catholic Church is becoming quite difficult, given its recent position regarding health insurance and birth control. While this position does not surprise me, as I well know the Church's position on birth control, the most recent debate is clearly a way for the Church to intervene in US electoral politics and one that troubles me in very significant ways.

Spirit Journey

"Home" as a Site for Healing and Transformation

Elisa Facio

"Home" can be unsafe and dangerous because it bears the likelihood of intimacy and thus thinner boundaries. Staying "home" and not venturing out comes from woundedness, and stagnates our growth.
　　—GLORIA ANZALDÚA, "(UN)NATURAL BRIDGES, (UN)SAFE SPACES"

Spirit journeys generally entail a search for explanations, understandings, and fulfillment. In my own spirit journey, some lessons, even those that were dubious, rendered healing, catharsis, and transformation. And there were others that left me confused, betrayed, and wounded, but also more inquisitive about my spirituality as an Indigenous Chicana. My spirit journey also brought a deepened sense of understanding about Chicana feminism and spirituality. I believed then, as I do now, that naming myself *"Chicana"* is spiritual in that I am committed to the transformation of my community, the larger society, and myself as a US woman of Mexican Indigenous descent.

However, a self-determined identity means little if we do not live up to the significance and integrity of the name with pride. Hence, I wanted to learn to live my life as a spiritual journey in an informed, respectful, and humble way. Like most Chicanas, I have used my own inner resources and creativity to live and express my spirituality, which is *Indígena* inspired and guided (Medina 1998). At present, I understand spirituality as the essence of living, how we move through life to become human and be human. This form of spirituality requires recognizing and valuing ourselves first and foremost as human beings. Also, we must understand and respect our relationships and "radical interconnections" to other people, plants, animals, and Mother Earth (Anzaldúa 2000).

59

The spirit journey discussed in the following autoethnographic essay illustrates critical engagements with various sites, spaces, and places regarded as "*home.*"[1] I deploy the metaphor of home to describe physical, spatial, and temporal locations ranging from participation in *inipi* and *temazkalli* ceremonies to negotiating my own body as a spiritual medium. The word "home" usually engenders descriptors such as safety, comfort, protection, and stability. The physical boundaries of home are tangible, thus presenting the image of a dependable, reliable site. However, home can also be a site of disappointment, betrayal, violence, anguish, and uncertainty. Home sites, as we know them, usually attempt to negotiate the binary of their energies, but these sites are also in constant flux. Home in this discussion refers to various sites with fluid physical boundaries. Home is not found in one location, but can be found in many places and spaces. The cultural and social boundaries are critically interrogated as I try to understand the multiple identities associated with these various sites, spaces, and places of home.

Given this understanding of home, the essay illustrates both my struggles and my catharsis in understanding how the various sites and spaces regarded as home can be spiritual, healing, and transformative. This is significant because interrogation and negotiation of these interstitial spaces can provide opportunities to deploy spiritual activism. The challenge is to unearth the healing properties of these various sites of home. In order to heal and transform in radical fashion, one must also know how we belong to these sites and spaces called home. This is a significant aspect of spiritual journeys. I argue that our interrogation and negotiation of these sites can provide opportunities to deploy spiritual activism as a radical ideology for social change.

To complement the character and features of home as described in this essay, I draw from the works of Gloria Anzaldúa and AnaLouise Keating. Anzaldúa used the word *nepantla* to theorize about liminality or the spaces between worlds. Nepantla is a Nahuatl word meaning *tierra entre medio* or in-between spaces. Anzaldúa associates nepantla "with states of mind that question old ideas and beliefs, acquire new perspectives, change worldviews, and shift from one world to another." Accordingly, transformations occurring in this in-between space are characterized as an "unstable, unpredictable, precarious, always-in-transition space lacking clear boundaries" (2002b, 1). Because the sites of home discussed in this essay constantly shift, I draw from Anzalduan thought in regarding home as *tierra desconocida*: "Living in this liminal zone means being in a constant state of displacement—an uncomfortable, even alarming feeling. Most of us dwell in *nepantla* so much of the time it's become a sort of 'home.' Though this state links us to other ideas, people, and worlds, we can feel threatened by these new connections and the change they engender" (3).

Home Sites

The places of home described in the following sections continue to hold significance for my healing, recovery, reconciliation, and transformation. Since 1996, my spirit journey has taken me to various sites of home that reveal interconnectedness between personal and political violence(s).[2] Experiences of violence cannot be categorized into simple dichotomies of personal and political, primarily meaning private and public. Personal and political violences are interrelated, interdependent. Violence has no rationale; therefore we should not impose or deploy linear ways of thinking in our healing and reconciliation. Obviously, though, we must be politically strategic in eradicating violence(s) in women's lives. As noted by Angela Davis at the INCITE! conference in Chicago, 2006, violence is a powerful ideological conductor.

The realities and bodies of violence have been relegated to secrecy within the folds of our psyches, communities, and the state. The construction and culture of violence in the United States have rendered *talking* about violence as a dialogue, which has been taken for granted. Chicana *cuentos y pláticas* (stories and conversations) about violence spontaneously and emotionally erupt in unexpected spaces; driving with friends to a social event, sharing meals with *colegas* at conferences, sharing "humorous" commentaries about violence to circumvent painful memories. Our dialogues are cautious. We fear overwhelming feelings of emotion, the emotional hangover, the political targeting of communities of color as the primary perpetrators of violence, the unresolved issues of *familia*, self-hate, feelings of unworthiness, sadness, and disappointment.

Inipi Ceremonies

My spirit journey began in 1996, when my friend Roberta invited me to an inipi ceremony focusing on women's healing.[3] I arrived early and helped the other women in preparing the lodge; a dome-shaped structure made of tree twigs and branches, covered with blankets and tarps. Inside, a small circular fire pit held the hot rocks. Once all the women were inside the lodge, a woman of wisdom, a respected elder, would pour water onto the rocks to create a very hot vapor. The rocks, actually small boulders, represent the energies of our grandmothers, grandfathers, and ancestors (*abuelas, abuelos y antepasados*) who have crossed over. It is believed the rocks guide all those who enter the lodge with their praying.

I immediately felt a sense of comfort with my surroundings, the presence of the lodge, the fire pit, and the women. I felt as though I had finally found a safe place, a home, to learn and flourish as an Indigenous Chicana. Ironically, once in the lodge I suffered tremendously and was extremely humbled by the ceremony. The vapor was extremely hot. I felt claustrophobic and very anxious. But through the prayers and strength of all the women in the lodge, I remained inside for the entire ceremony. I learned I had a long, arduous spirit journey ahead of me. Walking the "red road" was going to be a lifelong challenge. Most important, I learned a valuable lesson about healing. To heal involves a radical transformation of the body. Since the initial Inipi, significant life experiences have turned me to Coatlicue (celestial deity of all Indigenous deities), the Creator, Tonantzin (known today as the Virgen de Guadalupe), and my antepasados (all relatives who have passed) in search of healing and transformation as an Indigenous Chicana.

The Yakama Indian Reservation

My desire to learn more about Chicana feminism and spirituality became prominent in my life after receiving tenure in 1997 from the University of Colorado at Boulder. I experienced a range of emotions associated with the process of promotion: elation, self-doubt, anger, emotional exhaustion, and illness. I was relieved that I had survived nearly seven years of academic violence. And I felt betrayed, hurt, and angry for not being respected as a brown woman, a Chicana activist scholar.

I first identified my academic experiences as *violence* during my tenure sabbatical at Washington State University in Pullman in 1997–1998. To put it succinctly, the academic environment's corporate model of capitalist/militaristic socialization is unhealthy, demoralizing, and dysfunctional. I felt, and continue to feel, that I had to physically prepare my body politically, and spiritually before stepping onto the Boulder campus. We all have our rituals in negotiating the toxicity of the academic environment, ways of resisting and surviving. More specifically, we may find ourselves in constant states of anger, self-doubt, senseless direction, invisibility, political and cultural involvement, speaking our Chicana dialects of Spanish in safe spaces or performing all of the above. It is a constant struggle not to allow the university to undermine my spirit journey, my resistance, and healing. Patrisia Gonzales (2012) argues that to submit ourselves to sites of violence(s) such as the university is to obstruct and mutilate our female energies and spirits and basically to (re)victimize ourselves once again to legacies of violence.

I found it ironic that my tenure sabbatical fellowship took me back to my birthplace, the Yakama Indian Reservation, after nearly thirty-five years. I was born in Toppenish, Washington into a household of poverty, alcoholism, and domestic violence. My *abuelito's* (grandpa) life experiences in Wapato, his love for his children and grandchildren, and his wisdom as an elder convinced my father to move to California when I was just three years old.[4] I was perplexed by returning to a place I physically and emotionally considered a site of home. Wapato, a small town of nearly three thousand people located on the periphery of the reservation, is poor and is isolated from Yakama, the largest town outside the reservation. Given that my grandparents migrated from Mexico and traveled via Colorado to Washington, I wanted to learn more about our place as "uninvited guests" living on an Indian reservation.

I drove the four-hour trip from Pullman to Wapato nearly every weekend to be among my extended family. A few of my *tios* (uncles) married Yakama and Pendleton Indian women and are/have raised Indigenous/mestiza/mestizo children on the reservation. Few of the Mexican families who immigrated to Washington in the 1940s remain in Wapato. Children and grandchildren of these families have relocated to places outside the reservation. And it is primarily poor Yakama Indians and Mexican immigrants who reside on the reservation today.

During my weekend visits, I realized the importance of documenting a history that could be lost and of witnessing a legacy of genocide, which the state conducts through punitive policies and economic underdevelopment. However, the hard truth of confronting generations of alcoholism and domestic violence surfaced with and among *familia* (family). My body's memory of violence and the historical legacies of violence our bodies harbor shrouded my very existence. Conversations with family and friends seemed to always include some discussion of the violences that the women in our family experienced. Drinking at weekend gatherings was excessive, many times leading to fighting among the men and some women. There were the phone calls in the middle of the night from the local sheriff's office informing us of yet another relative arrested for drunk driving.

Weekends on the reservation were occupied with the local police department arresting numbers of Indians/Chicanos/Mexicanos, and some women, for disorderly conduct related to alcohol consumption. The local City Council reported in 1998 that nearly 65 percent of the city budget had been disbursed for "safety" via crime alert programs. Related to alcoholism is the issue of violence, particularly domestic violence. Individuals found guilty of such offenses are ordered to enroll in "anger management" classes, sponsored by none other than the police department, for anywhere from six months to one year. If the guilty party in any way verbally or physically abuses their partner during the probationary period, they are subject to arrest. These are but two of many examples reflecting the role of state policies as genocidal practice, as reflected in alcoholism and domestic-violence programs targeted primarily toward Indians and Chicanos on the reservation.

The state is supposedly responsible for the protection of all its citizens. Given the racist, sexist, and homophobic character of the state, the state is incapable of providing civil protection, including community programs and agencies established to "protect" and "guarantee" Indians, Chicanos and Mexicanos against harming themselves. Analyses of state policies as genocidal practice are in no way attempts to decenter the debilitating impact of violence on the human spirit, the personal journey in healing and reconciliation. Genocidal practices mandated by the state are only a continuation of neocolonial control and manipulation of Indian people culturally, economically, and spiritually. The contradictions and possibilities of our historical moments must be recognized and acted upon. As noted by Ward Churchill (1992), to harbor the personal journey places one as a bystander to "crimes against humanity." I am not advocating that every individual afflicted by alcoholism and domestic violence organize politically and strategically, but those of us who are fortunate enough to deconstruct violence in our lives or have the ability to act constructively have a responsibility to do exactly that.

The privatization and commodification of violence against our communities, especially against women, must continue to be critically assessed. Rehabilitation and educational programs, as opposed to punitive measures such as probation and state-imposed monetary investments (jail/prison, police/military, state-controlled community agencies), should be seriously considered in antiviolence efforts. We need to contest privatization of violence against women and challenge the depoliticizing of the movement (INCITE! 2006).

Turning our attention back to the genealogy of my spirit journey, I realized some twenty years later that simply leaving my parents' home immediately after graduating from high school in 1976 did not curtail the influence that violence and alcoholism would have on my psyche. Nor would understanding how centuries of colonial domination have afflicted Indigenous communities be enough to walk a spiritual path or the "red road" with dignity. I was given the opportunity to return to the reservation to finally face my demons or internal darkness after so many years of confusion, complexity, contradiction, and pain.[5]

Patrisia Gonzales argues that the memories of violence our bodies have harbored have been revealed in the lives of many women. She states, "life has a way of speaking to us through other people and the land, mother earth" (2000, 2). These memories have revealed themselves to me through my abuela (my grandma), my mother's and tias' (aunts) looks of despair after violent encounters with their husbands, male language and discourse used when talking about the sacredness of familia, our struggles as Indigenous/Chicana/

Latina academics, the Zapatista women in Chiapas, the *jineteras* (sex workers) in Cuba, the women in Iraq and Afghanistan, and the number of Mexicanas murdered and physically and sexually enslaved along the US/Mexican border and throughout North America.

In her book of essays, *Yellow Woman and a Beauty of the Spirit* (1996), Leslie Marmon Silko writes, "the beauty that Yellow Woman possesses is the beauty of her passion, her daring, and her sheer strength to act when catastrophe is imminent" (70). She writes of the Laguna Pueblo belief that Thought Woman is Creator and she thought up her three sisters and they came into being, and together they are Mother Creators. The Mexica feminine healing energy is referred to as Tlazolteotl. And it is believed it works through many women. More specifically, Patrisia Gonzales (2012) writes that for some of us it takes time for Thought Woman or feminine healing energies to create the ability to heal our bodies from legacies of violence. It was not until my late thirties that I finally embraced, situated, and became a "student" in healing from the violence(s) I had experienced.

Learning to Pray—Stones People's Lodge

When I returned to Denver in 1998, I shared what I experienced in Wapato with a few close friends, friends walking the "red road." Rocky Rodriguez, a respected Indigenous Chicana community member, activist, teacher, and sister, invited me to attend lodge, a place where I would continue to learn how to pray, to heal, and to transform. I began to attend lodge almost weekly.

Despite my suffering during the first lodge I attended, I felt absolutely at home. The Inipi or stones people's lodge became another significant spiritual home. The stones used for the Inipi are the spiritual energies or our grandmothers, grandfathers, our antepasados, and the four directions including the Sun and Mother Earth. The ceremonies were conducted in Lakota, and unfortunately I did not understand anything being said. However, those leading the ceremony made me feel welcome, as English was also spoken to explain certain elements of significance—such as the meaning of the stones, the color of the robes, tobacco ties, and the food and water shared among us. During prayer, I would place my hands firmly on Mother Earth and let her energies run through my body as I prayed for help, guidance, and health. On one occasion I was frightened by the energies moving throughout the lodge. One elder told me that being in lodge was the safest place on earth, as the lodge represents the womb of Mother Earth. This is why many people suffer during lodge. Through our prayers we experience a rebirth. And as many of you know, the rounds of ceremony do involve praying, suffering, and rebirth, if you will.

Also, I could sense the uneasiness of other people, particularly the men. I must admit that many times I would count to see if there were more men than women in the lodge. My friend Elena and I would look at one another knowing that we had to pray for strength for our brothers. Then during one ceremony the elder pouring told the men to thank us women for our energies as women and creators of life. I continued to pray for my brothers, but began to focus on my own healing.

With each ceremony I attended, I began to suffer more and more. I cried and sobbed as silently as possible because I did not want my sisters and brothers to carry my pain. I knew the person pouring could "hear" and feel my pain. However, in women's lodges or ceremonies I sobbed without inhibitions. Despite any differences that exist among us, we carry the legacies of a colonial past and live today as neocolonial women. The historical wounds of rape, genocide, and racism experienced by our foremothers always seem to surface during women's lodges. Thus, in temazkalli ceremonies, we suffer as Chicana Indigenous women spiritually engaged in a decolonial process.

My body began to feel the pain of my memories. Sufferings from a lifetime of violence had finally surfaced. My body was forcing a *limpia*, a spiritual and physical cleansing of my body, mind, and spirit. My body forced me to rid myself of the *susto*, the trauma and fear resulting from the molestation I experienced as a child. Susto is considered soul loss; a part of our soul remains in the past. I had to revisit the past in order to understand the female energy moving throughout my body.

Today, I realize this important lesson has become absolutely vital for my future. I learned that my kidneys and liver were degenerating. My kidneys were suffering from the oppressive conditions of a neocolonial woman and a woman/child victimized by violence and sexual abuse. My liver was no longer able to withstand the frustration, rage, and anger that consumed my body for so many years. When first told by western physicians that my condition was unpredictable and could not be treated, I obviously was scared, angry, and confused. Why was this happening to me? Remembering conversations with my tias, I now believe this illness was a gift; the gift to heal, grow, and move onto the fourth age of life as an older Indigenous Chicana Otomi woman.

The lessons learned in lodge and a life-changing event taught me to value my life. I was worthy simply because I am a human being. I had to forgive my former perpetrators, but most of all I had to no longer remain silent because of self-imposed feelings of shame. I learned from curanderas/curanderos (medicine women and men) that my body was medicine. I had to learn to bring the medicine out of my body and pray to the Creator inside of me to heal my memories and illness.

Since then, I have done many things to heal, such as using yerbas, having acupuncture and limpias, consulting with curanderas/curanderos, and participating in inipi and temazkalli ceremonies. I consider all these types of healers and healing as my guides, my teachers helping me to rebalance my life. One of the greatest gifts of knowledge given to me was about walking/ living the red road. I learned during ceremony that walking the red road is not difficult. What makes it difficult is the world that exists outside the path that complicates and confuses our journeys. I continued to pray in the stones people's lodge, to participate in summer solstice ceremonies and ceremonies honoring youth and the importance of adolescence in the life cycle, and support sun dancers at Sun Dance, as well as sisters and brothers making recommitments on the hill, more appropriately referred to as "vision quests."

Through my movement within various spiritual communities, I was invited to pray in a temazkalli. I was told that in temazkalli there would be the opportunity to learn the ways of the people of the south, the Mexica people. Having remembered my abuelito telling me to never forget I was Indian, I saw that here was yet another opportunity to search for my spiritual self. It was through prayer and song in temazkal that connections between Mother Earth and Tonantzin were made. As part of my spiritual understandings and experiences, I have come to embrace La Virgen de Guadalupe as the feminine energy of Tonantzin.

Also, many times the people who led ceremony or poured called themselves two-spirit. There were special ceremonies that focused on understanding the violent oppressive nature of heterosexism and homophobia. Our challenge as heterosexuals was and continues to be contributing to the eradication of oppression and hatred toward two-spirit relatives. With respect to lesbians, Lara Medina states that two-spirit women who (re)capture their own spiritual authority and autonomy are engaged in a political act of self-determination as patriarchal systems of domination are circumvented. Furthermore, she argues "(re)defining 'where we locate our spirituality' subverts dominant cultural norms which traditionally place spiritual authority in the hands of male mediators who can easily orchestrate a monopoly over the sacred" (1998, 195). In the *Calmecac* ("school of learning" in Nahuatl) to which I belong, respect for two-spirit communities is an important value. Inés Hernández-Avila, for example, refers to this value as a respect for difference. She states "differences such as sexual preference were respected, and in many cases tribes assigned great significance and powers to gays" (1992,164). In both inipi and temazkal, two-spirit sisters and brothers were accepted with respect, primarily among the more politically conscious Indians.

My spirituality, like that of others, is informed by different cultural influences, namely Indigenous and Catholic. Since the age of fourteen, I have questioned the teachings and practices of the Catholic Church. However, it was not until years later that I could comfortably call myself a "cultural Catholic," meaning that I still take part in Mexican expressions of Catholicism such as baptisms, *quinceañeras*, weddings, novenas, and funerals out of respect for my mother and for the sake of maintaining good family ties. However, I wholeheartedly reject the white male Euro doctrine that dictates religion. It was my niece's quinceañera, where my goddaughter wore high-top white leather army boots under her white dress, praying in temazkal with my friend Olga, and conversing with my tio Alfredo about our indigeneity, that led me to Toluca, Mexico, where I learned of my Otomi heritage.

Moving Toward *Indigenisma*

In January 2001 I traveled to Toluca, which is about an hour northeast of Mexico City, and met my Otomi relatives. For nearly twenty years, I held in my memory the conversation I had with my abuelito about our Indigenous ancestry. My Otomi brother Thaayrohyadi met me at the international airport in Mexico City. From there we traveled by bus to Toluca. When we arrived at the bus station, unbeknown to me, there were about a dozen or so Otomi relatives waiting to greet us. I was adorned with a *corona* (crown) made of evergreen and white roses, and a beautiful lush *colliar* (similar to a long necklace) also made of white roses and evergreen. I felt so honored and loved as my relatives made great sacrifices to welcome me at the bus station. Also, this public welcome defined a place for me as an Otomi woman. I overheard people in the bus station saying, "that's a tradition among the Otomi people." As I left the bus station with Thaayro, I was so overwhelmed with emotion that I began to cry.

Later that afternoon, we drove through the sacred lands of our ancestors. I asked Thaayro why it had taken so long for me to come home. He stopped the car and said "because now is the time for you to be here." We stopped again and looked at a set of mountains, which embrace the memories of the Otomi people. We arrived in Temoaya to share a meal with his mother—chicken mole, *arroz*, and blue corn tortillas. After our meal, I had the honor of trying on traditional clothing from the region. I was given a beautiful belt that Thaayro's mother made. Later that evening, Ester (Thaayro's wife) and I prayed and bathed in a temazkal as our ancestors have bathed for over forty thousand years. We entered a U-shaped figure made of bricks and wood with vapor coming through an opening at the front of the temazkal. We prayed for guidance and health. We used soft flat rocks to cleanse our bodies of the negative energies that lead to illness, arrogance, and disrespect. That night, I bathed and slept in the ways of my ancestors. I felt so very much at home.

Once I returned to the United States, I found myself questioning the legitimacy of having been "given" an Otomi identity. I thanked Coatlicue, the Creator, antepasados and Tonantzin every day for this gift of knowledge and guidance in living and walking my path, now, as a Chicana-Otomi woman. The issue of legitimacy, not choice, in relationship to my identity became an issue. The real issue, however, was one of fear. In other words, I asked myself "how do I responsibly honor and share this knowledge so that our communities heal and transform?" In my conversations with sisters like Patrisia Gonzales, Rocky Rodriguez, Olga Gonzales and Adriana Abarca, they replied that it is our responsibility to know where we come from and to validate that knowledge respectfully and humbly.

The remnants of colonial imperialist domination were haunting me, threatening my resistance to countering a fragmented memory that was centuries old. Part of the healing involves understanding the place of that identity as part of our essence or spirituality. We all know that colonial imperialist definitions of "Indigenous" have hindered our understanding of the complexities of colonization and Indigenous relocation and settlement. Obviously, this is not a uniform process, but the outcomes are similar. Understanding the complexities of Indigenous relocation and settlement can facilitate the reunification of all Indigenous peoples of the North and South.

As previously mentioned, I practice a spirituality influenced by the teachings of the Calmecac, my Otomi relatives, and Catholicism. I constructed an altar in my home nearly fifteen years ago. My childhood friend Elsa died of lupus and the altar was built in her honor. Today the altar has burning candles to La Virgen de Guadalupe or Tonantzin as I call her, a small statue of Saint Jude, Mother Cabrini, Santo Nino de Atocha, Saint Peregrine, and a small wooden doll I happened to find dressed in Indigenous clothing; I call her Tlazolteotl, the Mexica feminine healing energy. There are a number of other items on my altar, such as sage, copal, a prayer box, and prayer sticks. All these sacred objects I consider medicine. Our task is to balance the multiple and diverse cultures that inform our daily experiences. As Gloria Anzaldúa says, "the effort to work out a synthesis requires the ability to live in more than one culture, to make sense out of contradictory values, and to create a way of life which transcends opposing dualities" (Medina 1998, 195).

My spirituality informs my understanding of Chicana feminism, and how I want and need to live as a Chicana-Otomi woman. A spiritually based Chicana feminism is a terrain or site where the complexities of identity, resistance, healing, and survival are negotiated. Such terrains are essential in moving Chicana feminism forward as a transformational politics. We need to ask ourselves, "what can I bring to this life?" We need to be active, not passive observers of life. To only resist is to remain in a male-energy mode; to heal is to transform, and transformation involves the feminine principle. The decolonization of our bodies and the reclaiming of our spirits is a struggle for our human rights as women. This healing is part of our journey in what Anzaldúa (1987) called mestiza consciousness and Ana Castillo (1994) calls *Xicanisma*. The discussion of the term "Chicana" put forward by Norma Alarcón has also been influential in this process. Citing Anzaldúa (1987), she writes, "The name Chicana is the name of resistance that enables cultural and political points of departure and thinking through the multiple migrations and dislocations of women of 'Mexican descent.' The name Chicana is not a name that women (or men) are born to or with, as is often the case with Mexican, but rather is consciously and critically assumed and serves as a point of redeparture for dismantling historical conjunctures of crisis, confusion, political and ideological conflict, and contradictions of the simultaneous effects of having 'no names,' having 'many names,' not 'know(ing) her names,' and being someone else's dreamwork" (1998, 374).

It is in this space called Chicana feminism that I began to create my ability to see my body as a site of physical and political resistance.

Cancer Journey

On May 9, 2002, my body was afflicted with cancer. The next evening, after a complicated surgery lasting more than nine hours and requiring two blood transfusions, I initially felt absolutely betrayed by the Creator. I felt hurt, angry, discounted and devalued as a human being. I immediately called my friend Bea, a Sun Dancer, to guide me through my confusion. She arrived within the hour, performed a brief ceremony, and told me I had every right to feel angry. More importantly, I learned it was my challenge and responsibility to prepare for my cancer journey without abandoning my spirituality. I could no longer just simply intellectualize my experience; as with violence, cancer has absolutely no rationale. Hence, my relationship with my body took on a new meaning, which elicited questions of purpose, fate, and my identity as an Indigenous Chicana cancer patient.

Interrogating and negotiating this relationship proved to be an exhausting emotional, physical, and spiritual process. The medical establishment's attempts to claim my body as primarily existing on physical energies undermined the *bodymindspirit* balance needed to resist, survive, and transform. Additionally, my attempts to build a sense of home within my body were thwarted by oppressive Catholic notions of punishment. Asking the infamous, but standardized and binary questions of Catholic doctrine, "why did this happen to me?" or "what did I do to deserve this?" only placed my healing space within the patriarchal confines of organized religion. Such spaces or sites call on the individual to humbly acquiesce to their so-called fate in life. In my efforts to create my body as a home site, the medical-industrial complex and Catholicism elucidated yet another challenge and alienating confrontation with the relationship between medical violence, my body, and spirituality.

In retrospect, my survival and transformation largely depended on reclaiming my body from within a nepantla space. Anzaldúa specifies her intentions regarding the concept *nepantla* as follows: "To theorize unarticulated dimensions of the experience of mestizas living in between overlapping and layered spaces of different cultures and social and geographic locations, of events and realities—psychological, sociological, political, spiritual, historical, creative, imagined" (2000, 176). As noted by AnaLouise Keating, "nepantla" refers to liminal space(s) where transformation can occur, and where spaces and times are characterized with great confusion, anxiety, and loss of control (2005, 6). Placing my body in the process of nepantla, which involves liminality and change, provided me with ways with which to negotiate identity-related issues as an Indigenous Chicana and cancer patient, as well as epistemological concerns about my body as a home site of healing and transformation.

Even though the nepantla space demands isolation and seclusion, it can lead to new forms of community. Keating states that these new forms of community are "seen most prominently in the work of las nepantleras: those who travel within and among multiple worlds, developing transformative alliances" (2005, 7). *Nepantleras* are described as threshold people, agents of change, spiritual activists who employ liminal states of consciousness and ways of thinking as they enact their visions. After nearly a decade of battling cancer and cancer-related health issues, negotiating my body as a nepantlera guided me in reclaiming my Chicana-Otomi existence, which has been instrumental to my current status as a cancer survivor/thriver. Healing and transformation are part of spirituality regardless of our physical and emotional states.

In creating my body as a site of "home," Edén Torres helps me to understand the *resilient indigenisma* that took form and continues to develop in this nepantla space. Torres states that "this resilient indigenisma is most often missed by mainstream audiences and cultural critics seduced by the promise (and sometimes economic rewards) of multiculturalism and diversity" (2003, 39). She continues with her argument by drawing from the work of Elena Avila, who claimed that "identifying with this indigenisma has a communal function beyond a romantic longing for post-modern complexity" (Torres 2003, 39, quoting Avila 1992, 69). Today, I feel I can now better contribute to the healing of our communities and society in general. The outcome has simply been the following lesson: *Spirituality is Revolutionary; Revolution is Spiritual*; and the foundation of this space is love, revolutionary and spiritual love.

I build on Aleticia Tijerina's argument that revolutionary and spiritual love can connect us to others to "perform human acts." She concludes her essay "Notes on Oppression and Violence" by stating, "Each moment we recall the vision of love *we commit an act of resistance against the oppressor*" (quoted in Torres 2003, 46, quoting Tijerina 1990, 179).

In conclusion, my intention was not to write about being a victim and the transformative acquisition in embracing the fluidity of revolutionary and spiritual love. However, in (re)visiting the violence(s) in my life, subsequent implications for my spirituality, pain, anger and/or victimization were left to the direction of the West, thus taking me to the energies of the East to heal, transform, and learn to love and be loved in revolutionary and spiritual ways. Thus, I find myself moving among the energies of the East as I continue to learn about spirituality and implementing spiritual activism in my daily life. Deploying spiritual activism involves self-reflection and self-criticism in how I share words with people, and how I respond to and attempt to acknowledge respect for all living energies as part of my own survival. In particular, I consciously engage in manifestations of spiritual activism by organizing and participating in communal teaching ceremonies such as the temazkalli, the university classroom, and the community in which I reside. The home sites discussed in this essay are places where spirituality was consistently negotiated in a nepantla state. Hence, various home sites were recognized and embraced as places of radical healing and transformation leading to spiritual activism.

Notes

1. Anzaldúa describes *autohistoria* as "the genre for writing about one's personal and collective history using fictive elements, a sort of fictionalized autobiography or memoir; an *autohistoria-teoría* is a personal essay that theorizes" (Keating 2005, 6).

2. In this essay violence(s) refers to all forms of violence—economic, physical, social, cultural, spiritual, racial, and sexual.

3. A brief definition of Mexica prayer lodge according to an Apache Sun Dance elder: *Tema(li)ztli + calli = temazcalli*. *"tema" "tomar un baño de temazcal"* "to bathe in the temazcalli," so the verb "to sweat in the lodge" is actually *temaliztli*. It is important to note that there are variations of spelling throughout the literature referencing this Indigenous name for sweat lodge, but the editors have chosen temazkal and temazkalli for consistency throughout the anthology.

4. Anzaldúa stated that "coincidence" is a word of the colonizer. Coincidence does not allow for us to accept or even raise the possibility of spiritual energies or forces.

5. Drawing from Nichiren Buddhist practice and ideology, "internal darkness" refers to personal issues or wounds that a person harbors.

PART TWO

The West

Feminine Energies

Next we turn to the West, the place of water, associated with feminine energy and endings or the completion of a cycle. A three-part poetic narrative sets the tone for the following essays, which document the authors' spiritual journeys while offering methodological and pedagogical tools grounded in the West. Berenice Dimas's "Queeranderismo" boldly maps the human capacity and political need for healing across generations in ways that recuperate our multilayered selves, including our sexual, erotic-spiritual selves. Evoking the healing maternal waters of the *orisha* Yemaya—"Durante una ceremonia con Yemaya / My mother's womb walls spoke to me" (77)—in "I Was a *Curandera* Before Birth," Dimas offers us a decolonizing spiritual imaginary where we are invited to envision the possibility of healing the violences experienced by our ancestors, and thus ourselves and future generations. She leads us to the present, showing us how past wounds can linger and make themselves known in unexpected ways. Through the private and communal spaces and tongues of what she calls "Queeranderismo," "[c]*uranderismo* in motion for queer *cuerpos y espíritus*" (79), Dimas powerfully holds up hope for learning how to be our own conscious *curanderas* capable of healing historical, intergenerational, and present-day traumas. She closes this ongoing healing cycle with "Under the Blankets of our Bed," an ecstasy-filled "re-remembering of our two-spirited ancestral way of loving" (79).

Unsurprisingly, several anthology contributors elaborate on the preeminent Virgin of Guadalupe-Tonantzin, a powerful sacred figure representing the feminine energy of *la mera mera* Madre, Our Mother, the Mother Earth. While C. Alejandra Elenes focuses on the deployment of "borderland/transformative pedagogies" in part 1 and Brenda Sendejo's emphasis is the development of research methodologies, both frame their spiritual inquiries and *conocimientos* through the prism of their relationship with Guadalupe-Tonantzin. In this section, Sendejo discusses the various ways that coming into a new consciousness about Tonantzin-Guadalupe are what she defines as "methodologies of the spirit," the building of knowledge about spirituality through reflecting on one's "spiritual development, experiences, and trajectory" (84–85). In "Methodologies of the Spirit: Reclaiming Our Lady of Guadalupe and Discovering Tonantzin Within and Beyond the *Nepantla* of Academia," Sendejo analyzes the ways that critically reflecting on "the new knowledge about spiritual connections, intimacy, and healing among and between women that emerged from [her] research experience" (85) helped her develop a deeper understanding of spiritual formations, including her own. Building on Chicana/Latina/Indigenous praxis and taking the "insider/outsider" researcher discussion into new terrains, Sendejo, "a Texas Chicana conducting anthropological research *on* and *with* other Texas Chicanas" (85), shows us how our research can be a spiritual process and how our research can benefit from our spirituality.

Oliva M. Espín, in "Saints in the Cuban Heat," is also primarily guided by the feminine energies of the West. She begins her essay by stating that in the course of a life full of dramatic change and uncertainty, two strands have remained constant, shaping the backdrop against which she has made decisions and weaving other strands of her life. One is the guiding force of spirituality and the other the sustaining force of feminism. The author notes that writing about the presence of women saints during her Cuban childhood led her to weaving the strands of women, feminism, and spirituality. The following question is addressed throughout this essay: Why have the lives of women saints created this peculiar point of convergence of the main strands of her life? In the writer's life she has been witness to how faith and heroism work together in the stories of these women. Espín notes how she has been captivated by the intricacies of these women's lives, their courage as well as their weakness, their childishness as well as their maturity, and above all, doing what they believed was right regardless of their fears or the opinions of others, including male authorities in the Church and family. She proclaims that her spirituality has grown against the grain of traditional beliefs. Thus, the writer makes available her own memories as a tool to better understand the transaction between the stories of women saints and her life narrative.

Irene Lara's essay also focuses on the relationship with feminine sacred energies and the engagement of such spiritual figures in relation to the cultural and biological maternal bodymindspirit as a generative place. In "Sensing the Serpent in the Mother, *Dando a Luz la Madre Serpiente*: Chicana Spirituality, Sexuality, and Mamihood," Lara reflects on the challenging process of trying to bridge sexuality, maternity, and academic life as part of an erotic spirituality. Drawing on Anzaldúan thought and the decolonial feminist work of others who (re)claim holistic Indigenous approaches to womanhood, sex, and spirit, including through the feminine energies of Cihuacoatl, Guadalupe-Tonantzin, and Tlazolteotl, Lara discusses the ways she tries to forge an erotic-spiritual life path and strives to integrate her whole self as a thinker, writer, teacher, mother, lover, and spiritual activist. Described by some as the place where one's serpent skin is shed, the West is an appropriate place to house Lara's essay, which engages the multivalent serpent symbol while meditating on the ongoing process of renewal, transformation, and the remaking of a fluid yet grounded and whole identity. As part of exploring erotic spirituality and what she calls "serpentine conocimientos," as well as their relationship to sustaining a life committed to social justice, Lara infuses her essay with the language and images of spirited desire and erotic spirit.

Queeranderismo

Berenice Dimas

I: I Was a *Curandera* Before Birth

I was a curandera before birth
Un maíz prieto swimming in my mother's womb
With warm liquid sabor a rebeldía
Floating through la sangre de mi cuerpo

I was a curandera before birth
One of the first signs of love
Manifesting in the middle of walls
That were once raped and abused
Consistently
For an entire childhood

I was a curandera before birth
Recovering ancient dreams
De historias sobrevividas
Y sentimientos heridos
Queriéndose curar

I was a curandera before birth
Healing layers of pain
From generations within
My mother
My grandmother

My great grandmother
All victims of rape

and, I know
I carry
Those
memories
In my skin

Durante una ceremonia con Yemaya
My mother's womb walls spoke to me
Me confesaron
"Mija, I was not ready to let you go.
Tenia tanto dolor
Y tu calor
me estaba curando.
Cuando llego el tiempo dejarte ir
tu empujabas y yo no me habría.
Nuestros corazones ya no podían.
That's why nos tuvieron que abrir.
Cortarme a mi
Sacarte a ti
Tu vida, comenzó como una lucha ganada
Pero con heridas"

I was a curandera before birth
And I am a curandera now
Channeling generational trauma
Listening to its voice
Feeling its pain
Helping my mother heal
Helping myself heal
Remembering
That our bodies are not disposable
That our existence is hope
That we are worth living
That we have something valuable
to share with the world
That we need to heal
For our next seven generations

I am a curandera now

And every time my mother smiles,
I see generations of survival[1]

II: *Curando Memoria Recuperando mi Alma*

She grabbed my legs and held me tight. Fucked me from behind. My fingers quickly gripped tight to the sheets holding on with all their strength. Tears dripped as I shut my eyes and waited for that moment to be over. At the time, everything that was happening felt right, painful but right. I thought I was exploring my sexuality. Pushing the boundaries of my comfort by allowing her to touch me in that way.

When I got home I took off my clothes and looked in the mirror. I saw my legs bruised and my back scratched. Suddenly the aching burning sensation on my skin spoke to me. Asked to be heard. I ran in the shower and felt the warm water caress me while I cried. I touched my body, held myself, and apologized. I thought to myself, "How did I get here? Why would I let myself experience something that I knew did not feel good to me?" In those moments of confusion, I went back to childhood memories of my mother hitting me. Getting home from working two, sometimes three jobs, and releasing her frustration and anger at me. As the oldest of three in a single-parent home, there were a lot of expectations that I had around the house. So, in those moments where my *niñez* interrupted my responsibilities, I felt that leather press against my skin. For years those memories were repressed. I was always scared of telling someone because I felt nobody ever really understood the complexity of my family. I was afraid that my mother would be judged before being understood. She did so much more for me and those were rare occasions, but they were also a part of my experience growing up.

As I became older, I understood where my mother's pain and frustration came from and why I was a victim as much as she was. With time, we began talking about those experiences and expressing our pain to each other. However, it was not until I experienced similar physical pain with another woman that those memories came back.

Sitting on the floor in my shower I realized that the experience was beyond exploring pleasure for me. It was about healing a "comfort" with physical pain from a woman that I had internalized, and recognizing a trauma from being hit as a kid. Now I am beginning to explore the pain and interrogate how those memories inform my sexual interactions. I am learning how to openly communicate what is pleasurable and what is not with my partners. It is so rare to have open conversations about domestic violence and about intimate-partner violence in queer relationships. It is also rare to take those conversations to a deeper level and talk about generational sexual trauma and its relation to how we develop and explore our sexual desire. These conversations with myself and with others are helping me heal. It is a process I call "Queeranderismo." *Curanderismo* in motion for queer *cuerpos y espíritus*. A space to heal our memories, desires, and experiences by interrogating how our past informs our present. In these conversations we have the potential to heal for our future generations.

III. Under the Blankets of Our Bed

I can feel
My lips Swollen
Pulsating
To your calorsito
Sweet movements between my legs
And in that moment of orgasmo,
My spirit left my body
Entered another frequency of time
looking at you and me
two women of color
touching, feeling, kissing each other
something that our eyes are not used to seeing
watching us together is a decolonizing experience
a re-remembering of our two-spirited ancestral way of loving

as your tongue sang lullabies,
versos de liberation between my legs
labios started speaking their own language with you
I couldn't control their cumming in your mouth
and it made me nervous

you see, i'm a thinker, a pensativa soñadora
always distracted by my own thoughts
and your lips' conversation between my legs
was new for me because my body took control
and it didn't ask for permission

you've taken me to a place

where memories are speaking
about security, control, and need

feeling secure about controlling my sexuality
because at times in my life i haven't had control
being raped and having your body violated
does something to you
to how you see your body
to how you express your sexuality

so control over my cumming evolved from
healing the wounds of violation

my "need to control" came from deeply wanting to experience something
    different with my sexuality
needing to be in control and feel secure were my escape . . . or my
    empowerment i thought . . .

but today, i realize that i have much to heal
and in the most gentle and beautiful way,
i'm learning under the blankets of our bed
how to let my body speak,
express itself
ooze as it desires
not thinking about when or how i should allow it to cum.

Notes

1. Note: the term *Queeranderismo* is something I have been exploring with my good friend Beto De León. I want to acknowledge both our contributions to naming such an intimate healing process as we are experiencing in our lives. Beto, *gracias* for being part of this journey with me.

Methodologies of the Spirit

Reclaiming Our Lady of Guadalupe and Discovering Tonantzin Within and Beyond the Nepantla of Academia

Brenda Sendejo

My current spiritual journey began several years ago, in my late teens and early twenties, with the independence that came with leaving home and entering the world of the university in Austin, Texas. I was adamantly and in some ways defiantly redefining myself and my place in the world, as I navigated the plethora of new knowledges and experiences that came my way. A turning point came in an anthropology class, not in learning about the lifeways of South American Indigenous groups, or the linguistic patterns of African herdsmen, but in learning about the cultural practices and beliefs of another group: Mexican Americans. To say I was pleasantly surprised to learn of Mexican American history and culture outside the Alamo narrative, and to see myself and familiar cultural practices reflected for the first time in the pages of a book, in lectures, and in films is a gross understatement. I was profoundly and forever moved. Little did I know that this served as the early foundation for a life path that would lead me to academia and on a deeply profound and unexpected spiritual journey.

During these formative years, as I cultivated a love for the study of Mexicana/o and Chicana/o history and culture, I also avoided attending Catholic Church services, separating myself from the religious tradition in which I was raised. At that time, it was not out of a sense of anger but out of a sense of apathy. Nothing about the Church moved me. Apathy evolved into skepticism as sermons touting the fear of God began to bother me more and more. My strong convictions about social justice, in particular gender equality, were developing, and some questions I had about religion in my teens once again emerged. I questioned many things the priests said, much to my family's dismay. Catholicism did not meet my political or spiritual needs, so I drifted away from it. I began to feel the need for some kind of spiritual practice. It was just something that I felt—the need for spirituality and the need for a deeper connection to my own spirit, something Catholicism failed to provide. Yet I had no other spiritual tradition to which to turn. I started to feel the effects of being devoid of a spiritual belief system and felt that I had been robbed of a part of my cultural heritage. I was angry at the patriarchal institution that had judged and oppressed me and those I love.

I brought this internal battle with me to graduate school and it flourished there—my decision to disassociate myself from what I considered the hierarchical, homophobic, and sexist ways of the Church was almost immediately validated. Since those years leading up to graduate school—my late twenties and early thirties—various changes have transpired. I have grown into a full-fledged "former Catholic" and taken on all that goes with that, including contending with subtle and sometimes not-so-subtle remarks from family about my choice.

For instance, one day I told my father about my decision to study women's spirituality. He responded, "But *mi'ja*, you aren't spiritual." Tears welled up in my eyes. While in my mind I knew that for my father being spiritual meant being Catholic, I still could not help how very deeply that statement affected me. It pained me a great deal. However, in that moment my father actually demonstrated a very important point to me, something that I would not come to fully realize until later: the difference between being religious and being spiritual. Understanding the differences and similarities between the two and exploring how they manifest in people's lives, including my own, is part of my current spiritual quest and life's work. This includes conversations that dad and I now have about how it was that he came to be so close to *la virgencita*, as he calls her. He does not know, he tells me, but he prays to her daily at Mass and has several images of her up on his walls. He has lit enough candles to her in prayers for my health and well-being to light a football field at night. And it gives me comfort.

The Loss of Our Lady: My Estrangement from Guadalupe

In graduate school I studied the history of the Catholic Church—how clergy historically oppressed Tejanos through racial and ethnic oppression and how Church dogma and discourses functioned to suppress women and their sexualities. This explained much to me on a personal level. I related to feminist readings of authors who had liberated themselves from such holds—the mere possibility was an epiphany for me. But I also came to realize that through the process of severing myself from the Church I was also experiencing loss. In rejecting the Church I rejected everything that went along with it, including a part of me, a part that is deeply entangled with my Mexican American identity.

This raised uncomfortable questions for me about home, family, society, and who I was. For years I was conflicted about being drawn to Our Lady of Guadalupe. It is painful to recall those moments growing up—that I ever felt ashamed to be Mexican American.[1] Overcoming internalized shame and feeling pride for my heritage was a long and arduous process. The simultaneous longing for and resistance towards my Mexican-American Catholic religious upbringing complicated this process of reclaiming my heritage and ethnic identity immensely. Even as I learned about Our Lady of Guadalupe's history and read the scholarly interpretations and analyses of her, I was still cultivating resentment towards the Church—and she, sadly, was in the path of that resentment and fell victim to it as well.

When my maternal grandmother Victoria died, around the time I began graduate school, I so desperately wanted to call upon Guadalupe for help, for healing, as my grandmother once did. Grandma Vita was a devout believer in Guadalupe and in her ability to help women and their families. I thought invoking Guadalupe would bring me closer to my grandmother, who I desperately missed, but I resisted, conflicted because up to that point I had cultivated the narrow belief that Catholicism as a whole was sexist, oppressive, and a symbol of weakness. I had not yet been exposed to the fact that Catholicism was more dynamic than that, and that there was a difference between one's personal faith and the man-made institution of the Church. I was not yet equipped to reconcile my grandmother's devotion and belief with my misguided interpretation and disillusionment with Guadalupe. I allowed this disillusionment to inform my conclusion that Guadalupe too, signified the patriarchal church hierarchy. I made my decision: I no longer needed her.

For a very long time I thought that "they"—the patriarchal church establishment—stole her from me. But I allowed it to happen. My distance from the Church grew, as did my distance from Guadalupe and anything else that represented the Church. With her went part of my identity, part of the history that I had recently reclaimed and so desperately clung to, trying to remain connected. As I learned more about my Chicana history and heritage, the worse the pain of losing her became. I was now drawn to every aspect of my heritage, much of which I denied and some of which was denied me growing up in a predominantly English-speaking household in a middle-class suburban neighborhood. But something about her being a woman, the familiarity that overcame me when I saw her image, and the absolute and unfaltering devotion to her by the women in my family and my father made it difficult to deny her.

I was so torn. The pain swelled as I envisioned my grandmother and how she would feel to know I rejected something, someone she so revered, someone who carried her through the darkest of days, *la virgen*. In a sense I associated her with my grandmother, so I wondered if by rejecting *la virgen* I was rejecting my grandmother. It felt like the ultimate betrayal. Because my grandmother's death coincided with the development of my intellectual and feminist consciousness, the feelings of guilt for denying part of my grandmother's legacy ran very deep.

Chicana Feminist Thought, Ethnography, and New Possibilities for Embracing *La Virgen*

The realization that my ethnic and religious identities are interwoven came as I began to see that the Church no longer met my spiritual needs. So what did I do with this knowledge? I began to better understand it through various Chicana feminist texts and realized that I was not alone in my experience. Ana Castillo describes it well: "Although the Catholic Church as an institution cannot, for a number of reasons, guide us as Mexican Amerindian women into the twenty-first century, we cannot make a blanket dismissal of Catholicism either. Rejecting the intolerant structure of the Church does not automatically obliterate its entrenchment in our culture" (1994, 96). Here Castillo illuminates the tension that ran so deep within me due to the "entrenchment" of Catholicism in my culture. It is this very tension that came to impact numerous aspects of my life, including relationships with people I love.

My once contentious relationship with Guadalupe symbolizes a tension between my Catholic identity and my developing Chicana feminist identity, but it also provides the context for my discussion of methods for understanding spiritual life from an ethnographic perspective. By way of autoethnography and *testimonio*, I will discuss my own spiritual journey and religious transformation and the various ways that coming into a new consciousness about Guadalupe are what I describe as methodologies of the spirit.[2]

Methodologies of the spirit include those experiences that occur over the course of conducting research and that contribute to the researcher's knowledge about spirituality, the production of spiritual epistemologies, and the uses of spiritual practices.[3] Knowledge production around the spiritual occurs in the space where researcher and participant intersect and overlap, and where the researcher's own spiritual development, experiences, and trajectory help to inform the research being conducted. Methodologies of the spirit offer a model for doing ethnography inspired by methodologies employed by Indigenous scholars who acknowledge that the spiritual practices and world-views of research participants are foundational aspects of everyday life (Denzin, Lincoln, and Tuhiwai Smith 2008). Methodologies of the spirit acknowledge corporeal and spiritual experiences as key sites of knowledge production. They constitute a holistic and historically informed approach that accounts for moments of connection and understanding between the researcher and those with whom she works as vital sites of knowing.

In considering such new spaces of knowing, I am also inspired by a borderlands *mestizaje* framework that involves "centering and listening to *el cuerpo y experiencias en nuestro analisis*," and which acknowledges that theories must come from this kind of method of researching the everyday lives of people. This framework attends to the fact that our bodies and experiences can be "powerful sources and sites of knowledge and identity negotiation and production" (Saavedra and Nymark 2008, 256–57). The concept of methodologies of the spirit was inspired by my own positionality as a Texas Chicana conducting anthropological research *on* and *with* other Texas Chicanas and the new knowledge about spiritual connections, intimacy, and healing among and between women that emerged from my research experience. On several occasions my interactions with *las mujeres* broadened my understanding of women's spiritual formation and subsequently, my own.[4] The methods I employed show that the bodies of Chicanas/Tejanas/Mexicanas, including my own, are sites of knowledge. They hold memories of lifetimes of social struggle, identity formation, and redemption.

In this essay I also discuss how I constantly (re)negotiated my place in academia in a state of *nepantla*, the uncomfortable and liminal in-between state of which Gloria Anzaldúa speaks, which signifies a painful transition between two or more states of being.[5] The state of nepantla that I inhabited within academia would also end up being a space that led me to a pivotal moment in my own spiritual journey. This is represented in my reclaiming of Our Lady of Guadalupe and discovery of Tonantzin. In the process of seeking to decolonize the acts of collecting and telling stories of the "other," I would come to locate a sense of self; that is, of who I am and how I construct my identity as a spiritual being. In this process of self-discovery, I came to locate new knowledge about the cultural production of spirituality among the Texas Chicanas whose spiritual lives I explore. I interweave this life experience into the narrative of the woman who helped to facilitate this process of self-discovery for me and who inspired this study, Alma. In doing so I aim to provide insight into her spiritual transformation, her role as a spiritual teacher to many, and the ways in which the realms of religion and spirituality have been and continue to be political for Alma, the other women participants in my research, and myself.

This knowledge about the spiritual was gained by employing methodologies of the spirit—the researching and gaining of new knowledge about spiritual practices and beliefs, at times where the researcher's and the participant's lives intersect. I juxtapose the roles of informant and researcher in this essay in order to show how I—a Texas Chicana studying Texas Chicanas—gain reflective insight into the spiritual experiences I study in part by reflecting on my own. While the roles of researcher and informant appear separate on paper, in reality there are moments when they collapse into one; I often get the sensation that I am at once the researcher and the informant.

Because of this, my experience has involved navigating the nepantla that is academia for me. As a "native" anthropologist, in some senses I see certain moments in the lives of the women with whom I conduct research as mirrors into my own history, a history that I am still unfolding.[6] At times I see a connection between my spiritual exploration and that of the women in my study, particularly in stories of how they reconcile their own activist, spiritual, and feminist identities with the religious traditions of their pasts. Other times their stories raise provocative new questions for me, such as how Catholic Chicana feminists reconcile their feminist perspectives with their institutionalized Catholic devotion.[7]

My individual subjectivity at once informs and is informed by my work. This is a fluid and at times unstable and unnerving state—a nepantla state—for while I am drawn to embrace it and those moments where my own life offers insight into the lives of my informants, at times affording me a sense of self-fulfillment, I am also trained in objective research practices. So my academic journey has entailed seeking the balance between the two.

Our Lady of Guadalupe-Tonantzin: Active Symbol of Chicana Resistance

A lens with which to investigate how women mold a sense of self is their relationship to Our Lady of Guadalupe. Because Guadalupe is the most recognized religious icon among Mexican and Mexican American Catholics, understanding women's relationship to her illuminates a great deal about their relationship to religion and their experiences navigating certain power structures within the religious realm. I analyze my own relationship to Guadalupe as a springboard for understanding other women's experiences. This involves reimaging Guadalupe on my own terms and reclaiming her after years of feeling anger and pain caused by the previously mentioned disillusionment with aspects of the Catholic Church doctrine that I found exclusionary and antagonistic.

In subsequent years I became increasingly frustrated with the Church's antichoice perspectives on reproduction and discriminatory views on homosexuality. I rejected Catholicism, the faith I was brought up in from birth and that still surrounds me today. As I described earlier, part of my rejection of Catholicism involved rejecting Guadalupe and misinterpreting her as a symbol of Catholic patriarchy, which left me estranged from her and, in a sense, from my ethnic identity.

In ways similar to the journeys of other Chicana feminists, including that traced by C. Alejandra Elenes in this volume, I reclaimed Guadalupe as an integral part of my spiritual and ethnic heritage by reestablishing my relationship to her, which involved acknowledging her pre-Columbian antecedent, the Nahua earth goddess, Tonantzin. This process was facilitated in part by my newfound identity as a Chicana feminist and interest in the rich historical legacy of Chicana feminism and activism, my entrance into academia, and the relationships I have formed with the women activists in my study.[8] In the following section I offer an anthropological analysis of my own personal reflection on the tensions that arose when I tried to reconcile my religious cultural upbringing with my politicized Chicana consciousness. This is one of many experiences—presented here as a methodology of the spirit—that informs my personal and professional understanding of the ways that religion and spirituality function in people's lives.

Religious Recollections: Cultural Memory and the Power of Place

I have resisted entering churches in such a way so many times that, in retrospect, it almost has a ritualistic quality about it. For a number of years I resisted Catholicism when I traveled in Mexico, and more often than not these acts of resistance involved *la virgen*. During this period the various cities I visited for research and leisure became sites where a particular kind of internal conflict materialized. Perhaps it was the anonymity that I took with me to Mexico on these trips that allowed this tension to surface in such a way. The following recollection about my last visit to Guanajuato is illustrative of these kinds of experiences.

The scenario goes like this: I walk down the steep hill from the home where I am staying towards the *centro*. As I look up and my gaze meets the horizon I see the first one up close. Upon first glance something inside me is triggered; a sense of familiarity and nostalgia rush over me. I see the long narrow steeple first and then the rest of it materializes as I make my way down the hill. It is gorgeous—pristine, tall, ornate, old, Spanish. I begin going through the motions. I slow my steps and consider it for one second, then decide, no. I am off, suppressing the urge to enter. I approach the second one about five blocks down. This one is a deep hue of yellow with white trim. A long set of stairs leads up to the heavy, wooden, open doors. A large copper bell rings loudly from above.

This sacred building that cradles the bell is situated amid carefully manicured gardens, surrounded by cafés and government buildings along cobblestoned streets. During my stay in Guanajuato I have noticed that there is constant activity there—a mass, a wedding, or a *quinceañera*. Adults and children constantly flow in and out over its threshold, especially on the weekends. When the sun sets just right it is one of the most beautiful sights, nestled against the backdrop of a multicolored sky with small colonial-style buildings in the foreground. I walk closer, close enough to sneak a glimpse inside yet far enough away to assert my physical and mental distance, or so I think. My eyes make contact with the marble floor and they follow the long aisle bordered by pews all the way up to the altar. A large cross with the crucified Jesus hangs on the stark white wall above the altar. Bouquets of colorful, fragrant flowers are everywhere to be seen.

I notice that I am drawn more to churches that feature Our Lady of Guadalupe in place of a crucifix. In these instances it is harder not to step inside. This particular moment in Guanajuato, however, is not one of those times and I resist: "No. I don't need to," I tell myself, "it's silly. I don't *need* to go inside." Still, I keep the idea in the back of my mind, and the thought lingers—"What could it hurt? No one will ever know." Who this "no one" is, I have yet to discover. I continue: "Just go in for a minute . . . one minute." The internal battle continues and I convince myself that it is not right. It is hypocritical. So usually I walk by and do not stop. I do not listen to the part of me that longs to go in. However, the scenario generally plays out differently when I approach churches where *la virgen* is represented. There, a more intense familiarity overcomes me, making it more difficult to resist the urge to enter. I cannot help but ponder why. In the moments I cannot resist the temptation, why is it that I find solace staring at her as I sit alone in the last pew at the back of the quiet church?

As an anthropologist, I interpret the meaning behind the aforementioned scenario and consider, for instance, the historical and social contexts out of which my behaviors emerge. I consider my acts in light of how Chicana/Latina women navigate systems of power around race, class, and gender that function to control them through discourses such as those circulated about Marian purity. If I step away from this experience as far as it is my own, I consider how a researcher assessing a set of events such as this would respond. I ponder the qualitative interview questions she would ask of the "informant." What would she conclude from her sociohistorical examination of the symbolic action behind the woman's understanding of the Guadalupe story, her use of a home altar, or the carrying of her grandmother's rosary and simultaneous rejection of Guadalupe?

The researcher might consider what such religious acts and rituals do; that is, what kinds of meanings they produce, circulate, and communicate (Geertz 1973). She would analyze how they are shaped by each of the woman's various subject positions—Mexican American, feminist, Chicana, Tejana—and the history of her relationship to Catholicism—how it functioned in her life. The investigator would explore why such acts occur within this memory-place (Flores 2002), a site where the subject's mere presence there evokes such powerful memories that it *does* something to her, affects her in such a way.

Navigating the nepantla of academia has involved making sense of the dual researcher-informant identity in which I at once occupy insider and outsider positions (Zavella 1994, 1997). In doing so I acknowledge the inevitable moments of tension that surface in conducting such research, such as knowing how and when to step out of my researcher role; while I may identify with research participants in some ways, there are times when that may inhibit insight rather than facilitate it (Rosaldo 1989). The delicate balance in the relationship between informant and researcher, however amicable, can be compromised.[9] Aware of these issues, I envision this project as an opportunity to elicit new knowledge about Chicana life and spiritualities in the space where self and other overlap and methods of conducting decolonial anthropological and feminist research practices are realized.

Inspirations for Crafting a Methodology of Spirit within Academia

Numerous scholars have inspired my commitment to conduct socially responsible research that places women's lives at the center of narratives and my conception of new methodologies with which to do so. This deep belief in social justice and equality informs my identity as a Chicana scholar-educator. Like many other Chicana/Latina/Indigenous scholars, my life experience and feminist pedagogies, epistemologies, and praxis are the framework through which I see the world and articulate my values and beliefs in both my professional and personal lives.

Chicana/Latina/Indigenous feminist scholars have demonstrated that one's spiritual and academic lives do not have to unwind along divergent roads

(Anzaldúa 1987; Medina 1998; L. Pérez 1998; Denzin, Lincoln, and Tuhiwai Smith 2008). There will always be instances where the two roads converge, where the on-the-ground lived experiences of social actors intersect with those of the researcher. This occurs with this project by way of Chicana spiritual practices that seek out a holistic and decolonial way of understanding and living in the world. Gloria Anzaldúa examines these subversive spaces where knowledge, *conocimientos*, emerge, and where the subversive power of ancient ways of knowing and being that "challenge official and conventional ways of looking at the world, ways set up by those benefiting from such constructions" manifests (2002a, 542). Anzaldúa's call for spirituality as a form of knowledge also shifts who is understood as the producers of knowledge.

So as I ponder what this space is for me and those women with whom I share it, I also know that together we are producing new knowledge in academic territory that has traditionally excluded us and dismissed the importance of our spiritual histories, practices, and knowledges, such as methodologies of the spirit. It is in such a terrain that navigating the nepantla of academia occurs. So as we mold and then occupy these third spaces (Anzaldúa 1987) the question of whether we as scholars can achieve both personal and professional fulfillment without severing one from the other continues to be explored. I envision such spaces as opportunities to challenge old epistemologies and create new ones, where personal understanding and growth occur *alongside* the production of academic knowledge, not in isolation from it. I come to this conclusion based on my own fleshing of the spirit that informs and is informed by my positionalities as Chicana-Tejana, student, scholar and educator.

In the next section I will introduce one of the people who occupies this new subversive space with me. I will discuss how she and I go about unearthing new knowledges together, while achieving personal fulfillment and spiritual and intellectual growth, and how in the process we achieve a deeper understanding of self and challenge conceptions of "other."

The Spirit Speaks: Meeting Alma

As I mentioned previously, there are numerous moments when my spiritual and academic lives intersect. For example, I did not intentionally set out to study spirituality in graduate school. In fact, I often say that it chose me. It was an interesting—yet in retrospect not surprising—turn of events that led me to choose religious and spiritual practices of Texas Chicanas as the subject of my life's work. The irony in doing so is that on a personal level, as I have discussed in this essay, the spiritual is an area that has perplexed me for years and served as a source of anxiety and frustration on so many levels. Even more ironic is that this would take place within the university walls, where I once questioned the core of my being and my place within academia.[10]

It would, surprisingly, be within this context—where I experienced the fracture of mindbodyspirit—that I would grow and heal. This is in large part thanks to the amazing group of women who entrusted me with their rich and powerful stories and who generously gave of their time and themselves so that I could become a scholar. These women, to whom I was drawn by way of my academic work, help create scholarly knowledge on Chicana history and spiritual cultural production and in doing so, have inadvertently helped me to locate answers to questions about my own spirituality, contributing at once to my academic and personal growth.

As I will continue to explicate throughout this essay, the scholarly research and my personal (re)search are not mutually exclusive, but rather very much intertwined. The realm of academia has become a place where I am reconnecting with a part of myself that I thought was forever lost. Of all places in the universe, fleshing the spirit occurred there.

While I am appreciative of the many women who assisted me with this research project, one person in particular inspired me to choose Chicana-Tejana spiritualities as the topic of my dissertation research. My journey to Alma and this project began in 2006 with my participation in an oral history project about the political lives and contributions of women actively involved in electoral politics during the Texas Chicano movement.[11] While Alma's political narrative was enormously engaging, I remember being particularly struck by another narrative that emerged—her spiritual narrative. I was intrigued by Alma's story of having left Catholicism in the years following the movement, her period of "spiritual dormancy" and her eventual arrival at the practice of shamanism. She would later tell me in reference to her transition, "The church no longer meets my spiritual needs." Something about Alma's experience spoke to me; I was intrigued by the idea of leaving Catholicism for another spiritual path. It was not an option I thought to consider prior to meeting her.

Alma had experienced the effects of church patriarchy and racial and gender discrimination firsthand, growing up in a small North Texas town. Considering Alma's spiritual transformation within the context of her experience as a pivotal actor in the Texas Chicano movement in the 1970s raised a number of critical questions for me about the relationship between women's politics and their spiritualities, both of which I contend are informed by the material conditions of their lives. At the time I met Alma I was studying Tejanas of the World War II generation and their contributions to the development of a politically aware Chicana generation (Sendejo 2009). Once I met Alma, I shifted my focus toward Chicana spiritualities.[12] This shift would come to impact my life in more ways than I could have ever imagined.

Since Alma and I started working together I have come to know her as a friend, confidant, and teacher who is showing me how she healed herself, how she helps to heal others, and how I can heal—mentally, physically, and spiritually—from life's various traumas. Alma's life work is healing and teaching. She is a gifted healer and a spiritual teacher to many. She is a giving, nurturing, and gifted soul. Her spiritual practice and beliefs are informed by strong convictions on social justice, including equality based on gender, class, race, and sexuality, as well as the responsibility each of us has to care for and honor the earth and her resources. Through her ways of being in the world she helps me to understand connections between social justice activism and spirituality and the ways the two inform each other. That is how she is helping me for "research purposes," but this also informs my thinking on a personal level. She knows how to live to the fullest, and does so with the greatest degree of integrity, generosity, and compassion for all living beings and for the earth. These are her gifts and she shares them with me and with numerous others.

Through her teachings Alma has educated me about many aspects of life, including feminism, motherhood, spirituality, the environment, health, and healing. One day she taught me something that shook me. In a powerful moment she at once brought clarity to my research questions about women's spiritualities and to questions regarding my own spiritual path. My feelings about the Church came up one day in a conversation with Alma, with whom I share the experience of a Mexican American Catholic upbringing. She explained in her intelligent, compassionate, and unassuming way that I could open my formerly closed heart to a greater spirit through the feminine face of God, and that I could do so through understanding Guadalupe on my own terms, separate from the institution of the Catholic Church.[13] She said I could reject attempts by the Church to subjugate women and still hold on to Guadalupe as a symbol of feminine power, strength, and liberation. She explained that the Church does not have a monopoly on Guadalupe; that la virgen was not originally connected to the Church and she does not have to be now.

I came to see that I could reestablish my relationship with Guadalupe without compromising my feminist principles. Alma explained how she knows Guadalupe as Tonantzin in a way that aligns beautifully with my Chicana feminist sensibility. I could call upon her on my own terms, in my own space, for my own needs. I no longer had to keep a distance from her. I was finally able to reconcile my feminist perspectives with my ethnic and cultural identity. The hegemonic power of the Church that worked to suppress my spiritual creativity, personal independence, sexuality, strong moral convictions, and relationship with Guadalupe lifted. With this epiphany, I began the process of feeling whole once again and of healing my formerly fragmented spirit. This decolonial, feminist process of reclaiming Guadalupe led me to Tonantzin.

My experience and Alma's guidance speak to a process of self-making, or how we construct/produce ourselves (Ortner 1996, 1–2). This is a process that many Chicana/Latina/Indigenous women, including several of my study participants, have gone through. Perhaps it is because we share a mestiza consciousness (Anzaldúa 1987), a fluid and fractured identity that Dolores Delgado Bernal states, with regard to Chicana college students, is negotiated "in relationship to their language, culture, communities, and spiritualities" (2006, 128) that I can have this connection with women such as Alma. Drawing upon personal insight, I better understand the making and remaking of Chicana life. What I just described is the type of lived experience characterized by a "tolerance for ambiguity" (Anzaldúa 1987) that leads Chicanas to have such internal conflicts. It is what Anzaldúa means by inhabiting spiritual, geographic, psychological, ethnic, and sexual borderlands. From such a position I, as a Chicana ethnographer, gain deeper insight into the questions I should be asking about Chicana life.

Scholars such as Irene Lara (2008a, 2008b) address the decolonization of the spirit through the process of understanding Guadalupe as Tonantzin and seeing Guadalupe's Indigenous identity as symbolic of the postcolonial process of healing colonial wounds. Lara's concept of Tonanlupanisma as a decolonial theory and method is useful in understanding how "Tonanlupanista artists invoke and reconfigure feminist and Mesoamerican Indigenous thought and iconography to heal the colonial and patriarchal misrepresentation of women's spirituality and sexuality as popularly configured by the Christian 'virtuous *virgen*/pagan *puta* dichotomy'" (2008b, 63).

Guadalupe-Tonantzin's multiple meanings are shaped by the numerous individual desires and needs of women to heal and to partake in an anticolonial spirituality that connects them to a sacred Indigenous/mestiza worldview (Lara 2008a, 2008b). Guadalupe-Tonantzin also serves to reconnect women to a spiritual and cultural past. Laura Peréz elucidates an important point about the connection between spiritual worldviews and ethical perspectives: "Unlike the institutionalized religions that have colluded with patriarchy and class-exploitation, the spiritualities constructed in contemporary Chicana writing and art express egalitarian world views that are inseparable from questions of social justice, with respect to class, gender, sexuality, culture, 'race,' and environmental welfare" (1998, 39). The relationship between moral and ethical perspectives—that is, personal politics—and the "spiritual world-view" of which Peréz speaks is represented in the narratives of several women in this study, including Alma. They too are writers, artists, scholars, and activists negotiating questions of social justice that are inseparable from their spiritual practices and beliefs.

While I too engage in such work, the decolonizing of *my own* spirit had never before crossed my mind. While I was familiar with the literature about such processes, I had not conceived that I was capable of making such a move, not until Alma opened up the possibility for me. This is Chicana-feminist praxis functioning on the ground level, in the everyday lives of Chicanas. I believe it enables me to better see and more clearly understand what is happening in the spiritual borderlands and liminal zones that women occupy, and to know that other similar spaces of discovery await me. *This* is a methodology of the spirit, one that Alma and I cultivated together.

Knowing Alma and understanding her perspective on Guadalupe-Tonantzin in relation to what I have learned in my own studies grounds Chicana feminist theory in a very palpable way for me. Why was learning that I could still identify with Guadalupe after all these years so powerful for me? Because of the anger and hatred I held onto for so many years, which had built up more than I realized. Reasons for my anger and resentment run deep. I am learning to trace those energies to the correct sources. I now realize that I must learn to forgive and begin the processes of healing in which so many who have been negatively affected by religious patriarchy must engage. In doing so, I work towards creating social change rather than punishing myself and cutting myself off from a very important part of my Mexicana/Chicana/Tejana identity and heritage in the process. I knew these feelings were so deeply ingrained because of the unbelievable sense of relief I felt when Alma led me to Tonantzin. At that point my soul took a long, deep breath. I embraced the sense of relief and once again embraced her, Guadalupe-Tonantzin.

I owe a great debt of gratitude to Alma and others who, through their work as educators, writers, and artists and by way of their own experiences, expand our understanding of the world and each other and help us to heal.

Healing my fragmented spirit and becoming whole again inform my understanding of Chicana/Latina spiritual experiences. Understanding feminism, specifically Chicana feminism, in nonbinary terms—where I can at once be devoted to Guadalupe while still enacting feminist principles of gender equality—is one way this is accomplished. Such insight leads me in the direction of unearthing new types of knowledge and ways of knowing. For instance, it led me to want to explore the experiences of Chicana Catholics and Chicana feminist Catholics[14] and how they reconcile their perspectives on patriarchy and male hierarchies within the Catholic Church with their religious devotion and ethics of social equality.[15] But as I piece together my spirit and make it whole again, I struggle with the imposed researcher-informant binary and my transgressing of its boundaries.

Beyond the Researcher-Informant Binary: Locating Spiritual Epistemologies

Last night my soul took a deep breath. I allowed myself to be. Just be. The moon was full and so was my soul. The beat of the drum calmed me and the singing soothed me. Scholarly debates about appropriation and authenticity floated up and away in the red glow of the fire's ashes and deep scents of burning sage and rosemary. I went against my intellectual sense of reason that tells me to be very careful not to blur the line between informant and researcher, which I had not experienced crossing in such a way before. I crossed into that forbidden territory, shedding my researcher skin but leaving on many other layers. I was relieved that I was capable of negotiating my various positionalities in such a way. I was hesitant to go, but after several e-mails about monthly full moon gatherings, I finally gave in, because I needed to and because I wanted to. And it was real; I was real, they were real, and it was genuine in the most comforting of ways.

This reflection is inspired by a journal entry I wrote the day after attending a full moon ceremony at Alma's house in 2006. This scene illustrates some of the early tensions I felt in thinking I needed to separate parts of myself, tensions that characterized my nepantla state within academia. Since then I have been to several other events, including women's *temazkalli* and full moon ceremonies.[16] Both provided great sources of emotional support and spiritual fulfillment during very trying times. But in both instances I could not help but question if I was being dishonest in any way by attending—because while I am genuinely interested in such events and believe in their healing potential, I could not help but feel that I had to make a conscious effort to separate my personal reasons for being at these events from my professional interest in them. I remember worrying that I was betraying the groups I was joining and thinking, "Can I separate the two, just like that? What if I am not able?" I had the objective academician in me struggling with the Chicana feminist scholar side who reminded me that I did not need to separate the two, but just let it all fall into place, since my intentions were rightly placed.

I needed these moments and the healing and support that they and the people who gathered brought me. Preparation of exams was intense and at times utterly overwhelming. It took a toll on my mind, body, and spirit. Luckily,

I listened to my intuition and left my reservations at the door, allowing myself to nurture my spirit. I am so very glad that I did. Once inside, everything fell into place and I benefited from these communal, supportive ceremonial spaces. I found clarity and the internal conflict melted away.

Since that first experience at Alma's home several years ago, I have engaged in numerous ceremonies and spiritual gatherings with her and with a community of women I have since met. My own spiritual path is solidifying and I am content. This is in large part due to the fact that in the recent past I came to face personal loss like never before in my life. I searched desperately for a path to healing. And once again Alma was there, to help my partner and me pick up the pieces and mend our severely broken hearts and spirits.

It was this recent event and a new understanding of loss, personal suffering, and the dire need for spiritual healing that confirmed for me that the antiquated notion of the research-informant binary must be rethought. My relationship with Alma is so much more than an anthropological debate, especially within the context of our loss and the personal journey of healing that she has shared with me. The connection between us transcends western academic notions of self and other, demanding new methodological and theoretical spaces within anthropology and other disciplines to take into account the profound mindbodyspirit connections of and between "researcher" and "informant" that elicit new knowledges and ways of knowing.

I contend that these spaces of personal connection and experience offer immense insight into religion and spirituality as powerful arenas of social action and social change that extend beyond western epistemological understandings of ethnographic research. We must challenge and change dominant paradigms as such in order to locate new and varied epistemologies (Delgado Bernal et al. 2006; Denzin, Lincoln, and Tuhiwai Smith 2008) that deepen our understanding of cultural practices and the sociocultural issues that they represent.

The intimate relationship that I developed with Alma and the conditions out of which it emerged are forms of knowledge—spiritual epistemologies—that I explore within the context of scholarship that addresses insider-outsider dynamics. As described by Kamala Visweswaran (1997) in her overview of the development of feminist ethnography, in the wake of both Moraga and Anzaldúa's *This Bridge Called My Back* (1983) and Anzaldúa's *Making Face, Making Soul* (1990) feminist ethnographers developed ways to think and work through their multiple positions (Behar 1993; Narayan 1993; Visweswaran 1994). Visweswaran states that these scholars refer to themselves as "'halfie' or 'hyphenated' ethnographers, describing how mixed parentage, ethnic heritage, or racial positioning have shaped their ethnographic identifications" (1994, 613).

As I consider how I as a Chicana researcher deal with studying "her own" and, in some ways, herself, I reflect on this history of feminist ethnography and address issues of representation that I confront as a Chicana conducting research on Chicanas. In addition to proposing a new space for understanding our relationships to our "informants," I also consider where I/we fit within the realm of an established tradition of the study of spirituality and religion within anthropology, one that has customarily addressed religious and spiritual practices and beliefs of the "other" (Turner 1967; Geertz 1973; Durkheim [1912] 1995). I consider how the stakes have changed now that I, we, have at once become and study the "other."

I am guided by feminist scholars in anthropology (Zavella 1987, 1994, 1997; Behar 1993; Visweswaran 1994, 1997) who precede me in exploring women's lives and engaging in methods of research that draw attention to common experiences and relationships between researchers and informants rather than stressing divisions within anthropological projects. I am also inspired by the insights of Chicana/Latina/Indigenous ethnographers who engage critical questions about insider-outsider status that are particularly relevant to my own experience (Zavella 1987; Behar 1993; Russel y Rodríguez 1998; Hurtado 2003; Téllez 2005; Denzin, Lincoln, and Tuhiwai Smith 2008). These works merit attention because they represent a realm of scholarship that engages questions of subjectivity, situated knowledges, and multiple planes of difference.

I contend that the types of new knowledges that emerge out of such projects occur in part because these works, undertaken *by* women of color *on* women of color, embrace the realities of complex research relationships. Analyzing the experiences of women of color sheds light on our own experiences while broadening our understanding of the social relations among women and the diversity of their experiences. For me this new knowledge production comes by way of locating a source of personal knowledge about my own spirituality within the anthropological research project.

The choice to use my personal voice in this essay and to write about my experiences was not an easy one for this anthropologist. But as I struggled with the fear that I might inadvertently privilege my voice in this essay, I am reminded that my experience serves as a source of knowledge. As the editors of *Telling to Live: Latina Feminist Testimonios* (2001) note about the use of the personal voice in testimonio: "the stories show how knowledge of and from their [women's] everyday lives is the basis for theorizing and constructing an evolving political praxis to address the material conditions in which they live. . . . These *testimonios* offer the language of Latina intellectuals as an alternative site of knowledge" (ix–x).

So I move forward in this uneasy yet necessary task of sharing my own story, as it is a praxis that indeed delves into the material conditions of life, forms of knowledge that have shaped and informed my understanding of other women's spiritual experiences, such as Alma's. My work and the conception of methodology of the spirit is inspired by these and other Chicana/Latina/Indigenous scholars who have set the stage for drawing on such feminist methods in order to broaden our understanding of social life (Anzaldúa and Keating 2002; Delgado Bernal et al. 2006).

I reflect on the distance I keep from the Catholic Church together with the distance I am taught to keep from those with whom I work. In both cases I am taught to remain detached, to not venture too close, just to watch it/them from afar. Both have felt uncomfortable at times—contrived, false. As I reestablish my relationship to Guadalupe, I also consider what it means to be a Chicana anthropologist studying something that engages new questions about the external world and simultaneously my internal world. In some ways, early on, being a feminist and not understanding the profound impact that my racial and ethnic identity had on my sense of self separated me from a part of myself that so significantly and profoundly defines who I am—a Mexican American woman with roots in Texas. Engaging *Chicana* feminist theory and praxis, including honoring my history and ethnic heritage while enacting my principles of social equality, has brought things back into perspective. This perspective has been enlightening, allowing me personal fulfillment and a deeper understanding of the social processes and cultural practices that I live and study at the same time.

While some of the women in my study, such as Alma, have broken with traditional religious practices in the wake of donning a Chicana feminist consciousness, I have also learned that some activists leave Catholicism only to return to it later in life on their own terms. This is to say that this realm of life I study is multilayered, complex, and ever changing. It consists of seeming contradictions, and at the same time provides great moments of clarity about Chicana/Latina social life. As for me, I am learning to identify these new spaces. I do so by analyzing women's different spiritual paths—both within and outside of organized religion—from my various vantage points in order to learn about the whole realm of Chicana/Latina spirituality in Texas, lest the research be incomplete. As far as my own journey goes, Guadalupe has evolved into Tonantzin and I have found a sense of peace and stability in that. I have reconciled my feminist identity with my Catholic identity by reconfiguring and resignifying aspects of my cultural traditions in ways that hold meaning for me.

As I reflect on the course of events in my life that bring me to this moment, it is no surprise that my life path led me to focus on spirituality as my work. So in the end, or rather the beginning, twenty or so years following that first introduction to Mexican American studies, it is here, within the walls of academia in a space where it intersects with spirituality, that the circle is complete. Guadalupe is once again by my side and I am getting to know her as Tonantzin. I grew tired of the anger and tired of the feeling that I was missing a part of my soul. So finally, within the space where self and other converge, I reclaim her. I reclaim her in terms that decolonize her, assisted by Chicana/Latina/Indigenous scholars, Alma, and so many other women in my life. In doing so I have ripped Guadalupe free from the grasp of powers that seek to oppress women in her name. In doing so, I work toward the decolonization of the anthropological research project through spirituality.

As I move forward in my research, I see Guadalupe-Tonantzin through the eyes of a Chicana feminist who calls upon her past to make sense of her present. I see my mother, Gloria, my grandmothers, María and Victoria, and my great-grandmothers, Concepción, Petra and María, in Guadalupe-Tonantzin's strength, endurance, compassion, and subversiveness; qualities that characterize the spirit of la Chicana, la Mexicana, la Tejana. This spirit lives on within me and through the women who surround me. She is the candles they lit for me during my years of schooling and she is the prayers they say for my health and well-being. She is the fifteen-year-old worker in the cotton fields on a hot, South Texas summer day and the underpaid pecan sheller working in harsh conditions for pennies. She is the World War II machinist working the graveyard shift, dodging catcalls and building muscle from doing "man's" work. She is the young girl feeling ashamed of only knowing how to speak Spanish and the young woman ashamed of not speaking it well enough. She is a symbol of the feminine energy of the West—a resilient energy that manifests in the struggles and successes of generations of women in my family. She is the legacy of all the *mujeres* in my life who have had her by their sides. She is strength and love and *mujer*. She is mestiza, Tejana, Americana. She is us, she is them, and she is me. I am not willing to give her up—she is part of me and part of a historical and cultural heritage that defines me.

Understanding my own spirituality in these terms, on a deeper level, and embracing rather than denying the ways that it both informs and is informed by my work helps me to better understand experiences of other women. The collaborative cultivation of knowledge in which we engage holds much promise. And as I have learned, knowledge can be located in the most unexpected of places, sometimes where self and other reside as one and, in my case, where reclaiming Guadalupe entails discovering Tonantzin.

Notes

1. Chicana/o friends and other Latinos of my generation who grew up in Corpus Christi, Texas, also relate to this experience. As discussed by many scholars, this kind of internalized shame over being Mexican American is the confluence of a number of factors,

including the historical development of a city's racial/class climate and processes of acculturation that can accompany Mexican American social mobility. See Vallejo 2012.

2. After developing the concept of methodology of the spirit on my own, I discovered an earlier discussion of the phrase in "My Soul is a Witness: Affirming Pedagogies of the Spirit" by Cynthia B. Dillard, Daa'iyah Abdur-Rashid, and Cynthia A. Tyson (2000). The authors explore the meaning of spirituality within the context of how African American women educate and research. Dillard reflects upon her own experience within the context of a research project she conducted with graduate students who examined how Dillard enacted spiritually infused teaching. Our uses of spiritually inspired methodologies correspond in some ways, such as our shared attention to reciprocity and caring within research relationships, yet differ in that while Dillard considers methodologies within the context of pedagogy in academia, my central focus is the use of methodologies of the spirit in gathering data during field research and their impact on relationships between researcher and participants. Elsewhere I discuss how spiritual epistemologies manifest in my teaching and other academic endeavors (Sendejo 2011, 2013).

3. In "In the Presence of Spirit(s): A Meditation on the Politics of Solidarity and Transformation," Inés Hernández-Avila (2002) reflects on her process of writing, and how she must pull back the various layers of her identities, such as professor, *Nimipu* (Nez Perce), India MexicanaTejana, mother, and lover, to arrive where she writes from a place of spirit. Her discussion of spiritual epistemologies and how personal transformation can inform our understandings of the world and, in turn, promote social transformation, is important foundational scholarship that informs my concept of methodologies of the spirit.

4. Ruth Trinidad Galván's (2006) insightful discussion of "pedagogies of the spirit" is related to methodologies of the spirit, which acknowledges that spiritual knowing—or knowledge about spirituality and spiritual experiences—can emerge from spiritual interconnections between researcher and participants. Pedagogies of the spirit consider how *campesina* spiritual epistemologies shaped the pedagogies they enacted in daily life and in their spaces of collective organizing—for example, in inclusion of prayer in meetings and the adoption of a spiritual approach to how they interact with one another and learn from and teach one another. I employ pedagogies of the spirit in my approach to doing anthropology by bringing my own "way of knowing and being in the world" and spiritual epistemologies to my research (Trinidad Galván 2006, 163). The new experiential knowledge that emerges as a result and between research participants and myself is the result of employing methodologies of the spirit.

5. Anzaldúa addresses nepantla as a space of transition where various ways of thinking come into conflict with one another in a way particularly relevant to this essay: nepantla is "where you question the basic ideas, tenets, and identities inherited from your family, your education, and your different cultures. Nepantla is the zone between changes where you struggle to find equilibrium between the outer expression of change and your inner relationship to it" (2002a, 548–49). Also see Jessica Heredia's and Gloria González-López's essays in *Bridging: How Gloria Anzaldúa's Life and Work Transformed Our Own* (Keating and González-López 2011) for discussions on navigating the university as nepantla experiences.

6. See Patricia Zavella's (1987, 1997) work on conducting research with Chicana informants for a discussion of the complexity of "native" anthropology. In both my case and Zavella's, while we may share one or more social locations with our research participants, there are still different aspects of our identities that prevent us from fully ever

being "native" anthropologists. Also see Kirin Narayan (1993), who asks if anyone can ever really be a "native" anthropologist.

7. See Sendejo (2013) for an in-depth examination of the spiritual and activist trajectories of three Tejana activists: Martha P. Cotera, María Elena Martínez, and Susana R. Almanza. The work draws from the aforementioned ethnographic research project and the praxis of spiritual activism employed by Gloria Anzaldúa. I use spiritual activism to analyze patterns of spiritual change among the three women and to discuss how it is reflective of their political and feminist sensibilities, as well as tied to the material realities of their lives.

8. It was Martha Cotera's seminal text, *Diosa y Hembra: The History and Heritage of Chicanas in the U.S.* (1976), that initially opened my eyes to the historical legacy of Chicanas and our Indigenous, feminist, and activist identities.

9. See Ruth Behar's (1993) discussion of her relationship of "fictive kinship" with her informant and comadre Esperanza as an early challenge to conventional anthropological research methods. Also relevant are the challenges that arose with Karen McCarthy Brown's insider-outsider status as described in *Mama Lola: A Vodou Priestess in Brooklyn* (1991). McCarthy Brown describes her approach as "the product of unconventional methods of anthropological research and writing" and claims "that more extended, intimate, and committed contact between the researcher and subject can undercut the colonial mindset of much anthropological writing" (2002, 127–28).

10. Chicana/Latina scholars have articulated the obstacles we face in our university experiences. See, for example, Latina Anónima 2001, Lara 2002, and Holguín Cuádraz 2003.

11. "Alma" is a pseudonym. My writing of this essay was the first time I reflected upon my relationship with Alma in published form. Whereas I use Alma's given name in another essay that has since been published elsewhere (Sendejo 2013), Alma and I together made the choice to use a pseudonym for this particular essay. I wish to honor that choice and where we both were in our lives at that time.

12. This proved to be a natural transition. I soon came to learn that the experiences of the World War II–generation Tejanas who are mothers of the Chicanas I currently study are very relevant to my current work. Spiritual and religious practices among World War II–generation Tejanas greatly inform my research on changes and continuities among the spiritual practices of their daughters.

13. On Guadalupe-Tonantzin as the "feminine face of God," see Castillo (1996, xvi) and Rodríguez (1996).

14. See Medina's (2004) work on Chicana/Latina religious activism in the Catholic Church and Isasi-Díaz and Tarango (1988), who discuss Hispanic women's engagement in liberation theology and feminism within the Catholic Church.

15. I explore this in depth in my dissertation, an ethnography examining Chicana religious and spiritual experiences (Sendejo 2011).

16. A temazkal is a large clay and brick enclosure with hot rocks inside that produces steam and heat used for healing and purification purposes. See Facio, Medina, Villegas, and Gonzales's discussions of the temazkal in this volume.

Saints in the Cuban Heat

Oliva M. Espín

When I was a girl of eight or nine, during another hot and humid Christmas season in Havana, *los Tres Reyes Magos*—the Three Kings or Wise Men who bring presents to children on January 6, the feast of the Epiphany, in many Catholic countries—brought me a small book: *Niños Santos*. I was already an avid reader; *Niños Santos* became my constant companion. I read its stories so often I could recite the lives of the young people it contained from memory. Around the same time, a film on the life of Rose of Lima, the first canonized saint of the Americas, became a success in Latin America. *Rosa de América*, a black-and-white feature film, triggered my fantasies about sainthood. Watching Rosa on the screen after reading about her in *Niños Santos* made saints even more real to me.[1]

I was mesmerized by Argentinean actress Delia Garcés playing the role of Rose of Lima. Garcés was a beautiful woman, as Rosa was supposed to have been. She played many other glamorous roles in Argentinean cinema but none made her as famous to the Latin American public in the 1940s as Rosa. Her beauty made sainthood seem like an attractive possibility. Her long dark curly hair, so much like mine, made me think I could be like her if I tried. Maybe if I behaved like her I could become as beautiful and as good as she was. And Rosa was Latin American, not European like the other saints I was hearing or reading about. This made her particularly attractive to me. The incessant tremors of Cuban political history, the distant echoes of life-and death-dramas in the politics of other Latin American countries, were present even then when I did not have a full understanding of all those events. As you will read later in this essay, Cuban history with a big *H* has been a most important determinant in the course of my life. I think my child's intuition, no matter how unformed, made me understand that I had more in common with Rosa than with all those European saints.

Then, when I was ten or eleven, I watched the now-legendary film in which Ingrid Bergman played the role of Joan of Arc, and for days after I passed the time jumping on furniture carrying my banner, a broomstick with a rag tied on one end, pretending to be Joan of Arc conquering fortresses. While Joan of Arc evoked fantasies of achievement in my childish mind, Rosa had built her sanctity through acts of self-mutilation.

Many decades later I learned that because women's bodies were presented as sinful, impure, and imperfect by centuries of cultural and religious discourse, many women equated sanctity with controlling and reducing their bodies. Therefore, women who aspired to sainthood showed the power of their spirit through the mutilation or even annihilation of their bodies. Such control was the best demonstration of the strength of their souls (Espín 1998). But as a child I did not have a gender analysis of Rosa's behavior. Imitating Rosa meant hurting my body. I was lucky enough not to wear a veil that could hide a crown of nails or clothes that might conceal a locked iron chain around my waist as Rosa did. Instead I filled my school shoes with beans, knelt on pebbles to pray whenever possible, and ate foods I strongly disliked. I even went long hours without drinking water in the Cuban heat, while dreaming about founding a religious order named after Saint Rose of Lima. I spent hours designing the habit my nuns would wear, making it as beautiful as possible: white pleated chiffon, trimmed with black velvet at the neckline, the sleeves, and the waist. I guess I wanted to be a fashionable saint!

I had read other stories and fairy tales and seen other films about young female heroines. Indeed, Disney's *Snow White* was the first film I saw. But the stories of young women devoted so deeply to God that they reached the Catholic Church's pinnacle of sanctity captivated my imagination. Transforming the world in which they lived or the lives of others looked a lot more attractive than marrying an unknown prince. I liked that they played an active role in their own lives, instead of waiting for that prince to wake them up with a kiss. What I wanted most in the world was to be a saint. I fantasized about being some self-sacrificing martyr or hermit, playacting the roles on a daily basis. The saints who stimulated my imagination most were women. The intricacies of these women's lives have stayed with me.

Yet the saints were not the only catalysts in my life. My childhood memories are also full of "snapshots" of my budding feminism. One anecdote remains vividly present. I was five; my sister and I were playing with my two cousins on the porch of my paternal grandmother's house, watched closely by one of my father's sisters. The four of us were about the same age, three girls and one boy. In the course of our play talk, I referred to the four of us as "*nosotras.*" My aunt corrected me, saying the right form to use was the masculine "*nosotros*" because my male cousin was part of the "we." Although at the time I had no idea what sexism was I quickly responded to her that it did not make any sense: Manoly was only one boy and we were three girls, we were the majority; the feminine form should prevail! How my aunt responded, I cannot remember, but I imagine she probably said the rule was the rule regardless of what I thought.

In the course of a life full of dramatic change and uncertainty, these two strands have remained constant, shaping the backdrop against which I have made decisions and into which I have woven other strands of my life. One is the guiding force of spirituality; the other is the sustaining force of feminism, both present in my life even before I had a word for them. The stories of women saints are one way I have found to connect spirituality and feminism.

Sainthood, Spirituality, and Mysticism

Why have the lives of women saints created this peculiar point of convergence of two main strands of my life?[2] I believe that it is because I have seen how faith and heroism have worked together in the lives of these women. They set out to do what they believed God wanted from them, regardless of what others thought. Obviously, whatever they believed to be God's wishes was dictated by their own thinking. And even though they could not fully abstract themselves from the influence of their cultural milieu—as no one fully can—they used the tools of their culture to implement their own will in the name of God. In rather contradictory ways, they used negative cultural and religious gender norms to challenge what was expected of them as women. It must have been the paradox at the center of the saints' lives that attracted me. I remember having an inkling that even the most apparently submissive among them had challenged authority.

Most of the stories and narratives about saints, particularly those presented to little girls as role models, portray them as compliant, obedient, self-sacrificing masochists, faithful to the dictates of authority, completely neglecting or denying the fact that their behavior frequently challenged the norms and expectations placed on them as women. But once I grasped that they understood their lives through the lens of their historical and cultural contexts, these women's stories had the opposite effect on me. They were examples of the effects a "passionate spirituality" (Dreyer 2005) could have on the development of a "radical wisdom" (Lanzetta 2005) unique to women's spirituality.

Reflecting on their capacity to alternatively accommodate and rebel against patriarchal dictates of the Roman Catholic Church, I found that their experiences, despite the differences in historical circumstances, were frequently close to mine. Their femaleness, like mine, presented specific limitations and provided specific avenues to spiritual achievement. They became models of self-assertion and rebellion against arbitrary dictates of authority for me, because my perspective on the stories of these women goes against the grain of established traditions.

Although the human developmental journey is widely different in various historical and cultural settings, in many ways, saints are like us—down to earth. Their gritty resistance to authority and sometimes stubborn conformity can illumine our own lives' struggles. All over the world and across generations, Christian girls (including Roman Catholics, Orthodox Christians, Anglicans, and many others) have been raised on stories of saints and a few other female heroines who have been presented to them as models to imitate. In Latin American countries, the feasts of patron saints, celebrated with processions, dance, song, and food punctuate the calendars of small towns and big cities alike.

As Meredith McGuire puts it aptly, "Religion [and spirituality], in . . . broad sociological sense, consist of how people make sense of their world—the stories out of which they live" (2005, 118). In Latin America, those stories are powerfully and deeply tinged with the historical and daily experiences of the materiality of life. For as McGuire elaborates, "All religions engage individuals through concrete practices that involve bodies, as well as minds and spirits" (119). The food, songs, and dances in honor of patron saints engage the bodies of participants and make the spiritual meaning of the ceremonies accessible to those who cannot rely on texts for their spirituality. Moreover, food preparation and eating—so important in Latin American culture and so intertwined with the lives of women in our cultures—"can be highly meaningful spiritual practices [that give us] a different appreciation of women's [spiritual] roles" (127).

The central focus of my spirituality, based in large part on what I learned as a child about some women saints who have been my role models, has grown against the grain of traditional beliefs and has helped me develop a relational perspective on the life of the spirit that, in turn, has brought me closer to my spiritual self and to my fellow human beings. True spirituality is, by definition, relational, since it is fundamentally about a relationship with whatever we understand "God" to be. And this in turn determines our relationships with other human beings. Spirituality is "embodied in ways that activate memory, deeply felt emotion, social connectedness and meaning" (Dreyer and Burrows 2005b, 63). In other words, there is a profound "materiality" to spirituality. My personal and professional choices have been guided by this relational spiritual perspective, albeit not always consciously. In these pages, I make my own memories available as a tool to understand the transactions between these women's stories and my own, as well as their possible significance for the spirituality of everyday human life.

Early on, I became more or less consciously aware that at the core of these women's lives was a profound personal connection with what they understood God to be. Indeed, sainthood is not about "religious" activities or roles, but about one's relationship with the Divine, which is what mysticism is all about. That relationship in turn brought them to active transformations in themselves and others. As the German theologian Dorothee Soelle says in her book about mysticism and resistance, "mysticism and transformation are insolubly connected" (2001, 89). For these women saints, "the experience of being with God [was] stronger than [their] fear or depression and stronger than all authority based on hierarchy or custom" (84); stronger than cultural and historical limitations imposed on them. And that strength, derived from their mysticism, is what made them saints.

From these saints' lives I intuited early in life that "a defining characteristic of Christian mysticism is that [it] impels a person towards an active rather than purely passive, inward life" (Sheldrake 2005, 287). Indeed, true Christian mysticism "is founded on the practice of common human everyday life rather than on private experiences or on purely devotional or ascetical exercises" (283) and it has nothing to do with political domination or the right-wing perspectives that seem to be associated with the word "Christian" these days. In fact, as Michel de Certeau (1992) asserts, saints, like the mad, stand for a kind of otherness and live on the social and even religious margins. Their otherness gives them the ability to defy conventional sources of power and privilege. Women saints are, in their own unique ways, culturally and politically subversive. They may have "mouthed" and believed in culturally approved norms, and yet they lived their lives acting against those norms. For them, as for us, spirituality is a center from which to challenge structures of power and privilege, particularly as they affect women.

Feminism and Spirituality

"Redemption" for women is not about selflessness and submission. On the contrary, as theologian Rosemary Radford Ruether (1998a, 1998b) and others have made clear, for women, "redemption means overcoming patriarchal subordination of women in all its forms and creating societies and cultures of just and loving mutuality between men and women across classes and races"

(1998a, 13), because "redemption happens when we resist and reject collaboration with injustice and begin to taste the joys of true well-being . . . when life is lived in solidarity with others in mutual well-being, every act of sustaining life becomes a sacrament . . . whether it is bread broken and shared, sexual pleasure between lovers, tilling the ground, making a useful product or giving birth to a baby" (103).

Needless to say, my understanding of both spirituality and feminism has changed dramatically over the years. Both could have developed very differently or not at all were it not for the jarring changes and transformations of my life. The question of what to do with spirituality in a secularized world, of how to preserve spirituality without falling into the trap of fundamentalism that denies and suppresses the insights of feminism, remains alive for many women. The need to recover, revitalize, breathe life into faith traditions continues to be felt by many women, myself included, as this writing demonstrates.

In this process, I focus my attention on the individual experiences of these women and the specific details of their cultural and historical contexts. Any understanding of spirituality cannot ignore "the importance of gender and sexual orientation, race and ethnicity, class and social location, locality and nationality, as crucial factors in understanding culture and experience . . . and how these factors impinge on our understanding of the spiritual life" (Dreyer and Burrows 2005c, 367).

In my previously published work, I have written about immigrants/ refugees and Latina women from psychological and gendered perspectives (for example, in Cole, Espín, and Rothblum 1992; Espín 1997, 1999; Kawahara and Espín 2007, 2012; Yakushko and Espín 2009). Working as a professor at state and private universities, I have lived most of my adult life in the world of the secular academy, researching women's lives and studying the psychology of women of ethnocultural backgrounds less frequently considered as subjects by psychology. My teaching positions have been supported by public funds or by student tuition at private institutions for the training of psychologists. The professional institutions to which I have belonged have been committed to the nonsectarian study of psychology and women's studies. I have taught courses about women saints and presented this material at professional conferences, but in those settings it has not always felt acceptable to speak of the significance of this material for my own life.

I am now beginning to give myself permission to write as a spiritual person, even as I also write as a scholar. Thus I speak with two voices. I speak directly and unabashedly about some of the implications that this material has for my spiritual life. The seemingly small stories of my childhood and my encounters with these women saints create the thread that ties all these stories together.

But I also speak as a women's studies scholar recovering the rich and complex legacy of our foremothers. As a psychologist I am interested in what shaped these women's life experiences; as a woman, I am interested in what these experiences might have meant to them and might mean to us.

As I write in my two voices, I try to reach others like me who have been searching for ways to weave together their feminism and spiritual beliefs. Many women mistrust and reject traditional religion because its patriarchal positions have been a powerful source of women's oppression. Alternative forms of spirituality, such as goddess worship and nature-oriented rituals, have been developed or rediscovered in the context of the women's movement. Yet many women—feminists included—do not find adequate spiritual fulfillment in these approaches. For some women, more traditional religious beliefs continue to serve as a source of inspiration in their struggles for liberation. For them, as for me, such traditions remain a source of strength.

In the early 1990s, when I started teaching women's studies full time, my interest in women's stories and their lives crystallized in more expansive ways that took me beyond psychology or purely psychological interpretations of lives. Almost coincidentally, as I started using women's stories more actively in my teaching, I started remembering the saints' stories of my childhood and wondering about the meaning of my favorite saints' life stories. As women's studies scholarship recovered the stories of women's lives in history, literature, and anthropology, and as psychologists understood women's emotional experiences and psychological conflicts to be healthy reactions to oppression rather than pathological responses to individual mental health challenges, I began reading Teresa of Avila again.

Although it would be anachronistic to say that Teresa was a "feminist," her sharp understanding and critical interpretation of the constraints of women's circumstances remain relevant today. I had read Teresa's writing in high school Spanish literature classes in Cuba, but as I read her through different lenses, I began to see that Teresa was not the obedient daughter of the Church described to me as a child, rediscovering in her the story of a woman of stature in early modern Europe tenaciously struggling against Church authorities to fulfill what she believed to be God's will. Reading Teresa with this new understanding made me want to explore the stories of the other women saints of my childhood. My interest in these stories was fueled further by the importance of narrative and storytelling evident in the last few decades of research and writing in many academic fields.

As I write about saints, I find myself writing partly memoir and partly scholarly analysis of saints and sainthood. And I tackle the issues their lives present from the perspective of my main academic epistemological perspectives. Because I am a psychologist, I see human behavior through the lens provided by developmental, social, and clinical psychologies. Because I am a feminist I read all historical information about these women with a certain "hermeneutical suspicion" (e.g., Schüssler Fiorenza 1983; Schneiders 2005) that helps me see important information in the interstices, in what is not said by them or by other writing about them. Although I am not a theologian or a historian, the work of feminist theologians and historians illumines this exploration for me.

History and Life

Having grown up in a convulsed Latin America means I have lived immersed in contradictions, and each one of these women had something to teach me about contradictions. Moreover, my life has been marked by the experience of migration. As an outsider in many cultures I have experienced being "different," with all the positives and negatives involved. But even among those who shared my historical and cultural circumstances, I have felt an outsider more than once.

Since my early childhood, my family had lived a life of genteel poverty, no less harsh because it was hidden beneath the trappings of the middle-class life that my parents had known in their youth and wanted to believe they still enjoyed. Before I was born, my father had been a lawyer in the Cuban navy, a position he had earned after years of study and days of written examinations. Armed with his shiny white uniform and newly acquired credentials, he had married my mother shortly before the beginning of World War II and had had two daughters, thinking himself securely employed.

We had then lived half a block away from my mother's family in Santiago, in a house with a central courtyard full of trees around a gurgling fountain. I vaguely remember being placed in a big tin bowl that served as my boat as I floated round and round that fountain. I have a picture of myself—two years old, perhaps—sitting very properly at the fountain's edge.

Then, in December 1941, Fulgencio Batista—who had been elected president for the first time the previous year after several attempts at seizing power—"reorganized" the Cuban armed forces, and that was the end of my family's middle-class life. Batista fired my father and all other officers in the military known to be unsympathetic to his government. My father was left without a job and with a young wife and two daughters to feed—in Santiago, a city where the chances of employment were next to zero.

He had a teaching credential, and, with more hope than understanding, my father decided to start his own elementary school and commercial academy. Barely six months after Batista's action, we moved to Havana, to a flat above a house-painting store in a commercial district. There my father started his school. The patio with its trees and its fountain disappeared from my life, and I found myself, not knowing how, in a cramped space amid the traffic bustle of Havana.

The rest of my childhood took place in this space. My two brothers were born there. My sister and I had our first periods there. And there I built a world of fantasy in my head to compensate for the dreary and limiting surroundings in which I felt imprisoned. I spent my childhood surrounded by desks and blackboards, eating lunch and dinner quickly because our dining room had to be turned into a classroom for the afternoon and evening classes. I spent hours staying as quiet as possible behind forbidden doors so that my father's classes would not be disrupted by any sense of our presence. And during vacations and on weekends, when all the students were gone, I played at being Joan of Arc conquering castles for France, or some other saint engaged in some other heroic activity.

My parents had wanted to preserve the middle-class opportunities that would have been my siblings' and mine but for arbitrary political events beyond their control. So my father, using his church friendships and connections, had managed to get scholarships for my three siblings and me at private religious schools for middle-class girls and boys. There, even more than in my solitary adventures as Joan of Arc or some other saint, I learned to lead a double life. By day, I lived among girls who, at four o'clock, went back to homes with the porches, patios, gardens and garages that I pretended I also had. At the end of the school day, I retreated to the two rooms in the back of my father's school and, as quietly as possible, did my homework and read and fantasized in silence. The next day, I made sure none of my classmates knew where I had spent the night. Those years were an exercise in watching affluence close by but from the outside.

From the distance and vision provided by five decades, I believe I do not exaggerate when I think Joan of Arc not only saved France but also saved me. My fantasy opened the doors of possibility. Being Joan of Arc over desks and chairs, with my broomstick banner and ruler sword, gave me a taste for personal power and helped me realize that I could go anywhere and do anything without a chaperone. It also taught me graphically that sometimes women pay dearly for daring to be all they can be.

I have not saved any countries from invaders. And I am still here so, clearly, I have not had to pay for my challenging of societal norms by being burned at the stake. I am far from being a saint. Yet both the triumph and the pain of Joan's struggle have been present throughout my life. And even though I do not climb desks or chairs anymore, I continue to reach into the possibilities for personal power that Joan and other women saints, centuries after their death, introduced to me.

Some Final Thoughts

In addition to Joan, Rosa and Teresa of Avila and other women saints also became role models for me. Together, Joan of Arc and Catherine of Siena demonstrate that it is possible for women to have political influence despite the discriminatory practices that are still prevalent. Teresa of Avila and Edith Stein (canonized as Saint Teresa Benedicta of the Cross) point up the value and spiritual power of intellectual pursuits. Even little, quiet, unassuming Thérèse of Lisieux—the most popular female saint in the Catholic Church— who spoke to the pope in public after a specific injunction to remain silent in his presence, and who never hid her ardent desire to become a priest even though she was a woman, has something to teach me. The Latin American saints in particular, Rosa of Lima, Mariana Paredes of Quito, and Teresa of Los Andes, exemplify alternative ways to be Latina despite racial tensions, social injustice, and political upheaval, and point out the pitfalls of relying on individual, personal spiritual development in the face of our unique mixture of historical circumstances.

Sharing what I know and understand about women saints has become my passion and my work. I want my own appreciation of women saints to open doors for others as it has for me, enabling others to recover, as I have, some of the meaning and spirituality I had lost because of the rigidities of Church positions about women. De Certeau (1988) speaks about the ability of narrative to mold and revolutionize human situations. I want to share my struggle against the indoctrination in sanctimony and docility I received through the distortions of these women's stories, and thus to create a narrative that would transform the lives of other women. And I want to share my struggle to develop strength from the presence of these saints in my childhood imaginary; the many ways in which they led me to believe that many things were possible. In other words, I want to share my personal quest with other women. I offer these reflections in the hope that the stories of these women open doors for others as they have for me.[3]

Notes

1. Rosa was the only canonized Latin American female saint from 1671 until 1950, when Mariana de Jesús Paredes of Quito—almost her contemporary—was canonized. The third Latin American woman to be canonized was the Chilean Teresa de

Los Andes in 1993. After her, other Latin American women were canonized in rapid succession.

2. I am aware that the word "woman" is a noun, not an adjective. In several languages other than English (e.g., Spanish, French, Italian, German, the Slavic languages), the grammatical gender of the noun "saint" provides a feminine form, rendering the qualifier unnecessary. In those languages, the word "female" is frequently a term reserved for animals or a derogatory term for sexualized women. Therefore, I am opting consciously to use the word "woman" as a qualifier, rather than "female," a term that sounds pejorative to my ears and perhaps those of others.

3. Parts of this chapter have been published earlier and presented at several national and international conferences.

Sensing *the Serpent in the Mother,* Dando a Luz la Madre Serpiente

Chicana Spirituality, Sexuality, and Mamihood

Irene Lara

Settling for nothing less, our work, our relations, our art become sites hold-ing erotic spiritual power.

—LARA MEDINA, "LOS ESPÍRITUS SIGUEN HABLANDO:
CHICANA SPIRITUALITIES"

The snake is a symbol of awakening consciousness—the potential of knowing within, an awareness and intelligence not grasped by logical thought.

—GLORIA E. ANZALDÚA, "NOW LET US SHIFT . . . THE PATH
OF CONOCIMIENTO . . . INNER WORK, PUBLIC ACTS"

With the aim of thriving as a whole erotic being, my bodymindspirit always in the process of being in or moving toward harmony, beauty, and *"cono-cimiento"* (Anzaldúa 2000, 2002a), in graduate school I began to think about my writing as a prayer for social justice, healing, and the greater good. Inspired by the spiritual life lessons learned from many of my teachers, I began to con-sciously infuse my writing practice with gratitude, love, and hope (Lara 2002). When I struggled with connecting to my voice and getting my words onto paper on and off throughout the seven years that it has taken me to give light to this essay, I eventually remembered to return to this erotic-spiritual writing

113

practice and approach my work with the devotion of birth as a ceremony (Gonzales 2012).

But it is not always easy to practice what we know, to be self-reflective "spiritual activists" who work to "[connect] the inner life of the mind and spirit to the outer worlds of action" (Anzaldúa 2000, 178). Competing priorities, exhaustion (aka "multiple identity fatigue"), and internalized oppressions that lead to self-doubt and second-guessing oneself can get in the way—not to mention the sheer emotional and intellectual difficulty of reflexivity, meaning making, and confronting knowledge and "truth," including one's errors, limits, and contradictions. Moreover, the ethical necessity to take further action based on one's "conocimientos" (the insights and often subversive knowledges that we receive through "all of [our] senses" and by "consciously inhabiting [our] body and decoding its symptoms" [Anzaldúa 2002a, 542]), a process that is central to being a spiritual activist, entails its own personal and social challenges.

Needless to say, it sometimes takes me a long time to turn to my bodymindspirit toolbox, open it, discern what is needed, and proceed. Or simply to trust the process, which entails trusting myself. It is never a linear and not always a logical path, at least as framed within dominant western worldviews. Instead, like Anzaldúa who embraces the "snake [as] a symbol of awakening consciousness—the potential of knowing within, an awareness and intelligence not grasped by logical thought" (2002a, 540), I am learning to accept and welcome a more serpentine process of creating decolonizing feminist knowledge and art.

Indeed, I am learning to invite and expect the sinuous movements of what I call "serpentine conocimiento" in spite of any apprehension I may feel about diverging from dominant secular worldviews.[1] In fact, with time and study, my trepidation has subsided and faith in my journey has become stronger as I engage Indigenous "cosmo-logics, or deep foundations for making sense of the sacred processes of Life that our minds cannot fully understand or express" (221), as Patrisia Gonzales puts it in her contribution to this volume. This essay, then, is a documentation of my writing and knowledge-making process as an erotic-spiritual critical inquiry and method that contributes to Chicana/Latina/Indigenous women's decolonial feminist ways of knowing and teaching.[2] Hand in hand with the important work of developing culturally rich erotic-spiritual epistemologies and pedagogies, this essay explores the empowering significance of holistically theorizing *and* living one's conocimientos, which may serve others on their own historically, politically, and culturally grounded paths of bodymindspirit integration and action.

Engaging in such a holistic praxis, I assert, can be an erotic-spiritual, decolonizing act of healing internalized oppression and empowering our communities and ourselves as integral parts of the world. I concur with Laura E. Pérez, for whom "a decolonizing politics resides in an embodied practice rooted in lived and liveable worldviews or philosophies and is therefore in decolonizing relationship to our own bodies and to each other as well as to the natural world" (2010, 123). In this essay, I discuss my serpentine method and praxis through utilizing an *"autohistoria-teoría"* approach that blends autobiography, cultural history, and theory (Anzaldúa 2005). Specifically, I draw from Anzalduan engagement with "the serpent," a personally compelling cultural figure and Indigenous sacred symbol that represents "divine consciousness" (Anzaldúa 1999, 241) situated in the body and earth, to analyze some of the ways I have worked to sense and give birth to the serpent in me as a whole being—mother, daughter, lover, spiritual activist, teacher, and writer.

Serpentine Conocimiento

The concept "serpentine conocimiento" is inspired by Anzaldúa's engagement with serpentine cultural figures as well as by my studies of Mesoamerican/ Mexican Indigenous worldviews—including the interviews I have conducted with Chicana/Indigenous women who are considered healers, ceremonial leaders, and/or teachers and students of Indigenous oral traditions by their communities. The serpent, "who rubs the belly of the earth, moving as energy moves" (Hernández-Avila 2005, 233–34), is associated with the revered Mother Earth, as symbolized by Cihuacoatl ("Serpent Woman"), Coatlicue ("Serpent Skirt"), Tlazolteotl ("Divine Filth Eater"),[3] Tonantzin ("Our Mother"), and Tonantzin-Guadalupe as a transcultural, postcolonial, and decolonial figure in *las Américas*.[4] These and related figures are "honored elements of nature or sacred energies representing creation and/or destruction, sexuality, and motherhood within a Nahua religious cosmology" (Lara 2008a, 100), that is, within a holistic spiritual worldview that understands life and death and other dualities as complementary and ultimately as one or parts of the whole, instead of oppositionally binary, and that values all life as interrelated (Marcos 2006; Gonzales 2012).

As also discussed by Lara Medina in this volume, for Indigenous peoples such as the Hopi and Tohono O'odham serpents represent "feminine wisdom and earth knowledge" (178) and are entrusted to carry the people's prayers to the spirits. Indeed, within a Nahua Indigenous worldview, the serpent is associated with wisdom and justice particularly through Quetzalcoatl ("Feathered Serpent") known as "the sacred being of MesoAmerica who represents the highest plane, the highest energy to which humans can aspire" (Hernández-Avila 2005, 233). In Nahua thought, this "highest energy" is related to Quetzalcoatl's "dual duality" of being female/male and male/female and who is thus seen as androgynous and/or coupling with "his" feminine counterparts—Tonantzin, Coatlicue, and/or Cihuacoatl (Hernández-Avila 2005; Ruether 2005; Marcos 2006).[5]

If "conocimiento" is knowledge, awareness, and insight that "questions conventional knowledge's current categories, classifications, and contents" (Anzaldúa 2002a, 541) and validates spiritual inquiry as a way of knowing, then "serpentine conocimiento" centers knowledge and wisdom about and from the earthly and human-animal body—including conocimientos related to sex, sexuality, and the erotic—within the context of a holistic, nonoppositional Indigenous worldview that emphasizes duality, equilibrium, and fluidity, the connection between the earthly and the divine, and the understanding that all life is interconnected (Marcos 2006; Gonzales 2012). In *Borderlands/La Frontera: The New Mestiza* ([1987] 1999), Anzaldúa engages such serpentine imagery when she recognizes that it has taken her "forty years . . . to enter into the Serpent . . . and to assimilate the animal body, the animal soul" (48). This multidirectional process of integration and acceptance entails, as Anzaldúa suggests, "acknowledg[ing] that I have a body, that I am a body" (ibid.).[6] To love the body and trust the senses as sources of conocimiento can be a tremendous endeavor in a dichotomous culture and stratified society that mistrusts the body, deems it inferior to the mind and/or spirit, and negatively racializes, genderizes, sexualizes, and classes it by associating it with people of color, foreigners, women, queers, and the impoverished (Marcos 2006, Rendón 2009).

Moreover, it is significant that Anzaldúa takes back the body and its erotic power to know through the senses, including the intuitive sixth sense, through the image of the serpent, which in her work critically references both Indigenous and Christian-colonial connotations. Validating the spiritual dictum that human beings are related to all that lives, Anzaldúa is inclusive of all species while claiming the value of the human-animal body *and* soul. Indeed, serpentine conocimiento comes from "opening all of the senses" (Anzaldúa 2002a, 542), including through the emblematic tongue of the serpent, who depends on it to read her environment in order to survive and thrive.[7]

Drawing on Mesoamerican worldviews, such serpentine conocimiento also suggests a nonlinear engagement with knowledge; serpents do not move in straight lines. Serpentine conocimiento is knowledge learned through *movimiento*, by moving back and forth, swishing side to side, moving through multidimensional space, spiraling. When pregnant with a child, an idea for a book, the spark of an artwork, the will to politically organize, or any other way we as humans across sexes and genders can embody maternity as a positionality from which we create and not only biologically procreate, movement and embodied self-awareness can be essential to an empowering erotic-spiritual birth. In fact, integrating the image of "the writhing serpent . . . the very movement of life" (Anzaldúa [1987] 1999, 43) into the theory of conocimiento highlights movement in the concept of conocimiento, as also intended by Anzaldúa. As she states, conocimiento is "that aspect of consciousness urging you to act on the knowledge gained" (2002a, 577 n.2).

Moreover, in her presentations and writings, Anzaldúa (2002a) herself represented conocimiento as "Serpent Woman, known as Cihuacoatl, the goddess of origins" by sketching "a half-coiled snake with the head of a woman" and claiming that she represented "not the root of all evil" as in dominant colonial thought, "but instinctual knowledge and other alternative ways of knowing that fuel transformation" (543).[8] Interestingly, the fact that Cihuacoatl "was invoked in birth by Mexica midwives" (223), as Patrisia Gonzales notes in her contribution to this volume, links this feminine serpentine energy with birthing conocimientos, as I expand upon in this essay.

Challenging the projection of Christian colonial moral assumptions about Indigenous paganism and female transgression onto Indigenous figures—as symbolized by Eve who was associated with a demonized serpent—Anzaldúa engaged such serpentine imagery throughout her oeuvre. Visualizing "conocimiento" as "a little serpent," Anzaldúa offers us a powerful concept of "counterknowledge" akin to the "knowledge of the serpent in the Garden of Eden" that is unacceptable to dominant culture because "it makes you too aware, too self-reflective" and thus too threatening to the status quo (2000, 266).

As I discuss further on, Anzladúa also challenged Mexica imperialist interpretations of the serpent and the female as figures to be controlled. Instead, Anzaldúa focused on the ways that various cultures across time have negatively mythologized "some female origin figures" as ultimately socially transgressive for desiring knowledge and an expansion of consciousness, "including carnal knowledge (symbolized by the serpent)," and rewrote them as empowered figures "taking individual agency" (2002a, 543). Although she does not fully discern the cultural differences among the figures she discusses (Xochiquetzal, Eve, and Cihuacoatl), she celebrates their common "passion to know, to deepen awareness, to perceive reality in a different way, to see and experience more of life" (543).

Ultimately, serpentine conocimiento refers to knowledge informed by my desire to know *and* live what I am theorizing about in bodymindspirit. With Anzaldúa, I heartachingly acknowledge that "beneath your desire for knowledge writhes the hunger to understand and love yourself" (2002a, 543) *and*, I dare add, to be understood and loved by others. Within a spiritual activist framework, working to feed such hungers is a decolonizing healing act with transformative repercussions for both inner and outer worlds, which are in serpentine relationship with one another.[9] Contrary to those who would negatively deem such erotic-spiritual inquiry a "self-indulgent" luxury, a spiritual activist framework positively reclaims these self-loving and other-loving practices as necessary for creating personal and collective well-being within a global and cosmic community.

Embodying Serpentine Conocimientos: Enacting Erotic-Spiritual Change

As I was preparing to present an early draft of this essay for "El Mundo Zurdo: First International Conference on the Life and Work of Gloria E. Anzaldúa" in spring 2009, I felt deep anxiety about how in the world I would be able to carve out time in the midst of intense teaching and mothering schedules to do the actual writing and organizing of the presentation. In spite of all the hard-earned lessons throughout college and the tenure process, and my devoted reading of Anzalduan and other decolonial feminist thought, I would often succumb to my socially conditioned drive to suppress all of my senses and neglect my body in order to dive into my mind, as if that is the only space from which knowledge emerges. The facility or ease with which I tend to fall back on this pattern and push myself to work late into the night although I have to wake up early every morning, at the cost of my erotic-spiritual well-being, is a testament to how well I have learned the western educational system's disempowering lesson to privilege my mind as if it is fragmented from my whole being.

This wounding miseducation goes hand in hand with the disenchanted modern worldview that sometimes still usurps my ancient memory and blinds my "reptilian eye" that can "[look] inward and outward simultaneously" (Anzaldúa 2002a, 542). While I humbly relish my powerful ability to "see," think, focus, and write, and the intellectual and creative contributions these skills have allowed me to make as *ofrendas* to my audience, my well-being is ultimately sustained by balancing this physically tiring, time-consuming work with taking care of my body and spirit.

In the case of this conference presentation, it meant trusting my intuition to bring my youngest daughter Xóchitl–who was fifteen months old at the time—and my mother Dolores with me to San Antonio, Texas. Their presence and my need and desire to spend time with them ultimately ensured that I would stay grounded in my body and spirit and not delve solely into my mind by working around the clock before my presentation. To enact the visionary "*mundo zurdo*," I need all of me and I need to validate all of the work I do, mothering and daughtering included.[10] If not at an Anzalduan conference, then where?

Indeed, this experience taught me not only to have faith in my serpentine conocimientos, my instinct, and what my bodymindspirit sensed it needed and would need, but also in my ability to construct and share knowledge from these serpentine conocimientos. That May morning at my panel, not only did I speak about my scholarly-spiritual inquiry into creating an integrated Chicana mamihood, sexuality, and spirituality with PowerPoint slides on the screen, I did so while embodying what it can look like day to day: nursing Xóchitl while listening to the panelist before me, carrying my baby on my hip while presenting, enjoying her gleeful yelp upon seeing a slide of her sister, *papi, abuelita*, and self when I introduced my paper with *agradecimientos* for my family (whose caretaking help and supportive love makes my work possible)—then feeling my joy multiply as the audience laughed in response to her gleeful yelp, palpably connecting everyone in the room. Embodying my serpentine conocimientos meant letting go of fears that I was being judged and that I would be risking Xóchitl's well-being by allowing her to roam among the audience, and ultimately trusting my "beloved community," my witnessing village with whom I was sacredly "teachinglearning" simultaneously, as Maria Figueroa puts it in her contribution to this volume.[11]

That momentous conference day marked how "our work, our relations, our art [can] become sites holding erotic spiritual power" for me (Medina 1998, 193). I was able to resist the dominant lessons that split me and instead transform them through my writing, theorizing, and other ways of being, knowing, and acting in my life. My bodymindspirit insists it be so.

As a strategy for sustaining this conocimiento in a society in general and academy in particular that certainly prefers and at times demands that we suppress our erotic-spiritual powers because it is threatened by the empowering reverberations of love, joy, and justice they unleash, every time I return to work on this writing block–filled essay, I decide to read a prayer. It is written to and from my bodymindspirit, my "deeper self," my "true me," *la Antigua Diosa* who like Anzaldúa's serpent embodies "divine awareness" (Anzaldúa 1999, 241) and healing powers (Anzaldúa [1987] 1999, 200). This prayer helps me connect to what my sacred bodymindspirit knows; it helps me to believe that this inquiry into the serpentine connections between spirituality, sexuality, and motherhood needs to be out in the world and I am the one to birth it, from my *whole* being, with the help of my spiritual and flesh and blood midwives. *Dando a luz esta Madre* that I am and *Madre Serpiente* that I am becoming have been filled with a struggle for language. I desire more courage to truthfully express myself without self-censorship. I long for a bigger "beloved community" with whom to discuss these issues, creating knowledge and enacting erotic-spiritual change along the way.

In fact, I lament that I have found only a few radical mothers of color writing and talking about the ways one bridges one's spirituality and sexuality in the process of creating erotic wholeness á la Audre Lorde (1984), á la Ana Castillo (1994), á la Lara Medina (1998), á la Cherríe Moraga (2000), *and* á la Mesoamerican and Afro-Latina/o sacred sexual energies I have been inspired to study that continue to touch and embrace me.[12] Challenging the popular western belief that strips eros/love from the erotic and associates the erotic *only* with sex and sexuality, which is oftentimes negatively racialized and presumed to be deviant, these and other writers recover and expand the notion of the erotic to refer to that which has the potential to infuse our lives with a tremendously satisfying sense of being, purpose, and connection to ourselves and each other (Lorde 1984).

The erotic as "creative energy/power" (Medina 1998, 193) can of course relate to sex and sexuality, but nurturing one's erotic energy has many faces, including those that have nothing to do with sexual intimacy. This "creative energy/power" can relate to spirit and spirituality, teaching, writing, parenting, and more. Quoting Lorde, Medina writes, "the spiritual as the erotic is identified in the myriad of human experiences that moves what is 'deepest and strongest and richest within each of us'" and "provides a deep sense of satisfaction and connection to our capacity to feel, to create" (1998, 193).

Where is more of this work that engages spirituality and sexuality as erotic, interrelated aspects of the self, especially for mothers? I yearn for juicy details, step-by-step handbooks, and color illustrations! But on my best days, I am hopeful that as I persist on my winding serpentine path and insist on trying to return to the computer, to the classroom, to my partner, daughters, and entire family as a whole person—writer, teacher, spiritual activist, mother, daughter, lover—I am restoring what it means to be spiritual and sexual at once. I am working on reflecting the erotic-spiritual energy I ache to see in others. I am *sin vergüenza* saying: Yes, I want it all. I am faithfully saying: Yes, it is possible.

Embodying Serpentine Conocimientos: Rereading Anzaldúa with *Mami* Eyes and Cultivating an Erotic Maternal *Facultad*

Experiencing pregnancy, the birthing process, and being/becoming a mami to my kindergartener Xóchitl and fourth-grader Belén has led me to reread Anzaldúa's writings with my Chicana mami eyes. Often tired eyes, yes, but new eyes nonetheless that aim to not only see but, more holistically, sense through the "third eye." As Anzaldúa theorizes from her studies of many spiritual traditions, this primordial-like "reptilian eye" is representative of our ability to access knowledge through our intuitive spiritual awareness along-side making meaning by utilizing all of our senses, including a sixth sense accessed through *"la facultad,"* "the capacity to see in surface phenomena the meaning of deeper realities" ([1987] 1999, 60).[13] As Anzaldúa also recognizes, such conocimiento is born from reflected-upon material experience, which is related to the bodies we occupy in any given historical, cultural, and political context (2005).

Expanding upon Anzaldúa's "facultad" concept, Larissa Mercado-López's theorization of a "mestiza maternal facultad" (2011, 146) is particularly powerful and relevant, because the concept helps us validate and analyze the conocimientos that emerge from embodied "mestiza" experiences of mothering that take colonial-modern histories of racialization and transculturation into account. Mercado-López "propose[s] that the embodied experiences of mestiza maternity enable mestiza mothers to read their bodies in ways that challenge hegemonic constructions of motherhood, allowing for the creation of new traditions of empowered maternal identity" (2011, v). Like the writers she analyzes—Gloria Anzaldúa, Cherríe Moraga, and Laurie Ann Guerrero—I too find myself utilizing my "maternal facultad" as "a defense mechanism honed through the bodily and social experience of oppression and mother-hood" (v). In my case, consciously striving to integrate the erotic into my life as a mami or to be able to "sense" how the erotic is actually already present has helped me to hone my *erotic* mestiza maternal facultad and create new conocimientos that I do not think I would have otherwise.[14] Indeed, "la facultad" is also defined by Anzaldúa as "the ability to shift attention and see through the surface of things and situations" (2002a, 547).

Thus, in working to heal oppressive social experiences and challenge oppressive cultural ideologies and social structures, I cultivate an erotic maternal facultad that helps me to see through the dangers, act in spite of the fears, and "shift attention" to refocus purposefully on the empowering creativity of an erotic-spiritual mamihood. This is what sensing the serpent in the mother can look like. It is a springboard into decolonizing, self-loving, other-loving action. Moreover, I have found that *dando a luz a la Madre Serpiente* means birthing your own "healing spirit guide" (Anzaldúa [1987] 1999, 200) by summoning Her presence from within commingled with Her presence without, as I work to do through prayer, sharing my intentions, and being open to their/our serpentine movement and the possibly unexpected "sitios y lenguas (spaces and discourses)" (E. Pérez 1998) to which such movement leads.

The inspiration for my title, "Sensing the Serpent in the Mother," springs from Anzaldúa's call in the serpentine *Borderlands/La Frontera* for us "to unlearn the *puta/virgen* dichotomy and to see *Coatlalopeuh-Coatlicue* [the serpent] in the Mother, *Guadalupe*" ([1987] 1999, 106). She is referring, of course, to one of the preeminent sacred figures in las Américas, la Virgen de Guadalupe, and the many Indigenous Mesoamerican sacred energies that form part of her genealogy, including Coatlicue, Cihuacoatl, Tlazolteotl, and Tonantzin. Drawing on Mexican "indigenista" scholars who interpret the story and image of Guadalupe from a Mesoamerican Indigenous worldview, Anzaldúa writes Her name as "Coatlalopeuh." *Coatlalopeuh* is the Nahuatl name that some theorize the so-called goddess originally called herself when—as millions believe—she miraculously appeared. *"Coatl"* means serpent in Na-huatl and, as Anzaldúa documents, "lopeuh" means "the one who has domin-ion over serpents" ([1987] 1999, 49, 51), or as she interprets, "the one who is at *one* with the beasts" (51, my emphasis).

This direct link to Nahua thought was severed when the Spanish translit-erated "Coatlalopeuh" into "Guadalupe," a name the *cristianos* could hear, speak, and relate to within their Christian colonial imaginary.[15] Rather than elevating a divine figure's power over serpents as suggested by "dominion," Anzaldúa engages a Nahua worldview to emphasize the connection between this divine figure and serpents as "beasts." We are "related to all that lives" (Hernández-Avila 2002, 532).

As a great body of scholarship and endless cultural productions attest to, through the centuries Guadalupe became a polyvalent, contested symbol. However, as part of the Marian tradition that fashioned Mary as Eve's re-deemer, Guadalupe's dominant association with the impossible ideal of virgin motherhood and the construction of sacred womanhood as an iden-tity that does not value self-defining one's sexuality remains quite entrenched throughout the culturally Catholic *Américas* (Castillo 1994, 1996).

Unlearning the virgen/puta dichotomy is part of the decolonial feminist project that sheds light on the way that the split between women's spiritual subjectivity and sexual subjectivity is racialized. Simply said, from a eurocen-tric colonial perspective, the *vírgenes* or sexually proper women are presumed to be white and/or Christian and the *putas* or sexually deviant women are presumed to be Indigenous, mixed race, or primitively pagan (Lara 2008a). Thus, learning to see the Indigenous genealogies (represented by the serpen-tine Coatlalopeuh, Coatlicue, and Cihuacoatl) in the Mother (represented as the Virgin of Guadalupe), when they have been systematically denied, marginalized, and/or demonized, is a significant practice of healing the ra-cialized split between spirituality and sexuality for Chicana, Latina, and/or Indigenous women.

By fleshing the spirit and spiriting the flesh of her complex human and divine racialized "M/mothers," Anzaldúa aims to heal the internalization of a racist and heterosexist cultural legacy that particularly condemns the racialized female ancestors of the Américas. Recognizing the oppression that has led to some mestizas' denial and subjugation of their indigeneity and the systemic colonial/Church violence that literally pushed "the old spirit entities" worshipped by Indigenous/mestizo peoples into secret caves, behind altars, or underground, Anzaldúa insists on the decolonizing, healing value of reclaiming them as part of her genealogy and as her allies in the fight against intersecting oppressions ([1987] 1999, 53). She writes, "Las invoco diosas mías, ustedes las indias / sumergidas en mi carne que son mis sombras. [I invoke you my goddesses, you the Indians / submerged in my flesh who are my shadows.]" (53; my translation).

Anzaldúa argues that along with the subversion of other Chicana "Mothers," like the figures of La Malinche and La Llorona, the systemic "obscuring" of Guadalupe's "true identity" as a complex divine Indigenous figure representing sexuality, the body, the cycle of creation and regeneration, and the earth as a part of human motherhood and spirituality has worked "to make us docile and enduring" and "encouraged the *virgen/puta* (whore) dichotomy" (53). Thus, in Anzaldúa's decolonial feminist call for society to heal this *virgen/puta* split, that is, to no longer presume that women must either be one or the other and treat them and/or see themselves and each other accordingly, she directs us "to see *Coatlapopeuh-Coatlicue* in the Mother, *Guadalupe*" (106).

Working "to see *Coatlapopeuh-Coatlicue*" means becoming conscious about the Indigenous serpentine conocimientos of dynamic duality that these deities manifested before the seemingly imperialist Mexica (Aztecs) redefined their meanings from a patriarchal point of view that the Spanish colonizers further compounded in the early sixteenth century. By seeing the serpent as a symbol of the complementary duality of the spirit and flesh and the divine sexual aspect of the desexed mother Tonantzin-Guadalupe, one is potentially liberated from judging women and oneself based on a spirit-versus-flesh oppositional binary. Indeed, unlearning what I call "the pagan *puta*/virtuous *virgen* dichotomy" is nothing less than healing patriarchal and colonized constructions of female sexuality *and* spirituality (Lara 2008a). As aspects of identity, of full personhood historically linked together in the oppression of women, they must also be addressed together in order to forward feminist decolonial liberation and healing (Lara 2008a; Moraga 2000).

While I have been reading Anzaldúa since my first class as an undergraduate in 1991, not until I became a mother did I realize I had been analyzing her work with daughter rather than mami eyes, that is, from the positionality of a woman who had not experienced motherhood. While I am not claiming an essentialist perspective that suggests we are deterministically able to see and/or create conocimientos based on whatever our social locations or positionalities may be, becoming a mother has led to new experiences, new facultades, new erotic-spiritual critical inquiries, and so on continously in a spiraling serpentine fashion.

Yes, Anzaldúa's appeal to "unlearn the *puta/virgen* dichotomy" by learning about cultural figures and divine energies who embody sexuality *and* spirituality beyond the oppositionally binary way of configuring women and feminine sacred figures into either whores or virgins, had always been viscerally compelling to me. And yes, I had theoretically understood it, comprehended the need for it, and fashioned my research and teaching as a praxis that forwarded such decolonial unlearning and relearning. However, as I serpentinely became aware of embodying mestiza mamihood, my erotic maternal facultad emerged, allowing me to "shift attention" (Anzaldúa 2002a, 547), to see through my mami eyes, indeed to work to *sense* and create meaning through my whole being as a mami, daughter, lover, teacher, writer, and spiritual activist. So what can such decolonial healing look like when sensed through the positionality of serpentine mamihood?

Embodying Serpentine Conocimientos: Playing Tlazolteotl with my Daughters

Mesoamerican worldviews about humans and divine cultural figures who embody spirituality and sexuality at once offer a healing of the good spiritual woman/bad sexual woman western split that continues to impact our ideas about and behaviors toward girls and women in our patriarchal cultures. Such ideologies are internalized and dangerously directed toward ourselves as well as each other. When I think about deconstructing and healing from the *virgen/puta* dichotomy and cultivating practices that instead help us to sense the serpent in the mother and celebrate female sexuality and creativity, including for mothers, I ask myself: how do I effectively teach my daughters holism and multiplicity, harmony and fluidity, and spirituality and sexuality so that they do not have to "unlearn" the splits later on?

In this "Embodying Serpentine Conocimientos" section, I explore what I came to interpret as Tlazolteotl's erotic, healing presence in my life. Among the Mesoamerican genealogy of powerful Mothers, Tlazolteotl represents the rejuvenating, rebalancing generative and regenerative cycle of life. Patrisia Gonzales draws from the oral tradition when she authoritatively cites "la comadre Sylvia" who speaks of Tlazolteotl as "Mexica healing energy that absorbs ills and recycles and purifies life" (2003, 185–86). Typically represented as a squatting female figure giving birth in Nahua art, Tlazolteotl embodies "a duality of maternity *and* sexuality," in contrast to the western polarized binary (Cisneros 1996, 49). Indeed, she is considered a supporter of midwives, birthing women, and newborns (Gonzales 2012), as well as sexually active women. Moreover, in the *Codex Borbonicus*, Tlazolteotl is represented as giving "birth to a miniature version of herself," which also confirms her association with cyclical transformation and healing (Pasztory 1983, 184, 284). While I have "played Tlazolteotl" with both of my daughters, this next serpentine story initially emerged through the intimate medium of a missive to my firstborn:

Querida Belén,

One of your favorite games since you were about two and a half years old is to pretend that you are about to be born. "¿Jugamos que estaba en tu matriz?" ["Can we play that I was in your womb?"] you'll often ask me as we are getting dressed in the morning. After showering, I'll bundle you up in a decades-old Mexican San Marcos blanket, a deep burgundy-and-cream-colored blanket with an image of a deer that I carefully arrange around you so that only your eyes are peering out. Our ritual began as a way for me to keep you entertained while I brushed my long hair, applied lotion to my legs and arms, and stayed present while getting ready for the day. It quickly became an opportunity to teach you what it is like to give birth and for you to remember what it was like to be in my womb and then be born.

Now, as I retell the story, me llega el conocimiento that our game is also a ceremony that provides us both with a healing occasion to rewrite our birthing story to be less traumatic. Instead of the three hours of the last phase of me pushing and you trying to push through, of "panoltia," of conveying ourselves from one place to another, you are born within three minutes.[16] *Yahoo! Gracias a la Diosa. I give thanks to Tlazolteotl, the Nahua sacred energy of birthing and regeneration and patron to midwives and birthing women, who may very well have gifted us con esta ceremonia. A playful reminder that every day we are reborn. Every day we can work toward our own healing. Every day we can sense the serpent moving within us as mothers-daughters.*

As we play, sometimes I will pause during whatever I am doing to profoundly breathe, simulating the moments before you were actually born. Sometimes I hold my belly and lean back, open my mouth and my panocha, just like the Tlazolteotl-like Mesoamerican birthing figure on the altar. "I feel her coming, va nacer . . . here you come," I excitedly say as you synchronize your emergence from the tightly wrapped blanket into the light. We always celebrate when together we make our way through nepantla y aterrizamos, together we land, body-spirit together and transformed: "¡Yay, bienvenida a la tierra little one! Welcome to Mother Earth little one! We did it! This is you daughtering and me mothering at our erotic best.

Embodying Serpentine Conocimientos: Making Sense through *Panocha Pláticas*

For *sensing* the serpent in the mother to make a lasting difference, one needs to be willing to do the potentially hard work and proactively deal with the repercussions of *making sense* of this and other erotic-spiritual conocimientos. Evoking the serpent, Anzaldúa provides us with powerful kinetic imagery describing this inevitably transformative process: "every time she makes 'sense' of something, she has to 'cross over,' kicking a hole of the old boundaries of the self and slipping under or over, dragging the old skin along, stumbling over it" ([1987] 1999, 48–49). Such "sentipensante (sensing/thinking)" (Rendón 2009) self-reflection and conscious taking of further action is a physical, emotional, intellectual, and spiritual process that transforms identity, shifts our perspectives of reality, and is part of the serpentine "path of conocimiento" (Anzaldúa 2002a, 2005). Throughout her work, Anzaldúa discusses a potential precursor to such sense making as the "Coatlicue state," an incredibly challenging state of being, which she largely depicts as an internal, subterranean process dominated by feelings of isolation and despair. In her poem "Letting Go," for example, Anzaldúa describes what can be interpreted as occuring when you "cross over" from your relatively stable reality into a Coatlicue state sense of reality, full of uncertainty: "You've crossed over / And all around you space. / Alone. With nothingness" ([1987] 1999, 187).

Although being alone is not an intrinsically negative experience, and can actually facilitate meditative opportunities for transformation, I have consciously striven to create community to help me counteract my disempowered feelings of isolation. It is this desire for meaningfully making sense of my experiences—specifically, of becoming a mami in the midst of the academic tenure process—with my bodymindspirit intact and erotically flourishing that led me to cofound "Panocha Pláticas" in December 2006 with three other Latinas. Inadequately translated as "Vulva/Vagina Heart-to-Heart Talks," it is a spiritual and social justice-oriented, woman of color-focused yet not exclusive personal healing circle/support group and public workshop centered on "healing sex and sexuality in community" (Arredondo et al. 2007).

Panocha Pláticas is constructed as a bold and brave *"sitio y lengua"* (E. Pérez 1998) where participants are invited to let go of internalized social judgments and to risk being vulnerable by sharing ourselves and our stories in the service of creating healing conocimentos and forwarding social justice.

Because dominant western society teaches us to fragment our identities as well as disassociate our bodies from our spirits from our minds, we need ways to heal the splits and reclaim our bodymindspirits for ourselves and each other. In this loving, erotic-spiritual space, I am able to be and "sense" myself in all of my multiplicity. Indeed, Panocha Pláticas is a timespace where we live our interrelationship as we reciprocally see, hear, and generally "sense" each other and ourselves back into wholeness, make sense of our lives in historical, political, spiritual, and cultural contexts, and empower one another as spiritual activists.

I quote from one of the anonymous journal entries I included in the zine we cocreated and self-published to use during our workshops and allow it to speak for itself as an example of me sensing the serpent, allowing erotic energy/sexual desire to flow through my bodymindspirit, and responding to its call:

> *After becoming a mami, I yearned for panocha wellness. I was teaching a class on sexuality and I felt like a big farce. My own baby daughter was touching her panochita more often than I was touching my own. If I heard her at all, my panochita was saying: "Go get some sleep!" Having a healthy relationship with my panochaself means remembering that my erotic energy includes excitement over raising my daughter, teaching, and other acts of creativity. It means listening to her/me, with unconditional love. With joy in my panochaheart I share a particularly WONDERFUL healthy moment that came from listening to my panocha's desire for lovemaking. Listening to one's rockin panocha can shake things up. I was taken to a sacred place beyond good girl/mother/career woman expectations. The goddess Sacred Timelessness melted the tenure clock as a wave of sweet heat slowly spread into every single one of my dancing cells. I felt it, I trusted it, I went for it. Three times!* (Arredondo et al. 2007, 14)

Because the sexual aspects of our identity—particularly as mothers (be they biological mothers and/or "other mothers" who have a spiritual and social responsibility for raising children), as I am highlighting in this essay—are often denied, ignored, or fragmented from our whole erotic selves, to make a conscious effort to deeply listen to our sexual bodies can help us to transform ourselves, our actions, *and* the structures that occasion the oppressive dismemberment. As we present in our workshops, dominant western thought splits body from mind from spirit, but for some of us our othered and wounded panochas are even further split from the rest of our bodymindspirits, making it harder to lead empowered erotic-spiritual lives. Undoubtedly, for those of us who have been subjected to homophobia or transphobia, mistreated for not conforming to our gender or sex, or are survivors of sexual abuse working to love one's whole self—*panochitas* and *pititos* included—reclaiming our sexual/erotic/spiritual selves, reconnecting to our right to the erotic, to desire as part of our decolonizing, healing politics, can be a particularly long and difficult journey.[17] Yet it is a vital struggle, and by taking time from all of our roles and responsibilities to hold "Panocha Pláticas" we are insisting that we matter, that leading spirit-infused conscious lives matters, and that lovingly supporting one another matters.

Moreover, we are acknowledging that the conocimientos that we generate during our pláticas have repercussions for creating "actual change in the world" (Anzaldúa [1981] 1983a, 217). As I journaled, the s/Spirit of my panocha, if you will, was indeed "'a small still voice' within" (Anzaldúa [1981]1983a, 217, quoting Luisah Teish) that, once I made a conscious decision to listen to, became a resounding voice confidently asserting itself and its/my desires. In this moment, I engaged in "listening with raw openness" (Keating 2005, 249) to my other(ed) within, effectively dissolving the other/self dichotomy; that included no longer allowing dominant society's definitions of "good girl/mother/career woman" to have power over me. The goddess I named Sacred Timelessness was my serpentine ally in this process, and for her healing gift, I thank her.

Serpentine Conclusion: Methodology of the Erotic Spirit and Spiritually Activist Erotic Mothering

As I worked to articulate in this essay, the construction of conocimientos about spirituality goes hand in hand with reflecting on how my spiritual development is related to my erotic/sexual development and vice versa. Thus, I am engaging in what Brenda Sendejo in this volume calls a "methodology of the spirit": the production of knowledge about spirituality that integrates analysis of the scholar's reflected-upon "spiritual development, experiences, and trajectory" (84–85).

But more precisely, I am engaging in a methodology of the erotic spirit. I think it is imperative for the interrelated decolonial feminist/social justice, spiritual activist, and CuranderaScholarActivist movements in which many of us participate to work to heal the inherited presumed splits between spirituality and sexuality, spirit and body, conceptually *and* in our own lives by engaging in a methodology of the erotic spirit.[18] Critically decolonizing and (re)turning to the erotic-spiritual worldviews of Indigenous, mestiza, and other women of color and respectfully engaging them in ways that attend to contemporary contexts and needs can be a pathway for doing so. Striving to embody such serpentine conocimientos both provides erotic energy that we can ride in the service of erotic-spiritual social justice and can serve as an example that others may find helpful as we cocreate our own interweaving erotic-spiritual life paths.

Conscious that sexuality and the erotic have been split from the presumably superior, masculine realm of spirituality in dualistic, patriarchal cultures, and aware of the adverse effects that such a gendered and racialized dichotomy can have—keeping us as women of color from feeling whole, connected, empowered, and loving/loved—I join others in reclaiming the erotic as the spiritual and the spiritual as the erotic. However, in relating to the erotic as a more fluid "creative energy/power" (Medina 1998, 193) and reframing it as a spiritual experience, I have found that one risks marginalizing sex and sexuality as aspects of the erotic because of how deeply the dichotomy has been internalized. If decolonial feminist scholars, artists, healers, and activists have been consciously or unconsciously complicit in denying, marginalizing, and/or invalidating spirituality and sexuality as interrelated aspects of who we are as "whole" erotic beings, how can we work to ensure that it becomes part of our decolonial feminist politics? What gets in the way of having it all? How can we heal the pernicious splits between the erotic, sex, and spirit and thereby improve our quality of life, that is, the quality of our erotic-spiritual relationships with our selves, with each other, and with all that lives?

Moreover, how does healing the splits empower us, and thus inspire and energize us to engage in even more erotic acts of creativity and conocimiento that advance socially just, spiritual activist worldviews? Indeed, acts that connect us to our spiritual *responsibility* to do so? Relatedly, how might participating in social justice/spiritual activist movements that are infused with holistic erotic-spiritual perspectives stimulate healing itself?

Yearning for answers and a community with which to enter a dialogue about these concerns, this essay is an invitation to storytell with and listen to one another. While I reflect on my path and some of the ways that I have integrated my spirituality and sexuality as a mother, lover, scholar, teacher, and spiritual activist and thus striven to live my maternal, "erotic spiritual power" (Medina 1998, 193) and cultivate my serpentine conocimientos, this essay does not necessarily provide the answers I initially sought. More importantly, it is an ofrenda culled from my reflected-upon observations and experiences.

Let us ask questions from, and pursue our inquiries with, our whole body-mindspirits. Let us give ourselves permission to have high expectations for a full, erotic life and let us support each other, prioritizing our personal and collective well-being as "whole" people in relationship to all that lives. As significantly, this essay is a call for creating more spaces to storytell and listen to serpentine spirituality-sexuality-mamihood conocimientos across our different social locations as a way to create new critical knowledge with the potential to empower one another to participate even further in creating more equitable, personal, social, and, dare I say it, yes, *cosmic* change. Such cultivation of our erotic power will help us to advance personally and globally healing visions of social justice and take actions in solidarity with the people and the Earth working toward justice.

Developing such bodymindspirit practices and serpentine conocimientos entails asking ourselves many questions, and framing our inquiry as an erotic process: What is my spirit telling me? What is my body telling me? What is my body that is spiritual and sexual telling me? What is my bodymindspirit, which is me, telling me? By recentering our inquiry in ways that trust the conocimientos of intuition and feelings alongside our ability to reason, our questions aim to decolonize our bodymindspirits, decolonize knowledge, and contribute to a methodology of the decolonizing erotic spirit. Because our bodymindspirits, our "selves" are of course also constructed by our social, cultural, and historical locations and experiences, in ways that we may or may not be conscious of, the cultivation of conocimiento must also entail careful discernment. I am not talking about second-guessing what we "sense," I am saying that engaging in such inquiry also means reflecting on the potential limits to knowing through our bodymindspirits that are, for example, mediated by power dynamics, histories of wounding, and internalized oppression and dominance. There may or may not be a "pure" bodymindspirit. Regardless, we cannot ignore that it is a powerful site of meaning making, and thus it behooves us to try to generate conocimiento through all of our senses.

In a 2002 plática with Gloria Anzaldúa that I hold close to my heart I asked her if she ever felt there was a love that got away. We were at her Tonantzin-Guadalupe meditation tree along White Cliff Road overlooking the Santa Cruz bluffs, in the middle of a walk she tried to make every day as part of her healing practice. It was there that she shared with me that "*bueno, not a lover, but a child, sí.*" Sometimes she wondered what it would have been like to be a mother, the procreating kind. The last communication I had with Gloria a few weeks before her untimely passing in 2004, which I imagine as a shedding of her latest serpent skin on the way to renewal, was her email of congratulation on the birth of my first daughter. "You must be so ecstatic and in love" she wrote to me a few weeks after Belén was born. I was and continue to be deeply in love with my daughters, a feeling that is still incredibly fresh. While I did not really know the extent of deep love I could feel for my children until I experienced it, I suppose I imagined it was possible. However, I certainly did not know that I would also be capable of falling deeper in love with my *compañero*, or myself. Is it because as I love more, love is reflected back at me? Is it because I am in awe of my awesome ability to have created and birthed life? Is it because becoming a mother has brought me closer to knowing what it is like to feel the unconditional love and compassion of the Mother, *la mera mera*, to both receive and gift it?

Becoming a mami still feels like being in a world of continual (re)generation, where I continually grow and shed my serpent skin. Where I enter and allow myself to be entered by the serpent. Where I know myself to be Serpent Woman.[19] This is a world that is always ripe with the potential of practicing serpentine conocimientos as a form of spiritual activism. I know that I would be a different kind of mother without Gloria Anzaldúa's theoretical and spiritual tools; the new ways of seeing and sensing the world, literal reimaginings that sometimes effortlessly came to her and that at other times she worked very, very hard to imagine and then articulate, in order to share with all of us. I thank her for her ofrendas, for helping me to work toward sensing the serpent in the mother and as the mother, to nurture the serpent's presence within and in others. This is a continual process that brings me closer to knowing myself and closer to knowing wholeness; and in doing so, brings me closer to knowing you, as part of my envisioned "beloved community" of people striving to erotically act in spiritually activist ways. In what ways are we all Serpent Women? In what ways can our lives and work be strengthened by respectfully nurturing our and each other's serpentine conocimientos?

It is appropriate that I started to write about spiritually activist and erotic mothering inspired by Gloria Anzaldúa, one of the "mothers" of Chicana feminism who insisted on the need to address the multiplicity of our spiritual and sexual subjectivities. I offer my autohistoria-teoría as an Indigenous informed Chicana feminist example of working to heal the subject/object, masculine/feminine, virgin/whore, asexual mother/sexual woman, procreator/creator, sacred/secular, spirituality/sexuality splits. May my ofrenda engender healing personal and social change for you and future generations. It is my desire that we all heal from the *sustos* and *arrebatos* that keep us distrusting and fearing the power of the serpent in the mother, the spiritual as the erotic and erotic as spiritual—that is, from distrusting and fearing "this depth [of feeling] too much to examine the possibilities of it within [our]selves" (Lorde 1984, 54).

This is my invitation to dialogue and these are my decolonizing feminist *deseos*: May mothers, broadly speaking, and allies to mothers work together to infuse our world(s) with the energy of the erotic maternal honoring our spirits and bodies always. May we help one another respectfully remember old ways and create new ways to live erotically as all who we are and are becoming. May we devotedly nurture our maternal erotic-spiritual facultades and serpentine conocimientos. May we be gifted with the healing knowledge of la Serpiente, allowing our selves to accept the Serpent within, envelop her, and rejoice in her/our medicine.

Notes

1. The concept of "serpentine conocimiento" is rooted in Chicana/o literary and activist engagement with Indigenous philosophies. For example, in the early 1970s, Teatro Campesino's Luis Valdez famously engaged *"pensamiento serpentino"* in his manifesto-like poem of the same name. Such serpentine thought emphasizes cycles, continuums, unity, connections, and holism, in contrast to oppositional binaries, and is believed to be drawn from the Maya-Quiché origin story documented in the *Popol Vuh* (Valdez 1990; Broyles-Gonzáles 1994). In "Writing with Crooked Lines" in this volume, Laura Pérez notes that Valdez traces "pensamiento serpentino" to the "Maya linguist," Domingo Martínez Parédez (29).

2. The development of an erotic-spiritual epistemology and pedagogy is informed by many texts by women of color, including, among others: Lorde 1984; Castillo 1994; Medina 1998; Morales 1998; Anzaldúa 2002a; Alexander 2005; Delgado Bernal et al. 2006; Rendón 2009; and Maparyan 2012. In this volume, Elenes, Figueroa, Sendejo, Medina, and Pérez contribute to the communal discussion.

3. Along with Patrisia Gonzales, who draws on Martha Ramírez-Oropeza and other scholars and/or keepers of the oral tradition, I recover a more complex understanding of Tlazolteotl as a divine regenerative force. Instead of negatively and decontextually defining her as "Filth Eater" and associating her with sins and sexual perversion as the Spanish colonists did, Gonzales emphasizes that Tlazolteotl's "connection with waste is better explained by the principle of composting" (2012, 98). Citing a lecture by Ramírez-Oropeza, she further explains: "Tlazolteotl has two manifestations based on either waste or love: Tlazolteotl from *Tlazolli* (waste) *tetl* (stone) *ollin* (movement) or Tlazohteotl from *Tlazohtla* (love) *teotl* (stone) *ollin* (movement). . . . Both manifestations—and the actions contained or signified within her name—result in the ultimate act of regeneration and cycles of creation" (98).

4. In writing "Tonantzin-Guadalupe," I use a serpentine cord between Tonanztin and Guadalupe as a visual marker of their connected *and* distinct cultural histories and social meanings. As such, differing, overlapping, and new meanings of the serpent link and separate the "Mother" figures in Chicana feminist culture. Drawing on Fernando Ortiz's original theorization of the term, I use "transcultural" to describe these figures as part of a legacy of cultural loss, cultural persistence, and the creation of hybrid cultural forms, all mediated through power relations. See Lara (2008a, 2008b).

5. It is important to emphasize that this concept of nonoppositional duality or "dual oneness" that embodies both feminine and masculine principles as complementary and ultimate as one permeates Indigenous Mexico and originates in Ometeotl, a two-spirited deity understood as the pair Omecihuatl and Ometecutli. As Sylvia Marcos writes, "Most Mesoamerican deities were pairs of gods and goddesses, beginning with Ometeotl, the supreme creator whose name means 'double god' or dual divinity . . . Ometeotl was thought of as a pair whose feminine and masculine poles were, respectively, Omecihuatl and Ometecutli, the Lady and the Lord of Duality. Born of this supreme pair, other dual deities, in their turn, incarnated natural phenomenon" (2006, 16).

6. Although it is beyond the parameters of this essay to discuss, it is important to note that Anzaldúa also engages Jungian philosophy in her discussion of the serpent, the "Shadow Beast," and the "Coatlicue state." Moreover, as further evidence of the serpent's and Indigenous serpentine thought's formative influence in Anzaldúa's thinking, it is important to note that she titled one of her early manuscripts "La Serpiente que se come

su cola [The Serpent Who Eats her Tail]: Life and Death Rites of a Chicana Lesbian" (University of Texas at Austin Library, 1982).

7. I invite further theorization of the erotic-spiritual link between the serpent's tongue, the transformative power of language, and the human tongue's association with sexual pleasure. See, for example, Anzaldúa's "Speaking in Tongues: Letter to Third World Woman Writers" ([1981] 1983c).

8. In a published interview I had with Anzaldúa in 2001, she also discussed "forbidden or unacknowledged forms of knowledge" represented in an image she used during some of her talks with "a treasure chest in the background" and "the coiled serpent, con la cara y cabeza de mujer" as "la Llorona" in the foreground. She shared: "to me this image symbolizes Indigenous knowing or the knowing of other nondominant cultures," including the "knowledges you bring in your body and your soul and your spiritual practice [that] are not accepted" by dominant culture (Anzaldúa 2005, 49–51). Although the figure reprinted in this interview is not the exact transparency Anzaldúa is referring to, it does include a serpent taking a bite of, presumably, the fruit of forbidden knowledge. The additional transparencies she used may be found in her archive at the University of Texas at Austin (http://www.lib.utexas.edu/taro/utlac/00189/lac-00189p1.html).

9. As Inés Hernández-Avila analyzes in the poem "La curandera," Anzaldúa also depicts serpents as "healing spirit guides" who teach *la curandera* and her apprentice, "helping them shift their own consciousness so they can facilitate their miracles of healing" (2005, 237). I am also reminded of Cherríe Moraga's (2000) powerful discussion of the need to feed all of our hungers.

10. For Anzaldúa, "el mundo zurdo" was her utopian vision of a space where people "from diverse backgrounds, often with very different needs and concerns, co-exist and work together to bring about revolutionary change" (Keating and González-López 2011, 242–43. See Anzaldúa 1983a; Keating 2002b; and Keating 2005).

11. The phrase "beloved community" was frequently used by Martin Luther King, Jr. to evoke his vision of a loving and just world where all people treated each other with compassion and actualized the knowledge that we are all indeed relatives and interconnected. While King was grounded in a Christian worldview, "beloved community" has also been used more broadly to describe this spiritual, social justice vision that resonates with Gloria Anzaldúa's concepts of "spiritual activism" and "el mundo zurdo." See AnaLouise Keating's discussion in "Pedagogies of Invitation: From Status-Quo Stories to Cosmic Connections" of Reanae McNeal's use of "beloved community" to refer to her students and invite them "to see themselves as interrelated and connected" across their diversity (2013, 184).

12. See, for example, Gonzales 2012; Marcos 2006; Moreno Vega 2000. Also see "From the Four Directions: The Dreaming, Birthing, Healing Mother on Fire," a sister performance/poetry piece to this essay forthcoming in the anthology *This Bridge Called My Baby: Legacies of Radical Mothering*.

13. For an excellent discussion of Anzaldúa's engagement with a diverse array of spiritual traditions, including esoteric practices, see Pérez 2012.

14. Amber Kinser (2008) has a wonderful discussion of the concept of a "maternal erotic" and the tensions it creates in the lived experiences of mothers, but she does not analyze the ways one's racialized cultural embodiment of the maternal specifically matters.

15. Indeed, "Guadalupe" already existed as the name of a Marian virgin from Extremadura, a region in southern Spain from which many of the sixteenth-century invaders

originated. An enormous body of Guadalupe-Tonantzin–related scholarship exists, attesting to Her historical and continuing significance. For some recent discussions see Lara 2008a, 2008b; Estés 2011; Román-Odio 2013; Sendejo and Elenes in this collection.

16. According to historian Emma Pérez's (1998) Tejana lesbian interviewees, "panocha," a vernacular term for vagina and/or vulva, has Nahuatl roots. I have not been able to corroborate this conocimiento passed on through the oral tradition other than finding a similar-sounding word, *"panoltia,"* in an online Nahuatl-French dictionary after the *Dictionnaire de la langue nahuatl ou mexicaine* by Rémi Siméon (1885) that defines panoltia as "to pass, to convey something [or] someone from one place to another." http://sites.estvideo.net/malinal/nahuatl.page.html. Accessed June 21, 2012.

17. As eloquently explored by Berenice Dimas in "Queeranderismo," who links such sexual wounds and woundings to the effects of intergenerational trauma, such healing work is possible and essential. Also see Aurora Levins Morales on "reclaiming the wounded erotic" (1998, 118).

18. Representative writings from these movements include the following: decolonial feminism/social justice, L. Pérez 2010; Fernandes 2003; spiritual activism, Anzaldúa 2002a; Keating 2008; Keating and González-López 2011; Maparyan 2012, Sendejo 2013; CuranderaScholarActivist, Gonzalez et al. forthcoming

19. See Ruby Chacón's mesmerizing artwork that directly evokes la Serpiente: "Self with Serpent" (2001) and "Self as Cihuacoatl" (2001). http://www.authorstream.com/Presentation/aSGuest18092-184980-ruby-chacon-presentation-june-2006-rubypresentationjune2006-entertainment-ppt-powerpoint/. Accessed October 3, 2013.

PART THREE

The North

The Direction of the Elders

We turn to the North, the place of the wind, associated with elders and the energy of maturity. It is the direction we often turn to for guidance from the ancestors. The North also powerfully supports our practices of introspection and reflection. As previously noted in the Introduction, some texts may reflect one or more directions. However, the poem "*Sacrificios*" by "artivist" Felicia Montes is largely guided by the energies of the North. "Sacrificios" speaks to the sacrifices women make in order to survive on a daily basis. Many times these efforts, or offerings, can lead to our bodies' destruction. Oppressive ideologies of gender and race are consistently negotiated within our conscious and subconscious states, or, as Anzaldúa noted, in the in-between, transformative space of *nepantla*.

Several contributors in this section directly or indirectly engage ancestral healing knowledge and their relationship to elders in their lives, such as their spiritual teachers or family members. For example, in "Chicana in the Zendo: Love and Power on the Spiritual Path," Alicia Enciso Litschi reflects on her complex relationship with her last Buddhist teacher, with whom she lived in a Zen center. She uses the metaphor of a love story to trace the progression of the spiritual path through stages of idealization, disillusionment, and maturity. In carefully exploring this relationship, Enciso Litschi considers how spiritual communities can shy away from candid discussions of power and authority. As the north can also be the direction where we release knowledge and open ourselves to new wisdom, Enciso Litschi's critical reflections are well suited here. Indeed, she shuns a romanticized vision of spirituality and spiritual communities by emphasizing how spiritual paths are rooted in the realities of our secular conditions, arguing that it is through this realization that spiritual maturity develops.

The general theme of needing to navigate one's created or blood family to construct one's spirituality is also exemplified in Michelle Téllez's essay, "'*Pero tu no cres en dios*': Negotiating Spirituality, Family and Community." This narrative draws from Téllez's family experiences to illustrate confrontations, which lend themselves to difficulties in negotiating her spirituality. She offers the concept of "borderlands epistemology" to understand the dialectical relationship between spirituality, family, and the larger Chicana/o community. Téllez offers us her testimony as an important theoretical and methodological guide in conducting research on feminism, spirit, and spirituality.

Rosa María Hernández Juárez's contribution to our spirituality discussion is multifaceted. She accompanies her two self-portraits, titled "Plum" and "My Pieces," with a personal essay, "Healing Introspections: Reaching Inside and Reconstructing Myself," that describes her journey from accepting that she is ill and needs help to confronting the reality of being on the bridge between life and death. Created as part of her healing process, Hernández Juárez's artwork serves as an example of the many expressive tools we utilize to heal and that help us to understand ourselves better and remake ourselves in the process. This meaning-making *testimonio* courageously examines Hernández Juárez's process of illness and wellness through a reclamation of her familial healing ways.

Similarly, Lara Medina's spiritual inquiry into her own and others' "source(s) of healing" is at the center of her "*Nepantla* Spirituality: My Path to the Source(s) of Healing." Seeking wisdom from ancestral knowledges, she elaborates on "nepantla spirituality" as an example of transculturation, the continuous encounter of two or more divergent worldviews. Drawing on Anzaldúa, Medina argues that the native-Self is recovered when the tensions of nepantla are understood and engaged; thus nepantla becomes a site of ongoing healing and transformation. Sharing medicinal knowledge and healing energy is also accomplished through poetry and performance.

Sacrificios

Felicia Montes

Flesh offerings
Come daily in Xicana ceremonies
As we skin our piernas,
Pluck our brows,
Beat out pelo,
And tat and pierce our piel

These not so sacred ways
Becoming reminders,
Marks of memory,
Wounds of wisdom . . .
As we come full circle
Becoming holy sacrifices
Within our own temples of worship.

Becoming the bread and body
With our own flesh and blood.

Chicana in the Zendo

Love and Power on the Spiritual Path

Alicia Enciso Litschi

An Introduction in Retrospect

I left my last Buddhist teacher in 2007. At the time, my departure did not feel
like a happy ending. I had been a full-time training resident at my teacher's
Zen center and was slated for ordination as a priest. Leaving was a complicated endeavor, and I was haunted by the desire to tell my story—feeling that
there might be an aspect of my experiences that could serve others on the
spiritual path.

   However, this has not been a simple story to tell. In six years, this essay
has known several iterations and accommodated the shifting perspectives
of my present-day life. Thus, what follows is undoubtedly an imperfect rendering of my relationship with my last teacher. I have struggled to piece
together a narrative that is—to the best of my knowledge—factually true
and also evocative of the emotions, conflicts, and spiritual lessons that
make this a story worth telling. As incomplete as this tale may be, it is assur-
edly sincere.

The Spiritual Path as Love Story

Over the years, I have come to understand the spiritual path as a great romance. As with any good love story, it is about longing. The heart's longing
notoriously motivates us to do crazy things. Having fallen in love, we are willing to risk the inconceivable on the off chance that we have stumbled upon

138

that one exquisite salve for our inner thirst and hunger—whether it be a perfect relationship or a perfect spiritual path. Inevitably, however, the gap between our romantic fantasies and reality reveals itself in full. We are no longer so smitten. We are faced with the cruelty of falling out of love and into reality. This disintegration of fantasy is, I believe, where the true magic of any good love story lies. Indeed, that is the crux of my story.

If this is a love story, then the Catholic journey was my first taste of head-over-heels love. It began quite early. As a child I remember declaring to our parish pastor that I was going to be a priest one day. He chuckled and explained that my plans were impossible; the convent would be the more appropriate path for my unfortunate gender. Over the years, the theme of this incident played out repeatedly, and by the time I was in my mid-twenties, I could scarcely sit through a Catholic sermon without feeling the heat of offense surge through my body. However, the idea of not being Catholic felt like a threat akin to psychic homelessness. I was raised to be a good Mexican Catholic. That was my identity. Culture, religion, and family went together—a veritable replica of the Holy Trinity. I spent years avoiding the issue.

When I was twenty-six, I stumbled onto Buddhism. It began as a slow courtship, occasionally reading a few books, experimenting with meditation, but not much talking about it. Its concepts seemed so utterly foreign to me, and I found I could read an entire book about it without a shred of comprehension. Nevertheless, it drew me in, and I signed up for my first series of meditation courses at a Zen Buddhist temple in Chicago. A complete novice, I loudly fumbled my way into the temple on the first day of class, complete with shoes. A lovely Korean woman nodded at me, pointed at my shoes, and I suddenly realized all the barefooted people around me. I was horrified but hooked. Thereafter, things unfolded quickly. The year I turned thirty, I ended my long-term relationship, quit graduate school, sold my car, cropped my hair, put away my jewelry, and entered a Buddhist monastery. I may not have been able to be ordained as a Catholic priest, but I certainly could be ordained as a Buddhist one.

Buddhism was the solution to my Catholic dilemma. As my new love story, I fully expected it to be the quintessential remedy to the wounds of the past—the lover that undid the wrongs of all predecessors. In Buddhism I wanted a grand cure. I wanted to be free of the trappings of doctrine, power, control, patriarchy, racism, homophobia, classism, and any other form of unenlightened states of mind. This is, of course, wholly unreasonable. Nonetheless, albeit unconsciously, I was dogged in my stubborn drive to make Buddhism, its teachers, and its practitioners into something they are not—perfect.

Falling in Love

My last Buddhist teacher was an easy target for my idealizing fantasies. I quickly fell madly in love with her. It was not a sexual love; there was no sordid romance, but I easily projected onto her a sense of spiritual homecoming. She, I told myself, provided me with a spiritual context in which I finally could feel fulfilled and without moral complaint.

I knew my last Zen teacher simply as "Roshi," a designation for "teacher," which is formally transmitted through a lineage of masters in the Japanese tradition of Zen Buddhism.[1] Like many others, I was smitten by Roshi the moment I met her. She is not your typical Zen master. For one thing she is a woman, unapologetically fierce in her determination to elevate the place of women in Buddhist leadership. As a young adult she was active in the civil rights movement and outspoken about issues of injustice. Later in life, she founded a Zen center and formally began taking students. By the time I arrived at her Zen center, she was upfront about preparing to move into elderhood, discussing her need to find spiritual heirs who would carry her legacy. When I met Roshi, I felt a synergy between us and immediately told myself that I would be among those in the next generation to whom she could entrust all she had built.

My first encounter with her was in the dining hall on my first day at the Zen center. She motioned to me as I got up to wash my plate. All the pictures I had previously seen of her portrayed her with the shiny, bald head of a Zen priest. The woman before me had short, silvery hair but the same piercing blue eyes I had seen in the photographs. I was nervous, but she was friendly and flashed a disarming smile. She asked where I was from. When I mentioned having grown up on the US-Mexico border in Nogales, Arizona, she was immediately interested. She asked me if I spoke Spanish. Was I Chicana? Where was my family now? Did I go to college? Was I raised Catholic? She spoke a little Spanish with me and told me that Mexico is like a second home to her. She loves the people, the language, everything. Her eyes twinkled and said she was happy I was at the Zen center.

In subsequent conversations Roshi explained that, as a western woman, she was looking to provide new models for building Zen communities by more actively including women and people of color. This was perfect; everything I had wanted was encapsulated in one place, with one teacher. So it was decided: by the beginning of my second month at the Zen center, I had signed a contract promising at least the next eighteen months of my life to Roshi's community.

Everything seemed to fall easily and naturally into place. Soon after committing to Roshi, I was living in a private room (complete with Internet connection). Roshi accepted me as a postulant with plans to be ordained as a Zen priest within a year. Roshi even made a truly rare exception in insisting that I be granted membership in the center's prison project. At that point only the most senior priests and community professionals participated in this project, which established meditation programs in some of the state's prisons, jails, and juvenile detention facilities. It was a highly coveted opportunity, and even long-term residents and other priests had been unable to gain access to this project. Nevertheless, six weeks into my stay, I was already included in some of the most sought-after assignments and training Roshi had to offer.

Never in my life had I been so immediately—and rather extravagantly—welcomed by a person in authority. If I was in love, then it seemed like Roshi herself was also somewhat smitten. I did not question it and allowed myself to be carried by the rapidly moving current. Within weeks of my arrival, I had been promoted into a small circle of favored students. This whirlwind romance fit nicely into my fantasies. I was, I told myself, home.

Cutting through Delusion

In spite of my propensity for avoiding the obvious, it was not difficult to recognize the other factors at work. I began to observe that, as a Spanish-speaking Chicana from the border, I was an attractive commodity. The center was situated in an ethnically diverse landscape. However, like most US Buddhist communities, its members were largely white and upper middle class, which was a stark contrast to the center's understanding and promotion of itself as valuing diversity and multiculturalism. On some level, I was a public relations asset. There were several occasions on which this became evident. Early on, Roshi introduced me to some of the major funders of the center as "a Chicana from the border." No more, no less. When I attended my first meeting of the prison project, I had just finished introducing myself to the group when Roshi interjected, "Most importantly, she is a Chicana from the border and she is bilingual, which is why I invited her here."

It was clear, though not openly discussed, that my being Chicana was instrumental in my quick rise to the top of Roshi's list of favored students. Roshi was playing ethnic favorites, and for the first time in my life, I was on the winning side of the equation. The situation became more obvious when I recruited Miguel, my friend from Mexico, to the center. He was already an ordained Zen priest and was in search of a new community. Roshi paid for his move from Mexico, and he also quickly found favor with her. Immediately after Miguel's arrival from Mexico, Roshi took us out to dinner. Over enchiladas and huevos rancheros, she spoke to us of taking Buddhism on the road to Mexico and the border. We would be her companions and hosts.

Along with Miguel, I soon found myself in the politicized position of being the beneficiary of exceedingly public displays of favoritism. A few incidents made this uncomfortably obvious to the entire community. A few months into my stay, Soshin, our senior priest, left the center with little warning. It was a harsh blow to Roshi and a tremendous loss for the community. Roshi appointed Miguel to take Soshin's place as temple coordinator, and she named me as Soshin's replacement on the faculty of one of the center's most widely attended retreats. We were chosen for these roles above a group of students with more expertise and years of service to Roshi. Ironically, when it came time for me to serve on the faculty for the large retreat, Roshi did not assign me any teaching duties. She obviously realized that I did not have sufficient training to function in this capacity. Nonetheless, Roshi still introduced me as a faculty member during the opening ceremony for the retreat. She recited the familiar introduction, describing me as a Chicana from the border. She added that I had witnessed a great deal of suffering among my people. I was the colorful icing on the cake—there for show. I stood there silent, just nodding, smiling, and feeling a little more hollow inside.

On another occasion, Roshi sent a harsh email to Zen center residents stating that residents were wholly ungrateful for the training opportunities they were being given at the center. As a result, she would begin charging full-time residents tuition for the privilege of training at the center. She added that "for obvious reasons," Miguel and I would be exempt from having to pay this tuition. While Roshi may have intended this as a generous gesture, Miguel and I were horrified by the way in which she had leveraged our race to set us apart from the community in such an egregious manner.

These events were not lost on my fellow students. Understandably, tension and resentment began to circulate within the community. During a training session, one student sourly muttered under her breath that I was "a perfect student." On another occasion, one of the white priests candidly told me that I was one of Roshi's "pets" and that Roshi often treated people of color in this "special" way. Despite the obvious bitterness, I was grateful for her honesty. Her words gave voice to my own internal conflict around Roshi's excessive favor. She verbalized the fears that I had struggled to bury.

Falling Out of Love

At first I enjoyed the favored positioning. However, the favoritism slowly began to threaten the fantasy. There were costs to being a token or a pet. My favor was not only contingent on my being Chicana but also on my unswerving allegiance to Roshi. I was complicit in this game. I was the model Zen student. I followed orders, smiled when necessary, was stoic and silent when appropriate. I listened raptly, bowed with reverence, made her tea, and saved her pancakes for breakfast. I swallowed my opinions, bottled my disagreements. Above all, I did not complain; I made myself into a pet worth having. It was an old pattern of collusion. It was well-worn territory, back to my childhood on the border, where I had earned gold stars and A+ grades from the white teachers. That was my ticket out of the *pinche pueblo* border town—the ticket to a college education and career. I knew that role well. Sit down and shut up; do what the teacher says. She will make you a priest. Your family will be proud.

I had spent the better part of my twenties resurrecting my psyche and self-esteem from the role of the Chicanita who just smiles and acts nice. I had read the writings of Chicana feminist trailblazers. I had excavated a lifetime of rage over having stifled my voice and swallowed my words. I had battled it out with my internalized inferiority. I had learned to speak my mind a bit more and fight the important battles.

Yet, once I turned thirty, I had somehow managed to deliver myself into a situation where the spiritual path I pursued encouraged me once again to disown my opinions and serve willingly, happily, and humbly. This time it came in the guise of enlightenment. I was supposed to abandon my ego, let go of my attachment to outcome, and just be. I was told to heed my teacher's words and trust that my training under her would render me awakened. The Zen trainee in me adhered to the idea that I was on course, becoming a humble, altruistic, persevering Zen student. The Chicana in me felt painfully stifled and compromised—a sellout. This was not Catholicism, but these were my old wounds, familiar baggage, and reality rearing its unwelcome head.

I was not unique in my struggles around power, submission, and spirituality. Many of my fellow students knew this roller coaster well; many were similarly conflicted. Despite the monastic context, our lives at the Zen center were not immune from the pressures of hierarchy, status, and jockeying for position. Authority was both granted and withheld by Roshi. This was not a democratic system. As abbot, Roshi carefully constructed the power structure of the monastery, as is typically the case in the patriarchal tradition of Zen Buddhism. Consequently, just beneath the surface, the dynamic at the Zen center was marked by power struggles between priests and students in attempts to maximize their positioning within the administration of the center, within the resident community, and in relation to Roshi. Spirituality aside, what was at stake was the opportunity for career advancement in Zen and ultimately inheriting Roshi's legacy by possibly being named as one of her authorized heirs or even successor. There is no denying that the spiritual teachings of Buddhism permeated the fabric of our lives in the Zen center. However, our powerful conditioning as political creatures was also at work.

Leaving

The realities of politics at the Zen center—racialized and otherwise—were crushing to me. I wanted to be above the fray; I convinced myself that I was compromised, silenced, and in desperate need of retrieving my power. I rehearsed good reasons for leaving, reassuring myself that I could do more outside the system than within it. I decided not to ordain as a priest under Roshi and ultimately resigned myself to leave the Zen center after a thirteen-month residency. Telling Roshi my decision was a frightening prospect.

I met Roshi in a private, formal interview shortly after telling her my news. The frustration and anger were plainly displayed on her face. Her eyes were full of fire as she told me I needed to get over the baggage of my culture and my problems with institutionalized religion. I needed to stop acting like a victim. I knew she was disappointed and hurt, but her words ignited my rage. I stared at her without flinching and, for the first time in our relationship, could plainly see the river of conflict that had been surging between us just beneath the surface. I had acted like the good Chicana student, and she responded as the nice white teacher, but our roles concealed an ocean of resentment, guilt, and shame.

I left the Zen center without having a candid conversation with Roshi about the nature of our relationship. Today, having regained some of that stifled voice and still sifting through my troubled relationship to authority, I wonder how I might have brought this realization to Roshi. Could she have joined me in examining this? In the end, fear and shame prevented me from telling Roshi how I had experienced our relationship. I was afraid of her reaction, and I was ashamed that I had taken part in the dynamic from the start. As a result, Roshi would never know the full reasons behind my leaving. We each remained with our respective wounds—she felt abandoned and betrayed; I felt manipulated and used. Several steps shy of enlightenment, I left with petty excuses.

Testimonio

When I originally wrote this piece in 2007, I framed my departure from the Zen center as a type of declaration. I named it my *testimonio*, hoping my words would validate the experiences of others who have known the struggles of politics, hierarchy, and even racism in spiritual communities. I do not want to undermine that aspect of the story. Indeed, many western students have critiqued the patriarchal vestiges of Buddhist systems. In these power structures, teachers undeniably hold tremendous authority, and this has become problematic. Many students and teachers alike have discussed the explosive role of sexuality and gender in this dynamic (Boucher 1993; Dresser 1996).

In addition, increasingly there has been a surge of attention drawn to the issue of racism in American Buddhist communities. In 2000, the meeting of the Buddhist Teachers in the West focused on "Making the Invisible Visible: Healing Racism in Our Buddhist Communities." In preparation for that conference, many Buddhists spoke out about their experiences of spiritual journeys that were painfully impacted by encounters of overt and covert racism (Adams et al. 2000). A common theme was the tendency for these typically white liberal American Buddhist communities to hide behind a spiritual "colorblindness" as a way to avoid confronting palpable issues of racism (Gutiérrez Baldoquín 2000). In response to these critiques, there has been a move toward examining more inclusive ways of organizing Buddhist communities, invitations for white community members to examine their positioning of privilege, and a widening space for people of color to lend their voices and leadership to the growing Buddhist movement. (Gutiérrez Baldoquín 2004; Williams 2000). These dialogues and examination are necessary. Certainly my experiences at the Zen center reflected our community's anxiety and muteness around race, which contributed to deeply problematic power struggles and rifts in our communication.

All of these issues are, in fact, true and essential to confront in contemporary American Buddhism. However, these issues are not the reason I left Roshi, the Zen center, and my path to being a Buddhist priest. I left because my love story shattered, and hidden in that love story was my own uncomfortable relationship to power—my own reluctance to face reality fully without expecting anyone to save me from it. Roshi had not saved me and neither had Buddhism. In fact, they were just as messy as the rest of the world. Moreover, so was I.

Jack Kornfield (2000) writes that as students awaken to the betrayals that exist in spiritual communities, they become painfully aware of the degree to which they actually have betrayed themselves. This realization of self-betrayal is a ferocious fire of initiation. Roshi, it turns out, was right. I was—and still am—too quick to play the role of victim. My own hunger for power lay festering in the shadow of my role as teacher's pet. It was a hunger that I refused to acknowledge. As a result, I fed on the passive and indirect "favors" I gleaned from playing Roshi's favorite. Quite simply, I used Roshi. Too fearful of what it would mean to be grounded in my own authority, I clung to Roshi's robes, quick to reap the benefits of this association and equally quick to blame her when this arrangement soured. Clearly, Roshi and I both had blind spots. Mine provided just enough distortion to believe myself exempt from bearing equal responsibility in the way my relationship with Roshi disintegrated.

Growing Up

Leaving Roshi, my Zen center family, and my aspirations to be a priest quite simply broke my heart. Instead of sitting open to the rawness of that fractured state, my mind reeled to soothe itself with rational explanations. Those explanations may have merit but they did little to ease the pain. When I left the Zen center, I was unmoored. I had not only left my teacher, but the safety of an entire system to which I had pledged my spiritual longings. I had loved my life there, my friends, and Roshi.

While I was confident in my decision to leave, I stepped out of the temple into a secular world feeling completely ungrounded, without plans, and missing even the illusion of a fix-it-all spiritual solution. I moved to California with my partner at the time. Any attempts at meditation or Buddhist practice flooded me with waves of anxiety and bitter grief. In a desperate attempt to find a sense of spiritual solace, I even dragged my partner to Easter Mass with me a few months after leaving the Zen center. After the service, I collapsed into a sobbing heap in the car, utterly powerless over the raw spiritual ache that went unappeased. My partner—a lifelong Jew—looked at me dumbfounded, "Was the Mass really that bad?" she asked.

Clearly, the experience of being completely untethered is exactly where I needed to be. I was not only mourning the losses of my teacher, friends, and community; I was grieving the collapse of a lifelong delusion. I had entered the Buddhist path full of critique and frustration with Catholicism. I inserted myself into Buddhism with the wish that it might be the happy remedy to the failings of human nature. Much like the ecstasy of brain chemistry in the early stages of romance, my early years in Buddhism were blissful. Nevertheless, my fantasy had to end if I ever wanted to situate my practice in reality.

Whether she intended it or not, Roshi forced me to grow up. Just as we attribute our neuroses to our families of origin and wounded childhoods, so too we can link our spiritual obstacles and traumas to our flawed spiritual teachers and institutions. There will continue to be racism, sexism, classism, homophobia, elitism, and endless dances of power in the spiritual arena. We must be awake to these dimensions of our humanity. However, at some point, we have to claim our own personal and spiritual authority. Through Roshi and temple life, I was forced to dismantle my idealized view of spiritual practice. My friends from the Zen center and I joke that we are "ruined for life." We no longer have illusions of an idyllic mountain monastery in the desert, radiating peace and harmony. Indeed, the monastery is as abundantly flawed as the human psyches that take up residence within its walls. There is no spiritual ideal. With that discovery comes a momentary taste of freedom. Once the illusion is broken, then we are finally free to respond. For that glimpse of reality, I am grateful.

Regaining Love: Epilogue

Recently I realized that I no longer could remember where I had stored my *rakusu*—a square patchwork of cloth that is worn over the heart during meditation. A symbol of the Buddha's robe, the rakusu is given to Zen students by their teachers when students formally take Buddhist vows or precepts. Mine was given to me by Roshi, and written across the inside lining is the Buddhist name she gave me, Genshin. A fierce sadness seeped into my body as I sat with the thought that my rakusu could be lost—inadvertently slipped into a Goodwill box or left behind somewhere along the trail of my many moves. I scurried through the house, emptying the cupboards and drawers, venturing through dust balls and spider webs to search every possible hiding place. After a couple of hours, I let go of the search.

The practical need for my rakusu is all but nonexistent. I no longer regularly sit in meditation with a Zen community and have no plans to return to a disciplined study of Zen. Yet, the missing rakusu left an ache in my heart. Years in retrospect, interpreting my relationship with Roshi is a bit like a connect-the-dots exercise. I begin to see a larger mandala emerge. From this vantage point, I credit Roshi with catalyzing the trials and purification that ultimately oriented me toward my current spiritual path.

In the midst of my struggles with Roshi, there awakened in me a fierce hunger to uncover my spiritual roots as a woman of color. The journey began with a voracious appetite for feminist texts about the feminine divine. Most of these works were written by white women, leaving me to yearn for equivalent works by women of color. Consequently, I revisited Chicana efforts to reclaim Indigenous goddesses and reminded myself of the *mujerista* movement in theology. I reencountered Guadalupe, not as the Catholic Virgin Mary, but as the Great Mother, Tonantzin. As a woman of color, I felt deeply how a long history of patriarchal power intermingled with institutionalized religion had left our spiritual practices smothered, stripped, redefined, and molded into something blander and far less relevant to our lives.

While I had intellectually visited these terrains in the past, my trials with Roshi were the gateway to feeling these truths in my body. I left the monastery with a soul ache that was no longer theoretical. It took up residence deep in my bones and lodged in my gut. Under the guise of getting over Roshi, I began a healing path that turned out to extend way beyond the narrow view of my time at the Zen center. My path became one of reclaiming spirituality as a bisexual, borderlands mestiza. *Poco a poquito*, here and there, the process unfolded—meeting soul sisters and brothers, spending time in nature, sitting in illness, praying, and learning to trust my experiences. Years later, I now practice *curanderismo* and earth-based traditions with a community of *comadres* and elders who all have their own complicated spiritual journeys as women of color. In some ways it feels like a far cry from the Zen temple; in other ways it feels like a blink away.

In the tradition of the great Medicine Wheel, the direction of the North is the seat of the teachers and elders, our guides in wise and mature action. To this day, when I call in the sacred directions, I name Roshi as one of my teachers in the North, honoring her role on a path that challenged me to spiritual adulthood. The drama of my conflict with Roshi and the tenacity of her character became the medicine my practice needed. I now know that whether the setting is monastic or secular, my spiritual practice is as fundamental as breathing to me, and I can trust myself to honor it. My spiritual commitment is not dependent upon teacher, robes, temple, or creed. Being faced with the challenge of releasing those institutional structures of safety was as essential to me as a toddler being allowed to stumble in the ultimate service of walking.

I have returned to the Zen center a number of times in the last six years. For each of my visits, whether by happenstance or unconscious arrangement, Roshi has been out of town or our schedules have been impossible to coordinate. My last visit was with my husband, Matthew. I gave him a tour of the grounds, walking him through memories and landmarks. There are new buildings, subtle alterations to the daily routine, and fewer familiar faces among the residents. "When do I get to meet Roshi?" Matthew asked with a twinkle in his eye. I chuckled back, "I really do not know." The question now strikes me as something akin to a Zen koan—more a spiritual riddle than a scheduling issue. The more time that passes, the more my relationship with Roshi takes on the quality of a parable in which the ending no longer feels foreclosed, and I am left in wonder at the possible meanings.

I eventually returned to the search for my missing rakusu, convinced I could find it. Seated amidst a heap of boxes and bags I dragged out of storage, I suddenly had a flash of memory. Pulling out the stepladder, I retrieved a plastic box buried under photographs at the top of my closet. Wrapped in silk fabric, the rakusu sat folded into a cigar box for safekeeping. Instead of returning it to storage, I placed it on my altar near Guadalupe. Relieved, I ran my fingers across the hand-sewn patches, the imperfect lines precious reminders of the call to a spiritual life and its unpredictable crossroads.

Notes

1. Pseudonyms are used throughout.

"Pero tu no crees en dios"

Negotiating Spirituality, Family, and Community

Michelle Téllez

Introduction: The Borders between Our Hearts and Minds

I am reminded of one of my most lucid memories of Sunday morning Mass when I was nine or ten years old. I was wearing a blue flowered dress and pale blue tights. As we sang the hymn "Our Father," I stood tall between my parents and held their hands tight as we raised our arms up high. My voice was loud and clear and I vividly remember feeling absolutely exhilarated, directly connected to the Creator through our singing.

In this short narrative, I write about tensions I have felt with my family and larger community ever since I began to reconnect with my ancestral roots, *ceremonias*, and spiritual traditions. In the last twenty years, the ebbs and flows of these relationships have marked my journey in important ways. This *testimonio* is not about my quest to find answers to complex metaphysical questions or to define my spirituality; instead I focus on how I have related this spiritual journey to my family and community, a process that has been challenging but that has also taught me to fully live a borderland epistemology. I write from a particular position that speaks to who I am today. The process is ever evolving, but as I move toward middle age and understand my multiple identities as a daughter, sibling, aunt, community member, and mother, I have also come to understand the dialectical nature of our relations and ontological musings. Perhaps it is because I have now lived through the tremendous loss of both of my parents; the wound from my mom's passing is still so fresh that I find it important to note the fluidity of my journey.

Although I grew up in a bilingual, bicultural, Catholic home along the US-Mexican border, as a teenager I found myself isolated in a white working-class neighborhood. Despite the social and cultural differences between others, Catholicism offered me a sense of community with my peers. Yet as a young adult I found Catholicism to be antithetical to my evolving identity as a socially conscious and spiritual woman. Moreover, having ventured into the world of Indigenous ceremony and *danza*, I found myself estranged from my community. Instead of living in the liminal divide, I brought my spiritual experiments "home" with me. This piece will speak to the experience of bringing these practices "home."

Remembering that day in church, I pretended not to notice the snickering coming from a couple of girls that I had seen behind me. Were they laughing at my blue tights? Because I was singing? Because I was holding my parents' hands? I felt so spiritually elevated that I tried not to let them bother me. I remember this moment so clearly because it was the first time that I experienced two distinct yet equally important feelings that would come to inform my emotional and intellectual engagement with the spiritual world.

You see, while experiencing a moment of such faith, I was made to feel as if I was doing something wrong. It is precisely this disconnect, marked so vividly at such a young age, that I will speak to in this essay. I never came to know why I was ridiculed from afar by these girls, but I imagine it was their discomfort that caused it, a discomfort that must be similar to the one that my family has felt when I sought a spiritual path that was alien to their own comfort zone. It is appropriate that this chapter be placed in the section of the North, the place of the wind, associated with elders and the energy of maturity. Just as the winds carry messages through the seeds, the pollen, the birds, the monarch butterflies, and the seasons, I hope to bring a message in this chapter that underscores the ways in which spirituality can be understood in our relation to others.

Home

I was born and raised in San Diego, California. At around age nine or ten, my family and I moved from an apartment complex known as "Little TJ" to a house that we rented in an entirely different community.[1] I no longer had friends and family as next-door neighbors to play with. The brownness of my skin was also made apparent in this working-class community; although ethnically diverse, the majority of the families were white American.

I clearly remember dutifully praying daily during this time, hoping that through my prayers I would be bestowed with some friends. I felt completely isolated and spent a lot of time at the public library across the street from our house, allowing the stories of the many books I read to fill my days. The librarian became my closest friend.

Once I began attending the neighborhood school, the friendships came a little easier, but I still found that I felt detached from many of the kids because of the cultural differences that subtly played themselves out in our daily interactions. I eventually found common ground with the group of girlfriends who became my closest friends through high school because we were all raised Catholic.

As we grew up together, we could relate to one another on issues of sexuality, morality, having "strict" parents, and even the routinization of Catechism and weekend mass. We may have complained about the limitations that the Church and our parents imposed on us but we certainly did not question the doctrine itself; we accepted the principles as is. I, in fact, was steadfast in my beliefs that I was not to have sex before marriage and that I would never deface my body with a tattoo; I feared hell and did what I could to ensure that I would not end up there. I was baptized, had my first Communion, confirmed my faith (twice, I might add—once in Mexico and once in the United States) and came into "womanhood" at my fifteenth birthday mass celebration. In sum, being a "good" Catholic girl was an important part of my identity and, as my family would say, "*Lo único que te falta es casarte por la iglesia.*"[2]

I find myself now in my late thirties, a single mother to a beautiful daughter, with, yes, tattoos on my body and no plans to ever get married in the Catholic Church. My evolving spiritual beliefs are also closely connected to the politicization of my worldviews and while politics requires constant vigilance through a definitive stance, my spirituality sustains me through personal deep reflection. But it is in these times of personal deliberation that I realize I must also negotiate with the family and community from which I come; otherwise the process seems inauthentic and disconnected from the memories that continue to shape who I am. I am incapable of rupturing from my past and from the obligations that this history carries. Let me explain.

El Camino: "To go on that path, *se va descalzo* (you walk barefoot)"

When I started college I moved away from home and found myself in an environment where it was possible to be around Chicanas/os or Latinas/os more consistently again, and I was able to take my first Chicana/o studies class.[3] To learn about a history that had been denied to me throughout my previous schooling affected me not only intellectually and emotionally, but spiritually as well. I attended Mass close to campus and when I approached the priest with my queries, my doubts, my rage, the ineptitude of his response set me on a different path.

In many ways, living away from home facilitated the process of inquiry for me, since I did not have to explain why I did not attend weekly mass or why I was reading a religious text other than the Bible. Then my father suddenly passed away and the inability of the Church and its practices to soothe the pain of this loss further fueled my search at this time. That was my first fissure. It took many years to have the confidence to share with my family the critiques I had of the Church and my desire to seek out a different path. It was difficult to express myself as the youngest of my generation, the only one to have moved out of our hometown—and to explain the gendered implications both of these positions present. Eventually though, in my mid-twenties, I decided I could not keep these worldviews separate. By this time, I had become a *danzante* and had participated in various ceremonies (sweatlodges/*temazcallis*, healing circles, and dance ceremonies). So I slowly started talking about my experiences, primarily with my mother and sister, to whom I was closest. I wanted them to understand that these experiences made sense to me. In the beginning, my mother and sister tolerated my ideas because they saw them as a fad that I was going through and would eventually grow out of.

Yet to fully embody my spiritual path, I could not accept a disconnect from my family. Thus, I tried to include them, either by inviting them to ceremonies that I participated in or by just subtly including my viewpoint when there was a group or family prayer before dinner or a celebration. This choice implied interactions and confrontations that risked dismissal at best and ridicule at worst. Yet it was important for me to keep trying. In effect, this was my second fissure.

For example, several years ago, my mother came to visit me when I lived in New York City. The danza group I was a part of held a Mother's Day celebration that weekend, and I took her to and participated in the ceremony. At one point, she and I were standing in the middle of the danza circle and when I brought the copal towards her, perhaps to make light of her uneasiness, under her breath she said, "*Que . . . me estas sacando el diablo?*"[4] Despite the very serious nature of my intentions, and my frustrations, I could not help but laugh. This experience was so beyond her own worldview that in order to make sense of it, she had to make fun of it. After my mother's comment, I did not know how to reengage myself with the ceremony. Although I continued to participate, the experience felt compromised because I felt uncomfortable and frustrated. I had been very excited to celebrate my mother, but the disconnect that I felt with her manifested itself in my dance and in my own engagement with the rest of the ceremony.

Another time, while in graduate school, I was home visiting my family when we received the news that my uncle, my mother's brother, was very ill. As she expressed her distress, she asked me to pray for him but then, almost immediately, she said, "Ay, pero tu no crees en dios,"[5] implying that I could not pray and could not help the situation in any way. I tried to explain to her that just because I did not attend mass it did not mean I could not offer my prayers. But she dismissed me and walked away from the conversation. As she walked away, I felt frustrated but also sad that my mother saw my practices as vacuous and without faith. I had found substance in our Indigenous practices from our place of origin, Mexico, and I knew that these prayers I was carrying resonated deep within her, but she could not make the bridge between her religion and the memories she also had that connected her to the natural world.

More recently, in preparation for the birth of my daughter, a medicine man that I work with and I organized a welcoming ceremony in the home of my daughter's godparents. I was about seven months pregnant and the ceremony was to take place a week after Christmas. On Christmas Eve, as I approached the door to my sister's house, my brother came out to greet me with a rendition of a very racist and insensitive powwow dance and "Indian" chant while hitting his mouth. The implication of course being that the upcoming ceremony was a practice foreign to his Catholic-Christian ways. I was in shock and all I could muster was a "That is not very nice"; he laughed and said, "Oh, my crazy sister."

Crazy, of course, because I chose to honor my daughter's new life in a markedly different way than his—but also, his internalized colonialism became apparent in his response. Here perhaps was another fissure. Whereas I saw myself as decolonized, he vocalized what he and my other family members thought: that I was crazy. These are but a few of the countless examples that I can speak to. At one time, these negotiations were extremely painful for me, but because both my family and my spiritual journey are important to me, I had to find a way to embrace and feel embraced by both.

Conclusion: Sharing the Path

I know from experience that it is hard to walk a new path. By sharing these stories I am highlighting the real ways in which one's daily life, situated and contextualized within one's reality in spaces where one engages with spiritual paradigms that are much, much different from one's family of origin, can create tensions as well as a sense of confusion about oneself.

I began this essay with my girlhood experience in Mass where I was ridiculed for singing in church too loudly, somehow feeling that I was doing something wrong as judged by my peers. Despite my subsequent separation from the Catholic Church, that feeling of alienation stayed with me as I sought to connect with the traditions of my ancestors. I write this because I want to acknowledge that it is difficult to disrupt family expectations, even if your new path of choice is about reclaiming practices that are grounded in our own lost histories. If your family of origin has not challenged the ways in which Christianity was brought into our lives through conquest and force, I think it is still important to find ways to bridge these seemingly disparate positions. I am trying to highlight the contradictions that we must negotiate.

To be fair, there were moments in this path where I too have absolutely rejected my family's religion, where I refused to sit through a Mass that highlighted hypocrisies that seemed apparent only to me, and where I too grumbled under my breath. This is where I believe that a borderlands epistemology, understanding the dialectical nature of not only material reality but also spirituality and family, is useful. A borderlands epistemology conduces to the state of *nepantla*, of crossroads, of coming to a point where I can say that although I may not agree with the church my mom adhered to, I came to respect her relationship to it and her faith in God. But it is also true that I cannot wholeheartedly deny the ways in which my Catholic upbringing informs my own relationship to the Creator and all my relations. The embodiment of syncretism is how I mark this path.

By embracing this kind of thinking, this path of understanding has become much easier. I also believe that my family has begun to see that this life I am setting out for myself is not temporal, that I am committed to engaging in ancestral forms of spirituality and to raising my daughter in this new tradition that she and I will be creating together. Of course, these traditions and *ceremonias* are not actually new, but connect me to the very earth we walk on, here on this continent, indeed providing me with a sense of wholeness that I never felt as a member of the Catholic Church. It is through a stronger sense of self that my family and I can reengage.

In fact, after the birth of my daughter we participated in a water ceremony, a baptism up in the mountains for her and other children, and members of my family were present and supportive. Perhaps they made a few sly comments, but they were there and demonstrated their support and love through their presence. This journey has not been easy but I know that struggling with the tensions and inviting my family in, I have demonstrated a commitment and a desire for mutual understanding. By doing so, I have created the opportunity to walk these tensions together, a practice that will be an important life lesson for my daughter that I hope she will carry for herself and future generations.

Spirituality, in the end, is how we relate to each other as human beings, independent of theology. I feel this now when my daughter and I make altars for our ancestors, in the dances we do in ceremony, and in the prayers we offer to all of our relations. I am reminded of the words of Cherríe Moraga, who said, "To raise an Indian child is the most radical thing I could do."[6] Spirituality, for me, is a movement. One that recognizes that going against the grain requires strength but also acceptance. While I do feel there is a great absence in our lives because my parents have passed away, I know we continue to honor their lessons. Just recently, my daughter gathered some sage and an old photo of her "*bia*" and "*bio*" and made an altar in her bedroom because she wanted them close to her. In some ways my entire life has been a series of fissures, but in the end, perhaps through my daughter, and through the honoring of my parents, we come together as a whole. Life becomes our ceremony.

Notes

1. So nicknamed because the majority of the families were of Mexican descent; "TJ" is the abbreviation for the city of Tijuana, Baja California, Mexico, which borders San Diego. Others often use the term pejoratively.
2. "The only thing you have left is to get married by the church."
3. The section title is a quote by Sylvia Ledesma. Quoted in Roberto Rodriguez (2002, 32–33).
4. "Are you taking the devil out of me?"
5. "Oh, but you do not believe in God."
6. Said during a speech given in Chicago, Illinois, for the Incite! Women of Color Against Violence national conference in 2002.

Healing Introspections

Reaching Inside and Reconstructing Myself

Rosa María Hernández Juárez

Sick and in Need of Healing

In spring 2003, I became very ill. At first, I thought it was a bad case of the flu. After feeling very sick at work, I left for the day hoping to get better at home. I went to a drugstore to get some flu medicine. I distinctly remember standing in an aisle, looking for the difference between product A and product B, when I felt a sharp pain in my lower abdomen. Feeling faint, I paid for my things and went home to sleep.

By the third day, I could barely walk and I could not stand erect. Since I had not been able to relieve myself for at least three days (which is not normal for me), my stomach was completely distended and the pain was excruciating. I called in sick to work and asked my boss not to fire me because I was missing so much work. Being a friend, my boss was more concerned with my well-being and asked what she could do for me. Since I could barely stand, I told her I desperately needed a shower and asked if she could come to my house and help me get in and out of the shower. Both my manager and direct supervisor came over to help me. At a glance, they both decided I needed to go to the doctor. I was way too weak to resist.

As soon as my doctor saw me, he was alarmed. He did a few checks on me, but sent me directly to the emergency room where I was admitted with an unknown diagnosis. After many tests, the doctors concluded that I had a bowel obstruction, though it was a nurse friend of mine who first determined that the root issue was endometriosis. The endometriosis caused cysts in my lower abdomen. One of those cysts had burst and become infected. As the infection spread, it somehow pinched my intestine into closing, something like when you bend a garden hose to stop the flow of water. With a course of antibiotics, the infection in my lower abdomen abated and I was able to move my bowels, though barely, and I was sent home from the hospital. It had been quite a scare, since I had never been in a hospital my entire life. I was certainly scared and so were my family and friends. Everyone had rallied around me, and I felt deeply comforted by that. When I was discharged, I really thought it was all over. Yet even though I was supposed to be better, somehow I was not.

Eating became a painful chore. I clearly remember when a friend brought food over for me and I spent about ten minutes eating a small piece of onion about the size of a dime. I must have cut that piece about three times when I realized it does not take that long to eat so little. That night, by the grace of God, I had a houseguest. At about one in the morning, I began to vomit violently. My guest called my best friend and asked her to take me to the hospital. By the time my friends arrived, I was feeling very faint and everything seemed to blur. I went in and out of consciousness and began to see things in a strobe-light rhythm as I closed and opened my eyes to catch the important details of what was happening. I opened my eyes and my friends were at my house carrying me up the stairs to the sidewalk. I clearly remember telling one of my friends that I was really scared. I just remember her saying that I should be more afraid of *not* going to the hospital.

Next I was in the ER in a wheelchair and I was given a bucket to throw up in—which I thought was ridiculous since I had not eaten in days, piece of onion notwithstanding, and I had already been throwing up for what felt like hours. During the intake part of my ER visit, the nurse did not seem very impressed by me. Suddenly, I threw up in the bucket with a loud splash. I did not even open my eyes until one (or all) of my friends shrieked and asked if I had just thrown up blood. My head was already hanging down, yet it still took all of my strength to open my eyes and look into the bucket on my lap. When I saw the pool of blood, I whimpered a faint "Yea." At that point the nurse kicked it into high gear and rushed me to a doctor, with only one friend by my side.

I clearly remember when the doctor pushed a tube down my nose and throat. Just before the doctor began, my friend took my hand and the doctor thanked her for it. I tried to thank her too, but could barely see by then, much less speak. It is really the pain I remember. The doctor gave me water to sip so as to swallow the tube as he led it down my nostril, down my throat and into my stomach, but everything in my being wanted to reject the tube and even the water going down. Afterwards, I opened my eyes only once, to see my friend vomiting in the sink. The very next thing I remember, I was in a hospital bed, with tubes and monitors and my parents sitting at the foot of my bed. Frankly, I could not tell if I was still alive, dreaming, or crossing over.

I longed for my grandmother to heal me. Even with the medical experts that handled my care, I was lost and unsure as to where the healing was supposed to come from if I did not have a *curandera* to pull it all together. Who was going to pray over me? My grandmother had passed some years before and suddenly my parents looked so old and so small at the foot of my bed as I looked past the tubes that invaded me. They looked scared and I was lost. Who was going to heal me, put me together, make me whole again? Where does healing come from and how do you do it?

Deeply Rooted in a Sense of Spirit: Healing in the Borderlands

I was born in Tijuana and raised in Chula Vista, California. I grew up going back and forth between Mexico and the United States as if the border were just a fence in the backyard—which it was in a way, compared to the situation now. I was exposed to a duality found everywhere in life that was especially poignant in a border community. Even in healing, there was a split in how the "American" idea of healing was so different from the idea of healing that my family taught me. My dad came from El Salto de Juanacatlan in the state of Jalisco and my mom and grandmother came from León, in Guanajuato. They taught me what they had learned about healing.

Growing up, most of my medicines came from my mother's garden and the healing seemed to come from my parents themselves. I already believed that my parents hung the moon, so this power of theirs to heal me seemed perfectly logical. My dad had shown me how to pick all the herbs they grew so they could just send me outside to get whatever they needed, be it spices for cooking or herbs for healing (or even food for cooking, since they grew a good deal of the food we ate, including ducks, chickens, and their eggs).

My dad also taught me to pick leaves from the yerba buena (mint) plant to treat mild stomachache and discomfort so my mom would not get annoyed if I had a stomachache from eating too much. Sometimes my mom boiled chocolate in water with ruda (rue) stems and leaves for bigger stomach issues. If necessary, my Ma' María (my maternal grandmother) could treat me for *empacho* (gastric obstruction) by massaging my belly with oil as she prayed over me. Ma' María would finish by giving me a concoction that she made with olive oil and chicken or beef bones she had cooked, dried, then charred, washed down with a hot mint tea. The tea was my favorite part because it was sweet and warm and I knew the treatment was over. My grandmother would then instruct my parents as to what foods I could and could not eat, and I would feel better in a day or two.

As a child, I never broke a bone or had any major health issues outside of common childhood illnesses like the flu and chicken pox (although as I write this I realize that I had various stomach issues). I used to think that illness was something I was protected from by my natural healers. Not only did they heal me, they also healed all of the people from our family and community who came to see them when they felt sick.

As I grew up, our family used western medicine as well, but regardless of the method healing was always deeply rooted in a sense of Spirit. It was through a profound sense of spirituality that the healers and the ill found the internal and external resources to aid in a process that was ultimately bigger than us. It was Spirit itself that would provide. Every medicine/ritual/invocation was served in reverence. Yet I always had questions: How did they have so much Faith? How were they so sure?

Pulling Myself Together to Stay Amongst the Living

I still had many questions for my parents but I could not speak because of the tubes that came out of my nose and made everything painfully difficult. Even when I did try to speak, it felt like only air came out of my mouth. Where had my voice gone?

The first time I was admitted to the hospital, the doctors had mentioned the possibility of surgery; this time I knew it was for sure. First, we had to wait for me to stabilize because they did not want to operate on me while I had a fever. In the daze of so much morphine, I would hear the explanations of what the doctors were thinking and doing, but it was like a bad trip where the information would make sense and vanish from my mind, seemingly at the same time.

It was the nurses who actually helped me understand everything I underwent; angels of mercy. I was to undergo surgery to clear my bowel obstruction and to remove two cysts from my ovary, since my obstruction was caused by a burst cyst that had become infected in my lower abdomen and kinked my intestine in the process. An ovary is not that big, the nurses explained—only about one-half inch in diameter. With that information, I was expecting the cysts in my ovary to be the size of a cherry or maybe even a golf ball. But then I was told that one was the size of a plum and the other was the size of an orange. The congestion above the bowel obstruction was also about the size of an orange, and about to burst. My intestine had all but closed, and had I waited any longer I would not have lived to tell this. I have to admit that I waited too long to seek the help I needed. Without knowing or meaning to, I had endangered my own life by not taking it seriously early on. Or maybe it was not that I did not take it seriously—the pain was unbelievable and felt quite serious. I think I was just scared and feeling so lost that I did nothing.

For the first time in my life I felt that I had to fight for my life. I had experienced a number of near-death experiences before, but they seemed unreal—I could not grasp that my life could end at any moment. I had felt like a cat with nine lives; life just keeps coming. As everyone waited for my fever to abate so I could undergo surgery, it was the first time I felt like I was straddling some fence, like I had to pull myself together to stay among the living. I became scared of everything. I was afraid of what was happening to my intestine. It was surreal to think of being cut open to expose my bowels and my reproductive system. It was scary to realize that surgery was the best chance I had at saving my life. I was worried that I might slip away from the anesthesia alone. I was mostly scared of how a strange calm seemed to be calling me, as if all I had to do was let go, slip away, and it would all be okay.

My mom later said she knew I would be fine because of my willpower. I believe that Will is Spirit and the reverence that my mothers and fathers instilled in me is Faith. At first, I was sure I had left it at home or lost it somewhere along the way. I could not find it and that began to freak me out. I wondered if this was how I was going to die. I felt like hanging on was difficult and my fingers were starting to give. But somehow I was able to let the noise fall away and I found a thread of hope. As if calling from the distance, I heard something say that I was alive and God is in all Life. I found my strength within.

As I waited for surgery, I would do my best to focus on life and living. I would become very aware of the fact that I was still breathing, even of feeling the excruciating pain. I was aware of my thirst and thought, "I am alive because dead people do not have thirst. Do they? NO . . . they do not," I decided. I would try to feel every part of my body, an itch, a pain, a caress. I would move my fingers and toes in patterns, rhythms that felt comforting. I would relish the presence of my visitors and pray for them as well. I would think of things I loved and hold on to the feeling of love as much as I could. I would try to read life around me by noticing how everything seemed to buzz.

At first, since I could not speak, I would search in the eyes of my visitors for some sign of how I was doing. Then I realized that I was really just seeing how they were doing. After a while, I would focus on showing them that I was still here. I still had light and I still wanted to shine. I would talk to La Virgen de Guadalupe and one time, I think I even prayed to La India Maria (the famous Mexican movie character portrayed by actress María Elena Velasco). Pain and morphine make a powerful combination. I thought La India Maria had appeared to me, though she was really just on the television that hovered over my bed. But I was willing to talk (or imagine I was talking) to anyone or anything in the Spirit world that would listen to me: "I am here, I am here!" I cannot say who it was that actually heard my pleas, but I think it was life that I was reaching for. I had faith I could be with God in life or death, but it was life that I was interested in.

I had faith that I would come out of the hospital and live. I believed I would heal. It was perfectly clear to me that the plan was not as simple as the surgeons had made it sound. Though I had faith in their ability, I had to have more faith in Spirit and my place in it.

Before and after my surgery I was able to tap into prayer through the pain and the heavy medications. Prayer looks very different for different people, and I am not here to define it for anyone else but myself. But if we can agree that prayer is communion with a higher force that I refer to as Spirit, I found that communion in many places. We can walk and live and love in communion with Spirit as much as we want because it is abundant. That is the most amazing thing, really; Spirit is everywhere. The night of the surgery, I was sitting on my stretcher praying for life and healing. My doctor came to check in with me and was visibly taken aback by seeing me pray. He incredulously asked if I was actually praying (maybe he was insulted). I simply replied: "You do your part and I will do mine." He smiled with genuine appreciation and said he was happy to hear that. It left me wondering if other people do not pray before surgery, since that is a pretty good time to go for it.

Spilling Myself Onto Paper to Heal

One of the ways in which I found Spirit working to heal me was a need to draw. When I was sent home after my surgery and eleven days in the hospital, a good friend, seeing I could not really speak, offered me some colored pencils and paper. Though I had many racing thoughts, the pain medicine I was given seemed to block my words and I felt trapped.

The need to draw was more like a fever than anything else I can describe. In the weeks of my recovery from surgery, I would spill myself onto paper. A number of drawings came out of this process; it was an amazing place to go when everything else was so difficult and painful. My gut had been cut open vertically. My viscera had been pulled out to be examined and fixed. My intestines were then put back and the cysts were removed from my ovary. The

Figure 1. Rosa María Hernández Juárez. 2003. *Plum.* Charcoal on paper, 9×9 in.

back pain that comes with being immobile was unbelievable—at some point, the worst pain I had felt. This includes the pain of having to walk the same day as my surgery so that my entrails could reposition themselves properly. I went into a funk that could not be penetrated by words in either direction. Somehow drawing gave me a place to go, to explore. It gave me a place to be, a place where I could ask my questions and imagine whatever answers I wanted. I like to think that I was never actually alone in that place, but that Spirit itself was working there with me, through me.

Two drawings are most special to me. The one where I am reaching inside of me I call *Plum* (fig. 1) because it is from a dream where I pulled out my own cysts and found that they were an actual plum and orange. I like the idea

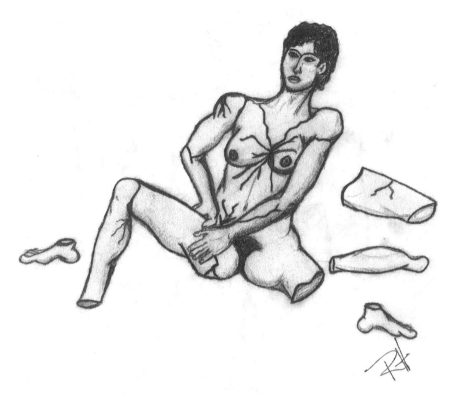

Figure 2. Rosa María Hernández Juárez. 2003. *My Pieces.* Charcoal on paper, 9×9 in.

of me being the one who reaches inside myself to extract that which endangered my life. I named the other drawing *My Pieces* (fig. 2) because I felt that I had been torn apart and had to pick up the pieces of my life, beginning with reconstructing my body. Again, I cherished the idea that it would be me who had the power to heal myself. Now I know that I am never alone at all because Spirit is with me in everything I do.

Healing Lessons

Thank God, my health is now good and I am strong. I know that being in touch with my body was essential in my recovery because it had so much to do with why and how I became so ill. I realize that as a survivor of childhood sexual abuse, I had disconnected from my body and had to learn to honor it. After many years of disassociating from my body and everything that came with years of abuse at the hand of extended-family members, I learned to hear what my body is trying to communicate. I learned that Spirit is inside me and in the people that came to be around me.

My recovery period also required Faith. Even though I was out of danger, I still had a long road ahead of me and I could not even imagine what was coming. There was so much of myself that I had to face and so much that I had to face alone. There were very few people who were able to be there for me, or who could even be clear about their limits. I told myself that seeing my pain was too much for people to see. Maybe it was people's fear of their own mortality that kept them away. There were even times I felt I was still taking care of others while I was in wretched pain. At first I could not understand what was happening. Eventually I realized that I had to let go of my fears about other people and focus on myself. I had to stay positive and not get lost in the depression and angst that tries to take over.

Not everyone ran, though. There were those who took care of my parents with rides to and from the airport, food, and even sitting with them while I was in surgery. Some spent the night with me at the hospital or brought me words and items of comfort. There were some people who helped me even while enduring their own excruciating pain. My father would do everything for me with so much love and patience even when my mom was freaking out. Though I saw the fear in my father's eyes, I was so moved by how he would push his fear aside so that he could still see me and what I needed. He once helped me bathe in a chair, since I was not allowed in the shower. I still tear up at the image of my father on his knees before me, washing small towels in warm, soapy water and offering me the warm towels as he fought back the tears in his eyes. As my father took care of me, I felt he was praying over me. I felt I had found my Curandero. He was never gone at all!

In another instance, after I was released from the hospital I had a friend take me to her house so that I would not be home alone. Even though she was experiencing a great deal of pain in her back, she took me up three flights of stairs. We both hobbled up the stairs—it was a sight, and I will never forget it because I felt her commitment. There are so many other ways I was helped and supported by my friends that I cannot list them all or thank them enough, really. I learned so much about what is healing about being with each other. When we really offer ourselves to each other, there is an amazing amount of healing that goes both ways. I learned so much about Faith in God, people, and ultimately, myself. I am forever grateful to those who were with me, even if we have gone our separate ways by now.

I feel that it is important to honor my healing and the people who were really there for me. To do that, I needed to honor myself. I needed to honor my body as an intelligent vessel that can guide me through this life. Though I already knew about eating well and getting exercise, the task was now to do these things consistently. I also need to love, pray, serve, and dance. The need to dance and rejoice no longer feels like a hedonistic indulgence but rather a spiritual necessity. My dad once told me that when you dance, you pray twice, or double (*"cuando se reza bailando, se reza lo doble"*). Dancing is the most sincere prayer I have.

I want to give back to my parents a way of reconnecting with an old way of doing things. I want to take them back to when they grew their own food and made their own remedies, because after so many years in this country they have let some of the old ways go. I want to learn everything they can teach me so as to not lose our traditions and our connection to nature, each other, and Spirit. I want to share this wealth of knowledge with those around me. Sharing myself in a new and more open way made the pain bearable, the healing possible, and life worth living.

Nepantla *Spirituality*

My Path to the Source(s) of Healing

Lara Medina

I write with the element of air, the wind, in my consciousness. The air teaches us to be fluid, to be flexible so that our strength and our stability do not become too rigid. We must be able to adapt when necessary, to flow like the wind, to be open to change, to be flexible with our plans, to be able to cleanse and renew ourselves. The air is the element of the North, the direction of the elders, of completion, and of wisdom that comes from moving through the cycles of life.

Writing about my spirituality is a challenge and an honor. I offer these reflections with humility and gratefulness for the paths that I have traveled to help me spiritually so that I can live in balance. As definitions of spirituality vary widely and can easily suggest something very abstract and elusive, it is important for me to define how I use the concept.

My definition of spirituality at this time is one's relationship with self, with others, with nature, with the universe, with the ancestors, and with the sacred source and great mystery of life and death. Spirituality is fundamentally about being in relationship; being aware of one's interdependence or connectedness to all that can be seen and all that is unseen. The integration of knowledge from our body, our heart, and our mind is required to be in full or complete relationship with all that is. We know or understand more fully when all aspects of our being are working together; when we trust our body and our heart as much as our mind. Our spirituality is a tremendous source of knowledge that determines how we understand and live out our human existence. As I am not always adept at integrating body, heart, and mind, the strength of my spirituality waxes and wanes but it is always a part of me, stoking the fire within. It is a way of life.

I have come to this understanding after years of living disconnected from others and from my self. As a child, I was not taught that relationships matter the most, that my heart has intelligence or that my body can talk to me, that art is healing, or that the earth is alive and that plants and animals have spirit that can help us. It took many twists and turns involving deep losses and amazing friends and healers who taught me, challenged me, and strengthened me to be fully in relationship, to heal my wounds deep within. The psychological consequences of colonization travel over many generations, yet can be healed.

I have also learned that spirituality must be nourished through community, creativity, compassion, and commitment. I believe that a collective spirituality based on compassion and justice can transform our world. I see a collective Xicana spirituality evolving in our communities, a spirituality that is "contesting the location of all forms of political, social and economical injustices," a spirituality deeply concerned with decolonizing our understanding of spirituality as "a private affair" (Brunal 2011, 180). It is a western construct to understand spirituality as strictly a personal matter. To do so depoliticizes spirituality and conveniently weakens its power. In non-western thought, spirituality is a way of life that impacts how we act in the world (Ritskes 2011).

In Xicana circles, I see healing rituals and ceremonies proliferating, artistic venues evolving, and groups rallying to unify against the forces restricting our human right to education and migration. It is a spirituality deeply rooted in returning to the earth/cosmic-centered Indigenous knowledge of our ancestors as a means of healing the wounds inflicted by patriarchal heteronormativity, racism, and capitalism. The return is not to a romanticized past, but to ancient epistemologies that value and understand fluidity and change; complementary dualities, yet ultimately a nonduality that exists behind all seemingly complementary opposites;[1] energies as the qualities of the elements calling us to be in relationship with the universe; the power of plant and animal medicines; the feminine as a distinct power; the feminine in balance with the masculine—a sacred complementary duality that exists in all; reciprocity between individuals and communities; and a "deeper power/mystery" in life that creates, destroys, and transforms.[2]

For Xicanas/os, this Indigenous ancestral knowledge is key to healing historical trauma; wounds we are conscious and not conscious of; wounds that have impaired our voices and our agency. Ancestral knowledge is key because it is a way of knowing and being in the world that values community and understands our interdependency. As Adelin Brunal writes in his reflections as an African Canadian, "To decolonise we cannot do so on our own; we need to work together as a community . . . and that same community needs support from other communities. . . . It is the same for the path to spiritual wellbeing" (2011, 180). But what does it mean to be in community? Community requires respect, gender and sexual equality, accountability, honoring women for their distinct intelligence and creativity, mechanisms to address conflict, and solidarity in seeking justice. As we belong to many communities and even communities within community, these values must be consistent as we navigate many spaces. A collective spirituality based on these values leads to "spirituality as resistance" (Ritskes 2011, 27); resistance to a paradigm of domination based solely on profit. And we resist to transform.

The paths I have taken to heal my wounds and nourish my spirituality have been greatly influenced by Audre Lorde's reflections on the erotic; feminist and liberation theologies; Mexican Catholic popular religiosity; Mesoamerican Indigenous, African, and Tibetan Bon Buddhist epistemologies and practices with the elements, and sacred energies in the universe and in our bodies. I am awed by the intersections between what I call southern and eastern ancient living knowledges that evolved from peoples living close to the land and the elements.

As Lorde wrote many years ago, spiritual, physical, emotional, intellectual, and political work is powered by the erotic, "a resource within each of us that lies in a deeply female and spiritual plane . . . that can provide energy for change" (1984, 53). This erotic/spiritual power can be activated through the diversity of creative acts we choose, whether they be emotional, mental or physical. Creativity opens the path to our spiritual consciousness, a consciousness that puts us in relationship with that deeper power within, among, and beyond. The *tlamatinime*, the poets and philosophical mystics of the Nahua ancestors, understood *in xochitl in cuicatl*, or *flor y canto* (flower and song), a *disfrasismo* or dual metaphor for the creative arts, as the true way of communicating with the sacred sources of life and death.

The Nahua culture, drawing on Toltec knowledge, also taught the importance of "the formation of citizens who were wise and firm, that is 'possessors of a face, possessors of a heart'" (León-Portilla 1992, 189). *In ixtli in yollotl*, or *cara y corazón*, face and heart, or mind and heart knowledge joined to form the character of the individual. I draw from these teachings to carve a spiritual path, a way of life. So I practice compassion, daily meditation to connect with the elements, heartfelt listening and conversation, creating ritual and ceremony, walking and cycling, eating nutritious foods, teaching to the heart and the mind, learning, creating art and viewing art, cherishing sexual pleasure, and a commitment to justice. When I create jewelry with the symbol of *teyolia*, or corazón, I reference the sacred energy and intelligence located within our hearts. The Nahua knew that the animistic energy located in the heart never dies, but upon the death of our physical body, this heart energy is stored in the sacred mountains. Cyclically the living invoked the teyolia to leave the mountains and renew the earth.[3]

When Xicana/o communities celebrate *Días de los muertos*, we are invoking the hearts of our ancestors to return to nourish the land and the dreams of the living.[4] This sacred energy keeps us connected to our *antepasados*, to nature, to the sacred sources, and revives our genetic and historical memories. The tradition of in xochitl in cuicatl, flor y canto, remains intact.

Nepantla Spirituality: Thriving in the Center

I offer reflections on some of the key encounters that have led me to better understand what nourishes my connection to the source(s) of life and death. On this journey, I have come to realize that I began in nepantla and I return to nepantla (a Nahuatl term meaning in the middle or the center), a site of both chaotic complexity and creative meaning making. With much gratitude to the work of cultural theorist and spiritual/political activist Gloria Anzaldúa and conversations with other great Xicana and like-minded thinkers and practitioners, I understand my present location in nepantla not as one of confusion or transition, but as a center space that is fluid, that is shaped by diversity, and that gives me and other "mixed race" persons the power to choose, critique, integrate, and balance our multiple cultural and biological inheritances. I speak of the spirituality that emerges from the middle, from the center, as nepantla spirituality.[5]

By all means, being in the middle also causes great confusion and conflict, as Gloria Anzaldúa articulated and visual artist Yreina Cervantez depicts so well (L. Pérez 2007, 37–45). Being in the middle requires body, heart, and head knowledge to make sense of and come to terms with the forces of colonization. Once processed, pain offers the challenge and opportunity to transform shame, confusion, and anger into creative thinking and healing action. We can choose to move through the shadow side of nepantla into the light within nepantla, or beyond the "Coatlicue state," learning from the lessons that the forces of creation and destruction offer. Cosmic earth energy or the mother Goddess, Coatlicue, creates space and time when experiences/situations collide and the resulting chaos holds transformative potential. It requires acknowledging the crisis, even embracing it with self-compassion, and entering into the internal space where transformation takes place. Coatlicue, as life- and death-force energy, offers the opportunity for us to discern the lessons hidden within the crisis. It is up to us to integrate them into our minds, bodies, and hearts. The end result offers tremendous transformative growth (Anzaldúa 1987, 41–51; 2002a).[6]

My Own *Nepantla*

Growing up in the mid-1950s to working-class Mexican-American Catholic parents exposed me to numerous power struggles regarding ethnicity, religion, class and of course, gender. We were a small family surrounded by Irish and Italian American Catholics in a northern California town. At home I heard arguments regarding how we should identify, with my mother claiming a Spanish identity, and my father claiming his proud *Mexicanidad*. Frequent trips to Mexico to visit my *abuelos* helped me to clarify my ancestral roots. I was also being heavily indoctrinated with patriarchal Catholic dogma and the infamous Catholic guilt taught so tenaciously in parochial schools yet to be enlightened by Vatican II. At the same time I was being nurtured by my mother's devotion to the divine female through the icon of Our Mother of Perpetual Help, and my grandmother's love for San Martín de Porres, an Afromestizo healer and canonized Catholic saint of Spanish and African lineage born in Lima, Peru in 1575.[7]

I realize now that I inherited my spiritual orientation to life from my mother and grandmother. They were both deeply religious women who trusted completely in a transcendent male God, his divine mother, and his saintly followers. Ironically, I learned from them to trust not in a male godhead but rather in the strength and power of women, both human and divine. As a young girl, I did not fully understand their yearnings for support from the *santos*, but I knew it was coming from a deep place within. I saw my mother pray with great devotion in front of her simple altar atop a bedroom dresser. I witnessed my grandmother's affectionate care for the icon of San Martín de Porres.

Later, as a young woman coming of age during the late 1960s, I rejected these spiritual relationships of my elders as mere superstitions. It was not until the 1980s, while studying Chicano liberation theology, that I understood the profound symbolism of the santos for maintaining relationships with the mystical and magical powers available to us from the spirit world. My mother's simple home shrine and my *abuela*'s ever-polished statue of San Martín were their way to take care of the divine and in turn receive protection and encouragement amidst their daily struggles. I had witnessed relationships based on interdependence and reciprocity, foundational Indigenous values.

My appreciation for Mexican Catholic religiosity grew when I formally studied Christian theology and saw how late-twentieth-century liberation struggles around the world were challenging eurocentric and western capitalist interpretations of Jesus's teachings. I finally felt comfortable in a tradition that had previously not allowed me to question it. Latin American liberation theology and then feminist theologies opened a path for me to reexamine the faith of my parents and grandparents. My return to the "official" Church in my late thirties surprised me, and it might have lasted if I had not experienced the racism and sexism of the US Catholic Church at first hand. I worked as a lay minister in a university in what appeared to be a progressive Catholic context, but my ministry to Xicana/o students was not appreciated by the institutional powers. After almost three years of being employed by the Church, I was forced to leave; my heart, mind, and body told me to continue on a spiritual path, but one not confined to the Church.

Spirit led me to other Xicanas who were also searching for the sacred feminine in their lives. We began to pray together and create ritual for our personal transitions. We began to name what we intellectually and intuitively knew, that the great mystery is of the feminine. Over time we understood the essential balance in all of life, that the universe is comprised of feminine and masculine energies, and that we have this sacred complementary duality within us. Writing our own prayers with woman-centered metaphors empowered us to name what we were uncovering. Looking back at these beginnings of a personal Xicana feminist spirituality reminds me of the process I have gone through to reclaim and heal my feminine sacred erotic powers. Praying to the divine mother is now very natural for me, and I have tried to pass this on to my daughter. Here is a simple prayer that I would say nightly with her:

> Madre Divina, Tonantzin Guadalupe, llena de gracia
>   Bendita eres tú, y bendita es la fruta de nuestras vientres
>   Madre Divina, Tonantzin Guadalupe, ruega por nosotras
>   Ahora, y cuando la muerte viene.[8]
>   [Divine Mother, Tonantzin Guadalupe, full of grace
>   Blessed are you and blessed is the fruit of our wombs
>   Divine Mother, Tonantzin Guadalupe, pray for us
>   Now and when death comes.]

My prayers have continued to develop and now emerge from a spontaneous place of gratitude for all that nourishes my life.

Temazkal Conocimientos

Meeting with other Xicanas to pray and bring ceremony into our lives led me to other women and men who practice the *temazkal*, the ancient Indigenous

Mexican purification sweat ceremony. This healing ceremony that is traditional to many but not all native peoples of the Americas has furthered my connection to the sacred elements of nature and the sacred masculine and feminine energies within and around us. The temazkal led me home to myself, to my fears, to my desires, to my limitations, and to my strengths. It is a *ceremonia* that brings me back to the earth, back to the elements of earth, fire, air, and water, back to the voices of my ancestors, back to my creator. I am grateful to the women and men who have shared and taught me this tradition.[9] As another Xicana says about her experience in the temazkal: "I felt like I was home. I felt like I went back five hundred years. I could feel the spiritual connection to those original ceremonies and to my ancestors, and I never felt like that before. I really felt a deep spiritual inner connection" (Virginia Espino, personal communication, March 1994).

I feel it is important to discuss the historical presence of the sweat purification ceremony among Mexican Indigenous peoples because there is misunderstanding in the Xicana/o community about the origins of the sweat ceremony and debate within some sectors of northern native communities whether Xicanas/os have the right to the ceremony.[10] Such misunderstandings can only cause divisions and fragmentation between native and mestizo peoples. While northern and southern purification ceremonies differ in terms of structure, material, and format, the Mexican temazkal and the Lakota *inipi*, as only two examples, offer northern and southern native and mestizo peoples a bridge for us to share our homes, our traditions, so that we all may return to the wombs of ancient healing knowledge.[11]

Elders and practitioners refer to the temazkal as "the mother of all medicines." At the time of the European invasions of the Americas the custom of purifying and healing oneself through ritual sweating was an integral part of the daily practice of many native peoples. The Spanish missionaries wrote extensively on the tradition they encountered in Mexico. Friar Diego Durán described succinctly what he witnessed: "These bath houses can hold ten persons in a squatting position. The entrance is very low and narrow. People enter one-by-one and on all fours" (Bruchac 1993, 17).[12] And Friar Bernardino de Sahagún observed that ritual participants prayed and chanted as the temazkal "restored their bodies, their nerves. Those who are as if faint with sickness are there calmed, strengthened" (ibid.). According to Joseph Bruchac, "For the Aztecs, the vapor bath was the favorite remedy for almost every ill" (16).[13]

Despite the presence of the sweat bath in parts of ancient Europe, Spaniards and other western Europeans from the fifteenth to the eighteenth century believed that bathing and sinfulness went hand in hand. The emphasis on bathing that the native people valued appalled the colonizers throughout the Americas. Combined with their fear of native spirituality, this explains their efforts to eradicate ritual sweating, which was a form of cleansing and praying.

The banning of the sweat bath in "New Spain" for native peoples, beginning in the sixteenth century, proved devastating to their spiritual and physical well-being. Bruchac cites a poignant example based on an interview with a Mayan elder called Tata Julian from the pueblo Todos Santos:

> In the college we had to bathe in cold water. I went to the chief and said, "Señor, it is the custom in my pueblo for the *naturales* to take sweat baths. Here there is no sweat bath. Will you give me permission to heat a little water for a bath?" He would not give me permission. After I had been there a year and six months, we all became sick with much *chor* [dysentery]. All of us were sick, sick every day. They gave us just tea; no coffee. Many *naturales* died. We became so weak that we could not walk. More and more of the *naturales* died. Then my thoughts went back to *Todos Santos*. I knew that if I did not escape I would never see my pueblo again. Señorita, as weak as I was, I escaped one night and I returned to my pueblo (1993, 20).

The pain and trauma experienced by this elder speak to the fragmentation that so many of our ancestors experienced as they were deprived of their traditions and ceremonia.

Spanish missionaries denounced sweat baths, and by 1873 the US government prohibited the tradition. Many native peoples in the United States lost the tradition over time; however, the Lakota managed to withstand colonizing forces waged against their sweat ceremony, inipi. During the Chicano and American Indian movements of the late 1960s and 1970s, the Lakota generously shared the tradition with other Americans, especially Chicanos/as who had lost knowledge of this medicine.

Xicanas in the Los Angeles area ran the temazcal or sweat ceremony that I participated in for fifteen years. We were trained in the Lakota tradition and had spiritual leaders from various traditions visit us over the years. Lakota, Mexica, Inuit, and Buddhist elders graced us with their presence and wisdom, sharing their ways and affirming our spiritual path. Our practice of the sweat ceremony remained Lakota at its foundation, but expressed Xicana cultural markers, because that is who we are.

When I enter the temazkalli and inipi on all fours and kiss the earth to ask permission to enter, I begin the return to my/our divine mother. Entering the temazkalli is re(entering) into the womb of the creative life source. Being enveloped by her warmth and immersed in the darkness of her womb enables us to purge ourselves of our burdens. Sitting in a circle in the darkness reminds us all of our inherent equality. It is a visceral returning to the unconditional love of the sacred mother and a return to our ancestors. Offering songs and prayers of thanksgiving to the four sacred cardinal directions of the universe, to the creator, and to one's ancestors opens the communication between the physical world and the spiritual realm. Prayers for one's personal needs and the needs of others are shared. The darkness of the womb frees us to pray openly, to share pain, sorrow, and joy. Many of us pray for our families, the world, and for specific help with our challenges. But gratefulness is always offered first before any divine assistance is requested. We express gratefulness for the ceremonia, for our ancestors who preserved the tradition oftentimes under great risk, or simply gratefulness for the day, for life, and for all of us who are present in the temazkal.

The lava rocks brought into the inipi embody the spirits of the ancestors. When the water is poured over them, they emit ancestral spirit and ancestral knowledge. The steam that is created offers the breath of the creator. Lakota Chief Lame Deer states, "The steam in essence is the Grandfather's breath combining together our prayers, the air, the water, the fire which is in the rocks, and our mother the earth" (Lame Deer and Erdos, unpublished manuscript, 2). The inipi ritual is divided into four parts or rounds coinciding with the four cardinal directions and the four stages in life. If a pipe carrier is present, the Lakota ceremony might include the sharing of the sacred pipe during the resting periods, particularly the third rest when the "door" of the sweathouse is opened.[14] The temazkal is often in two parts and the use of medicinal plants is more prevalent.

The process of sweating in the ceremony requires physical and emotional sacrifice. It is a process of letting go of one's fears, of working through material and temporal concerns. It is a process that requires trust, trust in one's creator, and trust in the ceremonial leader or water pourer. I have had the honor of being trained as a water pourer and I find that the responsibility requires love, respect, strength, intuition, flexibility, and humility. As water pourer, I lead in prayer, I invite the sharing of song, stories, or experiences, and I determine the pace of the ceremony based on the energies of the participants. It is a role that has challenged me tremendously, but at the same time gifted me with confidence and healing. When the ceremony is over, participants crawl out of the sweathouse, the womb, often feeling exhausted but at the same time reborn, renewed, purified, challenged, and fulfilled. "We rinse off and the sweat from our bodies is an offering of ourselves back to Mother Earth, who gave us life" (Lame Deer and Erdos 4). Sacrifice, reciprocity, and renewal underscore the dynamics of this purification ceremony.

Experiencing the temazkal has helped me to better understand the survival of Indigenous epistemology. Our interdependence is visceral and our relations with our *antepasados* come alive.

Pilgrimages Near and Far

Through Días de los muertos I also experience the interdependency between the living and the dead and my life is renewed and enlarged by this ancient Mesoamerican tradition. Since my mother, grandparents, sister, and father passed into the spirit realm I continue to call out for their help. Being present at most of their deaths gifted me with knowledge about how spirits travel. Hearing my name called out by my sister in the direction of her front door *after* her last breath convinced me that the dead do communicate with us and their conscious spirits do soar to other planes. I continue to receive guidance from my deceased loved ones. I continue to hear from my dead through signs, symbols, and spiritual mediums. The latter enables me to actually hear the conversations they wish to have with me. I feel their presence as we provide food and gifts for them at our domestic *ofrenda* and my daughter speaks her memories as we share a meal with our dead. Through stories we give life to the dead and in return we are renewed. Días de los muertos allows us to commune with our dead, a privilege our Indigenous ancestors knew so well.

My work as an academic provides me with many opportunities to travel in Mexico, Spain, and the Southwest, all my ancestral homelands. Some key experiences led me deeper into nepantla and enabled me to own the complexity of my spirituality and that of my Indigenous and mestizo ancestors.

Meeting with a Babalawo (a high priest of the Lucumí or Santería religion) in Cuba in 2002 affirmed the interactions I have with my dead. The Babalawo advised me to leave food out for my sister regularly, since she died feeling very hungry. Her spirit could enter our home if I left the window slightly open. Having not told the Babalawo anything about my sister, I was deeply moved by his advice, because my sister could not eat for six weeks prior to her passing.

My journey to stay in communication with the dead also took me on a pilgrimage to find the burial site of my maternal grandparents in Guadalajara, Mexico. Burial sites are sacred places because the bones of our ancestors reside there and hold their/our memories. This endeavor was filled with signs and guides along the way; not only did I find their tomb but also the crematorium for the poor where the ashes of my paternal grandmother lie. Reconstructing their deteriorating gravesite and commissioning a headstone for the *horno* holding the ashes of my *abuela* and those of nameless others fulfilled a family responsibility. Before my father's death he had not been able to provide a burial site for his mother. I was never told where she had been buried. Finding her remains and placing a marker with her name healed ruptured relationships between a mother, a son, and a granddaughter. My actions restored her and my father's dignity, and in return my heart was made whole.

This pilgrimage to Guadalajara also led me to the shrine of the first can-onized Mexican Catholic woman, nun, and nurse, Santa María de Jesús Sac-ramentado Venegas (1868–1959) or "Madre Nati," who healed impoverished and elderly people through her prayer and laying on of hands. As she was a relative of my traveling partner and dear friend Sybil Venegas, I benefited from firsthand knowledge about the healings Madre Nati provides. Sybil's grandchildren had been miraculously saved during a lightning attack that destroyed their home. Shortly after, Madre Nati appeared in dreamtime to their mother, Sybil's daughter. It was clearly a sign to assure her that her chil-dren and her life were being protected. We visited the shrine to Madre Nati at the hospital where she had healed. People from many regions in Mexico came and delivered *milagros* in thanksgiving for healings received. Mexican Catholics believe in miracles, in the intervention of the spirit world, in the care of the santos.

Madre Nati's life had been a testimony to her faith and to the divine work-ing through her. Her followers are now a testimony to a people's faith in the real possibility of healing through prayer. My prayers to Madre Nati always bring me guidance and protection. Placing her image on my home altar, lighting candles and sage offers a simple way to create space and time to give thanks, to ask for help, to feel at peace. Creating a shrine, an ofrenda for the santos and for the dead, brings ceremony and ritual into our lives.

Ceremony and ritual is about healing. As an individual participates in pri-vate or communal ritual, he/she experiences healing. The community experi-ences healing as well. If I am out of balance, my friends, my community can gather and pray for me, burn sage for me, sing over me, embrace me, and re-mind me who I am.[15] As Indigenous people, we do not exist separate from our communities or our families, but within them. Our challenge is how to main-tain balance between individual needs and communal needs. Strong, authen-tic, honest individuals make for strong and authentic communities.

A recent trip with Sybil to cycle in the Arizona desert led to an unexpected visit to Mission San Xavier de Bac in the Santa Cruz Valley, a bit south of Tucson. Established by the Franciscan Father Eusebio Kino in 1700 with the Tohono O'odham native people of the surrounding area, the mission sits like a white Mediterranean palace amid the toast-colored desert land. It turns out that the mission is a perfect blending of Moorish, Byzantine, and late Mexi-can Renaissance architecture. As we walked toward the edifice from the park-ing lot, I was comforted by the locals selling fried bread and tacos at makeshift stands. Once inside, we walked toward the front of the main church and I was completely awed by the native symbol system within and surrounding the main sanctuary. In the two side chapels adjoining the sanctuary I saw snake-skin imagery covering the walls from tile floor to high ceiling. I sat down in the side chapel and I quickly *felt* the serpent energy envelop me with its feminine wisdom and earth knowledge.

My mind began to race, for it was such a visceral experience of the creative agency within nepantla. The native artisans embedded their spirituality in the walls of this Christian sacred site and it was a clear coexistence of the symbol system, not a syncretism. From 1700 on in the Santa Cruz Valley of Tucson, Christianity shared the desert and was changed because of it. Although the artisans remain nameless, their voices speak through the sacred symbol of the snake. I wanted to tell Gloria Anzaldúa and hear her affirm the resistance of the Tohono O'odham in this desert temple.

As I sat longer I realized that the walls of the large *nichos* holding life-size santos were also covered with the snakeskin imagery and its energy moved my eyes upward to where, near the ceiling, a large round hole holds a sculpture of a female saint. Immediately, I remembered historical footage of the Hopi ceremonial snake dance that I had once seen. A sixteen-day ritual dance conducted in late summer required the ritual specialists to gather snakes from the fields in each of the four cardinal directions. The dancers then interacted with the snakes to entrust them with the prayers of the people and to ask them to carry their prayers to the spirits who bring rain for the crops. The dance also petitioned the spirits for protection from lightning shock, as snakes represent lightning. At the end of the lengthy ceremony, the snake dancers who had communicated with the snakes returned the reptiles to their snake holes.[16] From my nepantla perspective, the artisans placed the *santa* in the reconfigured snake hole and inscribed her with feminine snake energy. Just as their regional ancestors had done for generations, the missionized native artisans were communicating with the snake and its earth and sky knowledge, but now within the confines of the church building.

We continued on our journey to our planned destination, to the burial site of the Mexican curandera, Teresa Urrea, or La Santa Teresa de Cabora, in Clifton, Arizona. During graduate school I had become intrigued with the life of Teresa Urrea, and I had titled a research paper on her as "Healing Across Borders." As a daughter of a servant-class Indigenous (Tehuecan) mother and a middle-class mestizo father, Teresa had transcended the class and gender restrictions of prerevolutionary Sonora, Mexico. As a recognized healer who involved herself with the plight of the very poor, Teresa became the heroine of displaced Mayo natives in northern Mexico and the working poor. Her political commitments would push her into exile in the United States, where she was exposed to corrupt businessmen set on making a fortune off her healing abilities. Her social justice commitments remained strong among Mexicans in the United States, and eventually repercussions for her involvement in *Union Federal Mexicanos* in Los Angeles would force her into a more isolated life in the small copper-mining town of Clifton. Teresa continued to heal the working poor until she died from complications of tuberculosis at the age of thirty-three.[17]

Our arrival in Clifton took us back to an earlier time when wood-frame houses and small storefronts characterized the West. Surprisingly, the local cemetery was not easy to find, still less a marked gravesite with Teresa's name. Most surely we expected to find a shrine at the restored gravesite where it is reported that the scent of roses comes forth from the earth. Our search led us to a modern city hall and a Chicana administrator in the county recorder's office. Empathizing with our great interest in *La Santa*, this visible guardian angel/civil servant drove with us to the hidden cemetery and helped us to find the magical resting place of Teresa. Along the way, we learned how the townspeople are protective of her burial site for fear of possible exploitation and disrespect from outsiders.

Kneeling at the gravesite of this great *Mexicana* healer who had lived on both sides of the border and committed herself to bettering the physical, spiritual, and political struggles of the very poor touched and humbled us in a profound way. We offered sage and oranges to her spirit and watched an eagle soar overhead in the clear blue desert sky. Other devotees had left behind medals and rosaries in commemoration of their visit and their prayers. We both prayed in earnest that day. I asked for the healing of my mother-in-law, who remained in critical condition after enduring a brain aneurysm. It was hard to leave Teresa's resting place amid the tranquility of the desert mountains. The postcard photo I purchased of her with long, thick, black hair and a Victorian lace blouse now sits on my desk. I turn to her in prayer when I am in need of guidance, and I give thanks for the improved health of my mother-in-law. Both Teresa Urrea and Madre Nati have entered my life.

There are so many more experiences that have led me each time to a deeper encounter with the spirit world in our midst and thus a deeper understanding of myself in relationship. As I am not able to describe all of them in this essay, I will highlight another one that falls among the most profound: a journey to *España*, the fatherland, in 2004. Visiting Andalusia, or southern Spain, compelled me to confront the amazing complexity of my biological and spiritual *mestizaje*. Staying in Córdoba, the ancient capital city of Muslim Spain during the eighth to eleventh centuries, introduced me to just the surface of my hidden Arab, Jewish, and Iberian roots. Knowing that my paternal family name, Lara, could be traced back to a military family of Andalusia forced me to confront the contradictions of my existence. As mestizas, Chicanas emerge from the violent clash of cultures and people that confronted each other in Anáhuac, beginning in 1519 when the Iberians waged war first on the Mexica, then the Maya and the Inca, and all others who got in their way.[18]

Our history is usually presented in simple terms as white Spaniards versus brown Indigenous peoples. From my studies I knew that the story was more complex, involving mixed-race Spaniards, Africans, and Indigenous civil rivals. Being in the region of southern Spain where most of the conquistadors came from opened my eyes to the depth of the most refined Arab and Jewish influence on the culture and lineage of my Iberian forefathers and foremothers. Xicana/o mestizaje actually begins in Spain. Like an onion with many layers, our mestizaje goes much deeper than the simplified binary of Spanish and Indigenous.

Walking into the Mezquita, the seventh-century Great Mosque built by the caliph of Córdoba, Abd el-Rahman I, which at its peak was comparable to making a journey to Mecca in contemporary times, awed me in a way that has stayed with me. Countless hundred-foot-high arches supported by nearly nine hundred pillars (856 to be exact) towered above me, painted in a Moroccan red-striped pattern. The caliph had removed the columns from an ancient Visigothic basilica built over an earlier Roman temple. The diverse origin of these pillars explains the variety of stone on display: black onyx, grey granite, cream marble, and green jasper. How fitting for a city and a society that encouraged the interaction of its diverse population. Arab Muslims, Iberian Christians, and exiled Jews influenced each other in language, art, philosophy, literature, religion, and sex. According to María Rosa Menocal in *Ornament of the World* (2002), "Fruitful intermarriage among the various cultures and the quality of cultural relations with the *dhimmi* were vital aspects of Andalusian identity" (30).[19] The Mihrab, the sacred inner sanctuary within the Mezquita that held the Quran and possibly a relic of the prophet Muhammad, drew me in with its scallop-shaped dome adorned with intricate mosaics and golden tiles.

By 1236, the Iberian Christians took back control of Andalusia, and Córdoba began its decline from being the largest city and cultural/intellectual center of Europe. Emperor Charles V forced Christian *capillas* and icons into the architecture of the Mezquita and then tore down part of the mosque in order to build a cathedral inside. The Córdoban populace eventually stopped the destruction of this Islamic beauty and what remains is a jarring juxtaposition of Islam and Catholic Christianity within one sacred site. The tension and ultimate coexistence within the Mezquita speaks volumes to me of the same dynamics within the Xicana experience.[20]

One block from the Mezquita I entered into the Judería, the ancient Jewish neighborhood and came upon a small historic *sinagoga* where Jewish men and women would pray in separate quarters. I was struck by the visibility of the Jewish culture in the Spanish fatherland, a culture and a people whose contribution to my lineage has been completely hidden or, better said, denied. My stay in Córdoba has not let me forget that my spiritual and cultural mestizaje extends back to the rich soil, majestic sacred mountains, and highly developed (although stratified) civilizations of Mesoamerica, as well as to the magnificent mosques, humble synagogues, and refined (although patriarchal) cultures of the ancient Iberian peninsula.[21] Nepantla is where I was born and nepantla is where I remain.[22] More recently, nepantla has empowered me to learn from Tibetan Bon and Mexican shamans and experience deeper levels of healing for the layers of wounds I have carried.

Shamanic Healing and Learning From Masters

Three years ago I was invited to a weeklong retreat led by a Chinese American shaman of the Tibetan Bon tradition and a Mexican shaman of Kabbalistic and Indigenous traditions, both women. The experience transformed me, and I have continued the training. I am learning to work with energies, chakras, cleansings, spirit entities, the elements in nature, moon meditations, and much more and I am so grateful. Tibetan Bon has much in common with Mesoamerican Indigenous understandings of body, mind, and spirit. As the Indigenous religion of Tibet prior to the presence of Buddhism, Bon suffered the fate of most Indigenous religions around the globe. After the Chinese takeover of Tibet, training programs for Bon and Tibetan Buddhist monks began in India and Nepal. Both Tibetan traditions are now spreading throughout the world.

While it shares much in common with Tibetan Buddhism, Bon emphasizes being in relationship to the elements of nature and spiritual beings. In the words of Tenzin Wangyal Rinpoche, one of the first Bon monks to graduate outside of Tibet, and whose teachings I follow, the practices of the Bon tradition "enhance the quality of life, promote healing, and offer some protection from harm and illness. They can keep us alert rather than dull, relaxed rather than agitated. They can contribute to our health, vigor, and pleasure in life . . . However, the practices are most importantly used to develop spiritually. They change our perspectives about our relationships to the natural world and to our own experiences; they open and expand our views. And they support our meditation practices" (2002, xviii). I and other Xicanas have found this to be true.

Learning how to work with Reiki or spiritually guided life-force energy has also transformed my life and my ability to help others. As a healing practice given to humanity through the work of Doctor Mikao Usui in the nineteenth century and based on ancient knowledge in the sacred Hindu sutras, Reiki universal energy clears, balances, and aids in healing emotional, physical, and spiritual imbalances and ailments. However, according to Reiki principles, people must realize that healing requires the conscious decision to improve oneself, to take responsibility for examining one's life, take responsibility for healing, and take an active part in it.

As a Reiki practitioner, I integrate Reiki with *limpias* and blessings that I have learned from Mexican Indigenous traditions.[23] My healing practices embody nepantla, the middle space where diverse traditions and knowledge respectfully come together. Having the opportunity to share healing with others is a tremendous responsibility, one that I do not take lightly. What I have appreciated most from my teachers is their emphasis on working through one's ego so that the power that comes with healing does not become controlling or ego-centered power. I do not see myself as a healer, but as a Xicana on a path to learn how to live in balance in a chaotic world and how to share what I learn with others. My future vision is to study more deeply the intersections of eastern spiritual beliefs/practices with the southern spiritual beliefs/practices of ancient and living Mesoamericans.

Final Reflections: Chaos, Change, and Hope

These are dangerous and scary times. Recent legislative measures in Arizona drive home how much Mexicans and other brown people are still not wanted in this land of the brave and the free. Anti-immigration legislation and the banning of Mexican American studies and supposedly "subversive" texts like *Occupied America* by Rudy Acuña, *Ceremony* by Leslie Marmon Silko and *Pedagogy of the Oppressed* by Pablo Freire, all in the state of the saguaro cactus and with the motto, *"Ditat Deus"* or "God enriches," reveal the great contradictions in this country. As Professor Roberto Rodriguez of the University of Arizona points out,

> The mood here is not anti-immigrant. It is anti-Mexican. The racial profiling law has little to do with legalities; it is about the expressed targeting of red-brown indigenous peoples [those with] short, dark hair, dark eyes and red-brown skin. Spaniards are not at risk. . . . For years, those of us with red-brown skin have lived this reality anywhere along the U.S.-Mexico border. Nowadays, this anti-Mexican sentiment, under the veneer of anti-illegal immigrant fervor, is nationwide.
>
> This is about our bodies.
>
> This one is about our souls . . . it resembles the practices of the early European friars who deemed indigenous knowledge to be godless and demonic and destroy it completely (2010).

A collective and public spirituality is needed to resist these neocolonizing forces.

The United States continues to wage war in the Middle East, still remaining in Afghanistan where women and children suffer the most. The post-traumatic stress of returning US military men and women goes untreated. Despite warnings by the United Nations' Intergovernmental Panel on Climate Change, severe climate change, primarily due to human activity, is proving to have catastrophic consequences for the earth, its resources, and its inhabitants. Severe tornadoes, hurricanes, floods, and drought cause devastation across race and class divides, but the poor are most impacted. Public education for the youth of our working poor worsens at a deplorable rate. Teachers as well as students are pushed out due to lack of institutional support, low morale, and the threat of violence among other factors. A persistent recession, an unresponsive government, and an elite private sector exacerbate economic disparity, as the excess wealth of the rich increases alongside the homelessness of the working and unemployed poor. We live in dangerous and scary times.

Such chaotic times compel the just-hearted to balance the universe with critical organizing, good intentions, and good actions. Collectively we will make a difference and call humanity back to its original purpose. I look around and see my *colegas* working hard to educate our young people. Others are defending the rights of women and children, immigrants, and the working poor, and holding men accountable to respectful treatment of women. Our work gives me hope. Our work is our response to the chaos. We must take care of ourselves in the process. Nourish our spirits, find time to rest, time to create and appreciate art in all its forms, time to move our bodies, time to connect with the spirit world and the source of life/death within, among, and beyond. As Mexican curandera Estela Román orally teaches: "Each liberation that we receive is to prepare us for the next battle. We are constantly challenged. Do as much as we can in this life and pass it on to the next generation. We can enjoy life. There are times of peace and happiness, times of battle. We must know how to cleanse. Be open, humble and confident to help each other."[24]

As I complete this essay, I sit near Natural Bridges in Santa Cruz, California, where my daughter is now attending college. Raising children and seeing them out in the world on their own is truly a privilege and a sacred offering. This ancient rock formation along the shoreline is where Gloria Anzaldúa would often visit to reflect on her profound understandings. I am here communing with her spirit. Today the wind is gently blowing and cooling the warmth of the sun as the water crashes and embraces the stability of the rocks. All is in balance. Gracias Gloria for the paths you opened for us, gracias to my compañeras on this journey we call life, and as the Lakota tradition has taught me, *Mitákuye oyás' i*, all my relations, or *In Lak Ech, Tu Eres Mi Otro Yo,* You are my other self. We are all connected through spirit.

Notes

1. I have come to understand from eastern teachings that nonduality or an inherent wholeness exists behind what appears as differences or complementary opposites. The goal of "awakening" is to realize this wholeness in all that exists, the deepest meaning of "In Lak'ech."

2. I intentionally use "deeper power/mystery" rather than the common term "higher power." "Higher power" holds on to a hierarchical model of sacred energy and implies that this power is only beyond the human. "Deeper power" implies a power beyond, among, and within us, which is ultimately a great mystery.

3. For further discussion, see López Austin 1988.

4. I use the plural of *día* to emphasize the numerous days of preparation and celebration that are all part of the ritual and ceremony of honoring our dead in the Mexicano/Xicano tradition.

5. For further elaboration see Medina 2006; 2011.

6. I think the Coatlicue state can also be understood as the conflict that we unconsciously bring upon ourselves as a way to protect us from facing what is in need of transformation in our lives. I highly recommend Tenzin Wangyal Rinpoche (2011; 2012) for teachings and meditations to transform conflicts in body, mind, and heart.

7. See García-Rivera 1995 for a scholarly treatment of the saint.

8. The intent of my prayer is to name the divine mother, sanctify the fruits of women's bodies that emerge from our wombs, and honor the reality of death.

9. My first lessons in the sweat ceremony were from Lakota sister Jeanine Antoine, Xicana sisters Linda Vallejo, Patricia Parra, and Raquel Salinas, Xicano brother Steve Delgadillo, and other women in the Corazon family who maintained a sweat lodge for twenty years on Patricia's property in Highland Park, California. This sweat lodge was started by CinD Honesto and passed on to Patricia after CinD's battle with cancer and premature death in 1990.

10. Much of this discussion takes place orally, but there is a reference to it in Torres 2003, 193 n.101.

11. There are other kinds of sweathouses in the Americas, varying according to the ethnicity, tradition, region, and natural resources available. The Lakota inipi and the Mexican temazcalli are the most widely used today in North America. "Temazcalli" in Nahuatl means bathhouse or sweathouse. *"Tema"* means "to bathe" and *"calli"* means "house." See Bruchac 1993 and Bucko 1998.

12. For a study on contemporary efforts to preserve and document the temazcal in Mexico see Sánchez Morales 2003. I am grateful to my friend Steve Delgadillo for bringing this project to my attention.

13. The practice of sweating also thrived in ancient Europe, specifically among the Greeks, Romans, Scythians (who inhabited present-day Russia), Slavs, Scandinavians, and Celts, and also in the Arab world, ancient Japan, and parts of Africa. The Russian, Scandinavian, and African sweat traditions, in particular, had physical and spiritual therapeutic properties, as does the northern and southern Indigenous American sweat bath (Bruchac 1993).

14. The pipe is an extremely sacred object and is used "to remember the White Buffalo Cow Woman, and serves as a medium of purification and prayer" (Bucko 1998, 55). This holy woman appeared to the Lakota Sioux and gave them the sacred pipe, seven sacred rites, and knowledge about the sacredness of the buffalo and of women. The mythology of White Buffalo Cow or Calf Woman is recounted in Black Elk ([1932] 1979, 3–5). Also see St. Pierre and Long Soldier (1995, 38–42).

15. The theater production "New Fire," by Cherríe Moraga and Celia Rodriguez Herrera, authentically represents the healing power of ceremony. This play as ritual theater, performed at the Brava Theater in San Francisco in 2012, reflects Xicana spiritual consciousness as a way of life.

16. See Hirschfelder and Molin (1992, 270–71). For a historical photograph of a ceremonial snake dance, see Flaherty (1992, 50–51).

17. This very brief synopsis of Teresa Urrea's life is based on a collection of articles and primary documents. See Perales (2005) for one of the most insightful essays about Urrea's political activism and spiritual commitments.

18. "Anáhuac" is a Nahuatl term referring to the lands that the ancient Nahua inhabited. It is derived from the word "Anáhuatl," meaning ring. These ancient Mexicans believed that the earth was a large wheel or ring completely surrounded by divine waters. According to León-Portilla, early historians of Mesoamerica erroneously interpreted the central part of the present Republic of Mexico as the plateau of Anáhuac. In reality, "Anáhuac" referred to all of the land situated between the two oceans ([1963] 1990, 48).

19. In Arabic, "Dhimmi" meant the protected "Peoples of the Book," and referred to Jews and Christians who share Abrahamic monotheism and written scripture.

20. Controversy over the use of this sacred space continues, as Spanish Muslims protest for the right to pray within the Mezquita. Spanish Catholics fear a Muslim takeover or taking back of the shrine. What appears as religious coexistence belies contemporary cultural fragmentation (Wilkinson 2007).

21. For a similar reflection see, Martinez (2001). Also see Avila (1999).

22. I am inspired here by Anzaldúa's statement "I was born and live in that in-between space, *nepantla*, the borderlands" (1993, 114).

23. Estela Román, a Mexican *curandera*, has also been one of my trainers. See Román (2012).

24. Stated at a training session. Los Angeles, June 2011.

PART FOUR

The South

The Direction of Youth

Finally, we turn to the South, the place of the earth and the direction associated with children and youth. A number of contributors in this section write about their childhood memories and reflect on their experiences as youth from the vantage point of adulthood. They, like other contributors, remind us that we were all children once, playful, curious, with brilliant ideas, visions, and answers as well as wounds in need of healing. As the biological or cultural ancestors of the generations that follow, they share their stories and their gathered insights to also remind us that we as a society are responsible for all children, for teaching our youth. What will our legacy be?

We introduce this section with a poem by Sarahi Nuñez-Mejia, written soon after she graduated from college. "The Woman Within" describes a *conocimiento* process shared by many young women coming to consciousness during these years, particularly about their sexuality. She courageously takes us back to a dark, painful past; a past determined to obliterate the sexual and subsequently the spiritual woman within herself. Nuñez-Mejia reminds us of the critical interconnectedness between our sexuality and spirituality, and how each one of us must seriously interrogate our sexuality to heal and transform into our spiritual selves.

In her *autohistoria* "Creosote and Lavender," Angelita Borbón recounts her childhood as one grounded in an understanding that spirituality and identity evolve from one's relationship to the land, which in her case is the Sonoran Dessert. As she writes, "I remember my Tata's words, *'Tu eres el desierto porque eres de la Gente Original. Tu responsibilidad es cuidar al desierto, cuidar al Pueblo.'* I am a descendent of the Original People of this desert who have been buried here for centuries and *I am the desert*" (193–94). In one sweep, Borbón's creative personal narrative links her childhood remembrances as a formative time of spiritual inquiry with the embodiment of a land-based identity, reminding us that we all are responsible for taking care of the earth, which is to say, each other.

In "Coming Full Circle," Beatriz Villegas/Ilhuicatlahuili-Bea traces her spiritual path from childhood through various moments in her life story on both sides of the US-Mexico border, leading to her present role as a respected ceremonial leader in Chicano Indigenous communities. She begins her *testimonio* with haunting memories of being a child seeking God in the midst of violence, and takes her readers through a recounting of the spiritual and social challenges she faced as a Christian woman. Villegas traces "coming full circle" from the four-year-old who recognized the spirit world as her companion, to her work in the Christian Church in Texas and throughout Mexico, and back to her *curandera* grandmother's native spiritual roots, which Villegas has reclaimed as her own as an Indigenous woman.

Norma Cantú's essay, "Living La Vida Santa: My Chicana Spirituality and Activist Scholarship," mirrors our early reference to walking the red road. Her essay begins with a discussion of walking the ancient pilgrimage route, *el Camino de Santiago*, also known as *el camino francés*. During this walk, we can say that Cantú engaged in fleshing the red road; more specifically, as she notes, she came to know deeply that "every step along life's journey is indeed a step along a spiritual path" (202). The physical challenges Cantú encountered on el Camino de Santiago are significant in clarifying and informing her spirituality. Many times, physical challenges represent the obstacles we need to confront in order to maintain our spiritual *caminos* or walking of the red road. Cantú describes incidents from childhood to her present life that involve dreams, shift-changing, reincarnation, "soul traveling," and meditation. Drawing from Anzaldúa, these metaphysical energies and spaces contribute to spiritual imaginaries, which in this case, have influenced Cantú's scholarly work and academic activist position.

This direction and our anthology as a whole conclude with Patrisia Gonzales's contribution, "Anatomy of Learning: *Yauhtli, Peyotzin, Tobacco,* and *Maguey.*" This essay explores hidden texts of Indigenous medicinal knowledge in Gonzales's life story as an apprentice with Nahua *curanderos* and *parteras* and in her personal struggle to conceive a child. She connects or relates the pre-Columbian past to her present through storytelling and narratives regarding plants used today in birthing, and how they were recorded in inquisitorial efforts more than five hundred years ago. She offers the knowledge of the elders and oral tradition as a method equal to textual evidence to show the persistence of Mesoamerica in the lives of Indigenous peoples, including that of Chicanas and Mexicans who are spiritually undocumented Indigenous peoples.

The Woman Within

Sarahi Nuñez-Mejia

I remember that past and see the dark
I feel the screams and they don't stop
Lonely in fright I sense the dread
Confusion spreading through my head
Alone in chaos I tend to feel
I see the people yet don't sense them real
I fear to glimpse that disheartening past near
Which boils me up, I shed a tear
Alone I touch my hate that when it comes
It pumps my veins and scars my heart
I pray to God my wound to heal
I think God is deaf so I won't kneel
Then life showed me to let the past be
To heal myself and move within
To accept my spirit, and let the essence show
How to absolve the hatred and mend the soul
I had to forgive the people in my past
And I found that scars don't need to last
I understood I needed to unconventionally pray
And realized God was never in my way
In the dark no more, my love now shone
I discovered a spirituality I should have known
I began to grasp all it contained
Such as the flesh, body and soul it maintained

I see the world now; I am free to smile
I took a step towards spirituality's forbidden mile
By realizing that by itself it cannot win
Spirituality and sexuality intertwine without sin
Lifting confusion and dimming shameful tears
It erased resentment and released unseen fears
I began to understand the woman within
As maturity blossomed and my soul began to live
Alone I now know I'll never be
Now that I've found the person that is me
I understand I'm a sexual spiritual soul
As the woman within me continues to grow

Creosote and Lavender

Angelita Borbón

Creosote and lavender grow in my garden. I planted the lavender when my mother died. The creosote bush has been here since the Original People walked this desert and smelled her perfume after the rain. It is an ancient memory and this morning as I water my grandson's squash plant, I smell the rains he will know and I remember.

My first memory is the sound of a woman sobbing, wailing muffled *llantos al cielo*. I recognize the origin of that canto when I make those same sounds walking in a sandy arroyo looking for solace and reason: looking for my child lost in a silent hemorrhage. I feel alone but I know that I am not. Other women have walked this way before me. I follow their footsteps and cry for help. *Llorona, ayudame.* Heavy drops of rain fall from the dark sky crying for me *y me desahogo* and I am calm. The smell of creosote nourishes me and connects me to this desert of my birth and birthing and to my mother, Socorro Casanova Veliz.

She met my father in Copper Creek, a mining camp high in the Galurio Mountains. They married and moved to El Tigre, a village of red hills where they had two daughters, Marta Elena and Norma Gloria. My father wanted a son but my mother was happy with two daughters. There was a miscarriage, then another, and finally twin males stillborn just one year before my birth.

My mother grieved the ten lunar months of my gestation. This time she would not birth at home. In fact it appeared she might not birth at all. Two weeks past her time, and still she had no signs of my birth. So the company doctor made her go to Saint Mary's Hospital in Tucson. Fifty-five years later, before she died, she gave me the white pearl rosary she held in her hand praying in the car all the way into town. Praying in the room while they got her ready. Praying that she would not get sick if she ate the hospital food they gave her for dinner. Praying to the ancient ones still there in the shadows of Tumamoc Hill. I was born an hour later. Another girl.

After I was born my mother became very quiet. Most mornings she would sit at the kitchen table drinking coffee and staring out the window at the road on the hill. Every once in a while someone would walk by. I liked the view out the back door better. There was a giant saguaro with two big arms. He was my friend. My other friends were Rusty the dog who was half coyote, Pokey the tortoise who only showed up when he wanted to, and the noisy ravens on top of the neighbors' roof.

Rusty got rabies, so my dad had to shoot him. I stood on the kitchen table and looked out my mother's window. She tried to stop me from watching but my screaming was so loud that she had to let go of me and cover her ears. She left the room. I saw it all and when my dad entered the kitchen I could smell his rifle. He explained what would have happened if Rusty had bitten someone. He was protecting us by killing Rusty, he said. He was protecting the health of the People.

I did not cry. I dug a hole in the front yard with my father's pick and shovel and filled it with water. I put rocks around the edges and little branches of creosote in the water. Then I took off my clothes except for my *calzones* and got in the big puddle I had made. I extended my legs out straight and put my belly on the bottom. I kept my head up by leaning on my elbows. I called Pokey with my mind and I waited. I did this for days and finally on the day before my fifth birthday the tortoise finally came into our yard. He stayed a long time and was good company for me.

My mother's older sister, Hortensia Dunn, came to visit during this time. She thought El Tigre should build a swimming pool like the ones in Los Angeles, so that I would not have to swim in a puddle. I had heard my older sisters saying Tia Tencha lived in Hollywood and that was really far away. One morning my mother dressed me in good clothes instead of the play clothes I always wore. My Tia Tencha called me into the kitchen and with great ceremony she pinned a Miraculous Medal of the Virgin on my white blouse. It was hanging on a little gold safety pin with a pink satin ribbon tied in a bow. "This will protect you," she said. My mother nodded her head and looked pleased.

I went outside and sat in a chair wondering why I had to wear a skirt just to get a medal. The ravens were up on the roof making loud noises and hopping around. I wondered what they were saying. The neighbor had been fixing his cooler the day before and I saw that he had left the ladder leaning against the house. I decided to test my Miracle Medal. I climbed the ladder and stepped on to the roof. The ravens turned and when they saw me they started hopping all around. They were really funny and made me laugh out loud. Then they went to the corner of the house I could see from my front yard and one by one they flew away. I walked slowly around the roof looking at the cooler with the missing pads and the various pipes sticking out of the tarpaper roofing. I found two baseballs and threw them into the yard below. I ended up on the raven corner. I moved closer and closer to the edge until I could see straight down. I felt a wind blowing my skirt and a wind blowing at my back. I put my arms out like wings and I flew away. I landed on my hands and knees and rolled down the hill. Blood ran down my legs and into my socks. My hands were burning with pain and little rocks and sticks were embedded in the raw flesh.

I walked to the kitchen door and kicked it hard. I tried to pull the useless medal off my blouse and got blood everywhere. My mother opened the door and stared at me. I tugged at the medal, "This thing does not work," I told her. Then I told her what I had done. She picked me up and said, "What is wrong with you?" My Tia Tencha came over to see who was there and when my mother told her the story, she looked at me and the medal she had given me and proclaimed, "It is a miracle! *Es un milagro* she did not die. *La virgencita* saved her."

I spent the rest of the day waiting for my father to come home and letting my mother put plasters of herbs and ointments on my wounds. I did not speak. My mother greeted my father with, "Guess what your daughter did today?" He listened to the story with Tia Tencha's chorus of "Es un milagro. Es un milagro." Then he went to shower and change his clothes like he always did. Later he came into my room smiling and commenting on my serious face. "That medal does not work," I told him, and I extended my bandaged hands and legs out as evidence. He laughed so much that I started to laugh too. He decided that it was time for me to spend more time with my *Tata*. My Tata Rafael was the *leñero* in El Tigre, so I would help him gather firewood in the desert. I would also help him with the goats, and Tata would teach me everything that I needed to know.

That night I lay in bed listening to the baseball game with the others. The house was dark and the radio broadcast could be heard clearly in every room of our little house. I felt happy and more grown up that night.

I did not spend much time with my mother after that, because I left for my Tata's house right after breakfast and came home just in time for dinner. My father was right. Tata taught me everything I needed to know. In the desert gathering firewood I learned about plants and animals and I learned that I am the desert. I remember my Tata's words, *"Tu eres el desierto porque eres de la Gente Original. Tu responsibilidad es cuidar al desierto, cuidar al Pueblo."* I am a descendent of the Original People of this desert who have been buried here for centuries and *I am the desert*. My Tata told me that my responsibility is to take care of the desert and to help the People survive. He told me I would never be alone and he would always be with me even when he was gone from this time.

We played the Mexican card game *Kunkian* in the afternoon and I never won because my Tata played to win and he was a very good player. The playing cards came from Spain and each card was covered with beautiful drawings. He taught me about wine and sometimes in the evening before I went home he gave me a tiny little glass of port so I could drink with him.

My Tata never rushed. He was a very thoughtful man of few words. He showed me the virtue and beauty of working hard in balance and harmony with the cosmos. We walked together in a sacred way all the time without religion or medals. He was right. He never has left me. Even when the mining company forced us to tear down our houses and leave our orchards and gardens because their mineral rights superseded our property rights and El Tigre became a ghost town half buried by slag from the mine. Even when my father decided we would move to Tucson and he would drive forty miles to work in San Manuel so that my oldest sister Marta could go to the university. He has never left me because he is the desert. He speaks to me in the wind on my face and the colors of the sunset, and the smell of wet creosote.

His daughter, my mother Socorro, speaks to me now in the fragrance of herbs and spices and lavender and pearls and card games played to win. However, most of her life I was desert mud and rock hard caliche and screams against injustice. Kicking on back doors to get inside to testify and provide evidence that it was in fact true that the People were dying of unnatural causes. She did not understand me and would wonder out loud, "What is wrong with you?" Towards the end of her life she was able to accept my passion but still worried about me, especially because I never learned to cook. "What do you eat?" She would ask. Her domain was the heart of our home. She was *La Reina del Corazón de Nuestro Hogar*. All kitchens belonged to my mother.

On her deathbed, we understood each other perfectly without words. At her graveside, we sang "La Barca de Oro." *Adiós, mujer, adiós para siempre adiós*. I covered her coffin with fresh garlic, *chilitipines* and oregano mixed with rose petals and lavender and pearls. My sister Joni slipped a deck of Spanish playing cards into the grave as her coffin was being lowered.

Every Christmas when my grandson and I make cookies I wear one of her aprons. Hanging on a strand of freshwater pearls she would have loved, I wear the silver Hopi hand with a hummingbird and I remember her saying, "If it was mine, I would wear it every day." She was her father's daughter, a descendent of the Original People, and she is the desert in pearls and lavender.

Coming Full Circle

Beatriz Villegas/Ilhuicatlahuili-Bea

I do not like Wednesdays. I will never forget the terrifying experiences of every Wednesday night at my grandmother's house where I lived from the ages
of three to seven; I would be in the middle of my bed holding my one-year-
old brother Joel, waiting for my uncle Fernando. He would come into the
house just to scare me to death by crawling on his hands and knees, high-
heeled shoes on his hands making horrifying noises. Hours later, another
uncle, mi tio Natividad, would come in drunk, shouting, "Orphans, your
mother will never come back!" Then he would start molesting me. I prayed
every night for these things to stop. Then, one night when my uncle Fernando was asleep, a spirit dragged him by his feet all the way to the driveway.
He was so terrified that he stopped scaring me for a little while. There was no
one, no relative to turn to except for God and he answered my prayer by sending this spirit to help me. This affirmed to me that there is a Creator with
spirit helpers and a place where we will go after we leave this earth. Not too
many things changed after that, but ever since I was four years old the spirit
world has been my companion, my strength, and my guiding light.

My name is Beatriz Villegas, but my friends call me Bea, and, more recently, Ilhuicatlahuili-Bea. I was raised by my grandmother in Torreón, Coahuila, México, from the time I was three until I was seven. My grandmother,
Guadalupe Garcia Flores Rebolledo, a matriarch in all senses of the word,
was a strong woman of great faith and strong will. My grandmother's origins
explain her strength. My *abuela* Guadalupe was a Mexica *curandera* (healer)
Indian from Malinalco (better known as Chalma, Estado de México), an
enchanted place where the Mexica "Ninjas" were trained for war. My abuela

was abducted from her village by a Victoriano Huerta *guerrillero* during the Mexican Revolution. After the revolution, my *abuelos* moved to Torreón, a city that for many years I thought was where my family originated.

My grandmother had three sons and three daughters. Once, her youngest daughter Rafaela got very sick. Having no family and being so young, my grandmother had no one to turn to for help. She had heard of Baptist missionaries who prayed for the sick, so she went to them. They prayed for her daughter and she was healed. Out of gratitude, my grandmother adopted the Baptist religion. My abuela, being so eager to learn about this new religion, prayed for a miracle, the ability to read the Bible. As soon as she opened the holy book, she learned how to read and taught herself how to write as well. My grandmother was in her late thirties when my grandfather left her with six children and no financial income, but she supported the family with hard work, always teaching her children to live according to the Bible. Her example and guidance gave me the foundations to be spiritual and to be a tool in God's hand in helping others. At this age I really did not know about the native spirituality of this land, but I did discern that if you believed in God, the Great Spirit, he could help me as he helped my *abuela* to magically learn to read. Later I would learn how the Creator and his spirits can guide you to help people with their needs.

I was four years old when I had a vision of a spirit. I was on my way to the outside bathroom when I saw a young boy. There was a full moon, so everything was very clear to me. He was a teenager wearing overalls and a white shirt. He was trying to tell me something, but my fear was so great that I ran screaming and crying to my bedroom, jumping into the bed. My grandmother tried to console me when she noticed that I was burning with fever. The fever continued for weeks. She took me to the doctor, but the fever continued until my grandmother decided she was going to cure me the way her own Indigenous grandmother had taught her. Kneeling, she first prayed to God, asking for forgiveness for what she was about to do. Even though Christians had told her that *curanderismo* was evil and that she should never practice the gifts that she had, this was a matter of life and death. So she went to the market and bought a piece of *piedra lumbre* (fire rock). She took the rock and passed it over my body as she prayed. She then put it on the lighted coals where she used to make her tortillas. The rock on the fire started to take the shape of the young boy that I had seen. I got well, and after that, I continued to see spirits, some that I acknowledged and others that I preferred not to.

When I turned seven, I went to live with my mother in Ciudad Juarez, Chihuahua, which is El Paso, Texas's Mexican border city. She had married an Anglo from Fort Bliss, Texas. At this time I learned from my stepfather about racial prejudice; white was the color of supremacy, even though he was an alcoholic and a wife beater, and he did not provide for his family. The Mexica blood running through my veins made me stand up strong to him to defend my race and family. During this time with my mother, I did not have any apparitions or experiences with spirits, but I did have many nightmares and sleepwalking experiences. My mother had to lock the door from the inside so I would not leave the house.

My recollections of this time are mainly those of childhood activities. For example, I remember playing that I was a priest and the other children were my parishioners. I knew the Bible stories by heart and I would relate them to my friends. I would offer them little pieces of *piloncillo* and other Mexican candies as bribes so they would come to hear my sermon. At the end of my sermon, *los rociaba con agua*. Pretending it was holy water, I would sprinkle water on them as a blessing. They endured my sermons and antics in order to get the candy, but they also listened. To this day I still have some of these childhood friends.

At the age of sixteen, I went to La Buena Tierra, a Bible school in Saltillo, Coahuila, México. It was as if I wanted to run away from the gringo, my stepfather, and Anglo influences. I wanted to keep my Mexican culture and I stayed there for three years. From there, I went to the Instituto Evangelístico de México, a Christian seminary in Mexico City, where I earned a Bachelor's Degree in Christian Education. I served the Church of God for ten years as a missionary. During those years at the Instituto, I also interned with Wycliffe Bible Translators, translating the New Testament into different Indigenous dialects. I stayed with different Mexican Indigenous people, such as the Otomi in Puebla, the Tarasco in Michoacán, and the Rarámuri in Chihuahua.

During those internships, I experienced and witnessed healings and *limpias* done through ritual and prayer by the curanderos or *"brujos"*—the healers of the village, both male and female. A limpia is a cleansing of the aura with herbs to bring balance to one's energy. The missionaries used to scold me for spending time with the *"brujos" y "brujas" del pueblo*. They used to ask me if I was afraid of them, because they believed that they were capable of putting a curse on people. I would respond with "are not we serving the God almighty?" followed by the affirmation from the Bible, "If God is for us, who can be against us?" (Romans 8:31). During these times with the different Indigenous groups, I came to realize that my path was the ancestors' traditional ways and culture of this continent, *Ixachilatlan*. The rituals were not new to me, but part of me. I initially resisted these beliefs because of the evangelical religion that I professed at this point in time.

I did continue serving successfully in the evangelical church as a leader, a teacher, and as an instructor at La Buena Tierra Bible School. When I returned to Ciudad Juarez, I served as a pastor for two years and married an evangeli-cal minister. I moved to El Paso with my husband, and we had a booming ministry working with drug addicts at Victory Outreach. I gave birth to a beautiful daughter, Abigail Itzel ("Mist" in Mayan) whom I love dearly. After five years of marriage, we divorced because he was unfaithful and a poor provider.

According to Church rules, a divorced person, especially a female, could not minister in the Christian Church. I was angry at the double standard and even angrier when I learned that they had made a special dispensation so my ex-husband could continue as a minister. He received help from the Church, but I, the woman and mother of our child, did not receive any support. Since the Church had been my only source of income, I had to start a new career in order to support my daughter. My ex-husband never offered any economic help until the day he died.

At the age of thirty, I enrolled in El Paso Community College (EPCC) to learn the English language so I could find a job. During my first work-study employment at the college I met Carlos Aceves, with whom I had many con-versations about our Indigenous culture and the native ways of Ixachilatlan, the Valley of Aztlan. As we came to understand the *Tonalpohualli*, known as the Aztec calendar or the count of the days, the Nahuatl words that I had learned during my missionary internships all came back to me. Carlos was my first teacher in the *Mexicayotl*. After Carlos, I had many other teachers and spiritual guides like Tlacaelel, Acacio, and a very special lady, my En-glish instructor at EPCC, Teresa Duran. Ms. Duran was keenly aware of all things around her; she could hear the softest voice or slightest movement in the room when no others could. I believe she saw something special in me as well and so asked me to help with her healing. She guided me in the prayers and herbs needed for her recovery from a skin ailment that doctors had not been able to help her with before. She also mentored me with my academics and now we are very close friends.

In 1984 Carlos Aceves, myself, and many others founded *Kalpulli Tonal Teokalli* (House of the Creator), a Nahuatl Mexica community in El Paso. I was an active member of the *Kalpulli Tonal Teokalli* for twenty years, and now I am an active member of *Kalpulli Tlalteca*. Throughout all these years, I have hosted many ceremonies in my house, teaching our young ones to be proud of the legacy of our ancestors. I have a sweat lodge made of adobe where I conduct healing sweats and celebration sweats. My daughter and I started practicing the Mexica *danzas*, a dance to the beat of the drum in har-mony with our heartbeats to develop one heartbeat with Mother Earth. We are also part of the Sun Dance, a ceremony that consists of four days of fast-ing and praying from sunrise to sundown. As women we dance to support the warriors, the men. During the ceremony the men pierce their skin as an offering and in some communities the women do so as well. Our elders have taught us that women give their offering to Mother Earth through childbirth, so it is not necessary for us women to offer such pain. We are there to support the Sun Dancers with our prayer, fast, and dance. The Sun Dance creates such powerful energy that even a person who is attending as a visitor will undergo a positive change.

I did not have to learn these ways; they were embedded in my DNA. At my first Sun Dance, my daughter Itzel (who was eight years old at the time) and I went to the magical Malinalco. When we arrived at the small village, I saw children playing and two ladies waving at me. These two women, an old one and a younger one, seemed familiar to me for some reason or another. In order to get to where the Sun Dance was taking place, we had to climb a mountain that is called "la Montaña de las Aguilillas," Eagle Mountain. At the Sun Dance, I had visions of giants, and the eagles came to visit us every day. When I returned home, I visited my grandmother in Ciudad Juarez and told her of my experiences at the place that we had visited, Malinalco. She started crying and said, *"Esa es mi tierra, el pueblo en que naci"* ("That is my home town, the place where I was born").

There are no words to describe my feelings when I heard my grandmother's words. I found it inspiring that for my first Sun Dance I had gone to the place of my ancestors, the place where my grandmother was born. I also described to my grandmother the two ladies who waved to me. My grandmother told me that they were her mother and her grandmother who had been *curanderas* and her role models. Once again it was clear to me that I was following the right path, that my spirituality was not only in the Christian Church and that my life continued to be in God's hands.

At the present time, I have two grandsons, to whom I have given Mexica names. I am so grateful to my son-in-law Rick and my daughter Itzel, who agreed to the suggestion and loved the names that I gave them. The oldest, Elias Kuatonal (Solar Eagle), is fifteen, and the younger one, Nathaniel Ozelotl (Jaguar), is twelve; both follow the red path of respect and honor creation. My grandsons love the danzas and ceremonies; both had their tepee ceremonies when they were born. As Mexica, we have adopted the Northern Plains Indian tepee for use in some ceremonies, such as the naming and medicine ceremonies. It offers great shelter from the southwestern wind and desert sun. Elias can play all types of drums beautifully and often is asked to drum at our traditional ceremonies.

Also, at Hueco Tanks, here in El Paso, where we conduct many of our ceremonies, Elias Kuatonal was named the youngest warrior with the staff of the North, the eagle, by Gustavo Gutierrez, and with the staff of the South, the condor, by Francisco Melo, spiritual leaders of the Peace and Dignity Run. These Peace and Dignity Runs are intercontinental journeys that are conducted every four years to honor Native peoples' resistance to and survival of invasion, colonization, and genocide. I was one of the coordinators for the first Peace and Dignity Run in 1992, and throughout the years, I have been a faithful supporter of this ceremony.

I am recognized as the grandmother of Sun Dance in my community, and even when people meet me for the first time they feel comfortable calling me *abuelita*, grandmother. With this name I feel respected and loved. I am a holder of three sacred pipes: the Sun Dance pipe, the Grandmother Sun Dance pipe, and the Moon Dance pipe. I pour water in the sacred sweat lodges (*temaskal*) for the community and I am the founder of the Moon Circle, a group that empowers women with the Native American ways of the Moon, Coyolxauhqui, and the female side of Tonalpohualli. I have been entrusted to lead naming ceremonies, coming-of-age ceremonies, vision quests and traditional marriages. I do not call myself curandera, healer, or teacher although I have been given those titles by my community.

In October 2008 I did my first Moon Dance, Xochimeztli, with the *Abuela*, grandmother Tonalmitl at the pyramids of Teotihuacán in Mexico City. Tonalmitl is the one who gifted me with the name Ilhuicatlahuili, which means *Luz del Cielo* and is my destiny in a sense according to Mexica knowledge traditions documented in the Codex Borgia. The Moon Dance is a dance lasting four days from sundown to sunrise, each day beginning and ending with a sweat lodge. The women are so strong. The altitude and the cold harsh weather are hard on me. During my first years of participating, at times I thought I would not be able to finish my dance. As the night takes its course, we experience the magic of the unity of all the women: more than 250 dancers, all of us wearing the same white dress, making it hard to recognize anyone or make any distinctions because we all are one. When we dance, we are making a prayer with our feet, song, and spirit. If we are having a difficult time, the soft touch of my sisters to the right or to the left breathes life into me to continue. Also there are some men outside the circle supporting their duality (wife or girlfriend) by saying words of encouragement. Most of those men are also the fire keepers for all four days of the danza. The Moon Dance is a supernatural experience; the understanding that comes, knowing your self is out of this world.

After I go home, I still hear Abuela Tonalmitl saying, "*tiahui cihuas*," or "*movimiento mujeres*," "women are strong" in the middle of night. I have finished my first commitment—four years of Moon Dance—and grandmother Tonalmitl gave me a new name that I love: *Ilhuicatlahuili-bea*, which means "sky light." I will continue attending the Moon Dance every year of my life.

As Abuela Xöchicuamatzin teaches, *"En las noches de luna llena, las estrellas guardan su brillo para escuchar el canto nocturno de la luz blanca. Es entonces cuando las mujeres se entregan al movimiento armónico integrándose a la danza con el universo entero."* ("On full moon nights, the stars save their shine in order to listen to the white light's nocturnal song. It is then that the women devote themselves to the harmonious movement, integrating themselves to la danza with the whole universe." Co-editor Irene Lara's translation.)

I am honored to be the grandmother of the Sun Dance. I am recognized as an elder because of my age and experience in the traditional ways and the ceremonies that I have lived, learned, and experienced. It is my turn to pass this on to those who seek the traditional path. Most Native societies are matriarchal and in our Mexica ways women play a huge role in the ceremonies. We believe in duality. We are the keepers of the sacred fire. We conduct ceremonies and play an equal role. This is the way nature intended it to be and this is what we try to share. In December 2012 I was elected Tecutli (main representative, responsible for the Kalpulli Tlalteca as a whole).

I do feel that I have come full circle, the circle my grandmother—matriarch, a proud Indigenous woman who was taken from her village—began, but could not end. The circle I accept and embrace. The circle where I found respect, peace, and honor. I walk this path according to what the Great Spirit wants me to be because I have a life to share. Our philosophy as Natives of this continent is that we humans are one with creation.

Que su Luna sea brillante y sus sueños enseñanzas.

Living La Vida Santa

My Chicana Spirituality and Activist Scholarship

Norma E. Cantú

Walking the Path

On December 17, 2010, I began walking the ancient pilgrimage route, *el Camino de Santiago*, or *el camino francés*, as that route is known, from Saint-Jean-Pied-de-Port in France to Santiago de Compostela in northern Spain.[1] The ancient pilgrimage route winds its way to one of the most visited holy shrines in the world, Santiago de Compostela, where the alleged remains of Saint James are enshrined. As I walked the five hundred miles, I did not necessarily think of it as a spiritual experience—that was not my reason for making the trek—but that is what it became, and in the course of the pilgrimage a number of events transpired that reinforced and reaffirmed many of my core spiritual beliefs. Walking along the Camino, I learned many lessons and experienced countless spiritual connections—epiphanies, if you will.

One key lesson I learned from the Camino is that every step along life's journey is indeed a step along a spiritual path. Living any life, I believe, is a walk along such a path, for we are spiritual beings just as surely as we are physical beings. Few recognize this fact that was made so visibly manifest during my walk—I was aware of my body *and* of my spirit. I felt that my mind, body, and spirit were attuned during restful sleep as well as during the physical hardship of walking in the snow or climbing up some of the highest peaks—*el Pico del Perdón* or the village of O'Cebreiro—to traversing the *meseta* with its ferocious winds.

In this essay I explore how this sense of "spirit" has been an essence in my life's path and how I have come to this awareness through experiences I am classifying as auditory and visual hallucinations.[2] In narrating various incidents that may be classified as out-of-the-ordinary reality, surreal or extraordinary, I am laying out a framework for a discussion of my academic activist position. My writings, whether in literary or folklore studies, draw from the elements in my life; that is, as many writers do, I rely on my lived experience as fodder for my research and scholarly work as well as for my poetry and fiction. Instead of dividing these aspects of myself I seek to integrate them into a holistic and unifying self. Thus, the Camino has now become part of the resources I tap for framing theories of life and of literary or cultural analysis.

Coming to an Awareness of Spirit

I must have been about six or seven when I first became aware of this thing called spirit or soul. It baffled me. My family's devout Catholicism meant that my spirituality was tinged with Catholic dogma, while the folk Catholicism my grandmother practiced made it even messier. As I attended the *doctrina* where I memorized long prayers and the list of commandments that began "*Los mandamientos de la ley de Dios son diez*" I had many questions. The nuns and lay teachers charged with making sure that we were duly trained and ready to make our first holy communion had no patience for my questions, though, and I soon learned not to ask but to memorize the questions and answers as provided. "*¿Para qué hizo dios el mundo? ¿Cuáles son los sacramentos?*" Aside from confusion as to what the sacraments were, my utter bafflement at the idea that I would be eating the body and blood of Jesus in the Eucharist was only compounded by my disbelief that I could, in my frail, thin, six-year-old body, harbor God himself as Sister Consuelo taught us. But the theology and the official Church teachings formed only part of my spiritual training.

At home, my maternal grandmother Celia Ramón, whom we called Bueli, taught me an alternative spirituality based on a belief system that included *dichos* (*San Ramón ponle un tapón*), folk prayers invoking Catholic saints and soundly based on folk belief. Such prayers might help one retrieve lost items (thirteen Our Fathers to the *ánimas perdidas*), or ward off evils such as the dogs that roamed our neighborhood ("*Perro en ti, Cristo en mi, que la sangre de Cristo me libre de ti*"). Additionally, my family instilled religious and spiritual practices in us, such as praying the rosary daily, which ensured we would be in good favor with God. Bueli had a special devotion to the Virgen de San Juan and to la Virgen de Guadalupe. In fact, I still have the very image of the Virgen that she prayed to for healing or special favors.

My grandmother's devotion instilled a devotion to several virgins and saints in me: La Virgen de San Juan—both the one in Mexico, La Virgen de San Juan de los Lagos, and the one from San Juan, Texas—La Virgen de Sapopan in Guadalajara; La Virgen de Lourdes and La Virgen de Fatima; Santa Teresita; Santa Teresa de Avila; Santa Agueda; Santa Genoveva; and Santa Barbara. All have in some way touched me deeply, and I am indebted to them as I am to San Judas Tadeo, San Pancracio, and San José. In my kitchen I keep a statue of San Ramón and I find that I also have some connection to folk saints like Don Pedrito Jaramillo.

I did not seek the events that have led me to believe that there is more than what we experience with our physical senses. In fact, many of them terrified me. But I have also had occasion to be thankful for them, for it is through living through some harrowing and often inexplicable events that my own resolve and faith have been strengthened. I have chosen to share a few of these events to illustrate the kinds of experiences I have had and how they have shaped my spiritual life. The events can be grouped into out-of-body experiences, auditory and visual hallucinations, heightened awareness, and a feeling of oneness.

Messages: A Nun's Habit, A Sign, and Soul Traveling

I must have been about twelve when a powerful hallucination instilled such fear in me that I became silent about such things for a long time. I remember the day and the scene clearly: right after receiving communion one bright Sunday morning at San Luis Rey Church, I walked back to the pew where my siblings and my parents were kneeling, remembering to keep my hands clasped tightly and not to chew on the thin wafer. I closed my eyes and began my usual prayers—*Dios te salve María, llena eres de gracia*—or perhaps the longer prayer I had memorized from the evening rosary my family prayed each night—*Dios te salve, reina y madre, madre de misericordia*. In any case, I was feeling very holy indeed in the light blue cotton dress with the white collar that Mami had sewn for me. But then I opened my eyes and I was dressed in a heavy, thick, brown woolen habit. It was the color of my morning coffee before I poured milk into it—thick canned Pet evaporated milk. I began to think I had gone mad. *Loca*. I could imagine my father exclaiming, "*¡Estas loca!*" if I were to reach out and tell him; he was quietly kneeling on the same kneeler, head bowed in prayer. Not only did I see this garment, I felt its weight on my thin shoulders. I panicked, shut my eyes again and prayed even harder . . . but every time I opened my eyes, I was still wearing the heavy dark brown habit. This went on for quite a while.

Finally, at one point right before the end of the Mass, I opened my eyes and I was myself again, wearing the pastel blue dress with the white collar; the thin cotton was comforting. I was relieved, but I did not say a word to anyone. I was afraid that I would be called *loca*, deemed mad and sent away to *el manicomio*, a place I knew about from stories Bueli would tell us.

This first incident that I consciously remember brought even more questions to my young mind, and it was not the only time I felt as if I were in a trance, in another world. In retrospect, I think it must have been a bleed-though from another life. Many years later, during a past-life regression, I saw myself wearing the same habit. The reason I choose to share this incident now is that I know many of us have similar experiences, whether we are aware of them or not, and do not understand their significance. My past-life regression did not give me the answers I sought, such as, In what era and in what country did I live such a life? Is it due to that past life and my experiences with the Catholic Church that I vehemently shunned any suggestion that I might want to join a convent? I have had dreams in which I have been in a convent, and such dreams have usually sent me strong messages.

For instance, when I was finishing my master's degree and was preparing to leave Texas to pursue my doctoral work, I dreamed that I was the abbess of a convent and that there were some men who were going to kill us. Before the firing squad shot us, I went to each of the dozen or so sisters, looked into their eyes and said, "The spirit is eternal." The dream ended as I myself was shot and I felt the blood flow out of my body along with my spirit. I interpreted the dream as a sign that my current life was about to change and that I was "dying" to the old life. Curiously enough, whenever I have had dreams of dying I am about to make or have just made a major transition in my life.

In my dreams I often led an exciting and full life. When I found out about reincarnation, I felt I had found an answer to what I was calling my "incidents." But I never sought any of these events; they just happened. They always came just when I needed a sign, a reminder, or a nudge from my higher self—that is, the part of my being that serves as my guide and protector while on earth.

One such event happened even before I started my graduate studies. I had already decided to go on to a graduate program but I was full of doubts and fearful that I might not be good enough for graduate school. The morning when I was to take the Graduate Record Exam (GRE), I overslept and as I was rushing to the college where the exam would be administered, I drove by a creek where a bright yellow billboard with the word "TRUST" drew my attention. The billboard surprised me, since I took the same route every day and had not seen it before. Feeling solipsistic, I took the message to heart, relaxed, and tried not to worry when I kept getting red lights the rest of the way. I was almost thirty minutes late, but when I walked to the building, the other students were milling around waiting; the room was locked. Right after I arrived a harried looking man came with the key, opened the exam room, and we proceeded to take the scheduled GRE.

After the exam I drove by the creek looking for the bright yellow billboard that I assumed the Hare Krishnas, or perhaps another religious group, had put up, but to my surprise there was nothing there. I did not realize it at the time, but I had had a hallucination. I now consider it a sign that I would be fine in graduate school, that it was where I should go next along my life's path. During harrowing experiences in graduate school, I often recalled that event and found solace knowing that I should simply trust. I shared the story with a close friend who painted the word "TRUST" in block black letters on a yellow background as a going-away gift. I still cherish this reminder that indeed, all I need to do is trust.

It was even earlier, when I was in college, that I had my first out of body experience. In my twenties, I had several groups of friends: childhood friends, my office coworkers, my university classmates, and political activists, including a priest who soon became a good friend. One summer day, I went with the latter in his purple Taurus to deliver some materials from his parish to the Catholic sisters who ran the Ursuline High School. I remained in the car, and he went into the convent. Lazily daydreaming, I began looking up at the fast-moving clouds of that summer evening. And suddenly I was up in the clouds looking down at the car parked in front of the convent. At first I just enjoyed the sensation, but soon I became frightened and, not having words for what I was experiencing, I panicked. I felt a rush and a ringing in my ears as I found myself down in the car again looking up at the clouds, just as suddenly as before. I did not know about astral projection, sometimes referred to as "soul travel," nor had I ever heard of anyone doing this, so I once again remained silent and did not tell anyone. I was not as afraid as when I was a young girl and experienced the incident of the nun's habit, but I was still reticent and did not share the experience with anyone.

These events cemented my belief in things of the spirit that were not necessarily things of the Church. I learned to take heart and heed the messages, to be vigilant and to listen to the messages.

Speaking Out: From Spiritual Retreats
to Community Activism

While my priest friend and I often spoke of spiritual things, I never shared some of the deepest and most profound questions with him. Instead, I spoke to other women friends with whom I meditated. Cynthia—not her real name—moved to Laredo from New Mexico and we worked as volunteers to lead Search Retreats for youth in Laredo. I attribute my activist work to my working on these retreats. It was organizing the retreats in Laredo and later in Kingsville, where I honed skills that still serve me well as I later organized the women's group Las Mujeres and the annual conference Primavera, and as I now organize conferences for the Society for the Study of Gloria Anzaldúa. It was at a Search Retreat that I first delivered a public talk and found that I have a knack for public speaking.

Cynthia and I developed a deep friendship, and although I do not see her often, I still feel a deep connection with her. During the time we were doing volunteer work, we also began a meditation group. Becky, a friend who later walked the Camino with me, joined us sometimes. With them I could share my dreams and my ideas about reincarnation, as well as my doubts about the Church. While I was and remain deeply connected to the Virgin Mary and to Our Lady of Guadalupe, and have felt that they are my protectors and guides, especially Guadalupe—who in my mind embodies the female spirits of the Americas and therefore has a special connection with me, a daughter of the borderlands—I still had issues with the Church. I suppose at that point I was still not making the distinction between spirituality and formal religious institutions.

While engaged in the meditation group with Cynthia and Becky, I began reading about spiritual matters as well. I found the work of Edgar Cayce particularly illuminating. The books on him, especially *Many Mansions: The Edgar Cayce Story on Reincarnation* (1950), offered me a way of understanding what I was going through, and my meditation practice reinforced much of what I found in books.

The Seth books by Jane Roberts also helped me understand some of the experiences I was having. *Seth Speaks: The Eternal Validity of the Soul* (1972) came to me in the way other important books have, serendipitously and mysteriously through Becky. She was working on her masters' degree in social work in Denver, and I was working on mine in English in Kingsville, Texas. In those pre-cell phone days, we talked on the phone as often as our meager budgets would allow, and when we were back in Laredo for holidays we visited, talking nonstop. In the fall, probably some time during the Thanksgiving holiday of 1974, she told me about *Seth Speaks*, and I went looking for it in our campus bookstore, where browsing the shelves I suddenly felt the book hit me as it fell from an upper shelf. But I did not have the money to buy it, so I just leafed through it longingly and decided I would buy it after the Christmas holidays. I did not tell anyone about it. A friend of a friend gave me a ride home for the holidays, and as we were unpacking my luggage she handed me *Seth Speaks*. I was flabbergasted. "It is not mine," I explained. She looked at me, baffled. "Well it is not mine either and since you are the only other person traveling with me, it must be yours," and she handed me the book and drove away after making plans to pick me up in January to return to Kingsville.

I read the book during the break and found it comforting. It answered many of my questions, although it also raised many more. Principally, I still harbored questions about how to reconcile this knowledge of reincarnation and Akashic records that I had read about in Edgar Cayce's books with science and even with religious dogma.

Practicing Meditation

During those years, I was meditating daily for at least an hour, and I had many insights and truths revealed through meditation that still affect me to this day, some of which have helped me with health and emotional issues. For example, during one of my meditations I got the message not to eat tomato seeds and to take vitamin E. At the time, I was working in an office and often after my evening classes at the community college I would get together with my spirituality group, for Cynthia's young children would then be asleep and we could meet in her home. That day, I had been having some abdominal cramping that was not related to my PMS or to anything I had eaten. So I focused on the pain and then in my mind's eye I very clearly saw myself walking into Munden's, a sort of pharmacy and department store—the precursor of today's Walgreen's and CVS, the ubiquitous corner grocery store and pharmacy. I walked in and went directly to the pharmacy, where I asked for vitamin E. The clerk behind the counter reached back and handed me a small box that said "vitamin E" and a price. I also heard an inner voice say, "stay away from tomato seeds and drink water."

I believe I told a couple of friends about this vision and then quickly forgot it. A few weeks later, my mother called me at the office and asked me to pick up a prescription at Munden's on the way home. When I opened the door and walked in, I had a strange déjà vu and I recognized what was happening. I was wearing the same dress, and it was the same clerk as I had seen in the meditation session. As she handed me the prescription, I asked if they carried vitamin E. She swiftly reached back and gave me the exact same package I had seen in my meditation. The only difference was the price, which I remember being $1.50; it was now $2.89 (these are 1970s prices). I bought it, of course, and then remembered the instructions I had heard in my vision. From then on I stopped eating tomato seeds when possible—it is nearly impossible to extract them from salsas.

I believe my meditation has also helped me by keeping me in tune with my higher self—that part of myself that guides and protects me, as I mentioned earlier—as well as with the spiritual guides who also protect and guide me. During that time in Kingsville, Texas, I deepened my meditation and spiritual practice, and often my hour-long meditations filled me with peace and a sense of wholeness in which I was one with the universe. Many of my meditations were really prayer sessions since I was attending daily mass, at the time—first while my brother was in Vietnam, and then after his death as a coping mechanism. It was a place to be quiet and at peace. I learned many of the daily prayers that are still part of my spiritual practice during the 1970s when I was working in an office and going to college, although currently my prayer practice incorporates many more I have learned and developed over time. For example, I pray for the earth and send healing light to an image of the earth as a whole.

When I returned to Laredo in 1980, after graduate school and a Fulbright fellowship in Spain, I felt alone. Both Cynthia and Becky were gone from Laredo, and I was so busy finishing my dissertation and teaching twelve classes a year at the local university that I had little time to dwell on anything but my scholarly life. But during a second Fulbright fellowship to Spain in spring 1985, I met Ana Castillo, and thus began a friendship that has lasted all these years. For a spell while she was living in California, Ana convened a meditation group long distance. At eleven Laredo time every Tuesday night we would "tune in" through meditation for an hour or so. It worked fairly well, and I have fond memories of feeling connected to a circle of Chicanas who believed and felt as I did. But the circle disbanded soon after, and now it is only in the occasional dream that I share with Sandra Cisneros or Norma Alarcón that I feel that affinity or connection. We are all too busy and too involved with our lives. I like to believe that we are all following a path that only we can shape, as Machado so astutely wrote, "*caminante, no hay camino, se hace camino al andar* [traveler, there is no path, one forges the path as one walks it]."

Hearing Voices: Messages to Myself?

I moved to Kingsville, Texas in 1973 and it was there that I experienced my first auditory hallucination. I was alone in the small cabin my two roommates and I were renting for the summer; I was fixing a bowl of Cheerios when I distinctly heard a resounding voice exclaim "NO!" I was startled and perplexed, but thought no more about it after I checked that the radio was not on and that there was no one anywhere near the cabin. I ate the cereal, and within ten minutes I had a violent reaction. Vomiting and doubled over in pain I immediately connected the resounding "NO!" and my physical distress. In retrospect, it was probably a warning that I did not heed. On another occasion, I had no choice but to obey.

When I was living in Washington, DC, in the early 1990s I was mugged, and what could have been a very bad situation turned to be an affirming albeit frightful experience. I arrived at National Airport around midnight from a weekend trip to Guadalajara due to a flight delay, for I would never have booked such a late arrival. As soon as the taxi dropped me off at my house, it took off; I knew something was wrong because I had asked the driver to wait until I got in the door. Sure enough a tall, thin man wearing a hooded windbreaker approached me. I knew what was coming. The exchange was brief. "Give me all your stuff," he said, almost in a whisper. "No," I foolishly replied, almost shouting, "Go away!" He stood about two feet away; I could see something shining in his right hand, and that is when it happened: I heard a deep sonorous male voice say, "Give him everything." The instructions from self-defense classes came back all at once. Of course. The thing to do was not to fight, but to give him everything. But the voice? Where was it coming from? I can say that I felt it more than heard it. It was coming from deep within me.

As I was handing over my jewelry, briefcase, suitcase, and a shopping bag, I kept saying to him, "Not my book; it is in here," I said holding up the briefcase, "and I really need it." I had the page proofs for my book *Canícula* (1995) in the briefcase; I had been working on them during the flight and I was supposed to mail the book to the press the next day. He shook his head and picked up the suitcase and the shopping bag, having pocketed my watch, earrings, and rings. And off he walked as briskly as he could with the load. By this time I was trembling and crying; I rang the doorbell and knocked on my landlord's door. They lived in the basement; I had to walk up a few steps to my own front door. I could hear my cat meowing in my apartment. The police came and took a report, but they were not optimistic. "It happens all the time," the officer said, "chances are the stuff will be sold off soon and there is no way to track or recover stolen goods."

"Did he have a weapon?" he asked. "I do not know, but he was holding something shiny; I did not look too closely," I replied. "Was it a knife or a gun?" "I could not tell." The next morning, in the middle of making phone calls to report the theft of my credit cards and my checkbook, I received a phone call. The manager of an apartment complex two blocks away had found the checkbook with my phone number, and was calling to advise that I come over right away because some of my stuff was in the trash bin behind the apartments. It was Monday morning and the trash pickup was scheduled to come by any minute. I rushed over and burst into tears to see my clothes, purse, and other objects I had had with me the night before strewn all over the alley. I retrieved a clay *cazuela* (pot), a couple of bottle openers, and a bag into which I stuffed my underwear and blouses and whatever was not dirty or torn. I remember crying even more when I spotted my manuscript neatly stacked by the wall with a stone on top to keep the pages from flying—only the title page was missing. "He listened," I told the startled apartment manager who looked on as I picked up things, weeping uncontrollably. The voice I heard the night I was mugged stays with me. Sometimes I try to listen to it, but it eludes me.

Apparently it is only when I am in a crisis that I can hear it. I do not understand the impetus, but I am grateful it is there, this voice that offers advice. In some small measure, it suggests that an aspect of me that scientists have not yet been able to decipher is in fact watching out for me, sending me signs and communicating directly when I need such communication. I have often said that the next revolution—after the industrial and the technical—will be the spiritual revolution, which will happen when science catches up to ancient knowledge and traditions. Our ancestors communicated with and established connections to what we in our mechanized and scientific world cannot fathom. Science will one day "discover" their non-western ways of knowing and of being, and we will once again regain the ability to communicate with ourselves at all levels.

No One Does It Alone: *Comadres, Madrinas,* and Other Allies along the Path

Along my path, I have met many women who have shared their experience and knowledge with me and have thus enriched my spiritual path: the women of the women's group in Laredo, *Las Mujeres*, my students, friends like the ones I mentioned earlier—Becky, Cynthia, and Ana. But I would also add women to the list who with their work and their presence in my life have helped me navigate the troubled waters of academia and of activist scholarship: Gloria Anzaldúa, Enriqueta Vásquez, Terry Ybañez, Claire Joysmith, Ellie Hernández, Angela de Hoyos, Cherríe Moraga, Sandra Cisneros, Barbara Renaud González, Judges Hilda Tagle and Elma Salinas Ender, and many, many others. The list is really too long, but I must include those who have passed, members of Las Mujeres—Rosa Burgess and Rose Treviño—and my student and friend, Rosa Reyes. *A estas últimas, que en paz descansen.* I truly am grateful to them for their friendship and the many lessons they have taught me. It is these women—and some men—who have helped me forge my own path, a path of spirituality and activism.

I must also mention women who provided me a less Eurocentric view of the spiritual life. As I mentioned, because my childhood was suffused with Indigenous spiritual practices, mostly practiced by my maternal grandmother (who lived with us until she crossed over the summer before I was to enter fourth grade), I know many of the healing herbs and, whenever possible, I still grow the basics: *estafiate, ruda, romero, yerba buena*, and *albahcar* (sage, rue, rosemary, mint, basil) in my garden. Bueli also instilled respect for and a great connection to Mother Earth in me. But the public schools and the hegemonic class-based ethos of the border town where I grew up did not allow or nurture such a connection. Therefore, it was not until many years later that I came to a conscious awareness of my own indigeneity and how it had been erased from my identity.

For a few years the Indigenous Women's Network provided many lessons and opportunities that helped me regain that lost part of my self. I attended several gatherings at Alma de Mujer in Austin where Marsha Gómez, *que en paz descanse*, Cynthia Pérez, and many other *mujeres* introduced me to the sweat lodge and to the sacred rituals, which have also informed who I am as an activist scholar whose spirituality guides all action. It was at one of these gatherings that I reclaimed the Indigenous aspects of my *Chicanidad*. While I never accepted invitations to participate in *danza azteca* or *conchero* dancing, I was deeply touched to see such dancing, and since many *danzantes* were personal friends, I could see that they kept the Indigenous dance traditions. My work of more than thirty years with Los Matachines de la Santa Cruz in Laredo has also given me a deep connection to an Indigenous-based tradition.[3]

Another significant change point in my path toward a spiritual activist scholarly life occurred when I read Gloria Anzaldúa's *Borderlands* (1987), for I found many of my own thoughts and feelings in that book. Needless to say, Gloria and I became even closer friends after the book was published, and she taught me many things. When she passed so suddenly in May 2004, I was in Spain with friends after the *Congreso de Literatura Chicana*. Everywhere I went for the rest of the trip, I set up altars to honor Gloria's memory, and for nine days I did special prayers in her honor. Three years later, moved by many signs and inklings, I founded the Society for the Study of Gloria Anzaldúa: the first symposium was held in November 2007, and subsequently every eighteen months we have had a gathering of scholars, artists, and activists who seek to keep Anzaldúa's legacy alive. In many ways the Society and the *El Mundo Zurdo* conferences are the culmination of a spiritual activist practice that began many years ago when I saw myself wearing that habit, or when I led the first Search Retreat. But it is the collaboration of many others that make the conferences and the Society succeed.

All in all, I can truly say that I have been blessed to have encountered teachers along the way who have helped me understand my own spiritual path. It was a complex network of madrinas (godmothers) and comadres (intimate friends) who helped me forge my spiritual being.

Recent Lessons

Again it was Becky, whose friendship over thirty years has always been predicated on our affinity for things of the spirit, who more recently brought yet another element to my spiritual development. Becky had continued on a spiritual path; she had taken several classes, including training to teach a mini-soul cleansing class, when she was in Kansas for doctoral studies. I took the class when she taught it in San Antonio. It was also through Becky that I met Gwen Jones when she was giving lectures on angels at a local grocery store. Gwen spoke of coming to do spiritual work as a medical intuitive via her own experiences in England and how she was drawn to come to Mexico after seeing a traditional dance troupe perform in London. She moved to Mexico City, and it was there that one day, after being in Mexico City for two years, a man approached her on the street and said, "You have to come with me to meet my mother. Meet me here tomorrow and dress all in white."

She did as she was instructed with great trepidation, for she had been warned about the dangers of *el D.F.* But she was glad she followed her intuition and met the young man whose mother greeted her with "*Te he estado esperando dos años.*" The healer, who had been waiting for her for two years, proceeded to accept her into her family and into her circle of students. The woman, a *curandera*, taught her how to do much of the spiritual work she now does.

Gwen's story intrigued me. So immediately after the session, I approached her to schedule a session with her. After a brief moment, she responded that my angels told her I was not ready. I had too many things happening that summer, and it would be best to wait until later. I was disappointed, but happy that we would do it later. In August we held the session, and it was one of the most transformative experiences of my life. Since then, I have worked with Gwen on a seminar on the power of sound and of words. This collaboration began about the time of my father's transition as he struggled to cross over. It was Gwen's intervention that allowed him ultimately to have a smooth transition and to be at peace. Even this seemed to be a testament to the power of spirit, since my father, who did not speak English, and Gwen, who did not know Spanish, communicated via my cell phone and soon after he entered the last stage of his physical existence.

La Tercera Edad: Coming Full Circle

As I enter what in Mexico is called "la tercera edad" or the third age, I feel prepared for a deepening of my spiritual practice.[4] The fact that I turned sixty-four while walking the Camino de Santiago, as I entered my sixty-fifth year on earth, remains an important element in my life's path. A year later, when I turned sixty-five, I retired from my position at the University of Texas at San Antonio to take on a new challenge: to build a Latina/o Studies program at the University of Missouri, Kansas City. This move too is part of my spiritual path, and I feel that it was walking the Camino and all the lessons such a walk offered that prepared me for what follows in my life. Once again, I was confronted with inexplicable phenomena that reinforced my beliefs regarding faith, beliefs that now encompass much more than what that early catechism taught me.

In winter 2010, when I decided to travel the Camino de Santiago, Becky jumped at the chance to come with me. She had walked it four years earlier and was anxious to go back. She witnessed many of the small miracles that I experienced and that made the journey such a spiritual experience. At one time, coming into the town of Hornitos, I looked up at the bright blue sky and saw a strange cloud formation that shaped itself into the distinctive flourish of my father's signature. Tears sprang to my eyes and I felt my father's presence strong and real. On another occasion, as we were nearing the town of Rabé de la Calzadas, I was inexplicably moved to pray the rosary. I was walking alone and began praying, finishing the fifth mystery just as Becky caught up with me and we walked into the town. To my surprise, the *hospitalero* (caretaker) handed each one of us a Medal of Mary as we walked into the simple and clean *albergue* (pilgrim refuge). "This is Mary's town," he proclaimed, "and we offer her image to all pilgrims who come through here," he explained. It was not until later that night, as I was drifting off to sleep, that it occurred to me that Mary had instilled in me the desire to pray the rosary as we approached her village.

These are but two simple experiences that affirmed to me that the Camino de Santiago is a spiritual path and that my walking it was more than a mere physical exercise. But the Camino is only the latest of many events that affirm my beliefs.

I have been blessed every day of my life, and I honor the ancestors who have preceded me and whose DNA I carry, the many who have taught me and who guide me. Sometimes I acknowledge these ancestors with concrete actions. For example, I keep an altar in my home; it has an image of la Virgen de Guadalupe that my maternal grandmother owned. It is not anything fancy; in fact, the cardstock it was printed on has split and the image has yellowed behind the old glass frame. I remember this image of la Virgen de Guadalupe from my childhood, along with another that has disappeared from my mother's house, an image of la Virgen de San Juan de los Lagos. It is before Guadalupe that I pray, and it is this image that I light candles to and bring flowers to on special occasions. In December I set up an altar in my living room; it is at this same site that on the Day of the Dead I construct an altar or *ofrenda*. I have been building this altar every year since my father passed, and while at first it felt odd, since we did not grow up with the tradition of Day of the Dead *ofrendas*, it now feels intimate and essential.

In my tradition, instead of erecting altars, we would visit the cemetery and spend time by the tombs of all of our *muertitos*, as my grandmother would say, saying a few Hail Marys and Our Fathers plus the Apostles' Creed or some other prayer before communing with the person in silence. Of course, my prayers, gathered over a lifetime, seem to come to my lips almost automatically. When I cannot find an item, I immediately start praying the thirteen Our Fathers to *las animas perdidas*; if I go by a Catholic church, I cross myself, an involuntary reaction; and when I lie down to sleep, I often make the sign of the cross thrice on my pillow the way my Bueli taught me. I would venture to say that such habits constitute a spiritual practice, for in performing such actions I am also acknowledging the spiritual in everyday life. Praying, then, is also a continuous spiritual practice that has been part of my life.

Currently I am gathering my everyday prayers, including the prayer that I say when I pass roadkill, sending that sentient being to the light. Prayers have always offered solace and helped me cope with whatever has come my way. The prayer of Saint Francis is one of my favorites. Words have power; as a writer, I know this is true. So the spoken prayers that carry elements of gratitude and acknowledgment of the unseen powers are, to me, vehicles for voicing my need and offering gratitude for pleas granted. Becky and I thought about gathering our prayers when we were walking the Camino, and so I know it is a project that I am destined to complete, one more aspect of my spiritual life that for me is also my writing life.

My activism springs directly from my spiritual practice, since I am drawn to work on projects and to exercise certain tasks with a sense of mission. Knowing that I am here on this Earth reality for a purpose, knowing that my work in academia is intimately tied to my work on Earth allows me to live my life *con conciencia*, exercising *la facultad*, and doing work that matters.[5] These ideas come from Gloria Anzaldúa's work; they constitute what some scholars, including Chicana feminist scholar Theresa Delgadillo, have called a spiritual activism. I guess it could also be called activist spirituality—that is, living a holistic life focused on issues of social justice.

My work on adult literacy, for example, allowed aspects of my academic and political as well as spiritual life to come together. It may appear that I came to the literacy work by chance, but as I conclude this essay, I must affirm that I do not believe in chance. I was a recent PhD and working at a Hispanic-Serving Institution, Laredo State University (now Texas A&M International University), when the local NBC affiliate had a campaign for literacy. I met with the news anchors and over lunch pretty much designed and launched what would become the Literacy Volunteers of America–affiliated local program. For about two years, the "office" was the trunk of my car, and we were often housed in strange places—wherever we could secure office space for very little or no rent; not until we were able to secure space at Laredo Community College did I know the organization was solid. It is a project that continues to serve the community and to offer hundreds of adults the basic literacy tools to change their lives.

I have many anecdotes of how transformative such work can be, but I will share only one. It was the fall semester and I had recruited my linguistics students to volunteer as we tested the incoming literacy classes at the Colonia Guadalupe, a government housing project. Halfway through the testing, a woman in her eighties approached the table where I was registering potential students for the placement test that my students were administering. She openly and seriously looked me in the eye and said, "*No quiero aprender inglés. Solo quiero aprender a escribir mi nombre antes de morir* [I don't want to learn English. All I want is to learn how to write my name before I die]." Struck by her passion, I did not assign her an evaluator; instead I asked her to wait on the side, and as soon as I was done with the assignments, I sat with her at a desk and we practiced. First she practiced holding a pencil, then she tried slowly printing her name. In about an hour, she had mastered it. She hugged me, crying and pouring God's blessings upon me: "*¡Que diosito te lo pague!* [May God repay you!]" So, yes, spirituality and activist actions are related. We touch the spirit when we change the world with our actions, and it is spirit that "inspires" right action, especially our social justice actions.

Invoking those who came before and those who will come after, I close with a deep and humble sense of gratitude for life, love, abundance, grace, faith, guidance, family, friends, teachers, students, my activism and my writing. Finally, as always, I thank the creator for my life, the precious gift of being in this world.

Notes

1. El Camino de Santiago, the Way of Saint James, is one of Christianity's key pilgrimage routes, second only to the routes to Rome and Jerusalem. It actually predates Christian times and follows what are called "ley lines," that is, charged paths that have been traveled for centuries by people from Europe to see what they believed to be the

edge of the world, at Cape Finisterre. In winter 2011–2012, I blogged about the Camino and its impact on my life at *El Camino de Santago—An Immersion Memoir*, last modified October 27, 2012, last accessed October 8, 2013, http:// www.elcaminoayearlater.wordpress .com.

2. By using the term "hallucination," I realize that I am in dangerous waters. However, I certainly do not mean to use the term to elicit the common Eurocentric connotation of "illness" but instead to reclaim it to mean "a heightened state of awareness that allows for phenomena not experienced in customary fashion." "*Videncia*" might be a more appropriate term for what I am referring to, seeing with the eyes of the soul.

3. For further information on the Matachines tradition in Laredo, Texas, see Cantú (2009).

4. While the term "tercera edad" has been around a while, many now speak of a "cuarta edad," a fourth age that begins at eighty. Indeed many have found new life after eighty and are living well into their nineties; many more are reaching the century mark. I believe that those who do so with physical and mental abilities that allow them to function relatively well are pathbreakers who are preparing society for what is to come.

5. The ideas of *la facultad* and *conciencia* come from Anzaldúa's *Borderlands* (1987) and Anzaldúa urging us "to do work that matters" is from her essay, "Let Us Be The Healing of the Wound" (2003).

Anatomy of Learning

Yauhtli, Peyotzin, Tobacco, *and* Maguey

Patrisia Gonzales

The word has spread in the village. A *partera* is coming. My *maestra*, doña Filomena Cedillo Parra, comes to the village where I am staying with one of the *tatas* (elders) who is her *compadre de medicina*. These elders who have trained me represent that male-female balance so prevalent among traditional Indigenous peoples of Mexico. Each has provided me with a spectrum of knowledge regarding Nahua medicine, regarding birth, ceremony, *limpias*, *plantas*, and walking in balance and toward justice. Doña Filo has come to train another woman and me in midwifery because at the time of our instruction in 2005, there were no pregnant women in her own Nahua village. When I tell *el tata* don Aurelio Ramírez Cazarez, he says they will announce it on the village speakerphone near the church to spread the word, *que viene una partera*.

The elders know exactly which women are pregnant, a total of four. Notably, there is no practicing partera, or midwife, in the village, a place known for its traditional medicine. The last living professional partera—the much-respected doña Vicenta—had stopped catching babies. Doña Filo says she has come to teach us so that all this traditional birthing knowledge is not "taken to the grave" with her.

Doña Filo is a Nahua midwife. In June 2000, I met her in Brownsville, Texas, at the *kalpulli* (an Indigenous form of communal organization) where we would participate in a ceremony rarely witnessed in a lifetime, a Mexican Indian ceremony in which elders came from Mexico to recognize the ceremonial dance circle Grupo Coatlique, Mesa de la Virgen de la Luz. We reunited in a training on Mexican Traditional Medicine (MTM) at Nahuatl

University in 2001. Doña Filo would become my teacher and elder in tradi-tional birthing. From her I learned how to work with *maguey* medicine and purifying light. She taught me the power of *el ombligo y como juntar el pulso*, how to read the body's energy through the navel, and moon teachings of *la luna llena*.

As we await the women, we spend our days making tinctures and pomades, and mixing hot and "fresh" natured herbs (*bejuco de ajo* and *axihuitl*) to create a warm salve that is not too hot for pregnant women, who are consid-ered already in a "hot" state. Sometimes the women do not come to see us until ten-thirty at night, because that is when they can get there, but we are ready for them. And I learn to palpate the womb and listen to the heartbeat with a fetoscope or with my hands; I also learn various *recetas* (remedies) for scarred fallopian tubes (*manrubio*), to relax the uterus or to expel the placenta (*ruda* and *chocolate*), or, for extreme situations, *zoapatli*—the famous *cihua-patli*—in western botanical nomenclature *Montanoa tomentosa* Cerv., which was recorded in the *Florentine Codex* (Sahagún 1950–1982). She also teaches more techniques using the *rebozo*, a shawl, which is an instrument and a technology of MTM. Doña Filo and the tata discuss one woman who does not come because she is feeling too sick, even though the walk is short. The tata says that is one way the placenta *se enfría*, or gets cold, from the body not moving around enough. We partake in ceremonies, such as the *temazkalli*, or Mexican medicinal sweat lodge, and limpias, or purification rites. And at night with *pan y café*, the elders, the children of *los primeros* Zapatistas, re-count stories about Zapata and other cultural heroes of Morelos. I have been fortunate in my life to have been taught for two decades by this generation.

Long before I decided to pursue a doctorate, my journey to understand *las plantas* would lead me to many recetas and to *medicinas* such as *peyotzin*, *yauhtli*, maguey, tobacco, and *el poder de las flores*, the healing power of flowers in purification rites. To Indigenous people, the plants are medicines. These four *plantas*, or medicines—in fact, ceremonial plants—organize this story of how I learned their power and application. These plants are my guides in understanding fertility, pregnancy and labor, and general imbalances whether physical or spiritual. Plant knowledge is so important for Nahua cultures that we literally "plant" who we are, our *ombligos* (umbilical stubs), placentas, and names.

I first learned of "name planting" ceremonies from Andrés Ségura, the late elder of the Conchero Aztec ceremonial tradition, in 1991, when I was re-searching a book on spiritual social change (Gonzales 2003). Having docu-mented various name planting ceremonies in Mexico and the United States, I knew these were practices in the present tense.[1] Little did I know that my own *"olla" estaba fría* (my "pot" was cold). And as I stood over pots of burning *romero*, a warming plant, to "warm my pot," or was given other *recetas* in women's circles, or as ceremonies were performed for my womb, women shared their knowledge of fertility and birthing with me.

Through this ecological story of my practical and ceremonial relationship with traditional medicine, I place myself within the hidden and encoded Indigeneity of the Americas. As a journalist who chronicled Indigenous memory for two decades, I have lived the reemergence of Indigenous knowledge among Native peoples and Indian-rooted cultures in Mexico and the United States. This medicine story is among the "hidden texts" of which Florescano writes, hidden knowledge that remained silent and underground or dressed in Christian cloth in order to survive (Florescano 1994).

Midwife Angelita Borbón calls this medicinal knowledge a hidden medical system. I received instruction through this hidden medical system from the oral tradition, often obscured from the world of scholars, which I present here as an anatomy of learning among my peoples. This instruction led me to explore how the values in the codices and chronicles on birthing continue today and are part of a larger matrix of Indigenous medicine. I have received permission from the elders to write about this. My anatomy of learning is "data gathering" in Native science, where direct experience is valued over abstract understanding. This is an ecology of birthing and Indigenous medicine as I have grown to understand it within my own personal and collective context. Cajete connects such ecological knowledge to Native science: "Unless the cultural/ecological context of relationship is understood, one cannot fully comprehend a particular Indigenous technology. Without its context, the ideas of the people or the environment in which those ideas have arisen, the science of a people remains mysterious" (2000, 207).

These stories are held in stones, plants, or the eye of springs; they are unfolded in a medicine bundle, our elders' stories, or a "fertility place" (ibid., 125, 207) where we go to ask for a child. These practices are more than "folk medicine." I remember among the last teachings Segura imparted when my family saw him in 1996 was that the ceremonies and medicinal knowledge were scientific. Others have imparted similar ideas, noting they can be both scientific and spiritual.

In keeping with doña Enriqueta Contreras's guidance—both in oral tradition and now documented in Guerra Falcón (2009)—as a midwife we share the same story and one body with the earth, I include here stories and narratives, *recetas*, and rites that I learned about birthing as I, a childless woman, wanted to understand how to get pregnant and how to help pregnant women. As an herbalist and *promotora tradicional*, I was often asked to do *limpias* in the community and to prepare women for birth. This, coupled with my journey to learn traditional medicine, exposed me to numerous teachings, ceremonies, and *pláticas* (talks) with elders and traditional knowledge bearers from Indigenous people across the Americas who helped me fill my "blanket" with various approaches to women's health. (Traditionally among Native peoples, we may lay a blanket as a place to make offerings.)

Over the years I have bundled this knowledge with the ancient picture-book tradition of my ancestors, reading the books as medicinal texts from the gaze of a promotora. I work with many codices and numerous symbols of the great weaver, spider women, trees of life, and knots of wild herbs and serpents that form ombligos and twisted cords, where star beings and energetic practices emerge. In all of these formulas, I found life processes expressed in the medicinal knowledge of today in my world: medicinal practices around the navel as an energetic center, rebozos hanging as physical celestial cords to help bring down a baby, tree-crosses in our ceremonies.

In Mexico, my elders speak of *mistica* as a certain quality of knowledge that is experienced and emerges from experience. Mistica occurs when knowledge, mastery, or skill and mystery are joined.[2] I am trained in the practices of Mexican Indigenous medicine. This system of knowledge is a helix threaded by science and spirituality. I cannot, and choose not to, expansively describe what I have experienced when I work with the energies and powers of life. They are so profound that words cannot wrap around them. This is why so many Native peoples speak of the life powers as the Great Mystery, the Great Spirit(s), the Formers, the Life Makers, That Which Is Near and Close, and All That We Live For (to name a few) to convey our cosmo-logics, or deep foundations for making sense of the sacred processes of Life that our minds cannot fully understand or express.

Indigenous natural law(s) stress generosity, mutuality, and interdependence. Natural law is expressed in the cyclical nature of the four seasons, the physical processes of cellular regeneration, and the cycles of life-death and regeneration. Natural laws and Indigenous science are based on spiritual and ceremonial protocols with all life forms. They are agreements to live by that are expressed in our respectful interactions of prayers and ceremonies—prayers left for the waters, prayers carried in smoke, or the offerings of sacrifice left by our very bodies, as well as our human struggle to empty our hearts of *aires*, or "winds," in the form of envy, revenge, grief, judgment, resentment, and mockery. In accordance with natural law, the Moon asserts her influence over the tides of the ocean and the human body, over blood and amniotic fluids. As Mohawk midwife Katsi Cook (1992) notes, Grandmother Moon gives women their reproductive "authority." Similarly, astral forces such as Grandmother Moon and the Morning Star are part of the "authoritative knowledge" of Red Medicine. These authorities work in conjunction with the authority of elders and their lived experiences to establish ceremony as part of "authoritative knowledge" in birth. These protocols and sacred authorities form the original instructions of many Indigenous peoples; they establish teachings on how to conduct ourselves.

I have the first doctorate in my family, but I am not the first doctor. My great-grandparents were curanderos, *yerberas*, bone setters, and parteras. I like to reconfigure my letters. For me, my PhD means "promotora of herbal doctoring," "promotora of *huevo* (egg) doctoring," and "promotora of *huarache* doctoring," in honor of all the elders I have had to keep up with up and down *montes, pasto,* and jungle as they easily maneuvered the terrain in huaraches. They are the barefoot doctors of the Americas, healing bones and breaking fevers and *sustos*. The huarache doctors are *médicos Indígenas,* doctors in their own right—"root doctors" like my great-grandma Concha. Someday, after I have apprenticed for three decades, I may be able to say my PhD stands for "partera and huarache doctor."

I am the daughter of Kickapoo, Comanche, and Macehual peoples, raised in the Mexican/Xicana communities. In my early life, I was raised by my grandparents, who considered themselves "Indios." My maternal grandfather said we were Kickapoo, Comanche, and "Aztec." According to my grandpa, my American Indian relatives went into Old Mexico for refuge from the Indian Wars and married the Nahuatl-speaking peoples of Guanajuato and Zacatecas. On my father's side, we are also Kickapoo, and the descendants of the Mexican and Indian peoples who were in the landbase now known as Texas before it was a state or part of the country of Mexico. I descend from three generations of curanderos, parteras, and people "who know herbs," as my Uncle Joe said. My great-grandmother Concha was a tall, stout woman born in San Antonio in the mid-1800s, and a midwife who was fluent in both Spanish and English. I also have had the fortune of learning traditional medicine from the Nahua tatas and *nanas* (our words for grandfathers/ grandmothers or male/female elders) of Morelos, Mexico, who are my elders. Based on their ceremonial calendars, my *madrina* is Meyahuel, the spirit of the maguey and a guardian of the *yerbas* and healing.

In many ways, it is the mistica of the plantas, *las matas,* or the plant world that led me to birthing as an expression of Native science. Plants are part of human history. The plantas have been calling me for many years now, speaking to me in dreams or catching my spirit on a path. Plants have guided me in crucial times in my life, saving me from a life as a housebound invalid when I contracted an autoimmune disorder in 1989.

In "The Millennium of the Feminine," a brown paper that I wrote for the Women's Theological Center in 1993, I shared some of my experiences in self-healing: "So part of healing female energy requires bringing the medicine from within our suffering. As Paulo Freire said, it is our suffering that allows us to understand our life and the treasure of our dignity, our human-ness. And so in my reconstruction of my life, I began the cycle of creation" (2000, 3). This is the process of our natural laws: origination, transforma-tion, regeneration, return. I gained a deeper understanding of herbs then, as I relied on plantas, prayer, *ceremonia*, and various elders (Grandpa Ray, don Faustino, las nanas Zapatistas) to heal. I learned herbalism and how to work energy to heal myself, and by 1997, at the end of my recovery, I was under my own herbal self-care. I have worked with yerbas since the 1980s, first for my self-healing, and now as a community yerbera and promotora tradicio-nal. Plants are part of our oldest "body memory" and reveal a profound story about the human condition. Snake Woman, or Cihuacoatl, who was in-voked in birth by Mexica midwives, is also called Quilaztli, which is some-times translated as "abundant herb." My self-determination encompasses the natural world's sovereignty. Without their right to continue and thrive, I would not exist. The weave of platted grasses reminds us of the will of life to continue.[3]

Tlazolteotl's Escoba

Growing up, I have vague memories of my grandmother's *escoba*, or broom, for limpias. She would pray over it and use it in purifying "sweeping" of the body, and then use the huevo. Some escobas are made of plants and herbs, showing a continuity of acts and instruments with ceremonial brooms de-picted in various codices. She also had prayers for the water—which she and my relatives have used to cure drug addiction and alcoholism. As my mother recalls, "She prayed over everything." My earliest memory as a child was watching my grandma pray to the four winds at night. I realize now this was my traditional formation. Later, as I began in earnest to study *la medicina* (traditional medicine), first for my own healing and later as a promotora and apprentice herbalist, the elders in my family began to share family protection rites and precise ways in which my great-grandpa prayed to the four winds, as well as the medicines he used to "feed the spirits," with me. Like many other families considered "Mexican," our family held Indigenous knowledge pri-vately and expressed it in our lifeways maintained through traditional heal-ing knowledge.

For my grandparents who identified with their nations, being Mexican was "another kind of 'Indian.'" I learned recetas about my granny's "turtle medi-cine"; my other granny's *ventosas* (cupping); recetas for colds, for *frío* in the body and what to do "*si la sangre calienta*," or if the blood gets hot in a child from *mal ojo*; and how a troubled marriage can lead to the blood "going cold" and cause illness. I learned one of my grandpa's recetas for how to clear *mal energía*, or negative energy—small recipes and practices that were the staple of any family with a connection to the energies and the natural world. I carry tobacco prayers for rain, my grandparents' different ways to call the four winds, and how to cut and gather plants based on sacred directions and celestial positions, all of which is my personal legacy of being in relationship with my family and original relations.

While in ceremony with other Indigenous peoples, I experienced actions that were familiar to me. As I wondered when—and how—my father's family lost our Kickapoo tobacco that Mama Mencha grew, as I reckoned with the legacy of pain because my maternal Kickapoo great-grandmother was stolen from her people, I also tried to make sense of resonating experiences between my familial knowledge and other tribal people's medicine ways. I also found clarity in the distinctions.

As I deepened my relationship with the medicines, every instruction from an elder, every ceremony, my dreams, my experiences in nature, all became instructions in how to understand Indigenous medicinal ways. Sometimes, the teachings came as I helped tend the fire or clean the altar or place of offerings. All the while, I was also learning from traditional elders, ceremonial leaders, grannies, and curanderos at women's gatherings, workshops, Indigenous gatherings, and courses in Mexico and receiving teachings from my elders in the United States. I did not grow up traditionally, learning to do the ancient medicine as my relatives did their work. But I was treated with herbs and the huevo and lived within the atmosphere of their "doins." I have had to return to Indigenous relatives to learn these ways deeply. I am not a curandera or a ceremonial leader. I am a self-healer, an apprentice yerbera (herbalist), traditional birth attendant, and a promotora. Now that I have a doctorate, I follow Doctor Mario Rojas's model of a *promotora-investigadora*, which I learned in 2005 while taking some training from him on integrating traditional medicine because I wanted to experience how traditional medicine was adapting to new environments.

During my communal learning in the mid-1990s, I was part of a women's collective and kalpulli in Albuquerque (Kalpulli Izkalli), in which we began to recover and transmit the teachings of traditional medicine within our families. Several of the women had been apprentices for decades yet never named themselves curanderas, because they wanted to uphold the traditional ways through which such designations transpire—by being named by your elders or your communities. Sometimes because detribalized people have lost communal structures, there is a sense of the need to name oneself. Yet I recall the advice of one of my aunties, who would acknowledge herself only as the curandera of her vast extended family; a curandera does not name herself publicly, for it makes her powers vulnerable to various levels of attack. In my own family, my grandmother holds memories of being labeled the off-spring of *el brujo*, or the witch, because my great-grandfather was an extremely sought-after curandero. As we will see later, this tension of the *curandera-bruja* in many Mexican families is a legacy of the persecution of female healers.

I remember asking a ceremonial leader once for a limpia, and she responded that she could give me one or she could teach me how to do my own. Like a lot of women, I did not think I had the right or permission to do one, for that was the domain of elders. But as we gathered in our women's circle, we gave ourselves permission to heal ourselves. While we reclaimed the right to do this, we also asked for permission from our various elders, who guided us throughout the process. We were in our thirties to our fifties, and we knew better than to think we knew enough on our own, even though some of us had decades of experience. Some of the women had inherited *el don*, or the gift of healing, from their elders or were born with the power to doctor. As a result, we created what we believe to be the first promotora program on Mexican/Indigenous traditional medicine in the United States, in 1998.

As part of our vision, we adopted a phrase from the ceremonial leader Sylvia Ledesma: *"Curandera de yo misma."* Curandera of myself.[4] We knew it had not been that long since our teachings and ways had stopped being practiced, and some never did cease. As I became a promotora of traditional medicine, I saw how people, when gathered in a circle, would invariably remember a recipe or even ritual knowledge and old cosmological knowledge associating ecological phenomena with health and illness. From that experience, I concluded we could not have a resurgence of traditional medicine or *curanderismo* until we first revitalized *curando*, or healing our own bodies and those of our families. That family medicine is the foundation that allowed the teachings to continue in the first place. As Ledesma says, "healing is part of our self-governance."

I was contemplating how the plants are part of self-determination, establishing sacred relationships with life, when I found this passage by Cajete: "Plant cultivation was one of the primary reasons for the development of accurate calendars" (2000, 237). It reminded me of how Mesoamerican ceremonial calendars are based on the agricultural cycle and the cycles in the natural world. During the "sweeping of the roads" ceremonial period of purification, the midwives danced with bundles of herbs, marigolds, and tobacco. I thought of Malinalli, an herb or grass twisted like a double helix, which is a day sign on the calendar. I thought of Cihuacoatl's twisted hair, and again of Quilaztli. These twisted braids are energetic *trenzas* that connect what is above with what is below in energetic and physical umbilical cords of life. Hundreds of years later, we medicine keepers of the kalpulli dance with brooms and these same herbs during the same ceremonial count.

I remember traditional teachers advising us that to understand Indigenous medicine, we must study the calendars. While learning Nahuatl, I dreamed of Nahua symbols in a cave. A man was pointing them out to me. Florescano calls the calendar system a device that "set historical memory into motion" (1994, 58, 103). In Mesoamerican traditions, the past is living and remembered in the human activities of planting, hunting, and gathering of foods and medicines. I felt that something was being transmitted to me, though I did not know what. A Mayan medicine man once told me I would be an "autoridad de las plantas," someone who would defend and know the plants deeply.

Hidden Knowledge Speaks Up

In Mexico and among many cultures, "traditional medicine" is used to refer to a series of medicinal and healing practices that have been maintained over time:

> Traditional medicine in Mesoamerica is based upon knowledge and practices that originate from systems of thought and worldviews that are different from those of the West. This knowledge and these practices both derive from and provide the rationale for the daily activities of professional healers. These professionals vary in their characteristics from culture to culture, but throughout the ancient lands of Mesoamerica they are known as *curanderos*. The word "*curandero*" does not have a precise meaning. It refers to an individual's role as a healer while at the same time implying that this individual is not a medical doctor in the Western sense. A *curandero* is a person who cures, or who tries to cure, in accord with the ancient pre-Hispanic indigenous pattern, adding knowledge that has accrued for nearly five centuries since the Spanish Conquest. (Viesca Treviño 2001, 47)

Viesca Treviño and Noemi Quezada (2000) note that the "magical" aspects of curanderismo were emphasized in colonial writings. In fact, they were recorded because the dominant group wanted to eliminate what the Indigenous syncretic medical practices favored most (Viesca Treviño 2001). While MTM incorporated African and Spanish elements into its medicinal practices, it did not stop being Indigenous medicine. Some of it became more mestizo or Christianized, but its roots and trunk remained Indigenous.

The *curandero* is the product of the Conquest; indigenous medical specialists such as the Nahua *tícitl*, the Huastec *ilalix*, the Tzeltal *h'ilojel* and
Tzotil *h'ilol*, the Mayan *h-men*, the *ah cut* of the Pokoman, and its Quiché
equivalent, the *ah cun*, became diluted and homogenized. All of these pre-
Hispanic healers gradually became *curanderos*, with a single Spanish term
serving to overshadow cultural differences among them. Previous to the
Conquest, all of these healers had been doctors in the complete sense of
the term: specialists who solved the health problems of their own people
through activities ranging from attending to relations with the sacred to
the preparation of medicines (Viesca Treviño 2001, 47–48).

Indigenous medicine is always adapting to its circumstances. Indigenous
people took European grains and turned them into flour tortillas and fry bread;
tobacco tins became part of the regalia of the Anishinabe jingle dress. *Ruda*
(rue) and rosemary were adopted when Native plants were discouraged by the
oppressors because of their ceremonial uses (such as the herb *estafiate*), yet
estafiate continues to be used today, and ruda and rosemary are primary healing plants, even considered *plantas maestras*, or principal plants, by Indigenous
healers. They synchronized their preexisting knowledge with the European
and African influences of hot and cold, ancestor prayers, and various treatments for emotional disturbances. Many traditional healers say that Indigenous medicine and curanderismo develop from what is useful and accessible.
As I began to learn both natural medicine and Indigenous medicine, the advice I got from several of my elders was to know my foundation—what teachings grounded me as an Indigenous woman.

Today, traditional medicine in Mexico is still vibrant and undergoing
change. Some Indigenous elders use a pendulum for diagnosis; dousing has
appeared in cultures around the world but is especially popular today in alternative medicine. Other elders have adopted Bach flower remedies, a natural
extension of their vast knowledge of the curative, ritual, and ceremonial uses
of fresh flowers. They have not stopped doing Indigenous medicine because
of these complementary practices. They are Indigenous people grounded in
their relationship with the natural world.

Peyote, a medicine from Mexico, led to the formation of the Native American Church north of the border, yet curiously, Mexicans and Mexican Indians are often prohibited from using this potent medicine because they cannot
prove they are Indian, despite the fact that many in Texas are the descendants
of Chichimeca tribes and other Native peoples with an ancestral connection
to this medicine. This is, in good part, the consequence of being discursively
and legally defined out of the Native American category, often at the whim of
the United States. Such changing markers displace original peoples from the

historical consciousness in the following portion of a prayer. Among pre-Columbian peoples, peyote was greeted with the memory of its origins: "*can ichichimeco*," or "you who live in the country of the Chichimecos" (Aguirre Beltrán [1963] 1992, 139.)

MTM has not lost its vast knowledge of herbs, nutrition, or the energetic practices that are often combined as part of the treatment in the forms of limpias or ceremonies. A relationship with the four elements of life and the land persists. The practices of limpias, medicinal baths, and herbalism represent a landed relationship and often a particular relationship with land. In California, *pirul* may be used as a planta maestra, while in another place it may be *gobernadora* that is used. The plants also migrate with us as we move through the lands. I have had to adjust my limpias to different landscapes, using, for instance, more evergreens and cedar when I moved to Wisconsin's "tundra" for graduate school.

Plantas Calientes

"*Vamos a calentar tu olla*," said my friend Helga Garcia Garza as we walked to the *temazkal* to warm my pot at her family's kalpulli near Brownsville, Texas. "*Vamos a calentar tu temazkalli*." Her *familia* of *danzantes*, or ceremonial dancers, had learned from Ségura, and she and her husband, Jose Garza, are knowledge keepers of Indigenous medicine and ceremony. From Martha Ramírez-Oropeza, a cofounder of Nahuatl University, I would learn that *la olla*, the woman's uterus, is symbolized in the codices as a U-shaped pot on the moon. We would also participate in a 2002 ceremony led by Nahua curanderas at the "pyramid of the flowers." There, I was first exposed to the offerings of the women with their "pots," or bellies, filled with a baby at Xochitecatl (a few years before I would read about this place in books, I knew women were still going there to pray for babies).

At a gathering of Otomi in Denver, Colorado, an Otomi woman who did traditional medicine told me that as a result of being raped in 1984, my *matríz* "*volvio niña*." My uterus had become like a girl's, and therefore cold. The hot-cold principle of traditional medicine in Mexico is an ancient one, predating the Spanish introduction of its own hot-cold paradigm into MTM (López Austin 1988). Treatments using the four elements of life are often determined by this hot-cold paradigm. They can vary from teas to *baños*, or herbal baths, to massages with salves made with oils and herbs with specific hot/cold/neutral qualities, to eating or avoiding foods that are hot or cold in nature, and to using the temazkal. Hernández Sáenz and Foster record this paradigm in colonial medicinal knowledge of "cold in the womb" (2001, 44).

Cultures dense with symbols develop healing systems based on the opacity of symbols and cosmology that help to explain this hot-cold world-view. One of the shared symbols among many Mesoamerican cultures that still thrives today is the concept of the dual Creator, understood in Aztec/Mexica culture as Ometeotl: *Ome*—two; and *teotl*—sacred stone. This duality is constantly expressed in life as movement, which is created by the tension between the balancing of opposites: male-female; salt-sweet; acid-alkaline; day-night; solar-lunar; above-below; hot-cold. This is an energetic principle. Other Native cultures, such as Laguna Pueblo, also have male-female creators that speak to their cosmological understanding of balance. Thus, to have a name for Creator(s) that recognizes this duality indicates that this philosophical code is an organizing principle and the originating Indigenous source for this continuing healing framework. A prime example in Nahua medicinal thought is the pre-Columbian expression of sickness as "*in ehecatl, in temoxtli*," referring to cold, wind, and water as sources of illness and the signaling cosmic dualities: "This was a simple way of naming the two halves of the world from which most of man's illnesses came" (López Austin 1988, 275).

By examining the hot-cold paradigm, one can also see a system of Indigenous medicine that involves an integrated approach to healing and wellness. Aspects of the four elements are employed based on their physical and energetic properties and prescribed to balance the hot-cold state of the body. The four elements are applied internally or externally to purify and balance the state of life, depending on the nature of the imbalance. The four elements are used based on their unique nature. For instance, the properties of earth have an absorbing function. *Tierra*, or earth, itself is cooling and would be employed when a person needs something absorbed, as opposed to being fortified by fire. When I teach students about this property, I instruct them to place their palms facing the earth. Most will detect the gravitational pull of the earth. The elements of earth include food, herbs, flowers, and minerals that contain the hot-cold principle.

As a child, my mothers (grandmothers and mother) would tell me not to go *descalza* (barefoot) lest frío—cold—enter my body. To avert *aires* (airs), I could not go out with wet hair on a cold morning or in the evening. When I first started trying to get pregnant, the nanas would advise me not to eat cold foods. Many traditional midwives speak of pregnancy as a hot state. Cosminsky notes the Mayan belief that women carry more blood while pregnant, and blood is hot in nature (2001). One traditional curing practice that I have been taught is how to take care of a child who has gotten sick from being exposed to too much heat from a pregnant woman. The nana (grandmother) midwives teach that when a woman gives birth she is very "open," and cold can enter. After delivery, a woman is in a cold state from the loss of blood and expulsion of the baby and therefore should consume hot teas and hot food. Elders have also taught me that it is not recommended to use scissors when cutting the umbilical cord, because scissors are cold in nature. Elders may use obsidian for cutting the cord, and Nicolás León, who gathered a trove of birthing knowledge of Mexico in the 1900s, recorded this same Indigenous practice to guard against cold entering the child (1910).

This is an example of how Indigenous knowledge makes sense by establishing caution and making use of what is available. Jordan has documented how sometimes using a *vela*, or candle, often a traditional instrument to cauterize the umbilical cord, is better than using technologies introduced by western medicine (1997). In homes without electricity or running water, it can be difficult to sterilize metal objects, while a candle is readily available and can ensure a sterile implement. I have been taught by elders that traditional medicine evolves from what is nearby and makes sense.

When I was living in Mexico, I miscarried. I did not follow my mother's prescriptions for postpartum care. I did not wear the *faja*, or cloth wrap, long enough to protect my uterus, the usual ritual time of twenty to forty days. Some women adhere to twenty, based on the Native ceremonial calendars, and others up to forty, based on the *cuarentena*. Some say the cuarentena is the Catholicized forty-day ritual period used not only for the faja and *dieta* (a prescribed diet) following birth, but for other healing practices involving repeated use or application for restoration. However, it is also considered a ritual time of two twenty-day cycles. (Mesoamerican ceremonial calendars employ a twenty-day time period similar to the Gregorian calendar's month.) I walked around barefoot where cold and aires could enter my body. That, coupled with the sexual violation, caused the *frío a madurar*. Once coldness has matured, it is quite difficult to transform it. "*Por eso te entró mucho, mucho frío,*" doña Filo told me.

Yauhtli

I asked la nana Filo what kind of herbs or flowers to use in limpias or purification of pregnant women. As an herbalist and promotora de medicina tradicional, I was often asked to do limpias and prepare women for birth. "Yauhtli," she said. "Yauhtli loosens and releases." When a woman has a difficult labor, the nana burns yauhtli. Popularly known as *pericón* or *yerba anis*, yauhtli is recorded in the *Florentine Codex* (Sahagún 1950–1982). *Yauhtli*, or *iyautli*, translates as "an offered-up thing" or incense (Ruiz de Alarcón 1984, 250).[5]

A few weeks after this apprentice period, I did a limpia and blessing for an expectant couple and the father's mother to honor the "catching" of the baby by the entire family during their home birth. We used yauhtli, their eagle feather, and flowers, and the baby came that night.

One of my spirit sisters, Judy P., taught me how to bless a newborn baby with *limpias de flores*. Judy descends from Mayan and Aztec peoples. And though she came from the mountains of New Mexico, she taught me a ceremonia using flowers very similar to that of the Nahuas as recorded by Huber and Sandstrom in postpartum rituals involving Huastec, Nahua, Otomi, Tepehua, and Totonac midwives regarding the afterbirth, blood, and amniotic fluid (2001).

Regarding Nahua midwives from Ixhuatlan de Madero: "On the fourth day after birth either the midwife or a special ritual kinswoman [the *axochiteonaj*, or water-flower godmother] ritually cleanses the newborn child by bathing him in water in which herbs have been soaked" (Huber and Sandstrom 2001, 154). Though we were thousands of miles away, we were following similar principles. We were acting in the capacity of the axochiteonaj, the water-flower godmother. Other nanas and traditional teachers taught me the importance of flowers in limpias and baños, for children as well as adults. The importance of flowers in ceremonies is strewn across the Americas on gravesites and altars and the crosses of yauhtli that are made on September 28 in Morelos and left in *milpas* (cornfields) and crossroads. This coincides with "the sweeping of the roads" ceremonial time in the Mesoamerican calendars, when the fall winds come and fields are harvested and cleaned in preparation for the season's turn toward repose.

The *materia medica* for herbs related to pregnancy and birthing is vast, though herbs tend to be discouraged to protect the child. I turn to three other herbs, some of which have more ritualistic usage and are recorded in the early colonial records of Sahagún and Ruiz de Alarcón. 'Come. Let it be you soon, priest, Nine-[times]-rock-slapped-one [i.e., the tobacco]. Let us shoo away from here the yellow palsy, the green palsy.' With this she puts down the *piçiete* [tobacco] and sets her pregnant one to giving birth. But if for the good outcome of the childbirth she intends to avail herself of fire and incensings, which commonly are with copal or with the herb called yauhtli—that is, anise—where she says in the incantation 'nine-times beaten one.' . . ." (Ruiz de Alarcón 1984, 159).

When I have shared this passage from the 1600s in my discussion of the medicinal uses of tobacco, peyote, estafiate, and the maguey, some Native midwives have commented that among their tribal traditions in the north, they also employ tobacco or peyote when there is a difficult labor or to diagnose causes and actions. Ruiz de Alarcón (ibid.) recorded in his treatise that in order to facilitate labor, women "pick up the piçiete in the hand and crush it, and then they move the hand with the piçiete over the belly of the pregnant woman, especially over the fetus." *Iyetl* is "tobacco" in Nahuatl; *piciyetl* is "tiny tobacco." Andrews and Hassig, translators of the treatise, identify it as *Nicotiana rustica* and note that it is used to cure afflictions of the uterus.

When I shared that story with doña Filo, she commented, "*Fíjate que sí.* You wouldn't believe it, but it works. You just blow like this." And she showed how she puffs on the cigarette as an intervention to advance labor. Tobacco used in this physical and energetic manner is a technology of birthing because it is employed to move the labor, and therefore it is energy. Jordan speaks of how tools such as the rebozo massage to ease back pains, a birthing stool or hammock, or a rope for vertical birthing are more than "folk medicine." They are technologies of birthing. They also represent Native cosmology and a medical geography. The rope traditionally has been viewed as a connection to the cosmos, such as in the Mayan worldview, or as an ombligo that ties the woman to the cosmos, such as the ombligos or umbilical cords that tie female rulers to mountains and space in the codices.

Tobacco offerings, tobacco gourds, and tobacco flowers are recorded in the codices and on stone figurines, such as that of Xochipilli. Women are depicted selling tobacco in the *Florentine Codex* (Sahagún 1950–1982). Today, various medicinal practices using tobacco continue in Mexican Indigenous medicine. To introduce masculine energy, tobacco is burned near a baby. It is also used for burns, diarrhea, cuts, insect bites, and afflictions of the uterus, for incisions, headaches, inflammation of the spleen, toothaches, syphilis, snakebites, asthma, and dropsy, and to alleviate pain. It is used for protection or rubbed on the body for fatigue or as a form of prayer. Ruiz de Alarcón records a recipe for *tenexiyetl* (lime-tobacco) in a 1:10 ratio for *mal de frío* (illness caused by cold), or to be used with tomato for swollen throats and cysts (1984, 251). This energetic practice is an example of how Indigenous knowledge is a continuance today of the pre-Hispanic Indigenous patterns.

Again, midwives thousands of miles from each other know to use the plant toward the same ends. In our relationship with las plantas, we each grow to know it, in some ways uniquely. One people will use the same plant for something entirely different from another people, but they may also employ it for similar purposes. Through repeated use and experimenting with plants, peoples may also find similar uses thousands of miles away. These are examples of the correspondences that Indigenous peoples share with each other based on similar values, yet as distinct peoples. And there is also the sharing of knowledge via trade and cultural exchanges. The plants' connection to humans is also creative. The plants convey to us certain truths of their powers and uses and should not be discounted in how distant peoples may arrive at similar knowledge. They are cocreators with humans. They have been the cocreators of my own health. I have coughed before a sacred fire as *"la medicina"*—peyote—healed me when I faced a life-threatening illness, or said prayers during ritual times based on my life cycle and the natural cycle of the moon.

In colonial Mexico, peyote medicine was so revered and useful, female midwives and healers were prosecuted by the Holy Office of the Inquisition for employing it, and colonial records document its widespread use among Indigenous peoples of Mexico. Despite religious persecution of its users, its medicinal and ritual use continues today among numerous Mexican Indians from Huichol and Tarahumara, Native peoples of the north, and detribalized Mexicans and "Chicanos indígenas" who use it medicinally in homes with families as part of prayers or in large ceremonies. Grannies use it medicinally in some places in northern Mexico and South Texas, growing plants on their porches or yards.

Quezada (2000) records midwives in Mexico who accused patients of adultery by resorting to peyote to determine the cause of difficult labor. The Inquisition reviewed the case of one mother who consulted peyote herself to see whether she was pregnant. Andrews and Hassig translate *peyotl* as "a thing that glimmers, glows" (Ruiz de Alarcón 1984, 251).[6] Maximino Martínez notes that many Native cultures revere peyote as a Creator spirit and protector, wearing it for protection. Prayers to "Señor Estafiate," the Nine-times-beaten-one (tobacco) and *yerba María* or peyote are recorded in Inquisition documents. Ruiz de Alarcón notes that copal resin and flowers were left as offerings to peyote. It is a practice that continues today (M. Martínez 1959a and 1959b).

Peyote is called by various Native names: *peyotl, jicuri, piyolli piot, piule, peyori, peyot,* and *peyoztin,* which I was taught means "heart that glimmers." It was banned by a 1620 edict of the Inquisition. For their peyote use to survive, Native peoples called it by encoded Christian names, and it became associated with Jesus and the Holy Trinity, as well as Nuestra Señora, Santa María, Santa Rosa María, Yerba Santa María, and Santa María el peyote. Aguirre Beltrán ([1963] 1992) records how in Zacatecas it was called Yerba María, San Nicolas, San Antonio, and Cristo crucificado; in Saltillo it was called señor don Pedro; when it is called Rosa María, its masculine part is known as Rosa San Nicolas (reflecting the Native cosmology of male-female creative beings). The conquest records indicate how Indigenous peoples used sacred language and offered song and dance, much as is done today in many Indigenous communities of Mexico and the United States.

¡Tlazolcihuapilli
Cemicac inichipochtli
Yaolquil itonatiuh

yahuallan Yohaualli
Ahuayahuayan
can ichichimeco
Nixtlacuilolli!

¡Mujer Divina y hechicera
Virgen para siempre jamás
espiga guerrera del sol,
que presides el cerco de la noche,
donde es dios el lanuginoso cactus,
en el país de los Chichimecas.
Tú, la del rostro pintado de blanco!
(Aguirre Beltrán [1963] 1992, 141–42)

This prayer, loosely translated, calls on the "divine woman and bewitcher" who is "virgin for always" and presides over the night where a cactus is Creator. It is interesting to note that in this prayer Tlazolcihuapilli is one of the divine female beings associated with stars and the night sky. These beings are also the women who die in childbirth and accompany the sun and another manifestation of Tlazolteotl, the female guardian of midwives, pregnant women, newborns—the Great Weaver and Parturient of Life. Other prayers recorded by the Holy Office further exemplify the cloaking of this medicine in the name of the Holy Spirit as the petitioner asks it "to take me out of the tribulation in which I find myself" (Quezada 2000, 50). The supplicants prayed:

Santa Rosa María, en el nombre del padre,
Del Hijo y del Espíritu Santo,
Por la virtud que Dios te ha dado,
Te pido que me cures y saques del tribulación en que me hallo.
(Quezada 2000, 50)

After saying these words the petitioners were to eat the medicine and, in keeping with the Inquisition, use this Christianized frame—if you have a virtue from God, heal me, but if your virtue is from the devil, I do not want to see or hear you. Some three hundred years later, Martínez notes this Huichol prayer recorded in 1924:

Quí Tacuezi cati coerenguan; Teahuari-Touzi Zapagui yemi tirzu Urámaca; quiechuri nauaca, taramara atosame Quetzi-Nacague, no ari huame, utranaca, usimahuaca, ¡Casiguari, Huahquiri! Ecatehuiri Matzi, paricuta, muelleica huersica huerica huemari.

Ta-ta Cabaleno simuáname catagué erataguame. Ya anite ne tete, neatama: Neamatzina huahuatzari; Tatagui, cipirza guie huro caique, tutujaique, henemulleica tocari.

Huaquiri enesenemalluri yunaiparan nenulleican nemallellureine tucari maneari.

Buenos días, mi Creador, siempre cuida de mí comida hasta hoy lo has hecho. No permitas que Tehuari-Touzi (Espíritu del mal) se apodere de mi alma. Que la madre nube me defienda del fuego por dondequiera que vaya! oh, tú, nube del norte, del sur, del este y del oeste, juntaos para que con vuestro riego se fecunde la tierra que me da de comer!

Felices vosotras, nubes que nacéis del mar y de los ríos, de los ríos que Cuetzi-Nacague formó azotando las culebras. (1959a, 472–73)

The prayer continues: "¡Oh, gran Ta-tata-Cabaleno (espíritu del bien) que ahuyentas los espíritus del mal, dame licencia de vivir siempre sano!" (M. Martínez 1959a, 472–73).

This prayer invokes various creators and clouds that are born from the ocean and rivers. These beings bless the corn and harvests that come from the providence of the peyote as a result of prayers offered to this sacred entity. I include these peyote prayers to contextualize the importance that the Inquisition placed on its eradication and why it continues today to be called the great creator and life sustainer and therefore continues to be utilized in fertility of the earth and humans and in birthing rites. Some elders told me to take peyote to get pregnant. One recipe called for taking it based on my moon cycle, followed by a massage from a *sobadora*. Among Indigenous people in northern Mexico it is known as the giver of life and fertility (Schultes et al. 2000, 144). Winter records this recipe for stopping menstrual hemorrhage: a bit of peyote is boiled with rosemary and pecan shell. Only after the water is boiled is a very small piece of peyote added. The decoction is used as a douche and is given every other day until recovery (1968, 111).

Today, peyote is used medicinally for heart problems, rheumatism, kidney stones, toothaches, digestive problems, dream healing, fertility, enemas, purging of illness, fevers, fractures, as an aphrodisiac, and for therapeutic uses, divination, and protection (ibid.; Kelly 1965). Some recipes call for it to be eaten with sugar or *piloncillo*. It may be worn, drunk in a tea, used as a douche or an enema, or burned. Some Indigenous midwives continue to employ it to fortify mother and midwife and as a painkiller. Despite colonized thinking that continues to suppress its living relationship with Indigenous peoples, peyote continues to be used in subterranean cultural practices. Chicanos and "undocumented" Indians unrecognized by the nation-state on either side of the border refuse to relinquish their ancestral relationship with this powerful medicine that has medicinal and ritual uses, including in birthing and fertility. Schultes et al. record that its usage was still so prevalent in 1760 in San Antonio, Texas, that a priest published a list for converts that included the questions (which I translate here): "Have you eaten human flesh? Have you eaten the flesh of peyote?" (2000, 147). That these medicines are still used for medicinal and ritual purposes to affect physical aspects of healing, such as fertility and birth, indicates the resiliency of these traditions across time and dominance.

Maguey Grandmother: New Moon Dream, April 2002

Journal entry made while teaching a course on sacred geography at UCLA:

> I am with *hombres de medicina*. Abuelos Mayas. I feel I know them, two or three. One tells me, "*un espíritu te ha escupido.*" (But I am protected.) I look on the ground and see a large square marble slab. He goes to my feet. I'm afraid to look. On my left foot is an emblem in green, 3-D, of Meyahuel, her tree. On right, is a glistening, silvery white spiderweb— spiderwoman. I can see Tlazolteotl's silhouette in the web. Then I see a jefe (ceremonial leader) from Amecameca. He is showing me an *escultura de* Quetzalcoatl. It is cut in vidrio, several layers of cut glass or quartz, cutting into the air. I can not make out what he is trying to show me because it is so silvery light and shining. Were they showing me my medicine, that they are inside me, on me? Showing me the way?

"Today is a good day. It is a full moon," la nana Filo told me when I started my first lessons with her by being treated for infertility.

I came to Mexico knowing only her town. I was told to go see her early, as she rises before dawn to work. I arrived at five-thirty in the morning, asking for directions in her village as I went along. She has already gone to the market. Her land base is organized in the old way of the Nahua peoples, with relatives and children in their own homes, usually one or two rooms at most, where sleeping and much *convivencia* transpires. She has a separate cooking hut for her hearth, and her *fuego*, or fire, was one of the first things she proudly showed me when we met up again later. People who must depend on the fire for warmth and their food often have a deep knowledge of life science and how to use it for medicina. By life science, I mean a science of life or a scientific understanding that unfolds from your very existence depending on a direct relationship with the natural world.

She palpates my womb and uterus, showing me some teachings on the energetic role of the ombligo, or navel, and sharing recetas with me, different yerbas for frío en el matríz, cysts, and tumors, and for cleaning out uterine congestion. She spends all the next day gathering *pencas de maguey*, roasting the maguey leaves and curing them with the full moon. I am not to bathe for the three days that I apply this ointment topically, and am to clean only lightly with a washcloth and not cold water, else I will inflame. It is a treatment of extremely hot nature. We speak of the moon, and I ask her if she blesses the babies; she does, presenting them to the celestial forces, but silently, since many of her clients are Christianized. Later, when I read the sixteenth-century birthing narratives recorded by Sahagún in which the midwife blesses the newborn, I think in some fashion this is still happening; midwives or ritual keepers are still doing this. We speak more of limpias and blessing ways. Over the years, she has shown me various recetas with the maguey. Maguey, or *metl*, treats infertility, the immune system, muscular ailments, and the kidneys. *Miel de maguey* (maguey honey) also is used for infertility, and for diabetes.

For instance, the nana says, if a woman is about to miscarry, she administers a drink made from nine *picos*, or tips of the maguey, a gold ring, and red thread. When tata Aurelio hears this, he interjects that the receta comes from the story of the Tepozteco, a cultural hero of nearby Tepoztlan. He tells us the story that night; it takes a good hour to tell, and I am falling asleep. So I ask her to retell it to me so that I can remember it. The part of the story relevant here follows.

There was a maiden who ate a piece of corn. She got pregnant and her parents abandoned her baby, leaving it on a maguey. A little worm pricked a hole so that the baby could nurse from the maguey milk. Then the *ranitas* (frogs) made him a mat from tule reeds, but first the little ants made him a cradle from ants so that he could warm up. Some *ancianos*, or elders, passed by and found him, and they took him to raise as their own. The abuela drank *atole* of amaranth to have mother's milk, "*y el niño colgó*," the baby latched on. Amaranth is from the same family as *ajonjolí*, or sesame, the nana notes. Earlier, doña Filo had said that amaranth helps with mother's milk, as does ajonjolí. We can see how this story contains what Native peoples call original instructions, guidelines for food as medicine and how to live, as well as stories that reflect a sacred geography. Native intelligence is expressed in doña Filo's understanding of the moon cycle and its influence on the maguey both as it grows and as the moon exerts pressure on its liquids, and as the liquids strengthen into a decoction while under its watch again. Sacred formulas constitute a distinct expression of Indigenous science, and ceremonies and rituals are included as part of the process of "causality." From the Otomi to the Totonac, midwives perform a sacred charge in the heavens, burning copal incense in the celestial realms and guiding as divine beings.

Sacred Directions

Tepixinola—woman rock—is a ceremonial site that el tata said we must journey to next. Later that day, we would go into the temazkalli. Before, it had been too humid, and the wetness would have entered our bodies. He prepared the fire and the herbs for *curar el frío*. "Una partera sin un temazkall," he tells us, "no es partera." A midwife without a sweat lodge is not a midwife.

> Journal entry: Tepixinola Aug. 18–04: *Despertamos con el caracol*. We awoke to the sound of the conch shell calling us for ceremony.
>
> Doña Filo says my uterus has gone into place (after three of the *tratamientos con la abuela Maguey*). I took pink booties and roses as offerings. As we arrived to the "window," our tata pointed out her stone rebozo on the ground. "*Aquí empieza su rebozo*." There is the baby! A rock formed like a baby on its tummy with its rump up. Someone had taken its head. "And there, there is her skirt." It was tall and thick like a womb that had borne many children. Tepixinola was full of herbs and plants. *Doradilla* and a maguey grew in its stones. Roberto saw a *chuparosa* (hummingbird). A *tlacuache*—possum—left some markings. "He left its offering," joked doña Filo. "Whenever you see a dead tlacuache on the road, cut his tail for when you need it." (Possum tail is prepared to speed a labor and is recorded in Sahagún.) Long green braids of doradilla and other herbs hang like trenzas from her chichis, her braids and teats. The traditional offerings of mole in clay pots and toys and candles fill the shrine. We pray to the four directions holding colored candles for each of the cardinal points. I pray to Tepixinola and ask for a baby. Roberto tells her we have brought her an offering. My abuelos pray for us and for their own children. As we walk back, doña Filo gathers some of her favorite herbs, *capitaneja* and San Francisco. Along with *axhiutl*, she uses them for numerous ailments beyond fertility and birthing. As I look at Tepixinola, I see all the teachings there, grandmother maguey who has been healing me, several large thick spiderwebs—Tlazolteotl's weavings. I see trenzas like the ones I have promised to bring back from my baby. The medicine of tlacuache and hummingbird, and its love medicine. And I have faith. In *tratamientos*, the properties of earth are physical and spiritual, and ceremonies move spirit and body. As above, so below. May that which is above and that which is below heal this middle

world, this earth plane in my body. And even if it does not bring me a baby, let it help me be like doña Filo, a "maker of mothers."

I have often wondered why I am a carrier of culture in some way. I have been told by my elders that I am to be a "mother maker" like my great-grandmother. I am but an apprentice in these ways, primarily of the Mexican Indian teachings. Aside from the oral instructions I receive, part of my medicinal knowledge comes from the spirit world and in dreams. Often, I will find evidence of their truths in the physical world via books and teachings passed on to me, as I did on November 30, 2003, while researching Indigenous birthing.

Chevalier and Sánchez Bain record that the Nahuas of Veracruz have a practice of putting a newborn outside, leaving the child "in the yard immediately after birth as if it were unwanted." Mothers who have lost other children are encouraged to do this to strengthen the child's life force (2003, 68). Prior to reading Chevalier and Sánchez Bain, I had a dream that was beautiful and painful until I found this citation. And so I will share this dream as another form of evidence: in October 2003 I dreamed that I birthed a baby. I saw the entire birth, even felt it in my lower spine while I was dreaming. It was an easy birth. I did not need nurses. I decided to put my baby outside in the sunshine, but I left it out too long. When I returned, it was slowly dissolving into a golden droplet. I touched it, and with my finger I picked up its last drop of light. I inserted it in my womb. The divine midwives in the spirit world had sent a message.

Notes

1. Sometimes I waited for Ségura as he did his *curaciones* (healing work). One day, a young couple was waiting for him with their baby so that he could name him based on the ancient ceremonial calendars. The *Florentine Codex*, a thirteen-volume work that recorded Indigenous knowledge, speaks of the day keepers who read the ritual calendars and named children more than five hundred years ago (Sahagún 1950–1982). There are numerous glyphs in the codices that show the day keeper assigning a name.

2. Cajete also uses this term to explain Native science and knowledge.

3. As Cajete elaborates: "Plants present the life energy of the universe in their roots, stems, leaves, and flowers. In their tenacity for living in every location on earth, plants exemplify the operation of the natural laws of nature, of 'life seeking life.' At every turn, in every mode, and at every opportunity, plants seek to live their lives, and in their seeking, support all of life, including humans" (2000, 108).

4. Notably, many elders do not pronounce themselves curanderos, such as an elder who told me once, "Oh, no. I am not a curandera. I have been doing it only thirty-five years. My husband's the curandero. He has been doing it fifty." They have been named so by their communities.

5. *Tagetes lucida* Cav., of the Compositae family, is also known as *yerba anis*, *yerba de Santa María, pericon*, or sweet-scented marigold. It is a stimulant and an emmenagogue.

6. *Lophophora Williamsii* Lem. is of the Cactaceae family. It is a bluish-green plant with pale pink and white flowers. Famous for what western science terms its "hallucinogenic" properties, in particular when refined as mescaline, peyote grows in Queretaro, San Luis Potosí, Coahuila, Zacatecas, Chihuahua, and other places "del Norte," such as south Texas.

References

Adams, Sheridan, Mushim Ikeda-Nash, Jeff Kitzes, H. Margarita Loinaz, Jessica Tan, and Larry Yang, eds. 2000. *Making the Invisible Visible: Healing Racism in Our Buddhist Communities*. 2nd ed. Prepared for the Buddhist Teachers in the West Conference. http://www.eastbaymeditation.org/media/docs/6555_MakingTheInvisibleVisible.pdf.

Aguirre Beltrán, Gonzalo. [1963] 1992. *Medicina y mágia: El proceso de aculturación en la estructura colonial*. Jalapa, MX: Universidad Veracruzana.

Agyeong, Rosian, Margaret Brigham, Sabra Desai, Patsy Sutherland, Anne Wagner, and Njoki Nathani Wane, eds. 2011. "Feminism, Activism and Spirituality." Special Issue of *Canadian Woman Studies* 29(1/2).

Alarcón, Norma. 1998. "Chicana Feminism: In the Tracks of 'The' Native Woman." In *Living Chicana Theory*, edited by Carla Trujillo, 371–82. Berkeley, CA: Third Women Press.

Alarcón, Norma, Ana Castillo, and Cherríe Moraga, eds. 1993. *The Sexuality of Latinas*. Berkeley, CA: Third Woman Press.

Alexander, M. Jacqui. 2005. *Pedagogies of Crossing: Meditations on Feminism, Sexual Politics, Memory and the Sacred*. Durham, NC: Duke University Press.

Althusser, Louis. [1971] 2001. "Ideology and Ideological State Apparatuses (Notes Towards an Investigation)." In *Lenin and Philosophy and Other Essays*, 85–126. New York: Monthly Review Press.

Alvarez, Alma Rosa. 2007. *Liberation Theology in Chicana/o Literature: Manifestations of Feminist and Gay Identities*. New York: Routledge.

Anzaldúa, Gloria. [1981] 1983a. "El Mundo Zurdo: The Vision." In *This Bridge Called My Back: Writings by Radical Women of Color*, 2nd ed., edited by Cherríe Moraga and Gloria Anzaldúa, 217–18. Latham, NY: Kitchen Table, Women of Color Press.

———. [1981] 1983b. "La Prieta." In *This Bridge Called My Back: Writings by Radical Women of Color*, 2nd ed., edited by Cherríe Moraga and Gloria Anzaldúa, 220–33. Latham, NY: Kitchen Table, Women of Color Press.

———. [1981] 1983c. "Speaking in Tongues: A Letter to Third World Women Writers." In *This Bridge Called My Back: Writings by Radical Women of Color*, 2nd ed., edited by Cherríe Moraga and Gloria Anzaldúa, 165–74. Latham, NY: Kitchen Table, Women of Color Press.

———. 1982. "La serpiente que se come su cola [The Serpent Who Eats her Tail]: Life and Death Rites of a Chicana Lesbian." University of Texas at Austin Library. Accessed June 21, 2012. http://www.lib.utexas.edu/taro/utlac/00189/lac-00189p1.html.

———. 1987. *Borderlands/La Frontera: The New Mestiza*. San Francisco: Aunt Lute Press.

———. [1987] 1999. *Borderlands/La Frontera: The New Mestiza*. 2nd ed. San Francisco: Aunt Lute Books.

———, ed. 1990. *Making Face, Making Soul/Haciendo Caras: Critical and Creative Perspectives by Women of Color*. San Francisco: Aunt Lute Press.

———. 1993. "Border Arte: Nepantla, El Lugar de la Frontera." In *La Frontera/The Border: Art About the Mexico/U.S. Border Experience*, 107–114. San Diego, CA: Centro Cultural de La Raza.

———. 1999. "Interview with Gloria Anzaldúa" by Karin Ikas. In *Borderlands/La Frontera: The New Mestiza*, 2nd. ed., by Gloria Anzaldúa, 227–46. San Francisco: Aunt Lute Books.

———. 2000. *Interviews/Entrevistas: Gloria E. Anzaldúa*, edited by AnaLouise Keating. New York: Routledge.

———. 2002a. "now let us shift . . . the path of conocimiento . . . inner work, public acts." In *this bridge we call home: radical visions for transformation*, edited by Gloria Anzaldúa and AnaLouise Keating, 540–78. New York: Routledge.

———. 2002b. "(Un)natural bridges, (Un)safe spaces." In *this bridge we call home: radical visions for transformation*, edited by Gloria Anzaldúa and AnaLouise Keating, 1–5. New York: Routledge.

———. 2003. "Let Us Be The Healing of the Wound: The Coyolxauhqui Imperative—la sombra y el sueño." In *One Wound for Another/Una herida por otra: Testimonios de Latin@s in the U.S. Through Cyberspace (11 de septiembre de 2001–11 de marzo de 2002)*, edited by Clara Lomas and Claire Joysmith. Mexico City: Centro de Investigaciones Sobre América del Norte.

———. 2005. "A Daughter of Coatlicue: An Interview with Gloria Anzaldúa," by Irene Lara. In *EntreMundos/AmongWorlds: New Perspectives on Gloria E. Anzaldúa*, edited by AnaLouise Keating, 41–55. New York: Palgrave/Macmillan.

Anzaldúa, Gloria E. and AnaLouise Keating, eds. 2002. *this bridge we call home: radical visions of transformation*. New York: Routledge.

Aquino, María Pilar, Daisy L. Machado, and Jeanette Rodríguez, eds. 2002. *A Reader in Latina Feminist Theology: Religion and Justice*. Austin: University of Texas Press.

Aquino, María Pilar and Maria José Rosado-Nunes, eds. 2007. *Feminist Intercultural Theology: Latina Explorations for a Just World*. Maryknoll, NY: Orbis Books.

Arredondo, Sophia, Jessica Heredia, Irene Lara, and Eneri Arauz Rodriguez. 2007. *Panocha Pláticas: Healing Sex and Sexuality in Community*. San Diego, CA.

Asencio, Marysol, ed. 2010. *Latina/o Sexualities: Probing Powers, Passions, Practices, and Policies*. New Brunswick, NJ: Rutgers University Press.

Avila, Elena, with Joy Parker. 1999. *Woman Who Glows in the Dark: A Curandera Reveals Traditional Aztec Secrets of Physical and Spiritual Health*. New York: Jeremy P. Tarcher/Putman.

Ayala, Jennifer, Patricia Herrera, Laura Jiménez, and Irene Lara. 2006. "Fiera, Guambra, y Karichina! Transgressing the Borders of Community and Academy." In *Chicana/Latina Education in Everyday Life: Feminista Perspectives on Pedagogy and Epistemology*, edited by Dolores Delgado Bernal, C. Alejandra Elenes, Francisca E. Godinez, and Sofia Villenas, 261–80. Albany: State University of New York Press.

Baudrillard, Jean. 1998. "Simulacra and Simulations." In *Jean Baudrillard, Selected Writings*, edited by Mark Poster, 166–84. Palo Alto, CA: Stanford University Press. http://www.egs.edu/faculty/jean-baudrillard/articles/simulacra-and-simulations/.

Behar, Ruth. 1993. *Translated Woman: Crossing the Border with Esperanza's Story.* Boston: Beacon Press.

Black Elk. [1932] 1979. *Black Elk speaks: Being the Life Story of a Holy Man of the Oglala Sioux/As Told Through John G. Neihardt.* Lincoln: University of Nebraska Press.

Blake, Debra J. 2008. *Chicana Sexuality and Gender: Cultural Refiguring in Literature, Oral History, and Art.* Durham, NC: Duke University Press.

Boggs, Grace Lee, with Scott Kurashige. 2011. *The Next American Revolution: Sustainable Activism for the Twenty-First Century.* Berkeley: University of California Press.

Boucher, Sandy. 1993. *Turning the Wheel: American Women Creating the New Buddhism.* Boston: Beacon Press.

Broyles-González, Yolanda. 1994. *El Teatro Campesino: Theater in the Chicano Movement.* Austin: University of Texas Press.

——, ed. 2001. *Re-emerging Native Women of the Americas: Native Chicana Latina Women's Studies.* Dubuque, IA: Kendall/Hunt.

——. 2002. "Indianizing Catholicism: Chicana/India/Mexicana Indigenous Spiritual Practices in Our Image." In *Chicana Traditions: Continuity and Change*, edited by Norma E. Cantú and Olga Nájera-Ramírez, 117–32. Urbana and Chicago: University of Illinois Press.

Broyles-Gonzáles, Yolanda and Pilulaw Khus. 2011. *Earth Wisdom: A California Chumash Woman.* Tucson: University of Arizona Press.

Bruchac, Joseph. 1993. *The Native American Sweat Lodge: History and Legends.* Freedom, CA: Crossing Press.

Brunal, Adelin. 2011. "An Interconnected Path to Healing." In *Spirituality, Education and Society An Integrated Approach*, edited by Njoki N. Wane, Energy L. Manyimo, and Eric J. Ritskes, 169–82. Rotterdam, The Netherlands: Sense Publishers.

Bucko, Raymond A. 1998. *The Lakota Ritual of the Sweat Lodge.* Lincoln: University of Nebraska Press.

Butler, Judith. 1993. *Bodies that Matter: On the Discursive Limits of Gender.* New York: Routledge.

Cajete, Gregory. 2000. *Native Science: Natural Laws of Interdependence.* Santa Fe, NM: Clear Light Publishers.

Cantú, Norma E. 1995. *Canícula: Snapshots of a Girlhood en la Frontera.* Albuquerque: University of New Mexico Press.

——. 2009. "The Semiotics of Land and Place: Matachines Dancing in Laredo, Texas." In *Dancing Across Borders: Danzas y Bailes Mexicanos*, edited by Olga Nájera-Ramírez, Norma E. Cantú, and Brenda M. Romero, 97–115. Urbana and Chicago: University of Illinois Press.

Cantú, Norma and Olga Nájera-Ramírez, eds. 2002. *Chicana Traditions: Continuity and Change.* Urbana and Chicago: University of Illinois Press.

Castellanos, M. Bianet, Lourdes Gutiérrez Nájera, and Arturo J. Aldama, eds. 2012. *Comparative Indigeneities of the Américas: Toward a Hemispheric Approach.* Tucson: University of Arizona Press.

Castillo, Ana. 1994. *Massacre of the Dreamers: Essays on Xicanisma.* Albuquerque: University of New Mexico Press.

——. 1996. "Introduction." In *Goddess of the Americas/La Diosa de las Américas: Writings on the Virgin of Guadalupe*, edited by Ana Castillo, xv–xxiii. New York: Riverhead Books.

————, ed. 1996. *Goddess of the Americas/La Diosa de las Américas: Writings on The Virgin of Guadalupe*. New York: Riverhead Press.

Cerminara, Gina. 1950. *Many Mansions: The Edgar Cayce Story on Reincarnation*. New York: Signet.

Chabram-Dernersesian, Angie and Adela de la Torre, eds. 2008. *Speaking from the Body: Latinas on Health and Culture*. Tucson: University of Arizona Press.

Chevalier, Jacques M., and Andrés Sanchez Bain. 2003. *The Hot and the Cold: Ills of Humans and Maize in Native Mexico*. Toronto: University of Toronto Press.

Christian, B. Marie. 2005. *Belief in Dialogue: U.S. Latina Writers Confront their Religious Heritage*. New York: Other Press.

Churchill, Ward. 1992. *Fantasies of the Master Race: Literature, Cinema and the Colonization of American Indians*. Monroe, ME: Common Courage Press.

Cisneros, Sandra. 1996. "Guadalupe the Sex Goddess." In *Goddess of the Americas/La Diosa de las Américas: Writings on the Virgin of Guadalupe*, edited by Ana Castillo, 46–51. New York: Riverhead Books.

Cole, Ellen, Oliva M. Espín, and Esther Rothblum, eds. 1992. *Refugee Women and their Mental Health: Shattered Societies, Shattered Lives*. New York: Harrington Park Press.

Comas-Díaz, Lillian. 2008. "2007 Carolyn Sherif Award Address: Spirita: Reclaiming Womanist Sacredness into Feminism." *Psychology of Women Quarterly* 32(1): 13–21. doi: 10.1111/j.1471–6402.2007.00403.x

Cook, Katsi. 1992. "Grandmother Moon." In *Words that Come Before All Else: Environmental Philosophies of the Haudenosaunee*, edited by James Ransom, 139–42. New York: Native North American Traveling College.

Cosminsky, Sheila. 2001. "Maya Midwives of Southern Mexico and Guatemala." In *Mesoamerican Healers*, edited by Brad R. Huber and Alan R. Sandstrom, 179–210. Austin: University of Texas Press.

Cotera, Martha P. 1976. *Diosa y Hembra: The History and Heritage of Chicanas in the U.S.* Austin, TX: Information Systems Development.

de Beauvoir, Simone. [1952] 1989. *The Second Sex*. Translated and edited by H. M. Parshley. New York: Vintage Books.

de Certeau, Michel. 1988. *The Practice of Everyday Life* (vol.1). Berkeley: University of California Press.

————. 1992. *The Mystic Fable*. Translated by Michael B. Smith. Chicago: University of Chicago Press.

De la Portilla, Elizabeth. 2009. *They All Want Magic: Curanderas and Folk Magic*. College Station: Texas A&M University Press.

De La Torre, Miguel A. and Gastón Espinosa, eds. 2006. *Rethinking Latino(a) Religion and Identity*. Cleveland, OH: Pilgrim Press.

De Luna, Anita. 2002. *Faith Formation and Popular Religion: Lessons from the Tejano Experience*. Lanham, MD: Rowman & Littlefield.

Dechar, Lorie Eve. 2006. *Five Spirits: Alchemical Acupuncture for Psychological and Spiritual Healing*. New York: Lantern Books.

Delgadillo, Theresa. 1998. "Forms of Chicana Feminist Resistance: Hybrid Spirituality in Ana Castillo's *So Far From God*." *Modern Fiction Studies* 44(4): 888–916.

————. 2011. *Spiritual Mestizaje: Religion, Gender, Race, and Nation in Contemporary Chicana Narrative*. Durham, NC: Duke University Press.

Delgado Bernal, Dolores. 2006. "Learning and Living Pedagogies of the Home: The Mestiza Consciousness of Chicana Students." In *Chicana/Latina Education in Every-*

day Life: Feminista Perspectives on Pedagogy and Epistemology, edited by Dolores Delgado Bernal, C. Alejandra Elenes, Francisca Godinez, and Sofia Villenas, 113–32. Albany: State University of New York Press.

Delgado Bernal, Dolores, C. Alejandra Elenes, Francisca E. Godinez, and Sofia Villenas, eds. 2006. *Chicana/Latina Education in Everyday Life: Feminista Perspectives on Pedagogy and Epistemology*. Albany: State University of New York Press.

Denzin, Norman K., Yvonna S. Lincoln, and Linda Tuhiwai Smith, eds. 2008. *Handbook of Critical and Indigenous Methodologies*. Thousand Oaks, CA: Sage Publications.

Dillard, Cynthia B., Daa'iyah Abdur-Rashid, and Cynthia A. Tyson. 2000. "My Soul is a Witness: Affirming Pedagogies of the Spirit." *Qualitative Studies in Education* 13(5): 447–62.

Doetsch-Kidder, Sarah. 2012. *Social Change and Intersectional Activism: The Spirit of Social Movement*. New York: Palgrave Macmillan.

Dresser, Marianne, ed. 1996. *Buddhist Women on the Edge: Contemporary Perspectives from the Western Frontier*. Berkeley, CA: North Atlantic Books.

Dreyer, Elizabeth A. 2005. *Passionate Spirituality: Hildegard of Bingen and Hadewijch of Brabant*. Mahwah, NJ: Paulist Press.

Dreyer, Elizabeth A. and Mark S. Burrows, eds. 2005a. *Minding the Spirit: The Study of Christian Spirituality*. Baltimore, MD: Johns Hopkins University Press.

——. 2005b. "The Self-implicating Nature of the Study of Spirituality." In *Minding the Spirit: The Study of Christian Spirituality*, 61–64. Baltimore, MD: Johns Hopkins University Press.

——. 2005c. "Afterword: Emerging Issues and New Trajectories in the Study of Christian Spirituality." In *Minding the Spirit: The Study of Christian Spirituality*, 363–71. Baltimore, MD: Johns Hopkins University Press.

Durkheim, Emile. [1912] 1995. *The Elementary Forms of Religious Life*. Translated by Karen E. Fields. New York: Free Press.

Elenes, C. Alejandra. 2006. "Transformando Fronteras: Chicana Feminist Transformative Pedagogies." In *Chicana/Latina Education in Everyday Life: Feminista Perspectives on Pedagogy and Epistemology*, edited by Dolores Delgado Bernal, C. Alejandra Elenes, Francisca E. Godinez, and Sofia Villenas, 245–59. Albany: State University of New York Press.

——. 2011. *Transforming Borders: Chicana/o Popular Culture and Pedagogy*. Lanham, MD: Lexington Books.

Emoto, Masaru. 2005. *Hidden Messages in Water*. New York: Atria Books.

Ereira, Alana. 1992. *The Heart of the World: Elder Brothers Warning*. Montauk, NY: Mystic Fire Video. Videocassette (VHS).

Espín, Oliva M. 1996. *Latina Healers: Lives of Power and Tradition*. Encino, CA: Floricanto Press.

——. 1997. *Latina Realities: Essays on Healing, Migration, and Sexuality*. Boulder, CO: Westview Press.

——. 1998, April. "Rosa de Lima and Mariana de Quito: Women, Body, and Sanctity in the 16th and 17th Centuries." Paper presented at International Psychoanalytic Conference, "At the Threshold of the Millennium," Lima, Peru.

——. 1999. *Women Crossing Boundaries: A Psychology of Immigration and the Transformations of Sexuality*. New York: Routledge.

Espinosa, Gastón and Mario T. García, eds. 2008. *Mexican American Religions: Spirituality, Activism, and Culture*. Durham, NC: Duke University Press.

Esquibel, Catrióna Rueda. 2006. *With Her Machete in Her Hand: Reading Chicana Lesbians.* Austin: University of Texas Press.

Estés, Clarissa Pinkola. 1996. *Women Who Run With the Wolves: Myths and Stories of the Wild Woman Archetype.* New York: Ballantine Books.

———. 2011. *Untie the Strong Woman: Blessed Mother's Immaculate Love for the Wild Soul.* Boulder, CO: Sounds True, Inc.

Fernández, Adela. 1992. *Dioses prehispánicos de México.* Mexico City: Panorama Editorial.

Fernandes, Leela. 2003. *Feminist Practice: Nonviolence, Social Justice and the Possibilities of a Spiritualized Feminism.* San Francisco: Aunt Lute Books.

Flaherty, Thomas H., ed. 1992. *The Spirit World.* Richmond, VA: Time-Life Books.

Flores, Richard. R. 2002. *Remembering the Alamo: Memory, Modernity, and the Master Symbol.* Austin: University of Texas Press.

Florescano, Enrique. 1994. *Memory, Myth, and Time in Mexico: From the Aztecs to Independence.* Translated by Albert G. Bork, with the assistance of Kathryn R. Bork. Austin: University of Texas Press.

Fontana, David. 2003. *Psychology, Religion, and Spirituality.* Malden, MA: BPS Blackwell.

Frohlich, M. 2005. "Spiritual Discipline, Discipline of Spirituality." In *Minding the Spirit: The Study of Christian Spirituality,* edited by Elizabeth A. Dreyer and Mark S. Burrows, 65–77. Baltimore, MD: Johns Hopkins University Press.

Fukuoka, Masanobu. [1978] 2010. *The One-Straw Revolution: An Introduction to Natural Farming.* New York: New York Review Books.

Garcia, Alma, ed. 1997. *Chicana Feminist Thought: The Basic Historical Writings.* New York and London: Routledge.

Garcia-Camarillo, Cecilio, Roberto Rodriguez, and Patrisia Gonzales, eds. 2002. *Cantos al Sexto Sol: An Anthology of Aztlanahuac Writings.* San Antonio, TX: Wingspress.

Garcia Lopez, Christina. 2012. "Social Violence, Social Healing: The Merging of the Political and the Spiritual in Chicana/o Cultural Production." PhD diss., University of Texas at Austin.

García-Rivera, Alex. 1995. *St. Martín de Porres: The "Little Stories" and the Semiotics of Cultures.* Maryknoll, NY: Orbis Books.

Gardner, Howard. 2006. *Multiple Intelligences: New Horizons in Theory and Practice.* New York: Basic Books.

Gaspar de Alba, Alicia, ed. 2003. *Velvet Barrios: Popular Culture and Chicana/o Sexualities.* New York: Palgrave Macmillan.

Geertz, Clifford. 1973. *The Interpretation of Cultures.* New York: Basic Books.

Glazer, Steven, ed. 1999. *The Heart of Learning: Spirituality in Education.* New York: Putnam.

Godinez, Francisca. 2006. "*Haciendo que hacer:* Braiding Cultural Knowledge into Educational Practices and Policies." In *Chicana/Latina Education in Everyday Life: Feminista Perspectives on Pedagogy and Epistemology,* edited by Dolores Delgado Bernal, C. Alejandra Elenes, Francisca Godinez, and Sofia Villenas, 25–38. Albany: State University of New York Press.

Gonzales, Patrisia. 2000. "The Millennium of the Feminine." *The Brown Papers* 5(1): 1–14.

———. 2003. *The Mud People: Chronicles, Testimonios and Remembrances.* San José, CA: Chusma House.

———. 2012. *Red Medicine: Traditional Indigenous Rites of Birthing and Healing.* Tucson: University of Arizona Press.

Gonzalez, Alejandra, Irene Lara, Carolina Prado, Sophia Lujan Rivera, and Carmen Rodriguez. "Passing the Sage: Our Sacred Testimonio as CuranderaScholarActivists in Academia." *Chicana/Latina Studies: The Journal of Mujeres Activas en Letras y Cambio Social*. Forthcoming.

González, Michelle A. 2009. *Embracing Latina Spirituality: A Woman's Perspective*. Cleveland, OH: St. Anthony Messenger Press.

Guerra Falcón, Aida. 2009. *Medicina tradicional: Doña Queta y el legado de los habitantes de las nubes*. Coordinación y textos de Aida Guerra Falcón. Oaxaca, MX.

Gutiérrez Baldoquín, Hilda. 2000. "The Road Being Traveled: My Life and Times at San Francisco Zen Center (1990–2000)." In *Making the Invisible Visible: Healing Racism in Our Buddhist Communities*. 2nd ed., edited by Sheridan Adams, Mushim Ikeda-Nash, Jeff Kitzes, H. Margarita Loinaz, Jessica Tan, and Larry Yang. Prepared for the Buddhist Teachers in the West Conference. http://www.eastbaymeditation.org/media/docs/6555_MakingTheInvisibleVisible.pdf.

———, ed. 2004. *Dharma, Color, and Culture: New Voices in Western Buddhism*. Berkeley, CA: Parallax Press.

Hampe-Martínez, Teodoro. 1997. "Los testigos de Santa Rosa. (Una aproximación social a la identidad criolla en el Perú colonial)." *Revista Complutense de Historia de América* 23: 113–36.

Hanh, Thich Nhat. [1987] 2005. *Being Peace*. Berkeley, CA: Parallax Press.

———. 2010. *Together We are One. Honoring Our Diversity, Celebrating Our Connection*. Berkeley, CA: Parallax Press.

Hernández, Inés. 1988. "Cascada de estrellas: La espiritualidad de la chicana/mexicana/indígena." In *Este puente mi espalda: voces de mujeres tercermundistas en los Estados Unidos*, edited by Cherríe Moraga and Ana Castillo, translated by Ana Castillo and Norma Alarcón, 256–66. San Francisco: ISM Press.

Hernández-Avila, Inés. 1992. "An Open Letter to Chicanas." In *Without Discovery: A Native Response to Columbus*, edited by Ray Gonzalez, 153–166. Seattle, WA: Broken Moon Press.

———. [1997] 2000. "Mediations of the Spirit: Native American Religious Traditions and the Ethics of Representation." In *Native American Spirituality: A Critical Reader*, edited by Lee Irwin, 11–36. Lincoln: University of Nebraska Press.

———. 2002. "In the Presence of Spirit(s): A Meditation on the Politics of Solidarity and Transformation." In *this bridge we call home: radical visions for transformation*, edited by Gloria E. Anzaldúa and AnaLouise Keating, 530–37. New York: Routledge.

———. 2005. "Tierra Tremenda: The Earth's Agony and Ecstasy in the Work of Gloria Anzaldúa." In *EntreMundos/AmongWorlds: New Perspectives on Gloria Anzaldúa*, edited by AnaLouise Keating, 233–40. New York: Palgrave.

———. 2006. "Ometeotl Moyocoyatzin: Nahuatl Spiritual Foundations for Holistic Healing." In *Teaching Religion and Healing*, edited by Linda L. Barnes and Inés Talamantez, 127–38. New York: Oxford University Press.

Hernández Sáenz, Luz María, and George M. Foster. 2001. "Curers and their Cures in Colonial New Spain and Guatemala: The Spanish Component." In *Mesoamerican Healers*, edited by Brad R. Huber and Alan R. Sandstrom, 19–46. Austin: University of Texas Press.

Hirschfelder, Arlene and Paulette Molin. 1992. *The Encyclopedia of Native American Religions*. New York: MJF Books.

Hogan, Wesley C. 2007. *Many Minds, One Heart. SNCC's Dream for a New America.* Chapel Hill: The University of North Carolina Press.

Holguín Cuádraz, Gloria. 2003. "Lessons Learned from an Assistant Professor." In *Telling to Live: Latina Feminist Testimonios,* edited by Latina Feminist Group, 227–28. Durham, NC: Duke University Press.

hooks, bell. 1994. *Teaching to Transgress: Education as the Practice of Freedom.* New York: Routledge.

———. 2003. *Teaching Community: A Pedagogy of Hope.* New York: Routledge.

Huber, Brad R., and Alan R. Sandstrom. 2001. "Recruitment, Training and Practice of Indigenous Midwives: From the Mexico–United States Border to the Isthmus of Tehuantepec." In *Mesoamerican Healers,* edited by Brad R. Huber and Alan R. Sandstrom, 139–78. Austin: University of Texas Press.

———, eds. 2001. *Mesoamerican Healers.* Austin: University of Texas Press.

Huerta, Dolores. 2008. "Dolores Huerta on Spirituality. Interview with Mario T. García, June 1, 2007." In *A Dolores Huerta Reader,* edited by Mario T. García. Albuquerque: University of New Mexico Press.

Hurtado, Aída. 2003. "Underground Feminisms: Inocencia's Story." In *Chicana Feminisms: A Critical Reader,* edited by Gabriela F. Arredondo, Aída Hurtado, Norma Klahn, Olga Nájera-Ramírez, and Patricia Zavella, 260–90. Durham, NC: Duke University Press.

INCITE! Women of Color Against Violence, ed. 2006. *Color of Violence: The INCITE! Anthology.* Boston: South End Press.

Irwin, Lee, ed. 2000. *Native American Spirituality: A Critical Reader.* Lincoln: University of Nebraska.

Isasi-Díaz, Ada María. 1993. *En La Lucha (In the Struggle): A Hispanic Women's Liberation Theology.* Minneapolis, MN: Fortress Press.

———. 1996. *Mujerista Theology: A Theology for the Twenty-First Century.* Maryknoll, NY: Orbis.

Isasi-Díaz, Ada María and Yolanda Tarango. 1988. *Hispanic Women: Prophetic Voice in the Church.* Minneapolis, MN: Fortress Press.

Johnson, Robert A. 1971. *Owning Your Shadow. Understanding the Dark Side of the Psyche.* New York: HarperOne.

Jordan, Brigitte. 1997. "Authoritative Knowledge and its Construction." In *Childbirth and Authoritative Knowledge: Cross-Cultural Perspectives,* edited by Robbie E. Davis-Floyd and Carolyn F. Sargent, 55–79. Berkeley: University of California Press.

Kawahara, Debra M. and Oliva M. Espín, eds. 2007. *Feminist Reflections in Growth and Transformation: Asian-American Women in Therapy.* New York: Haworth Press.

———, eds. 2012. *Feminist Therapy with Latina Women: Personal and Social Voices.* New York: Routledge.

Keating, AnaLouise. 2000. "Risking the Personal: An Introduction." In *Interviews/ Entrevistas: Gloria E. Anzaldúa,* edited by AnaLouise Keating. New York: Routledge. 1–15.

———. 2002a. "Charting Pathways, Making Thresholds . . . A Warning, An Introduction." In *this bridge we call home: radical visions for transformation,* edited by Gloria E. Anzaldúa and AnaLouise Keating, 6–20. New York: Routledge.

———. 2002b. "Forging El Mundo Zurdo: Changing Ourselves, Changing the World." In *this bridge we call home: radical visions for transformation,* edited by Gloria Anzaldúa and AnaLouise Keating, 519–30. New York: Routledge.

———. 2005. "Shifting Perspectives: Spiritual Activism, Social Transformation, and the Politics of Spirit." In *EntreMundos/AmongWorlds: New Perspectives on Gloria E. Anzaldúa*, edited by AnaLouise Keating, 241–54. New York: Palgrave/Macmillan.

———, ed. 2005. *Entre Mundos/Among Worlds: New Perspectives on Gloria Anzaldúa*. New York: Palgrave Macmillan.

———. 2008. "'I'm a citizen of the universe': Gloria Anzaldúa's Spiritual Activism as Catalyst for Social Change." *Feminist Studies* 34(1): 53–69.

———, ed. 2009. *The Gloria Anzaldúa Reader*. Durham, NC: Duke University Press.

———. 2013. "Pedagogies of Invitation: From Status-Quo Stories to Cosmic Connections." In *Transformation Now! Toward a Post-Oppositional Politics of Change*, 167–88. Urbana: University of Illinois Press.

Keating, AnaLouise and Gloria González-López, eds. 2011. *Bridging: How Gloria Anzaldúa's Life and Work Transformed Our Own*. Austin: University of Texas Press.

Kelly, Isabel Truesdell. 1965. *Folk Practices in North Mexico; Birth Customs, Folk Medicine, and Spiritualism in the Laguna Zone*. Institute of Latin American Studies, University of Texas. Latin American monographs, no. 2. Austin: Published for the Institute of Latin American Studies by the University of Texas Press.

Kinser, Amber E. 2008. "Embracing the Tensions of the Maternal Erotic." In *Mothering in the Third Wave*, edited by Amber Kinser, 119–25. Toronto: Demeter Press.

Kornfield, Jack. 2000. *After the Ecstasy, the Laundry: How the Heart Grows Wise on the Spiritual Path*. New York: Bantam.

Lame Deer and Erdos. *Lame Deer, Seeker of Visions*. Unpublished manuscript.

Lanzetta, Beverly J. 2005. *Radical Wisdom: A Feminist Mystical Theology*. Minneapolis, MN: Fortress Press.

Lara, Irene. 2002. "Healing *Sueños* for Academia." In *this bridge we call home: radical visions for transformation*, edited by Gloria Anzaldúa and AnaLouise Keating, 433–38. New York: Routledge.

———. 2005. "Bruja Positionalities: Toward a Chicana/Latina Spiritual Activism." *Chicana/Latina Studies: The Journal of Mujeres Activas en Letras y Cambio Social* 4(2): 10–45.

———. 2008a. "'Goddess' of the *Américas*: Beyond the Virtuous *Virgen*/Pagan *Puta* Dichotomy." *Feminist Studies* 34(1/2): 99–127.

———. 2008b. "Tonanlupanisma: Re-membering Tonantzin-Guadalupe in Chicana Visual Art." *Aztlán: A Journal of Chicano Studies* 33(2): 61–90.

———. 2008c. "Latina Health Activist-Healers Bridging Body and Spirit." In *Spirit or Salvation. The Relationship Between Sexuality and Spirituality in Psychotherapy*, edited by Amy Mahoney and Oliva Espín, 21–40. New York: Haworth Press.

———. Forthcoming. "From the Four Directions: The Dreaming, Birthing, Healing Mother on Fire." In *This Bridge Called My Baby: Legacies of Radical Mothering*, edited by Alexis Pauline Gumbs, China Martens, and Mai'a Williams.

Latina Anónima. 2001. "Welcome to the Ivory Tower." In *Telling to Live: Latina Feminist Testimonios*, edited by Latina Feminist Group, 218–23. Durham, NC: Duke University Press.

Latina Feminist Group. 2001. *Telling to Live: Latina Feminist Testimonios*, edited by Latina Feminist Group. Durham, NC: Duke University Press.

Latorre, Guisela. 2008. *Walls of Empowerment: Chicana/o Indigenist Murals of California*. Austin: University of Texas Press.

León, Luis Daniel. 2003. *La Llorona's Children: Life, Death, and Religion in the Borderlands*. Berkeley: University of California Press.

León, Nicolás. 1910. *Compendio de la historia general de México desde los tiempos pre-históricos hasta el año de 1900.* Mexico City: Herrero Hermanos.

León-Portilla, Miguel. [1963] 1990. *Aztec Thought and Culture: A Study of the Ancient Nahuatl Mind.* Translated by Jack Emory Davis. Norman: University of Oklahoma Press.

———. 1992. *The Aztec Image of Self and Society: An Introduction to Nahua Culture.* Salt Lake City: University of Utah Press.

López Austin, Alfredo. 1988. *The Human Body and Ideology: Concepts of the Ancient Nahuas, Volume I.* Translated by Thelma Ortiz de Montellano and Bernard R.Ortiz de Montellano. Salt Lake City: University of Utah Press.

Lorde, Audre. 1984. "Uses of the Erotic: The Power of the Erotic." In *Sister Outsider: Essays and Speeches,* 53–59. Freedom, CA: Crossing Press.

Luna, Jenni Marie. 2011. "Danza Mexica: Indigenous Identity, Spirituality, Activism, and Performance." PhD diss., University of California, Davis.

Mani, Lata. 2009. *SacredSecular. Contemplative Cultural Critique.* New York: Routledge.

Maparyan, Layli. 2012. *The Womanist Idea.* New York: Routledge.

Marcos, Sylvia. 2006. *Taken from the Lips: Gender and Eros in Mesoamerican Religions.* Leiden and Boston: Brill Press.

———, ed. 2010. *Women and Indigenous Religions.* Santa Barbara, CA: Praeger Publishers.

Martinez, Elizabeth (Betita). 2001. "A Chicana in Spain: Remembering Our Arab Roots. *ColorLines* (Spring): 34–36.

Martinez, Maximino. 1959a. *Plantas utiles de la flora mexicana.* Mexico: Ediciones Botas.

———. 1959b. *Las plantas medicinales de Mexico.* 4th ed. Mexico: Ediciones Botas.

Martínez Parédez, Domingo. 1960. *Un continente y una cultura: Unidad filológica de la América prehispana.* Mexico: Editorial "Poesía de América."

———. 1964. *Hunab Kú: Síntesis del Pensamiento Filosófico Maya.* Mexico: Editorial Orion.

Matovina, Timothy and Gary Riebe-Estrada, eds. 2002. *Horizons of the Sacred: Mexican Traditions in U.S. Catholicism.* Ithaca, NY: Cornell University Press.

McCarthy Brown, Karen. 1991. *Mama Lola: A Vodou Priestess in Brooklyn.* Berkeley: University of California Press.

———. 2002. "Writing about 'The Other,' Revisited." In *Personal Knowledge and Beyond: Reshaping the Ethnography of Religion,* edited by James. V. Spickard, J. Shawn Landres, and Meredith B. McGuire, 127–33. New York: New York University Press.

McGuire, Meredith B. 2005. "Why Bodies Matter: A Sociological Reflection on Spirituality and Materiality." In *Minding the Spirit: The Study of Christian Spirituality,* edited by Elizabeth A. Dreyer and Mark S. Burrows, 118–34. Baltimore, MD: Johns Hopkins University Press.

McNeill, Brian W. and Joseph M. Cervantes, eds. 2008. *Latina/o Healing Practices: Mestizo and Indigenous Perspectives.* New York: Routledge.

Medina, Lara. 1998. "Los Espíritus Siguen Hablando: Chicana Spiritualities." In *Living Chicana Theory,* edited by Carla Trujillo, 189–213. Berkeley, CA: Third Woman Press.

———. 2004. *Las Hermanas: Chicana/Latina Religious-Political Activism in the U.S. Catholic Church.* Philadelphia: Temple University Press.

———. 2006. "Nepantla Spirituality: Negotiating Multiple Religious Identities among U.S. Latinas." In *Rethinking Latino(a) Religion and Identity,* edited by Miguel A. De La Torre and Gastón Espinosa, 248–26. Cleveland, OH: The Pilgrim Press.

———. 2011. "Nepantla Spirituality: An Emancipatory Vision for Inclusion." In *Wading Through Many Voices: Toward a Theology of Public Conversation*, edited by Harold Recinos, 279–94. Lanham, MD: Rowman & Littlefield.

Menes, Orlando Ricardo, ed. 2004. *Renaming Ecstasy: Latino Writings on the Sacred*. Tempe, AZ: Bilingual Press/Editorial Bilingüe.

Menocal, María Rosa. 2002. *Ornament of the World*. New York: Little Brown and Company.

Mercado-López, Larissa. 2011. "'I Feel a Revolution Occur in My Womb:' Mapping Cognitive and Somatic Transformation through Readings of Mestiza Maternal Facultad." PhD diss., University of Texas-Austin.

Moncada, Fernando F. 2009. "Soy Danzante." In *Cantos y Alabanzas: Yalhuaya, Naman, Huan Nochipa*, edited by Danza Mexi'cayotl. San Diego Kosoy, CA.

Moraga, Cherríe L. 1983. *Loving in the War Years: Lo que nunca pasó por sus labios*. Boston: South End Press.

———. 1996. "El mito azteca." In *Goddess of the Americas/La Diosa de las Américas: Writings on the Virgin of Guadalupe*, edited by Ana Castillo, 68–71. New York: Riverhead Books.

———. 2000. "The Dying Road to a Nation: A Prayer Para un Pueblo." In *Loving in the War Years: Lo que nunca pasó por sus labios*, 2nd ed., 195–213. Boston: South End Press.

———. 2011. *A Xicana Codex of Changing Consciousness: Writings 2000–2010*. Durham, NC: Duke University Press.

Moraga, Cherríe and Gloria Anzaldúa, eds. 1983. *This Bridge Called My Back: Writings by Radical Women of Color*, 2nd ed. Latham, NY: Kitchen Table, Women of Color Press.

Morales, Aurora Levins. 1998. *Medicine Stories: History, Culture, and the Politics of Integrity*. Cambridge, MA: South End Press.

Moreno Vega, Marta. 2000. *Altar of My Soul: The Living Traditions of Santería*. New York: One World.

Muñoz, José Esteban. 1999. *Disidentifications: Queers of Color and the Performance of Politics*. Minneapolis: University of Minnesota Press.

Nagler, Michael N. 2001. *Is There No Other Way? The Search for a Nonviolent Future*. Berkeley, CA: Berkeley Hills Books.

Narayan, Kirin. 1993. "How Native is a 'Native Anthropologist'"? *American Anthropologist* 95(3): 671–82.

Norris, Kathleen. 1996. *The Cloister Walk*. New York: Norton.

Ortner, Sherry B. 1996. *Making Gender: The Politics and Erotics of Culture*. Boston: Beacon Press.

Palmer, Parker J. 1998. *The Courage to Teach: Exploring the Inner Landscape of a Teacher's Life*. San Francisco: Jossey-Bass.

Pasztory, Esther. 1983. *Aztec Art*. New York: H. N. Abrams.

Pearce, Joseph Chilton. 2002. *The Biology of Transcendence. A Blueprint of the Human Spirit*. Rochester, NY: Park Street Press.

Perales, Marian. 2005. "Teresa Urrea: *Curandera* and Folk Saint." In *Latina Legacies: Identity, Biography, and Community*, edited by Vicki L. Ruiz and Virginia Sánchez Korrol, 97–119. New York: Oxford University Press.

Pérez, Emma. 1998. "Irigaray's Female Symbolic in the Making of Chicana Lesbian *Sitios y Lenguas* (Sites and Discourses)." In *Living Chicana Theory*, edited by Carla Trujillo, 87–101. Berkeley, CA: Third Woman Press.

Pérez, Laura E. 1998. "Spirit Glyphs: Reimagining Art and Artist in the Work of Chicana *Tlamatinime.*" *Modern Fiction Studies* 44(1): 36–76.

———. 2007. *Chicana Art: The Politics of Spiritual and Aesthetic Altarities.* Durham, NC: Duke University Press.

———. 2010. "Enrique Dussel's *Etica de la Liberación*, U.S. Women of Color Decolonizing Practices, and Coalitionary Politics Amidst Difference." *Qui Parle* 18(2): 121–46.

———. 2012. "The Performance of Spirituality and Visionary Politics in the Work of Gloria Anzaldúa." In *El Mundo Zurdo: Selected Works from the 2010 Meeting of the Society for the Study of Gloria Anzaldúa*, edited by Sonia Saldívar-Hull, Norma Alarcón, and Rita Urquijo-Ruiz, 13–28. San Francisco: Aunt Lute Books.

Principe, Walter H. 2005. "Broadening the Focus: Context as a Corrective Lens in Reading Historical Works in Spirituality." In *Minding the Spirit: The Study of Christian Spirituality*, edited by Elizabeth A. Dreyer and Mark S. Burrows, 42–48. Baltimore, MD: Johns Hopkins University Press.

Pui-lan, Kwok, ed. 2010. *Hope Abundant: Third World and Indigenous Women's Theology.* Maryknoll, NY: Orbis Books.

Quezada, Noemí. 2000. *Enfermedad y maleficio.* 2nd ed. Mexico City: Universidad Nacional Autónoma de México: Instituto de Investigaciones Antropológicas.

Ramos, Juanita, ed. 1987. *Compañeras: Latina Lesbians.* New York: Latina Lesbian Project.

Rayburn, Carol A. and Lillian Comas-Díaz, eds. 2008. *WomanSoul: The Inner Life of Woman's Spirituality.* Westport, CT: Praeger.

Rendón, Laura. 2005. "Recasting Agreements that Govern Teaching and Learning: An Intellectual and Spiritual Framework for Transformation." *Religion and Education* 32(1): 79–108.

———. 2009. *Sentipensante (Sensing/Thinking) Pedagogy: Educating for Wholeness, Social Justice and Liberation.* Sterling, VA: Stylus Publishing.

Ritskes, Eric. 2011. "Connected: Indigenous Spirituality as Resistance in the Classroom." In *Spirituality, Education and Society: An Integrated Approach*, edited by Njoki N. Wane, Energy L. Manyimo and Eric J. Ritskes, 15–36. Rotterdam: Sense Publishers.

Robelo, Cecilio. 1951. *Diccionario de mitología Nahuatl.* Mexico City: Ediciones Fuente Cultural.

Rodríguez, Jeanette. 1994. *Our Lady of Guadalupe: Faith and Empowerment among Mexican American Women.* Austin: University of Texas Press.

———. 1996. "Guadalupe: The Feminine Face of God." In *Goddess of the Americas/La Diosa de las Américas: Writings on the Virgin of Guadalupe*, edited by Ana Castillo, 25–31. New York: Riverhead Books.

———. 2002. "Latina Activists: Toward an Inclusive Spirituality of Being in the World." In *A Reader in Latina Feminist Theology*, edited by María Pilar Aquino, Daisy L. Machado, and Jeanette Rodríguez, 114–130. Austin: University of Texas Press.

———. 2004. "Mestiza Spirituality: Community, Ritual, and Justice." *Theological Studies* 65(2): 317–39.

Rodriguez, Roberto. 2002. *Codex Tamuanchan, On Becoming Human.* Albuquerque, NM: (self-published).

Rodriguez, Roberto Cintli. 2010. "War on Indigenous in Arizona." *New America Media*, May 17. http://newamericamedia.org/2010/05/war-on-indigenous-in-arizona.php.

Román, Estela. 2012. *Nuestra Medicina: De Los Remedios para el Aire y Los Remedios para el Alma.* Bloomington, IN: Palibrio.

Román-Odio, Clara. 2013. *Sacred Iconographies in Chicana Cultural Productions.* New York: Palgrave Macmillan.

Romero, Channette. 2012. *Activism and the American Novel: Religion and Resistance in Fiction by Women of Color.* Charlottesville: University of Virginia Press.

Rosaldo, Renato. 1989. *Culture and Truth: The Remaking of Social Analysis.* Boston: Beacon Press.

Ruether, Rosemary Radford. 1998a. *Introducing Redemption in Christian Feminism.* Sheffield, UK: Sheffield Academic Press.

———. 1998b. *Women and Redemption: A Theological History.* Minneapolis, MN: Fortress Press.

———. 2005. "Tonantzin-Guadalupe: The Meeting of Aztec and Christian Female Symbols in Mexico." In *Goddesses and the Divine Feminine: A Western Religious History,* 190–219. Berkeley: University of California Press.

Ruiz de Alarcón, Hernando. 1984. *Treatise on the heathen superstitions that today live among the Indians native to this New Spain, 1629.* Translated and edited by J. Richard Andrews and Ross Hassig. Norman: University of Oklahoma Press.

Russel y Rodríguez, Mónica. 1998. "Confronting Anthropology's Silencing Praxis: Speaking of/from a Chicana Consciousness." *Qualitative Inquiry* 4(1): 15–40.

Saavedra, Cinthya M., and Ellen D. Nymark. 2008. "Borderland-Mestizaje Feminism: The New Tribalism." In *Handbook of Critical and Indigenous Methodologies,* edited by Norman K. Denzin, Yvonna S. Lincoln, and Linda Tuhiwai Smith, 255–76. Thousand Oaks, CA: Sage Publications.

Sahagún, Bernardino de. 1950–1982. *General History of the Things of New Spain: Florentine Codex.* Translated by Arthur J. O. Anderson and Charles E. Dibble. Santa Fe, NM: School of American Research, Salt Lake City: University of Utah.

Saldívar-Hull, Sonia. 1999. "Introduction to the Second Edition." In Gloria Anzaldúa, *Borderlands/La Frontera: The New Mestiza.* 2nd ed., 1–15. San Francisco: Aunt Lute Books.

Sánchez Morales, Primo. 2003. *El Temazcal: Uso ceremonial y terapéutico.* Mexico: Instituto Tlaxcalteca de la Cultura.

Schneiders, Sandra M. 2005. "A Hermeneutical Approach to the Study of Christian Spirituality." In *Minding the Spirit: The Study of Christian Spirituality,* edited by Elizabeth A. Dreyer and Mark S. Burrows, 49–60. Baltimore, MD: Johns Hopkins University Press.

Schultes, Richard Evans, Albert Hofmann, Christian Ralsch, Alberto Blanco, Gastón Guzmán, and Salvador Acosta. 2000. *Plantas de los dioses: Las fuerzas magicas de las plantas alucinogenas.* Mexico: Fondo de Cultura Económica.

Schüssler Fiorenza, Elisabeth. 1983. *In Memory of Her: A Feminist Theological Reconstruction of Christian Origins.* New York: Crossroads.

Sendejo, Brenda. 2009. "Mother's Legacy: Cultivating Chicana Consciousness During the War Years." In *Beyond the Latino WWII War Hero: The Social and Political Legacy of a Generation,* edited by Maggie Rivas-Rodriguez and Emilio Zamora, 156–77. Austin: University of Texas Press.

———. 2011. "'The Face of God Has Changed': Tejana Cultural Production and the Politics of Spirituality in the Texas-Mexico Borderlands." PhD diss., University of Texas-Austin.

———. 2013. "The Cultural Production of Spiritual Activisms: Gender, Social Justice, and the Remaking of Religion in the Borderlands." *Chicana/Latina Studies: The Journal of Mujeres Activas en Letras y Cambio Social* 12(2): 58–109.

Seth (Spirit). 1972. *Seth Speaks: The Eternal Validity of the Soul*. Channeled by Jane Roberts; notes by Robert F. Butts. Englewood Cliffs, NJ: Prentice-Hall.

Shanley, Kathryn. 1999. "The Thinking Heart: American Indian Discourse and the Politics of Recognition." In *Race, Ethnicity, and Nationality in the United States: Toward the Twenty-First Century*, edited by Paul Wong, 256–76. Boulder, CO: Westview Press.

Sheldrake, Philip F. 2005. "Christian Spirituality as a Way of Living Publicly: A Dialectic of the Mystical and Prophetic." In *Minding the Spirit: The Study of Christian Spirituality*, edited by Elizabeth A. Dreyer and Mark S. Burrows, 282–98. Baltimore, MD: Johns Hopkins University Press.

Silko, Leslie Marmon. 1996. *Yellow Woman and Beauty of the Spirit: Essays on Native American Life Today*. New York: Simon & Schuster.

Silva, Dorsía Smith, ed. 2011. *Latina/Chicana Mothering*. Toronto: Demeter Press.

Soelle, Dorothee. 2001. *The Silent Cry: Mysticism and Resistance*. Translated by Barbara and Martin Rumscheidt. Minneapolis, MN: Fortress Press.

St. Pierre, Mark and Tilda Long Soldier. 1995. *Walking in the Sacred Manner: Healers, Dreamers and Pipe Carriers—Medicine Women of the Plains Indians*. New York: Simon & Schuster.

Talamantez, Inés. 1995. "American Indian Women: Seeing Red." In *Our Own Voices: Four Centuries of American Women's Religious Writing*, edited by Rosemary Skinner Keller and Rosemary Radford Ruether, 384–423. New York: Harper Collins.

Talamantez, Inés, M.A. Jaimes Guerrero, and Anne Waters, eds. 2003. "Indigenous Women in the Americas." Special Issue of *Hypatia* 18(2).

Téllez, Michelle. 2005. "Doing Research at the Borderlands: Notes from a Chicana Feminist Ethnographer." *Chicana/Latina Studies: The Journal of Mujeres Activas en Letras y Cambio Social* 4(2): 46–70.

Tijerina, Aletícia. 1990. "Notes on Oppression and Violence." In *Making Face, Making Soul/Haciendo Caras: Creative and Critical Perspectives by Women of Color*, edited by Gloria Anzaldúa, 170–73. San Francisco: Aunt Lute Books.

Torres, Edén. 2003. *Chicana Without Apology: The New Chicana Cultural Studies*. New York: Routledge.

Trinidad Galván, Ruth. 2001. "Portraits of *mujeres desjuiciadas*: Womanist Pedagogies of the Everyday, the Mundane and the Ordinary." *Qualitative Studies in Education* 14(5): 603-21.

———. 2006. "*Campesina* Epistemologies and Pedagogies of the Spirit: Examining Women's *Sobrevivencia*." In *Chicana/Latina Education in Everyday Life: Feminista Perspectives on Pedagogy and Epistemology*, edited by Dolores Delgado Bernal, C. Alejandra Elenes, Francisca Godinez, and Sofia Villenas, 161–79. Albany: State University of New York Press.

Trungpa, Chogyam. [1984] 2009. *Shambhala: The Sacred Path of the Warrior*. Boston and London: Shambhala Publications.

Trujillo, Carla, ed. 1991. *Chicana Lesbians: The Girls Our Mothers Warned Us About*. Berkeley, CA: Third Woman Press.

Turner, Victor. 1967. *The Forest of Symbols: Aspects of Ndembu Ritual*. Ithaca, NY: Cornell University Press.

Valdez, Luis. 1990. *Early Works: Actos, Bernabé and Pensamiento Serpentino*. Houston, TX: Arte Público Press.

Vallejo, Jody Agius. 2012. *Barrios to Burbs: The Making of the Mexican-American Middle Class.* Palo Alto, CA: Stanford University Press.

Viesca Treviño, Carlos. 2001. "Curanderismo in Mexico and Guatemala: Its Historical Evolution from the Sixteenth to the Nineteenth Century." In *Mesoamerican Healers*, edited by Brad R. Huber and Alan R. Sandstrom, 47–63. Austin: University of Texas Press.

Villanueva Toscano, Silvia. 2013. "Teaching as a Healing Craft: Decolonizing the Classroom and Creating Spaces of Hopeful Resistance through Chicano Indigenous Pedagogical Praxis." *The Urban Review* 45(1): 23–40. doi 10.1007/s11256-012–0222-5.

Visweswaran, Kamala. 1994. *Fictions of Feminist Ethnography.* Minneapolis: University of Minnesota Press.

———. 1997. "Histories of a Feminist Ethnography." *Annual Review of Anthropology* 26: 591–621.

Wangyal, Tenzin. 2002. *Healing with Form, Energy and Light.* Ithaca, NY: Snow Lion Publications.

———. 2011. *Awakening the Sacred Body.* Carlsbad, CA: Hay House Inc.

———. 2012. *Awakening the Luminous Mind.* Carlsbad, CA: Hay House Inc.

Wilkinson, Tracy. 2007. "Catholic-Muslim Strife Still Echoes in this Marble Forest." *Los Angeles Times*, March 28, A1.

Williams, Angel Kyodo. 2000. *Being Black: Zen and the Art of Living with Fearlessness and Grace.* New York: Penguin Compass.

Winter, Evelyne. 1968. *Mexico's Ancient and Native Remedies: A Handbook of Testimonials and Historic References for Modern Use.* Mexico: Editorial Fournier.

Yakushko, Oksana and Oliva M. Espín. 2009. "The Experience of Immigrant and Refugee Women: Psychological Issues." In *Handbook of Diversity in Feminist Psychology*, edited by Hope Landrine and Nancy Felipe Russo, 535–58. New York: Springer.

Zavella, Patricia. 1987. *Women's Work and Chicano Families: Cannery Workers of the Santa Clara Valley.* Ithaca, NY: Cornell University Press.

———. 1994. "Reflections on Diversity among Chicanas." In *Race*, edited by Steven Gregory and Roger Sanjek, 199–212. New Brunswick, NJ: Rutgers University Press.

———. 1997. "Constructing Ethnic Identity with 'Chicana' Informants." In *Situated Lives: Gender and Culture in Everyday Life*, edited by Louise Lamphere, Helena Ragoné, and Patricia Zavella, 42–61. New York: Routledge.

Contributors

Volume Editors

Elisa Facio is an associate professor in the Department of Ethnic Studies at the University of Colorado, Boulder, where she teaches courses on Chicana Feminist Thought, Chicana Indígena Spiritualities, transnational issues related to gender, race, and sexuality focusing on Cuba, and Age, Aging, and Generations. Elisa received her BA with honors in sociology from Santa Clara University and an MA and PhD in sociology from the University of California, Berkeley. Elisa's academic work is published in academic journals, anthologies, and encyclopedias, and her book on older Chicana/Mexican women titled *Understanding Older Chicanas: Sociological and Policy Perspectives* was published by SAGE in 1996. In collaboration with departmental colleagues Arturo J. Aldama, Reiland Rabaka, and Daryl Maeda, she coedited the anthology *Enduring Legacies: Ethnic Histories and Cultures of Colorado* (2011), to which she also contributed an essay. The American Sociological Association recognized her work on Cuban sex workers as an Outstanding Scholarly Contribution. Elisa is completing a manuscript tentatively titled *Race, Gender and Sexuality in Post-Soviet Cuba*. She is also a *promotora* working with older Mexicana/o, Chicana/o, and Hispana/o populations in Colorado.

Irene Lara is a Chicana scholar, writer, and teacher who recently celebrated her ten-year anniversary as a professor. She graduated from Stanford University with an Honors BA in American Studies, then the University of California-Berkeley with a PhD in Ethnic Studies and Designated Emphasis in Women, Gender, and Sexuality, and has served as an assistant then associate professor in the Department of Women's Studies at San Diego State University. Her scholarship on Chicana/Latina/Indigenous spirituality, healing, pedagogy, and cultural productions is published in journals such as *Feminist Studies, Aztlán: A Journal of Chicano Studies, Chicana/Latina Studies: The Journal of Mujeres Activas en Letras y Cambio Social*, and *Women and Therapy*, and in anthologies such as *this bridge we call home: visions for radical transformation* (2002) and *Chicana/Latina Education in Everyday Life: Feminista Perspectives on Pedagogy and Epistemology* (2006). She is currently writing a book titled *Decolonizing the Sacred: Chicana/Latina Spirituality, Sexuality, and Healing* and coediting a humanities-based Women's Studies textbook. As part of her work as a "CuranderaScholarActivist," Irene loves to cofacilitate the spiritual activist/reproductive justice workshop, "Panocha Pláticas: Healing Sex and Sexuality in Community," and guide her students in the "CuranderaScholarActivists in Academia"

Faculty-Student Mentor Program seminar. She also loves being mami to her beautiful daughters Xóchitl and Belén.

Chapter Authors

Angelita Borbón is a descendant of the Original Peoples of the land in southern Arizona and northern Mexico called the Sonoran Desert. She is a copper miner's daughter from a mining camp now a ghost town called *El Tigre* where she learned to never leave a baseball game before it is over because anything can happen, and never ever cross a picket line. Her belief in the possibility of the impossible, her respect for organized action, and the cultural and spiritual teachings of her Indigenous family form the conceptual framework of her Life and Work. In 1978, her education as a public health nurse at the University of Arizona in Tucson included a semester of independent studies in central Mexico where she worked with physicians and traditional healers practicing the Ancient Science and Medicine of Mexico. One of her experiences was living in the mountains with a *partera*/midwife, who blessed Angelita's hands and said, "*Hija*, whatever you do in your life, from now on, you do it as a midwife." Angelita is the midwife/creator of *Conciencia* Scientific Dialogue, an Indigenous methodology and practice designed to awaken consciousness and conscience.

Norma E. Cantú recently retired as a Professor of English and US Latina/o Literatures at the University of Texas at San Antonio to build a Latina and Latino Studies program at the University of Missouri, Kansas City. She received her PhD from the University of Nebraska, Lincoln. As editor of two book series—Rio Grande/Rio Bravo: Borderlands Culture and Tradition at Texas A&M University Press and Literatures of the Americas at Palgrave—she promotes the publication of research on literature and culture. She is the author of the award-winning *Canícula: Snapshots of a Girlhood en la Frontera* (1995), and coeditor of *Telling to Live: Latina Feminist Testimonios* (2001), *Chicana Traditions: Continuity and Change* (2002), *Dancing Across Borders: Danzas y Bailes Mexicanos* (2009), *Inside the Latin@ Experience: A Latin@ Studies Reader* (2010), and *El Mundo Zurdo: Selected Works from the Meetings of the Society for the Study of Gloria Anzaldúa 2007 & 2009* (2010). Dr. Cantú is currently working on a novel tentatively titled *Champú, or Hair Matters/Champu: Asuntos de pelos*, and an ethnography of the Matachines de la Santa Cruz, a religious dance drama from Laredo, Texas. She is founder and director of the Society for the Study of Gloria Anzaldúa and cofounder of the group of Latina/o poets, CantoMundo, as well as a member of the Macondo Writers Workshop.

Berenice Dimas is a queer Xicana, Reiki practitioner, and *estudiante de la vida* on a curandera life path. Her current work involves facilitating healing workshops in the community to help people regain hope and strength to continue changing the world. She specifically facilitates workshops with undocumented students, queer youth, social justice collectives, community/grassroots organizers, and activists. Her goal is to bring people together to start a healing process from generational poverty, memory of trauma, suffering, activist burnout, and healing for those coming out as queer to their familias. She also facilitates sessions focusing on healing physical wounds of the body and metaphysical layers of the self. Berenice is currently a high-school teacher in East Oakland

and is part of the Resisting Colonial Legacy and its Impact on Medicine (ReClaim) Health Collective. She can be contacted on Facebook as La Bere, and by e-mail at ms.b.dimas@gmail.com.

C. Alejandra Elenes is an associate professor of American Studies, Ethnicity, Race and First Nation Studies, and Women and Gender Studies in the School of Humanities, Arts and Cultural Studies at Arizona State University. Her research centers on the application of borderland theories to study the relationship between Chicana culture and knowledge, and how these theories relate to pedagogy and epistemology. She is the author of *Transforming Borders: Chicana/o Popular Culture and Pedagogy* (2011), published by Lexington Books, and coeditor of *Chicana/Latina Education in Everyday Life: Feminista Perspectives on Pedagogy and Epistemology* (2006) (SUNY Press: winner of the 2006 American Educational Studies Association Book Critics Award). She is also coeditor of the special issue "Chicana/Mexicana Pedagogies: *Consejos, Respeto y Educación* in Everyday Life" in the *International Journal of Qualitative Studies in Education* (2001). She has published articles in journals such as *Frontiers, Educational Theory, International Journal of Qualitative Studies in Education*, and *Feminist Teacher*. Elenes is honored to be part of this exciting anthology on Chicana feminist spirituality.

Alicia Enciso Litschi is currently a doctoral student in Counseling Psychology at the University of Texas-Austin with plans to graduate in 2014. Alicia's research interests center on psychospiritual healing and how communities create contexts of healing outside of formal mental health services. Alicia's research has been made possible by her *comadres* and *maestras* of the Alma de Mujer Center for Social Change in Austin, Texas who provide powerful lessons on what healing means in the cultural, political, and spiritual landscape of our current time. Alicia was born and raised on the Arizona-Sonora border, came very close to being ordained as a Buddhist priest, and now makes her home with her *esposo* Matthew. She continues to be amazed and humbled by the twists and turns of the spiritual journey.

Oliva M. Espín is Professor Emerita in the Department of Women's Studies at San Diego State University and the California School of Professional Psychology of Alliant International University. A native of Cuba, she received her BA in Psychology from the University of Costa Rica and her PhD from the University of Florida. She did postdoctoral work at Harvard University. Dr. Espín has worked on issues of immigrant women and Latinas and has trained psychotherapists for several decades. She has received many professional awards, has authored three books, and has coedited several others. Dr. Espín has recently turned her attention to the study of women saints and to the writing of memoir. Dr. Espín held a Fulbright Distinguished Chair in Gender Studies in Austria in 2010.

Maria Figueroa is a maestra, mama, danzante, teatrista, poeta, hija, hermana, and comadre, and makes her professional home at MiraCosta College in Oceanside, California as a professor of English, Literature, and Humanities. She is originally from the city most marginalized by the Orange Curtain, with roots running three generations deep in Santa Ana, California, where the rooster's crow awakens working-class dreams. With the spiritual and financial support of her familia, she is the first in her family to attend college, having graduated from UC San Diego (BA) and Dartmouth College (MA). She now makes her home in Encinitas, CA with her precious masterpieces, Cuauhtemoc and Esperanza Tonantzin.

Patrisia Gonzales teaches courses about Indigenous ways of knowing and Indigenous medicine as faculty in the Department of Mexican American Studies at the University of Arizona. She is also a member of the Native American Research and Training Center in the College of Medicine. As a W. K. Kellogg Foundation fellow, she explored community healing and as a member of Kalpulli Izkalli in Albuquerque, NM, she helped to establish the first promotora project on Mexican traditional medicine in the United States. For many years, she was a nationally syndicated columnist and has authored several books, garnering her human rights awards. Her most recent book, *Red Medicine: Traditional Indigenous Rites of Birthing and Healing* (2012) is part of the First Peoples Series: New Directions in Indigenous Studies through the University of Arizona Press. She is a godmother to dozens of Indigenous babies whom she helped bring into this world as part of her traditional practice.

Inés Hernández-Avila is professor of Native American Studies at the University of California-Davis. Dr. Hernández-Avila is a member of the National Caucus of the Wordcraft Circle of Native Writers and Storytellers, and she is active with the Native Traditions in the Americas Group of the American Academy of Religion. She is one of the six founders of the Native American and Indigenous Studies Association (NAISA). She served as the chair of UC Davis's Native American Studies Department and the director of its Chicana/Latina Research Center for many years. In 2008 she won an American Council of Learned Societies fellowship, sponsored by the Center for Contemplative Mind in Society, and in 2009 she received the Academic Senate Distinguished Teaching Award at the Graduate and Professional Level. Dr. Hernández-Avila's extensive scholarly and creative publications are widely read and cited in many disciplines.

Rosa María Hernández Juárez was born in Tijuana, Baja California, Mexico and was raised in Chula Vista, California by a loving, strong, humorous, spiritual, traditional, and untraditional family. Rosa received her degree in Chicano Studies at the University of California-Berkeley and has a career in public health and public service.

Cinthya Martinez is native to the San Diego/Tijuana border region and works as a high-school counselor. I am extremely grateful for my time with my teacher, Elena Avila, and to all the healers that share their knowledge with love. I am passionate about using these teachings with youth and helping them acknowledge their divine light.

Lara Medina is a professor in the Department of Chicana and Chicano Studies at California State University, Northridge. She earned her PhD from Claremont Graduate University in American History and a MA in Theology from the Graduate Theological Union. Her research and teaching focus on Chicana/o religious/spiritual practices; Chicana/o religious history; religion and social change; religion, politics, and art; oral history; family histories; and Chicana/o history.

Felicia Montes is a writer, performer, organizer, student, educator, and cultural activist who has worked with a long list of community organizations and art institutions including Self Help Graphics and Art and United Farm Workers of America. She is cofounder and coordinator of Mujeres de Maiz, a collective of creative women of color, and a member of In Lak Ech, a song and spoken word group of Xicana Indígena women. Having organized hundreds of cultural events for many artists and causes, her current goal is to focus more on her own creativity, finish her master's thesis in Chicana/o studies and continue teaching at local colleges.

Sarahi Nuñez-Mejia was born in Mexico City and raised in Los Angeles. She earned an MBA from Georgia State University and a Master of Management degree from the Sorbonne in Paris through an international dual-degree program. She currently has a career in consumer marketing working in the entertainment industry, focusing on the US Latino market.

Laura E. Pérez, an associate professor in the Ethnic Studies Department at the University of California-Berkeley, teaches and writes on US Women of Color, feminist and queer art, spirituality, and decolonizing politics. Pérez is the author of *Chicana Art: The Politics of Spiritual and Aesthetic Altarities* (Duke University Press, 2007). She cocurated, with Delilah Montoya, the multimedia exhibition *Chicana Badgirls: Las Hociconas* (Albuquerque, New Mexico, 2009) and curated *Labor*+a(r)t+orio: Bay Area Latina@ Arts Now (Richmond, California, 2011).

Brenda Sendejo is an assistant professor of Anthropology and faculty affiliate in the Feminist Studies and Latin American Studies Programs at Southwestern University. Her work examines how issues related to gender, race, sexuality, and social justice shape the religious and spiritual traditions, histories, and identities of Mexican Americans in Texas. Other areas of interest include Tejana Anthropology, Chicana Feminist Theory, and spiritual activist and feminist pedagogies and methodologies. She is currently working on *Spirit Stories: Narratives of Spirituality and Social Justice*, an intergenerational oral history project that brings together undergraduate students with activists involved in movements for social change in Central Texas since the late 1960s.

Inés Talamantez (Mescalero Apache/Chicana) is an associate professor of Religious Studies. Dr. Talamantez arrived at the University of California-Santa Barbara in 1979 from Dartmouth College to develop the area of Native American Religious Traditions. Since then she has developed ten undergraduate courses in this area of study and has taught a variety of graduate seminars. Indeed, the UCSB Religious Studies department is the only program that offers a PhD in religious studies with an emphasis in Native American religious traditions. Considered a foremother in the field of Native, Chicana, and Mexican spiritualities, Dr. Talamantez is a widely published scholar and respected mentor/teacher.

Michelle Téllez is an interdisciplinary scholar trained in community studies and education who teaches in the School of Humanities, Arts and Cultural Studies and the Masters in Social Justice and Human Rights program at the New College of Interdisciplinary Arts and Sciences, Arizona State University. In her twenty years of community engagement and activism she has been involved in multiple projects for change at the grassroots levels utilizing critical pedagogy, community-based theater, and visual media. Her writing and research projects seek to uncover the stories of transnational community formation, migration, and resistance.

Beatriz Villegas, who also goes by Bea and Ilhuicatlahuili-Bea, is a ceremonial leader and teacher of Mexica culture in the El Paso, Texas region. Recognized as an elder, curandera, and grandmother of the Sun Dance, she was one of the coordinators for the first Peace and Dignity Run and cofounded Kalpulli Tonal Teokalli (House of the Creator), a Nahua Mexica community. She also founded the Moon Circle, a group that empowers women with the Native American ways of the Moon (Coyolxauhqui), pours water in the sacred sweat lodge (Temazkalli), participates in the Moon Dance in Mexico, and leads naming and coming-of-age ceremonies, vision quests, and traditional marriages for the community. She presently participates in Kalpulli Tlalteca and works as a lab assistant at El Paso Community College.

Artist's Statement

Linda Vallejo

Standing Spirits, 1999
Acrylic on canvas
48″ (h) × 36″ (w)
from the collection of Paul Dillaway.

Standing Spirits is a painting from the series *Los Cielos* completed in 2000. This body of work made up of over fifty paintings exemplifies my experience in ceremony. The horizon line, the rising of the sun and setting of the moon were my inspiration.

Each year as we traveled down the rocky road to ceremony we could see the standing rock elders—tall, strong, and everlasting, reminding us of our ancestors and spirit guides. As we made the journey to complete our commitment we prayed to remember these standing spirits and to stand tall for our families, the earth, and the traditions.

In prayer we gazed skyward to see the standing spirits among the clouds—appearing and disappearing. Through our offering we hoped to emulate their illusive strength and courage. The sacrifice was hard and sometimes we would fall. It was then that we called on these spirits for inspiration, protection, and guidance. We asked to see ourselves clearly and to learn how to follow our true path.

Now, we can sit by the roaring ocean or a flowing landscape and remember the times that the standing spirits were our good guides and helpers. If we center ourselves and concentrate on the blessings we received and the lessons we learned we can renew our commitment to stand tall, be courageous and generous, live well, and find happiness.

"Standing Spirits" is a record of my memories in ceremony where I learned to love the circle and the joy of commitment. I offer "Standing Spirits" with my sincere hope that it will bring you inspiration, peace, and happiness.

Index

academia, spirituality research and, 85–86, 89–90, 107–11

activist scholarship, Chicana spirituality and, 202–16

African American diaspora, 11, 26–27

African plants, Indigenous medicine and, 227–36

"Aguila Blanca" (traditional danza Azteca), 40–42

Alarcón, Norma, 70, 209

altar making, spiritual pedagogy and, 37–39

American Indian movements, 173–75

amoridolor, xiv–xv

Anáhuac (Nahuatl term), 185n18

ancestral knowledge: Cantú's reliance on, 214–16; nepantla spirituality and, 168–84

anthropological research: complexity of native anthropology and, 100n6; feminist scholarship in, 97–99; spirituality and healing in, 9

anti-immigration legislation, 182–84

Anzaldúa, Gloria, xv, 6, 10–11, 13–15, 37, 96; "borderlands" concept of, 20, 34–43; Cantú and, 211–13, 215; decolonial feminism and, 75; "el mundo zurdo" of, 133n10; on "home," 59, 61; on love, 130–31; maternal facultad and, 120–24; on mestiza consciousness, 69–70, 93, 96; nepantla spirituality and work of, 44, 46, 100n5, 170–71, 178, 183; on personhood and integrity, 28, 33n17; serpentine conocimiento and, 24, 114–18, 120–24, 126, 132n6, 133n8; on spiritual activism, 54, 56

autohistoria: Anzaldúa's concept of, 20–21, 35, 59–60, 72n1; Chicana feminism and, 13, 84–86; serpentine theory and, 115

Avila, Elena, 9, 71–72

axochiteonaj (water-flower godmother), 231–36

Babalawo (Santería priest), 176

Bach flower remedies, 227

Baktun (Maya time tradition), xviii

baptism, Elenes's memory of, 48, 50

Baptist religion, childhood memories of, 196

"beloved community" concept, 119, 133n11

betrayal, spirituality and, 145–46

birthing, as creativity metaphor, xiii, 14

birthing traditions: Borbón's memories of, 191–94; Indigenous midwifery practices and, 218–23, 228–30, 236–38; Lara's teaching to daughters about, 9, 125; sweatlodge and, 65; yauhtli (herbal plant) in, 230–36

bodymindspirit: borderland pedagogies and, 53; colonization's impact on, xviii, 4; erotic-spiritual change and, 118–20, 128–31; family relations and, 152–55; hallucinations and, 204–16; home metaphor and, 20, 150–52; illness and transformation of, xvi, 12–13, 60, 62, 70–72, 157–66, 219; limpia (cleansing) of, 66; mamihood and, 74–75, 120–24; methodologies of the spirit and, 24, 27–29, 31n7, 32n8, 32n11, 36–39, 41, 54–57, 91–99, 103; nepantla spirituality and, 167–84, 203–4; *Panocha Pláticas* community and, 126–28; serpentine conocimiento and, 113–18; Tlazolteotl

bodymindspirit (*continued*)
and, 124–26; violence and, 62–65; Zen
Buddhism and, 138–49
Boggs, Grace Lee, 29–30
Borbón, Angelita, xvi, 14, 187–88, 191–94, 220
borderlands framework: Anzaldúa's
discussion of, 20; Elenes on spirituality
and, 47–53; family relations and, 150–51;
healing traditions and, 35–36, 159–66;
Sandejo's methodologies, etc., 85–86;
spiritual pedagogy and, 34–42; spiritual
praxis and, 54–57
Broyles-González, Yolanda, 46–47
Bruchac, Joseph, 173–74
bruja/brujandera spirituality, 40–42, 55,
197–201, 224–26
Brunal, Adelin, 168–69
Buddhism, 11, 19, 26–27, 135, 138–49
burial sites, nepantla spirituality and
sacredness of, 176–81

Cajete, Gregory, 31n3, 220, 225–26, 239n3
calendars, Indigenous medicine and, 226
Calmecac (school of learning), 67–69
Camino de Santiago, 188, 202–14, 216n1
cancer journey, Chicana identity and, 5–7,
20, 70–72
Cantú, Norma, xiii, xvi–xvii, 6–7, 188, 202–16
Casanova, Steve, 51, 57
Castillo, Ana, 4, 6, 46–47, 70, 120, 209
Catherine of Siena, 111
Catholicism: Borbón's memories of, 192–94;
in borderlands narrative, 48–53, 58n4;
Chicana feminism and, 81–86, 91–95,
152–54; community in, 151–52; Indigenous identity and, 67–72, 87–89, 203–4,
234–36; in mestiza culture, 45, 280–82;
nepantla spirituality and, 11, 171–72,
203–4; punishment concepts in, 70–71;
sexism and, 105–6, 139, 146–47, 198;
Virgin of Guadalupe and, 44–47; women
saints in, 103–11
Cayce, Edgar, 207–8
Cedillo Parra, Filomena, 218–19, 236–38
ceremonies, healing power of, 177, 185n15
Chicana identity: activist scholarship and
spirituality and, 84–86, 202–16; Buddhism
and, 140–49; healing traditions and,
159–66; nepantla spirituality and, 59–60,
168–84; sweat ceremonies and, 172–75
Chicana/Latina/Indigenous scholarship:
cancer journey and, 70–72; family tensions
and path to, 152–54; mamihood and,

113–31; researcher-informant binary and,
97–99; serpentine conocimiento and,
115–18; sexuality and, 113–31; spirituality
in, 3–15, 15n1, 39–42, 68–70
childhood: awareness of spirit in, 203–4;
Indigenous medicine in, 223–26; sexual
abuse in, 195–201; spirituality and identity
in, 187–88, 191–94
Christianity: nepantla spirituality and, 11, 27,
177–78; social justice and, 19. *See also*
Catholicism
Cihuacoatl (Serpent Woman), 75, 115–18,
122, 225–26
Cisneros, Sandra, 45, 209, 211
civil rights activism, spirituality and, 19,
28–29
classism, spirituality and, 6, 48–53
Coatlalopeuh (Nahuatal deity), 122–24
Coatlicue (Nahua Mother deity), 45–47, 69,
115, 122, 132n6, 184n6; nepantla
spirituality and, 170; *sentipensante
(sensing/thinking)* pedagogy and, 126–28
Codex Borbonicus, 125
Codex Borgia, 200
collective spirituality, nepantla and, 168–84
colonization: borderlands concept and,
35–36; cultural warnings concerning, 6,
25, 32n9, 32n16; Indigenous medicinal
knowledge and, 188, 226, 233–36; peyote
suppression and, 232–36; serpentine
conocimiento and, 117–18; spirit writing in
context of, 23–24; sweat ceremonies
banned under, 173–75
comadres/compadres, importance of, 41–42,
211–16
community: healing traditions and, 164–66;
power of, 4–5, 29–30, 54–57
Conchero dance tradition, xviii, 219–20
conocimientos: in Chicana scholarship,
113–15, 187; serpentine conocimiento,
115–31; *temazkal* conocimiento, 172–75
Contreras, Enriqueta, 220–21
Cook, Katsi, 221–23
Coyolxauhqui (Nahua Moon deity), 27, 45
Coyote, energy, xiv
cuarentena ritual, 230
Cuban culture, 74, 102–11
cuentos y pláticas (stories and conversations),
Chicana identity and, 61
cultural knowledge: religious recollection and,
87–89; spirituality and, 26–27, 31n6, 55
curanderismo: childhood memories of,
195–201, 213, 223–26; colonial knowledge

of, 226; healing traditions and, 148, 164–66, 188, 239n4; Indigenous medical knowledge and, 9, 39–42, 218–23; queeranderismo and, 79

danza ceremonies, xvi, 198; danzante azteca, 20, 39–42; Indigenous medicine and, 228–30; as prayer, 166; Téllez's experience in, 151–54; tradition of, 212; Villegas's participation in, 198–201
death, nepantla spirituality and, 176–81
De Certeau, Michel, 106, 111
decolonization: activist spirituality and, 128–31; methodologies of the spirit and, 26–27, 40–42, 85–86, 92–95; nepantla spirituality and, 168–84
Delgadillo, Theresa, 9, 215
Delgado Bernal, Dolores, 55, 93
Días de los muertos, 170, 176, 184n4, 215
dichos (San Ramón ponle un tapón) (folk prayers), 203–4
difrasismos, xiv
Dimas, Berenice, xv–xvi, 73, 76–80, 134n17
Diné culture, 27
disease, spirituality and, 66–68
divergent thinking, spiritual pedagogy and, 38
drawing, as healing tradition, 162–66
dual oneness, Indigenous concepts of, 132n5, 229

"The East" (Martinez), 19, 21–22
education: in Alejandra Elenes's borderlands narrative, 48–53; spirituality in, 36–42, 55–57
Elenes, C. Alejandra, xvi, 4; borderlands narrative of, 36, 47–53; on feminism and spirituality, 20, 43–57, 73–74, 87
"El Mundo Zurdo" conference, 118–20, 212
Enciso Litschi, Alicia, xv–xvi, 135, 138–49
environmentalism, nepantla spirituality and, 183–84
erotic: in Chicana/Latina/Indigenous scholarship, 26, 32n15, 113–31; *conocimiento* and, 114–15, 118–20
escoba (broom), for limpias (spiritual cleansings), 223–26
Espín, Oliva, 6, 8, 74, 102–11
estafiate (herb), in Indigenous medicine, 227, 231–32
ethics, spirituality and, 93–94

ethnographic research, Chicana feminism and, 84–89, 96–99
European plants, Indigenous medicine and, 227–36

Facio, Elisa, xv–xvi, 3–15, 59–72; cancer journey of, 5–7, 20, 70–72
faith, healing traditions and, 162–66
family: Elenes's borderlands narrative and role of, 48–53; as home site, 61; spirituality and, 4–5, 136, 150–56; violence within, 63–65
feminist theory: healing practices and, 222–23; methodologies of the spirit and, 9–10, 16n8, 93–95; nepantla spirituality and, 73–75, 106–9, 169; Pérez's discussion of, 26–27; Tonantzin/Guadalupe and, 47–53
Figueroa, Maria, xvi, 20, 34–42, 54
fire rock (piedra lumbre), 196
Florescano, Enrique, 220, 226
flor y canto tradition, 49, 169–70
flower rituals, in Indigenous medicine, 231–36
Foster, George M., 228–29
Four Directions (Indigenous worldview), spirituality and, xvi, 13–15, 17n15, 40–41, 56, 65, 133n12, 175, 178, 224
Freire, Pablo, 182, 222–23
Fukuoka, Masanobu, 31n1; on culture, 33n23
full moon ceremonies, researcher-informant binary and, 95–99

Gandhi, Mahatma, 19, 26–29
Garcia Flores Rebolledo, Guadalupe, 195–201
Geico, León, xvii–xviii
gender equality, spirituality and, 4
genocidal practices, recognition of, 62–65
Goddess of the Americas (Castillo), 46–47
Gonzales, Patrisia, 9, 14, 218–39; on learning, 188; on Tlazolteotl, xiii, xvii, 114, 132n3; on healing, 69; on violence, 62, 64–65
Grupo Coatlique, Mesa de la Virgen de la Luz, 218–19
Guerrero, Laurie Ann, maternal facultad concept and, 121
Gutierrez, Gustavo, 199–200

hallucinations, 204–16, 217n2
healing traditions: el don (gift of healing) and, 225–26; Indigenous medicinal knowledge and, 181–82, 218–23; Inipi ceremony, 61–62; in mestiza culture, 26–27, 195–201; methodologies of the spirit and, 9, 91–95, 157–66; Mexican

healing traditions (continued)
Traditional Medicine and, 228–30; nepantla spirituality and, 167–84; temazkal conocimiento as, 66–68, 172–75; Tibetan Bon tradition, 181–82
herbal medicine, Indigenous medical knowledge and, 218–23
Hernández Avila, Inés, xvii–xviii, 4, 6, 51–52; identity explored by, 67–68, 100n3; on "La curandera" (Anzaldúa), 133n9; on spiritual praxis, 55
Hernández Juárez, Rosa María, xvi, 136, 157–66
Hernández Sáenz, Luz María, 228–29
heterosexism, 67–68
Hijas de María Immaculada, 49
Hinduism: mestiza culture and, 26–27; social justice and, 19
home, spirituality and concepts of, 60–72
homophobia, 67–68
hooks, bell, 37, 54; on spirituality in education, 55–56
Hopi culture, serpentine conocimiento in, 115, 178
hot-cold paradigm, in Mexican Traditional Medicine, 228–30
Huitzilopochtli (Nahua Sun deity), 45

illness: cancer journey, 5–7, 20, 70–72; healing traditions and, 157–66
immigration: banning of Mexican-American studies and, 182–84; borderlands narrative and, 52–53; spirituality and, 109–11
Indigenous cultures: Catholic figures in, 45–47; childhood memories of, 188, 197–201, 212–16, 222–26; conocimiento and, 115–18, 172–75; medicinal knowledge in, 181–82, 188, 218–23, 226–36; mestiza spirituality and, 45, 51–53, 58n1; nature concepts in, 32n13; nepantla spirituality and, 59–62, 152–54, 168–84. See also Native American studies
Indigenous studies. See Chicana/Latina/ Indigenous scholarship
Inipi ceremony, 61–62, 65–68, 172–75
In Lak'ech (Mayan philosophy), 19, 184n1; in Chicana/o literature and culture, 33n22; Pérez's discussion of, 28–29
Instituto Evangelístico de México, 197
"interbeing," Pérez's discussion of, 28–29
interdisciplinary research, spirituality and healing in, 9–10
"interpellation," spirituality and, 25–26, 32n10

interstitial space, "home" and, 61
in xochitl in cuicatl tradition, nepantla spirituality and, 169–70
Islam, Chicana identity and, 180
Ixachilatlan rituals, 197
izta cuauhtli, 41

Joan of Arc, feminism and, 103, 110–11
Johnson, Robert A., 31n2, 32n11
Jordan, Brigitte, 230, 232
Judaism, mestizaje identity and, 180–81

Kabbalistic tradition, 181–82
kalpulli (communal organization), 218–19
Kalpulli Izkalli, 224
Kalpulli Tlalteca, 198, 201
Kalpulli Tonal Teokalli (house of the creator), 198
Keating, AnaLouise, 6, 16n7, 43, 60, 71, 128, 134n18
King, Martin Luther Jr., 133n11
knowledge creation, methodologies of the spirit and, 84–86

La Buena Tierra (Bible school), 197–98
"La curandera" (Anzaldúa), 133n9
Laguna Pueblo, traditional medicine in, 229
La India Maria, 162
Lakota culture, 173–75, 183, 185n14
La Llorona, 52–53, 123–24
La Malinche, 123–24
Lame Deer (Lakota Chief), 174–75
Lara, Irene, xvi, xix, 3–15, 74–75; on activist spirituality, 7–8; on bruja/brujandera spirituality, 55; decolonization of spirit and, 93–95; on pedagogical strategies, 38–39
Las Mujeres (women's group), 207, 211
Latin American New Song Movement, xvii
Latina studies. See Chicana/Latina/ Indigenous scholarship
learning, spirituality and, 26–27, 218–39
lesbian studies, 10, 67–68
liberation theology, 8–9, 169, 171–72
limpia (spiritual cleansing), 66; limpias de flores, 231; memories of, 197–201; Mexican traditional medicine and, 219–23; Reiki integration with, 182; Tlazolteotl's escoba and, 223–26; yauhtli used in, 230–36
literacy programs, spiritual activism and, 215–16
Lorde, Audre, 26, 32n15, 120, 169
Los Matachines de la Santa Cruz, 212

loss, spiritual healing and, 96–99
Lucumí religion, 176

Madre Nati. *See* Santa María de Jesús Sacramentado Venegas (Madre Nati)
madrinas, as allies, xxi–xxii, 211–13, 222
maguey medicine, 219, 231–32, 236–38
Malinalli symbol, 225–26
mamihood, in Chicana/Latina/Indigenous scholarship, 113–31
Manifest Destiny, 36
Marcos, Sylvia, 116, 132n5
Mariana de Jesús Paredes of Quito (Saint), 111
Marian tradition in Catholicism, Our Lady of Guadalupe and, 122–24
Martinez, Cinthya, 19, 21–22
Martínez Parédez, Domingo, xvi, 29, 33n22
materiality, sainthood and, 105–11
maternal erotic, 128–31, 133n14
maternal facultad, serpentine conocimiento and, 120–24
Maya tradition, xviii, 19, 26–29, 32n16
medicinal knowledge: childhood memories of, 197–201, 212–16, 223–26; hidden aspects of, 226–36; of Indigenous cultures, 9, 148, 188; training in, 218–23
Medicine Wheel tradition, 148
Medina, Lara, xvi, 4, 6, 8, 11; feminist theology of, 44–45, 47; on Indigenous identity, 67; on nepantla spirituality, 136, 167–84; on serpentine conocimiento, 115–16, 120
meditation, spirituality and, 208–16
memory, Our Lady of Guadalupe and power of, 47
Mesoamerican worldview: nepantla spirituality and, 180–81; plant knowledge and, 225–26; serpentine conocimiento and, 116–18, 120, 124–28
mestiza culture: Elenes's narrative of, 47–53; curanderismo and, 226–36; healing traditions and, 70–72; maternal facultad and, 120–24; nepantla spirituality and, 26–27, 38, 179–81; Virgen de Guadalupe in, 45, 93–95
methodologies of the spirit: in academia, 85–86, 89–90, 100n2; activist erotic mothering and, 128–31; reclamation of Guadalupe-Tonantzin and, 81–99
Mexican Americans: conflicted identity in, 82–84, 99n1; history and culture of, 81–82; nepantla spirituality and identity in, 171–72
Mexican Traditional Medicine (MTM), 218–19, 226–36. *See also* curanderismo

Mezquita (Great Mosque) (Córdoba, Spain), 180, 185n20
midwifery, Indigenous medicinal practices in, 218–23, 232–238
missionary work, Villegas's memories of, 197–98
Mission San Xavier de Bac, 177–78
mistica (knowledge quality), 221–23
mixed-race ancestry, spirituality studies and, 15n1
modernity, spirituality and, 6, 25, 32n9
Montes, Felicia, xvi, xix, 135, 137
Moon Dance, 200–201
Moraga, Cherríe, 10–11, 46–47, 96, 211; on child-rearing, 156; on hunger, 133n9; maternal facultad concept and, 120–21; serpentine conocimiento and work of, 120
Mujeres Activas en Letras y Cambio Social (MALCS), 11, 16n6
mujerista theology movement, 147
mysticism, sainthood and spirituality and, 104–6

Nahua tradition: calendars in, 226; female deities in, 45–47, 49; medicinal knowledge in, 218–23, 228–36; nepantla spirituality and, 26–27, 169–70; personhood and integrity in, 28, 33n17; serpentine conocimiento in, 115–18
name planting ceremonies, 219–20
National Association for Chicana and Chicano Studies, 12
National Women's Studies Association, 11
Native American studies, spirituality in, xv, 11, 26–27, 35–36
natural law, Indigenous medicine and, 221–23
nature, modern *vs.* Indigenous concepts of, 31n1, 31n3, 32n13
nepantla spirituality: Anzaldúa's discussion of, 100n5; centrality of, 61, 89, 170–72; family relations and, 136; healing and, 71–72, 167–84; methodologies of the spirit and, xiv–xvi, 13–14, 86–99, 176–81; Sendejo's discussion of, 74; temazkal conocimientos and, 172–75; Tibetan Bon tradition and, 181–82
nonviolent activism, spirituality and, 28–29
Nuñez-Mejia, Sarahi, xvi, 187, 189–90

Occupied America (Acuña), 182
ofrendas (offerings), 118, 176–81
Ometeotl (Nahua Dual Deity), 34, 132n5, 229

Otomi culture, 197; Facio's identity in, 68–70; traditional medicine in, 228
Our Mother of Perpetual Help, nepantla spirituality and, 171–72

pain, healing traditions and, 161–66, 208–16
Panocha Pláticas, 126–28, 134n16
patriarchy: in Catholicism, 4, 44, 49; healing and confines of, 70–71
Peace and Dignity Runs, 200
pedagogies of the spirit, 34–42, 95–99, 100n4
pensamiento serpentino, 132n1
"perennial philosophy," 27
Pérez, Laura E., xv–xvi, xviii, 9, 19–20, 23–30, 46, 93–94, 115
performance, identity and, 33n21
personal experience, spiritual praxis and, 56–57
personal identity, spirituality and, 4–5
peyote: in Indigenous medicine, 227–28, 231–36; prayers involving, 233–36
pilgrimage tradition, 49, 176–81, 188, 202–16
place, religious recollection and, 87–89
plant knowledge, 239n3; Indigenous medicine and, 225–26, 227–36; Mexican traditional medicine and, 219–23
poetry, spirituality and, 27
politics, spirituality and, 152
popxcomitl (Nahua incense burner), 41
post-Enlightenment philosophy, spirit writing in context of, 23–24
postpartum rituals, in Indigenous medicine, 231–36
power, spirituality and, 29–30, 145–46
prayer: danza as, 166; folk prayers (dichos), 203–4; healing traditions and, 162–66, 233–36; spirituality and, 119, 154, 214–16; at stones people's lodge, 65–68
promotora tradicional, 220–21, 224–26
psyche, spirituality and, 25, 32n11
purification rites, Mexican medicine and, 219
puta (whore or sexual deviant), Our Lady of Guadalupe and, 122–24
Pythagoras, 27

"Queeranderismo" (Dimas), 73, 76–80, 134n17
queer theory: healing rituals and, 73; Pérez's discussion of, 26–27; spirituality and, 17n11; spirituality in, 10
Quetzalcoatl (Nahua "Feathered Serpent" diety), 21, 115–16, 236

Quezada, Noemi, 226, 233
Quilaztli, 225–26

racism, Buddhism and, 142–49
rakusu, 147, 149
Rarámuri culture, 197
rebozo massage, in Indigenous midwifery, 221, 232
Reiki (life-force energy), 181–82
reincarnation, spirituality and, 207–8
relationships, spirituality and, 4
religious beliefs: cultural memory and power of place in, 87–89; in Elenes's borderlands narrative, 48–53; feminist spirituality research and, 3–4, 8, 105–11, 195–201; nepantla spirituality and, 169; social action and, 96–99
Rendón, Laura I., 36, 55
researcher-informant binary, spiritual pedagogy and, 95–99
ritual practices, healing through, 177, 185n15
Rodríguez, Jeanette, 6, 8, 44–47
Rodriguez, Roberto, 182–83
Román, Estela, 31n7, 183
rope, in Indigenous midwifery, 232
Rose of Lima (Saint), 102–3, 111
Ruether, Rosemary Radford, 106–7
Ruiz de Alarcón, Hernando, 231–33

sacred pipes, 175, 185n14, 200
sagrada velación, 42n1
Sahagún, Friar Bernardino de, 173, 231, 237
sainthood: childhood impressions of, 203–4; spirituality and mysticism and, 104–6; for women, 103–11
San Martín de Porres, 171–72
Santa María de Jesús Sacramentado Venegas (Madre Nati), 177
Santería, 9, 26–27, 176
Santiago de Compostela, shrine of, 202
science, spirituality and, 6, 32n8
Search Retreats, spiritual activism and, 206–7
Ségura, Andrés, 219–20, 228, 239n1
Sendejo, Brenda, xvi, 49, 74, 81–99, 128
sentipensante (sensing/thinking) pedagogy, 36, 126–28
serpentine conocimiento: active spirituality and, 128–31; cultural figures and, 114–18, 124–26; erotic-spiritual change and, 118–20; maternal facultad and, 120–24;

nepantla spirituality and, 132n1, 177–81;
origins of, 132n1; Panocha Pláticas and,
126–28; Pérez's discussion of, 30, 115
sexism, early experiences with, 104
Sexto Sol (Nahua time concept), xviii
sexual abuse, childhood memories of, 195
sexuality: in Chicana/Latina/Indigenous
scholarship, 113–31; Nahua female deities
and, 45–47; Panocha Pláticas and, 126–28;
serpentine conocimiento and, 118–20;
spirituality and, 10, 17n11, 187; Tlazolteotl
and, 124–26
shamanic healing, nepantla spirituality and,
181–82
Silko, Leslie Marmon, 65, 182
social justice: nepantla spirituality and,
178–79; Our Lady of Guadalupe as symbol
of, 47; Panocha Pláticas community and,
126–28; religion and spirituality and,
96–99; spirituality and, 4, 8–9, 19
Society for the Study of Gloria Anzaldúa,
207, 212
spaces: "home" as, 60–72; religious
recollection and, 87–89
Spain, Chicana pilgrimages to, 179–81
spirit journeys: Facio's account of, 59; as love
story, 138–49
spiritual activism: in civil rights movement,
28–29; conocimiento and, 113–15; defined,
16n7; ethnographic research on, 101n7;
interdisciplinary research on, 6–8;
participation in, 206–16; pedagogy and,
56; serpentine conocimiento and, 128–31,
133n11
spirituality research: Elenes's discussion of,
43–44; Chicana identity and, 59–60;
childhood awareness of spirit and, 203–4;
feminism and, 106–9; healing traditions
and, 167–84; interdisciplinary approaches
to, 8; methodologies in, 15n3, 16n4, 81–99;
sainthood and mysticism and, 104–6;
serpentine conocimiento and, 118–20
spiritual praxis, Chicana feminist pedagogy
and, 54–57
"spiritual warrior": Buddhist ideal of, 19;
Pérez's discussion of, 28–29
spirit writing: Pérez's discussion of, 23–24;
pilgrimage and, 202–3; self-identity in, xv
stones people's lodge, 65–68
Student Nonviolent Coordinating Committee (SNCC), 28–29
Sufi mysticism, 27
Sun Dance ceremony, 198–201

susto (trauma and fear), expulsion of, 66–68,
222–23
sweat ceremonies: Cantú's participation in,
212; Indigenous midwifery and, 238–39;
nepantla spirituality and, 172–75, 184n9,
184n11, 194n13; Villegas's participation in,
198, 200. *See also* specific traditions, e.g.,
Inipi ceremony

Talamantez, Inés, xvi, xviii–xix, 6
Tarasco culture, 197
teaching/learning, borderlands concept and
spiritual pedagogies and, 36–42
Téllez, Michelle, xvi, 136, 150–56
temazkal conocimientos, 172–75, 200, 219
temazkalli ceremonies, 66–68; cancer
journey and, 72, 72n3; in Otomi heritage,
68–70; researcher-informant binary and,
95–99; Téllez's participation in, 153–54
Tenzin Wangyal Rinpoche, 181–82, 184n6
Tepixinola (ceremonial site), 238–39
Tepozteco (cultural hero), 237–38
"tercera edad" (third age), Mexican concept
of, 214, 217n4
Teresa of Avila (Saint), 108–11, 204
testimonio: on Buddhism, 144–49; Chicana
feminism and, 84–86; spirituality research
and, 9, 11, 20, 34–42
Texas Chicano movement, 91–95, 101n7
theology, spirituality and, 3–4, 8
"theory in the flesh," 10–11
Thérèse of Lisieux (Saint), 111
Thich Nhat Hanh, 28
Tibetan Bon tradition, nepantla spirituality
and, 181–82
Tijerina, Aleticia, 72
tlamatinime (Nahua philosophers and
mystics), 169
Tlazolcihuapilli (Nahua deity), 234
Tlazolteotl (Nahua deity), 14, 45–47, 65,
69–70, 115, 122; colonial connotations of,
132n3; decolonial feminism and, 75;
escoba (broom) of, 223–26; Indigenous
midwifery and, 234–36; serpentine
conocimiento and, 124–26
tobacco, in Indigenous medicine, 65, 224–27,
231–36
Tohono O'odham culture, serpentine
conocimiento in, 115, 177–81
Toltec culture, nepantla spirituality and,
169–70
Tonalmitl, 200–201
Tonalpohualli (Aztec calendar), 198

Tonanlupanisma, Lara's concept of, 93–95
Tonantzin (Nahua "Our Mother" deity): activist spiritualism and, 9, 20; decolonization and reclamation of, 75, 81–99; in feminist borderland pedagogy, 43–57; Guadalupe as, 46–47, 92–95, 132n4; healing traditions and, 62, 67–68; Otomí identity and, 69; Sendejo's discussion of, 74; serpentine conocimiento and, 86–87, 115–18, 122; spiritual pedagogy and, 37–39. See also Virgen de Guadalupe
Torres, Edén, 71–72
transformative education, spiritual praxis and, 54–57
Treaty of Guadalupe Hidalgo, 35
trenzas (twisted braids), Indigenous medicine and, 225–26
Trickster, energy of, xiv
Trungpa, Chogyam, 28, 31n4
two-spirit identity, healing ceremonies and, 67–68

Union Federal Mexicanos, 178–79
Urrea, Teresa (La Santa Teresa de Cabora), 178–79
Usui, Mikao (Dr.), 181–82

Valdez, Luis, 33n22, 132n1
vela (candle), Indigenous medicine and use of, 230
Villegas, Beatriz (Ilhuicatlahuili-Bea), xvi, 188, 195–201
violence: in academic experience, 62–65; home sites and, 61; privatization and commodification of, 64–65
Virgen de Guadalupe: in borderland pedagogy, 43–57; Catholicism and, 44–47; Chicana/ Latina/Indigenous reclamation of, 8, 37, 73–75, 81–99; childhood memories of, 203–4, 207, 214–16; healing traditions and, 62, 69–72, 161–66; in Mexican culture, 44–47, 49; origins of, 122–24, 133n15; serpentine conocimiento and, 115–18, 122–24; Tonantzin identity in, 46–47, 92–95, 132n4. See also Tonantzin (Nahua "Our Mother")
Virgen de San Juan de los Lagos, 203–4, 215
virgin/puta dichotomy, 94, 122–24

walking the red road, as spiritual journey, 65–68
war, nepantla spirituality and, 183–84
will, mind/body/spirit and, xvi, 161
women: as saints, 74, 103–11; violence against, 62–65
Women's Theological Center, 222–23

Xicana. See Chicana identity; Chicana/ Latina/Indigenous scholarship
Xicanisma, 70
Xöchicuamatzin, 201
xochitl in cuicatl tradition, nepantla spirituality and, 169–70

Yakama Indian reservation, spirituality on, 62–65
yauhtli (herbal plant), 230–36
Yemaya, healing rituals and, 73
yerba buena, healing traditions using, 159–60
youth, spirituality and memories of, 187–88

Zen Buddhism, teaching tradition in, 140